LIFE IN THE EARLY CHURCH

STATUE OF THE GOOD SHEPHERD

Lateran Museum. Probably 3rd Century.
Found in the catacomb of Callistus.

LIFE IN THE EARLY CHURCH
A.D. 33 to 313

By

A. E. WELSFORD

LONDON
NATIONAL SOCIETY
S · P · C · K
1955

First published in 1951
Reprinted 1955
by The National Society and S.P.C.K., London

Printed in Great Britain by
Richard Clay and Company, Ltd., Bungay, Suffolk

TO

ST LEONARD'S SCHOOL

ST ANDREWS

"Ad Vitam"

"I am come that they might have life, and that
they might have it more abundantly."

John, 10. 10.

PREFACE

SOME twenty-five years ago, when I was a school-girl, I sat in church one Sunday listening to the second lesson:

" The kingdom of heaven is like to a grain of mustard seed, which a man took, and sowed in his field. . . . "

The words were as fresh, as simple, and as full of mystery as when Christ first spoke them to his disciples, but I could not see that they had anything to do with the Church as I knew it. Collects, sermons, chants, and psalms; bishops, vicars, curates: all the formality and all the organization of the Church seemed to me remote from the spirit of the Gospels. How could the one produce the other?

The answer, as I afterwards learnt, is to be found in the first two or three centuries of the Church's history, for by the time of Constantine the mustard seed had put out branches, roots, and leaves; the essential structure of the Church was already in being.

In finding the answer to my question, I found much else as well. There is a freshness in the Christian writings of this period which carries across the centuries something of the joy and assurance which possessed men in the early morning of our faith. To enter imaginatively into the lives of those who believed and suffered during the centuries of persecution is a heartening experience, for their pains and doubts, their endeavours, and even their failures were part of the growth and triumph of the Church. So this book has been written for pleasure—the pleasure of sharing with others a source of true delight.

There are, of course, many Church histories which cover this period. Some, intended for students, are too concisely informative to be read with much enjoyment.   Others are for scholars and are too long, too specialized, and often too costly for the ordinary reader.   The original sources, apart from the New Testament, are not easily accessible for those with little time to spare.   It is my hope, therefore, that this book will be of use to those who would like to know more about the Church's early history, but have no leisure for research.   Teachers, particularly, may be glad to have ready to hand material which they can use for lessons that will make the early Church live in the minds of boys and girls today.

Few people, certainly few school-teachers, can afford to buy expensive books.   This book is therefore published in two parts in paper covers to reduce the cost to a minimum. A single-volume edition in cloth covers will follow for library use.   Part I has an introductory chapter on the Græco-Roman world, and covers the period from Pentecost to the end of the second century A.D.   Part II carries the story down to A.D. 313, when the peace of Constantine ended the last great persecution.   It includes a chapter on worship in the early Church, and another on the everyday life of Christians in the second and third centuries.   The map is included in each part.

CONTENTS

CONTENTS

INTRODUCTORY

The Græco-Roman World

ATTEMPTING to understand the past is as fascinating and as baffling as it is to travel in a foreign country with only a scanty knowledge of the language. The people are so like ourselves, even in little things, so fully and entirely human, that we catch ourselves wondering whether any of the differences between us and them are more than skin deep. And in this mood of happy confidence we are suddenly faced with some incident or habit which reveals how utterly un-English these people are. Our eyes are opened to the fact that we are foreigners travelling among people of an alien tradition, and we see that it would take us years to know their thoughts and share them, if indeed we ever could. In this combination of likeness with unlikeness lies the fascination of travelling abroad, and the same is true of travelling in time, especially in that particular tract of time which was dominated by what we call Græco-Roman civilization.

No man can wander through every land, so the wise traveller looks at a map beforehand and perhaps consults a guide-book as well. He studies the whole region, and finally chooses the district which interests him most, and sets off to explore that in person. In the same way the student, with a map of the Roman Empire before him, obtains a bird's-eye view of the Ancient World before attempting to investigate any part of it.* He sees at a glance that its centre is the Mediterranean rather than

* See map at end of book.

I

Rome.   Romans, Greeks, Ionians of Asia Minor, Jews of
Palestine, Persians of the more distant East, Egyptians, and
the defeated Carthaginians have all contributed to this
composite civilization.   To the west, beyond the gates of
Hercules, lies an infinite waste of ocean, America as yet
undreamed of.   To the north are lands won from the
barbarians: Gaul is already thoroughly Romanized, but
the remote island of Britain, in the middle of the first
century, is not fully conquered, Boudicca's rebellion and
the massacre of the Druids are still to come.   Along the
Rhine the Roman legions keep perpetual guard against
the German tribes, who, pressed on by invaders from the
icy north and by yet more terrible hordes from the Siberian
steppe, are striving to fight their way into the prosperous
countryside of Gaul.   To the east lie lands of wealth and
mystery from which caravans return laden with spices,
silks, and rarities, and Magi come to reveal the secrets of
the stars.   To the south a strip of inhabited coast is bounded
by the vast Arabian and African deserts, save where the Red
Sea and the Persian Gulf open a route to India.

From Palestine, our travels in the track of the early
Church will take us through Asia Minor to Rome itself,
and later to Gaul, and along the North African coast from
Alexandria to Carthage.   We shall travel from city to city
rather than from country to country, for nationality matters
little within the Roman Empire.   From end to end of this
vast area there are no frontiers, no tariff barriers.   The
population of most of the large cities is cosmopolitan, and
no wonder, for travel has never been easier; the Mediterranean is almost free of pirates and an excellent system of
roads covers every province of the Empire.   Veterans
from the army are settled in numerous cities, dignified by
the name of Roman Colonies.   Not only Jews, but other
adventurous Eastern merchants, have established themselves in any place where money can be made, advancing

into newly conquered territory on the heels of the troops. African slaves, captured Germans, and Britons from the frontier provinces, Eastern dancing-girls, Greek scribes, all meet together in the Emperor's huge slave households and on the estates of the rich. Wandering philosophers tour the lecture-halls. It matters little in which city we receive our first impressions, for, despite local peculiarities, the main features of Græco-Roman civilization are everywhere the same. In the western provinces the cities are relatively new, built on the Roman pattern; in the eastern half of the Empire, where most of the cities are old, the same pattern has been imposed, but less rigidly, and Greek and oriental influences are stronger. It will be worth while to gather a few impressions of life in a typical Græco-Roman city before endeavouring to understand the impact of Christianity upon the pagan world.

The most striking thing about a Græco-Roman city is its beauty. To a traveller from the twentieth century the colonnades and temples gleaming white in the sunshine, free from smoke and soot, have an effect of dazzling purity. Looking down on the city from a nearby hill, he is struck by its orderliness. It is laid out on a rectangular plan, as well as the lie of the land will permit. The streets are straight, some wide, some narrow. The public buildings are for the most part grouped together in the centre of the city, and the whole is girdled by the city wall. Yet, for all the stiffness of the pattern, there is none of the dreary monotony of a modern industrial town with its long rows of mean and uniform houses. The residential parts of the city are cut up into blocks by the street pattern, but within each block individual builders have pleased their fancy. Private houses large and small, shops and workshops, are found side by side. Entering one of the main gates, our traveller follows a well-paved street leading to the centre of the city. He has to keep to the pavement, for the roadway is crowded with country carts bringing in vegetables and livestock to the market, with pack-mules laden with bales of goods for export going in the opposite direction, and with riders of every description.

Before he has gone far, our traveller is tempted to leave the main street and explore a narrow road that crosses it at right angles. Here there is no room for wheeled traffic at all. On each side are shops and unpretentious private houses, some of which are workshops as well as dwelling-places. Low penthouse roofs give welcome shade to the passer-by, and none of the buildings here in this provincial city is more than two stories high, though in Rome, where space is valuable, tall tenement blocks are common. The private houses present blank walls to the street, save for their doorways, for Roman houses are built on the Eastern pattern, in which the rooms look inwards, for coolness and privacy. But the small, open-fronted shops are gay, not only with wares, but also with inviting frescoes painted on their plaster walls. The scene resembles an Eastern bazaar, and here, too, no purchase can be made without protracted bargaining, which is the spice of life both to the seller and to his customers. Through an open doorway weavers can be seen sitting at their tall looms, each swiftly passing his shuttle through the warp before him. A little farther down the road a coppersmith is hammering in the inner room behind his shop. Across the road is a much larger establishment, a bakery, where several slaves are grinding corn by guiding the mules which turn three large stone mills, while other men are kneading dough in long troughs, or stoking the great brick ovens in preparation for the baking. Next door is a pottery shop, where nests of rough cooking-bowls, stacks of huge double-handled wine-jars with pointed ends, and piles of heavy mortars for pounding spices, stand on the floor, while on the shelves gleam the red " Samian " platters and bowls, the fashionable Roman dinner-ware, manufactured at first in Italy and later copied throughout the Empire. In the back room the potter is busy at his wheel, turning a cooking-pot in coarse clay, decorating it with a zigzag pattern as he does so. Our contemporary watches enthralled and, when at last he tears himself away and retraces his steps, he thinks rather wistfully that this busy little street combines most of the functions of a large department store, together with the work done by several modern factories, and is far more full of life and fun than they.

Turning again up the street that leads to the Forum, our traveller sees on every side evidence of the pride its inhabitants feel in their city. On one hand are the public baths, magnificently equipped with sweating-rooms, hot-water baths, a cold bath large enough to swim in, dressing-rooms, and an open exercise-court. All this, as the inscription over the door informs the passer-by, was built with the legacy of a prominent citizen, who also bequeathed an endowment fund, so that all, even the slaves, might enjoy the baths free of charge. On the other side is a school, the gift of a retired centurion, and near it a temple to Apollo lavishly restored by a successful merchant. Wherever he goes, fountains, statues, colonnades, and commemorative tablets serve to remind him that love of his city is as natural to a man of the Roman Empire as love of our country is to us. From the greatest to the least, the citizens have a common pride in the glories of their native place and a common delight in the enjoyments it affords. Preoccupied with these thoughts, our traveller has almost reached the entrance to the Forum when his attention is attracted by a crowd gathered at the foot of the steps leading to the Temple of Fortune. On the steps stands an uncouth figure: an old man with an untrimmed, lousy beard and the gestures of a tub-thumper is haranguing a fairly large gathering. His wallet, his filthy mantle, and the staff on which he leans show him to be a wandering Cynic, but one whom Diogenes might not have owned. He is winning applause by inveighing against luxury and praising the virtues of poverty and honest work, for his audience consists of slaves and poor artisans; great guffaws of laughter greet his coarse personal abuse of certain rich men well known in the city and his sly digs at the devotees of the gods.

After that noisy scene, the Forum, busy as it is, seems as quiet as a college quadrangle. It is a large open court surrounded by a covered colonnade where business transactions are carried on. At one end is the Temple of Jupiter, and on either side openings lead to other temples, to the basilica where law-suits are heard and to the Senate's council chamber. It is the administrative centre of the city, and the dignity of the architecture becomes its character. Between the graceful white columns of the colonnade are touches of colour, for the Forum is surrounded by statues of the town's past benefactors, the marble painted to look like flesh. Yet, despite every enrichment, the straight lines of both colonnade and temple retain their cool severity. As he gazes about him, the traveller perceives a group clustered around an orator in the porch of the Temple of Jupiter and, finding people more interesting than stones, he draws closer. This speaker is not of the Hyde Park stamp, and his audience consists of a number of young men and some well-to-do citizens who are listening with quiet attention, occasionally asking questions on difficult points. Joining the outskirts of the group, the traveller at first takes the discourse to be a lecture on the stars, but on hearing more he classes it as a sermon.

"Have you not often felt your soul uplifted as you watched the noiseless progress of the planets on their pathway round the earth?" the speaker is saying, clothing his ideas in a rhetorical style which is much appreciated by

his listeners. "Have you not reflected upon the endless cycle of the seasons, summer following spring, winter treading on the heels of autumn? Destiny rules all! In all things we perceive the workings of the Divine Reason. In Nature, the macrocosm, the perfect cycle of birth, death, and regeneration is endlessly repeated. In man, the microcosm, the pattern of the universe is reproduced upon a tiny scale. We, too, are born, we die, and shall in due course be born again. In man, as in the universe, a fiery soul animates the matter which confines it. What wonder that your souls are stirred when you behold the stars! The same fire burns in them."

Here our contemporary, finding something unaccustomed in these apparent commonplaces, interjects:

"What of the theory of progress, sir? How do you find room in this scheme of eternal cycles for man's slow evolution from the animals and his steady progress towards perfection?"

"Young man," replies the lecturer, "I can find room for no such theory. Nor would any wise disputant of the Schools attempt to uphold such a thesis. How could any but a fool suppose that man is progressing towards perfection? It is common knowledge that the Golden Age is past. Men of this present time are puny in stature compared with their fathers, puny in mind as well. Can any of our modern poets compare with Homer? Can I compare with Aristotle?"

Polite murmurs come from the audience, but his twentieth-century questioner persists:

"Then, sir, I am right in thinking that you believe the universe, and man with it, to be moving, not in a straight line from its creation to its goal, but in a weary, unalterable circle. Surely there is an end to all things. At last the earth itself will grow cold and life will perish on it. What then?"

" You err. The world will end in a fiery conflagration, and afterwards there will be a new heaven and a new earth."

" Then your system is not eternal."

" Indeed it is. The cycle of day and night is not less permanent because it is subject to certain regular variations within the larger cycle of the seasons. The conditions we now experience would be exactly repeated in the new earth. We should not know the difference."

Incredulously our contemporary asks: " You mean that men would still quarrel and thieve, commit adultery and fight on the new earth as they do on the old? "

" Wherever the divine spark of Reason is cumbered by a mortal body there will be passion and excess," the philosopher replies.

" But the spark of reason in man is divine. The Lord Zeus," he cries, pointing to the shrine within the Temple, " is in his own nature one great continuous fire. ' Our souls will not have reason to rejoice in their lot until, freed from the darkness in which they grope, they have not merely caught a glimpse of the brightness with feeble vision, but have absorbed the full light of day and have been restored to their place in the sky—until, indeed, they have regained the place, which they held at the allotment of their birth. The soul is summoned upwards by its very origin, and it will reach that goal even before it is released from its prison below, as soon as it has cast off sin and, in purity and lightness, has leaped up into celestial realms of thought.' " *

As he concludes his (borrowed) peroration, his hearers, much impressed, break into applause, and then, in awed silence, make way for him as he sweeps down the steps and stalks off across the Forum. Several senators sitting in

* Seneca, Ep. lxxix. 12. Quoted by Halliday, *The Pagan Background of Early Christianity.*

the shade of the colonnade rise respectfully to greet him as he goes past. The audience disperses, but one man turns to our traveller and says:

"Sir, I see you are a stranger, and I would be glad of further talk with you. Will you accompany me home? For my part, I am not yet sufficiently philosophical to be indifferent to the needs of the flesh, and at your age you should not be, either."

Gladly accepting the invitation, the traveller accompanies his new friend across the Forum. He observes that the other is a prosperous-looking man, between forty-five and fifty, with shrewd eyes and a wide, tolerant mouth. He talks with his hands as well as his voice, in Eastern fashion, and he talks continuously:

"I admired the way you tackled Apollodorus, indeed I did! I don't altogether agree with the man myself. He's too much of a Stoic for me. I incline towards Platonism myself." Here he looks quickly at his guest to see what impression he is making. "There is something cold about these Stoics," he continues. "Think how they dismiss the gods as mere personifications of aspects of Nature. They allegorize the life out of religion! When one of my old sea-captains returns safely from a voyage he goes up there to offer thanks." He points to the entrance to a temple set a little back from the street. "I dedicated a model of a ship there myself a few days ago," he continues— "a lovely thing of gold and cedarwood—and I sacrificed to Neptune for the safe return of a costly argosy. I'd like to hear our friend Apollodorus at his prayers on shipboard when the wind is blowing at gale force. I wonder whether he'd call on the Divine Reason then!"

The traveller laughs. "You are a merchant, sir, I take it?"

"Yes," the other answers. "When I was born Mercury was in the ascendant, and on the whole I have prospered.

I hope to do even better in the future. My wife and I had our horoscopes cast recently; very expensive, but well worth it. I know now that I should never launch an important venture on a Wednesday. If I had known that two years ago it would have saved me thousands."

" Indeed, sir," the traveller murmurs politely, suppressing memories of Lyndoe and his fellow-prophets in the Sunday papers, " and is your wife as strong a believer in astrology as you are? "

" Certainly she is," the merchant replies with enthusiasm. " She's a wonderful woman; knows far more about that kind of thing than I do. She takes religion seriously and has been initiated into the mysteries of Cybele. But with all that she's practical, and has quite a sound business instinct too. Now here we are. Come in and I'll introduce you."

The entrance to the house is modest enough. The doorway is flanked by two shop-windows, one of which is protected by a close iron grille, through which gleam jewels and gold ornaments, part of the merchant's stock-in-trade. In the dimness of the narrow vestibule the visitor catches a glimpse of a shrine, containing an image of Janus, guardian of the door, and on the wall there is a representation of Priapus, intended to avert the evil eye. A moment later they are in the cool and pleasant *atrium*. There are no windows in this pillared hall, but the centre of it is open to the sky, and through the opening, sun and rain alike pour down into a large marble basin, where a bronze nymph smiles at her own reflection. The traveller has barely time to notice the rich colours of the mosaic floor, a couple of substantial treasure-chests by the wall, and a little household shrine in one corner, when he sees his hostess rising to greet them from the stool where she had been sitting at her embroidery. She is a tall, graceful woman, at least ten years younger than her husband, and her naturally dark

hair is dyed the fashionable golden hue. She welcomes
the visitor with a quiet dignity, which seems natural to
her, and then excuses herself on the plea of giving the slaves
directions to hasten lunch.

The merchant leads the way to the *peristyle*, a cloister
surrounding a small but lovely garden.   Opening off this
are several rooms, one of them the dining-room.   Here,
after slaves have brought water and bathed their hands and
feet, the two men recline on couches and chat.   One side
of the dining-room is open to the peristyle, and the scent
of roses blows in from the garden, together with the peaceful music of the fountain.   The traveller learns that the
merchant's name is Caius Sentius, and that his wife Julia
comes of an aristocratic family.   In a few minutes she
rejoins them, followed by a short, swarthy man with a
dark beard, whom Sentius introduces with a flourish as his
household astrologer.   Over a light repast of bread,
cheese, wine, and fruit, the traveller entertains his host and
hostess with tales of the land he has visited far out in the
ocean, beyond the Pillars of Hercules : there tenement
blocks are several stories higher than they are in Rome ;
carriages dash through the streets without having horses
to draw them ; artificial light turns night into day.   The
merchant and his wife listen enthralled, but the astrologer,
doubtful of the stranger's intentions, is critical, and now
and then interrupts with questions which show him to be
a man of considerable intelligence.   The traveller, to his
surprise, discovers that he is not a charlatan, but a man
who has inherited a long tradition, half priestly, half
scientific.   The distinction between magic and applied
science is unknown to him, and most of his conclusions are
wrong, being based on false assumptions; but he believes
much, though not all, of what he says.

A turn in the conversation brings up the subject of
slavery and the condition of the free plebeian workers.

The traveller expresses a great desire to see for himself how these men live. Sentius pauses for a moment and then chuckles, for an idea has occurred to him which affords him a good deal of amusement.

" Look here," he says to the traveller. " If you really want to study low life, how would you like to go with my butler to his club to-night? "

" I should like it immensely," the traveller replies. " But will that be all right? Will your butler and his friends mind? "

" Not a bit," says Sentius. " They'll be delighted. I'm their chief patron, and I ought to be present myself, but there's a municipal banquet to-night which I must not miss. You can represent me at the Neptune Club. You'll find them a very decent set of fellows: a few slaves, some freedmen, and some of the poorer plebeians who do not belong to any of the trade associations—about sixty members in all. It's a burial club, of course; wouldn't be legal otherwise. Some masters don't allow their servants to belong to any association outside the household, but I think it's good for them. Keeps them out of the low taverns and bawdy-houses and makes them contented with their lot. Stands to reason a man must have some social life, even if he is a slave, poor devil! "

" You say you are the patron of this club. Does that mean that you help it financially? "

" Oh, yes; I've done quite a bit for them in one way and another. You see, the entrance fee to the club is about sixteen shillings, and the monthly contributions are trifling. These chaps can't afford much. I built their dining-hall for them, and I'm going to bequeath the ground round it to them on condition that they tend the tomb I'm building there for myself and my wife. I'm leaving them some money, too, to keep an annual feast on my birthday. I like to think that I shan't be forgotten, or Julia either! "

" When you are free from the encumbrance of the body, Caius," his wife interrupted, " you will lose these earth-born desires. Soaring above the spheres of the planets, your spirit will be reunited with God, from whom it came."

" That's all very well for you, Julia, my dear," says the merchant, laying his hand affectionately on his wife's arm. " You are an initiate, one of the chosen of God. But I doubt I'll ever be that. There's too much earth and too little fire in my composition. To tell the truth, I'd rather sit here with you whom I can see and touch and love, than soar through a heaven of light. Anyhow, I'd like to think of those good fellows eating and drinking and enjoying themselves on my birthday. It's a good way to be remembered. But I'll call Clodius." Turning to his guest, he adds: " He can have the afternoon off to take you to the circus. You'll have time to see the last couple of races. Clodius will be an excellent guide there, at any rate. He has a friend in one of the racing stables, I fancy, for he has given me tips before now."

In answer to his master's summons, Clodius appears, and listens to his instructions. He obeys his orders with alacrity and, after the traveller has warmly thanked the merchant and his wife for their kindness, the two set off together in the direction of the circus.

At first Clodius is too doubtful of the stranger to talk freely. He answers his questions very civilly, but volunteers nothing. But the traveller's friendly manner, his readiness to stop at a tavern for a cup of wine, and his interest in everything, soon have their effect. Clodius becomes more expansive. " After all," he reasons to himself, " this traveller is only a man the master picked up in the Forum, probably no more than a freedman, if the truth were known, and none of us is likely to meet him again."

" Have you been long in the service of Caius Sentius ? " the traveller asks.

" Ever since his father bought me in the market at the age of nine," Clodius replies. " The master was a young man of eighteen then, and I was given to him on his birthday."

" You have a very good place with him, I should think."

" I have that. I could have bought my freedom a couple of years ago, for, besides my earnings, a good many tips and perquisites come my way. But what's the use? I'm happy as I am. Besides, I'd rather save a bit more, and be able to buy in my wife and the two children at the same time."

" So you are a married man, are you, Clodius? "

" In a manner of speaking, yes, sir. You know we slaves can't be legally married; but she's the same as a wife to me. We've always been true to each other, and the master gave us a slap-up feast for our wedding. I shan't forget that day as long as I live. The master's all right: quick-tempered, but generous. The mistress is the fly in my ointment. Hard as nails, she is, and gives my poor woman a bad time if her dresses aren't just to her taste."

" I thought Lady Julia was an initiate of the mysteries, with a soul above all mundane matters," the traveller remarks.

Clodius snorts and utters what sounds like a profanity, but the words are mercifully lost in a great roar of applause from the crowd watching the races. By now the two have almost reached the entrance, and Clodius hurries the traveller along, saying that they will barely be in time for the two last events. Clodius is known to the gatekeeper, and soon they are sitting panting among the other spectators, on one of the stone seats which are built in tiers around the arena.

The traveller looks round him with interest. He estimates that there are between ten and twelve thousand spectators; all talking eagerly and exchanging bets in the interval between the races. The course itself is a huge rectangular space divided lengthways by a row of statues.

" What are those statues for? " asks the traveller, turning to Clodius.

" Why, haven't you seen a race-course before? " asks Clodius pityingly. " They're the spine round which the chariots drive, and those columns at each end mark the turning points. The drivers keep as close to the spine as they dare, but it's at the turn that most of the accidents happen."

" What are those dolphins for? I can count seven of them."

" Oh, those are to mark the progress of the race. One is removed at the end of each lap," answers Clodius. Shifting a little, he shows the traveller a similar dolphin roughly outlined on the stone seat. " Emblem of the ' Neptune Club,' " he says. " The master likes the dedication of the club to Neptune on account of his trading interests, and we like it because we're all dead keen on racing. So everyone's pleased. Let me introduce a couple of the members," he continues, leaning across the traveller to attract the attention of those sitting on his far side. " Here's Quintus, who mends the sandals of the aristocracy, and Balbus, who's always pleased to give you a hair-cut." He adds with a swagger, " This gentleman is one of my master's friends. I'm showing him round, and he's coming to our festival tonight."

A shout from the crowd cuts short the civilities. The presiding magistrate has risen and is waving a white cloth, the signal for the start. The folding doors at the end of the arena open, and instantly four chariots emerge and their drivers whip their horses to the gallop. The charioteers wear the colours of their factions, white, red, blue, and green, and the crowd yells itself hoarse as each man encourages the driver of his fancy. In the third lap the driver of the leading chariot, the red, takes the turn too sharply. His wheel catches the stone base of the pillars and his chariot overturns, flinging him under the hoofs of the four galloping horses of the white chariot, which is attempting to pass. He is trampled to death, while the drivers of the blue and green factions seize their chance to take the lead and compete for victory. The traveller, sickened by this accident, has no further interest in the race, but the crowd is in a frenzy of excitement. A few shrieks from the women spectators and groans of disappointment from supporters of the red faction greeted the catastrophe, but it seems forgotten even before the body of the dead driver is dragged from the blood-stained sand. During the last lap people stand on the seats shouting, " Go it, blue! ", " Whip 'em up, green! ", to the surviving competitors. As the green chariot passes the winning-post, Clodius drops back on to his seat with a sigh of satisfaction.

" That's what I call a good race," he says to the traveller —" exciting from start to finish. I always say there's nothing like a chariot race to give you a real thrill."

Quintus, the shrivelled little shoemaker, having settled a brief argument with Balbus about the payment of a bet, joins in: " Every man to his taste, Clodius. I'd rather have a show of wild beasts and gladiators than the best chariot race in the world."

Turning to the traveller he explains: " I used to live in Pompeii before I came here. Wonderful shows they had there! The gladiators were from the best schools in Rome and there were tigers, leopards, and bears, all regardless of expense. Talk of thrills! Those games were something to look forward to. But these Greeks here are a soft lot. Some of them would rather watch boys running races than see a good fight."

" Then don't you have gladiatorial shows here at all ? "
inquires the stranger. " I thought I saw a placard advertis-
ing one in the town as we came through."

" You did," agrees Quintus. " The Proconsul is
holding three days' games here in a fortnight's time. There
will be twelve pairs of gladiators, a leopard hunt, criminals
given to the beasts and a heap more besides—a real good
show it promises to be. But that's a rare thing here. If
we get two or three such shows a year we are lucky. It's
all the fault of these highbrows. Why, when they wanted
to build an amphitheatre in Athens, one of the philosophers
there, Demonax was his name, told them they'd better first
destroy the Altar to Pity. That finished it. The City
Council turned the whole idea down. Even here, where
we are not quite so strait-laced, there are some who
grudge us poor chaps the bit of fun and the free bread that
makes our lives worth living."

The beginning of the last race ends his grouse, and the
traveller is left to his reflections. He feels as a man might
who stoops to pet a tabby cat and finds a tiger cub instead.
This crowd, which reminds him of football matches and
race meetings at home, has a touch of ferocity, a lust for
blood, unknown at a Wembley Cup-tie Final or at the
Derby. To his relief, the races end without further mis-
hap and, at the suggestion of Clodius, all four of them make
their way to the public baths. Pleasantly relaxed after the
bath, they stroll together through the exercise-court,
watching the people coming and going.

" Aren't you going to take this gentleman sight-seeing,
Clodius ? " inquires Balbus. " Where are you going after
the feast tonight ? "

" Where could we go at that hour ? " asks Clodius curtly.

" Plenty of places," says Balbus, with a knowing leer at
the stranger. " The city's just beginning to wake up
then, if you know where to go." Then, nudging Clodius

in the ribs, he adds: " Why don't you take him to the gardens of Aphrodite? That's a show place if you like! All the visitors want to go there."

" You know well enough why I won't, Balbus," replies Clodius, with evident annoyance. " I'm a decent married man, and I don't go to places like that, or take others there either."

" The wife wouldn't let you, I suppose," grins Balbus. " You're the hen-pecked husband all right. I'd be ashamed to own it if I were you."

" Here, that's enough of your teasing," Quintus interrupts. " Let Clodius alone. You don't want him to black your eye again, do you? He's a lot more sensible than you are. Those places aren't for the likes of us. It's all very well for the rich to amuse themselves with wine and dancing-girls night after night, but a poor man can't run to it. I like a good time, same as another. But what I say is, ' Have your fling at the Saturnalia and the Feast of Bacchus, but attend to your business the rest of the year.' "

Balbus, fingering the *phallus* that he wears round his neck as a charm, only laughs. He is watching a pale, effeminate-looking young man, who is just then crossing the courtyard.

" There's one of the rich men you're talking about," he says to Quintus. " That's young Vitellius, one of the Emperor's boon companions. He's divorced one wife already, and by what I heard last week, when I was working at his town house, the present one won't last long."

" We'll be late for the feast if we stay gossiping here much longer," says Clodius, interrupting him, and, to the traveller's satisfaction, they set out forthwith for the club.

They pass the Forum and continue along the road which Sentius and the traveller took in the morning, as far as the entrance to the Temple of Neptune. A vacant plot nearby has been made into a garden, and there a number of other members have already assembled. The traveller notices a half-built tomb of considerable magnificence, and rightly guesses that this is the monument which Sentius has designed for himself and his wife. Clodius, with more timidity than he has hitherto shown, approaches a group of men who are standing apart from the rest. These are officers of the club, men of higher social status than the ordinary members. One is a soothsayer, two are doctors, and the fourth is a well-to-do freedman. When Clodius explains to them that the traveller is a friend of the patron, and his representative for the evening, they welcome him cordially and invite him to preside, an honour which he hastens to decline. The soothsayer, upon whom this duty devolves, then gives the signal for the start. In silence the members, about fifty of whom are present, form a procession and, bearing flaming torches and the emblems of their club, they pass with due solemnity out of the garden, along the street, and up the steps leading to Neptune's temple. Standing before the sanctuary, the priest awaits them. He receives their offerings—modest gifts of fruit and corn, for the men are poor—and on their behalf burns incense before the altar. Then, with the same formality and silence, the procession returns, re-enters the garden, and halts, while the president makes offerings at the garden shrines. At one side is a long two-storied building, which the traveller had taken to be the fraternity's dining-hall; this they now enter. But, to his surprise, he finds that the interior of the lower room has the appearance of a dove-cot. The walls are lined with niches, most of them vacant, but a few filled with funerary urns. It is a *Columbarium*— the club's common burying-place. Here the club's officers strew roses and leave offerings of food and drink for the departed spirits. Then, the ceremonies ended, the members file upstairs to the dining-hall. Here the members recline on couches, taking their places in strict order of precedence, and before the banquet begins a distribution is made of small sums of money, the gift of the patron. The traveller is embarrassed and surprised to see that his share is larger than any of the others; the four officers receive twice as much as ordinary members, and the slaves least of all. The President then makes an announcement. He has heard with regret of the death of one of their members. The funeral will take place the following day, and he trusts that all those who are able will attend. This is their pious duty, and a small sum will, as usual, be paid to each mourner. He also reminds two members that their monthly subscriptions are in arrears and that they will be suspended and lose their right of free burial if they do not pay up soon. This necessary business over, the banquet begins. Reclining on the soothsayer's right, the traveller can look down the room and see the evident enjoyment of the members, slaves and citizens alike. None are men of wealth or position, some can be sold in the market or beaten to death at their master's whim, but this is their hour of freedom, when, in the joy of fellowship, each becomes an individual who matters, not for what he has, but for himself. " What were the first small Christian communities but burial clubs like this? " the traveller thinks to himself, absently crumbling a piece of bread in his hand. His neighbour passes him a cup of wine, which he sips and passes on, and as he does so the scene before him fades from his mind's eye. Folding up the map of the Roman Empire, which is spread out before him, he opens his Bible at the Acts of the Apostles, and begins to read again the familiar story of Christianity's first impact upon the pagan world.

CHAPTER I

JERUSALEM: BORN OF THE SPIRIT

JERUSALEM was crowded with pilgrims. They had come from throughout Judæa, from Galilee, from beyond Jordan, and from farther afield than that. There were Jews from Mesopotamia and from still farther east; many had come from Cappadocia, Pontus, Phrygia, and other provinces in Asia Minor; others were from the Jewish quarters of Alexandria, and from the district round Cyrene in Libya; some were from the heart of the Empire —Rome. Most of them were Jews by birth, though some were proselytes, converts to the Jewish faith, and all had been drawn to Jerusalem by their desire to keep the feast of Pentecost in the holy city, where, in the courts of the Temple, they might come as near as mortals dare to the presence of God Himself. There were plenty of shrewd business men among them, merchants and financiers, wise in the ways of the world and familiar with the power of Rome. But all who were Jews by birth remembered that they were descendants of Abraham, who through faith had left the prosperous city of Ur to travel into the unknown in search of the Promised Land. They, like him, were children of the promise. They looked for the day when God would vindicate His people, when the Gentiles would be humbled and the Chosen People glorified. The power of Rome did not daunt the imagination of men whose forefathers had been delivered by the hand of God from Pharaoh and delivered again at a later day from captivity in Babylon. Egypt was no longer a mighty empire;

Babylon had fallen; Rome, their present oppressor, might soon be stricken as these earlier foes had been. Then the Messiah, the heaven-sent deliverer, would reign in Jerusalem upon the throne of David and the age-long purpose of God would be accomplished.

The feast of Pentecost is the second of the three annual Jewish festivals. Many of the pilgrims from distant lands had come up for the Passover seven weeks before and had stayed on, so that they might celebrate Pentecost also in the holy city before returning home. During Passover-tide the popular longing for the advent of the Messiah had been wakened from a smouldering dream into a flaming reality. A certain Jesus of Nazareth had been hailed by the people as the Lord's Anointed and been brought in triumph into the city. Many had believed that he was indeed the Messiah who should restore the kingdom of David and free the Jews from Roman rule. But the Jewish authorities had remained unconvinced. They saw very clearly the folly of rebellion against Rome; nor were they disposed to believe that a carpenter's son from an obscure village was indeed the long-expected Messiah. The Scribes and Pharisees, those whose business it was to study the law and interpret ancient prophecies, had given their report on the man and his teaching after a prolonged investigation. They had dogged his footsteps ever since he first became famous as a miracle-worker in Galilee, and they had nothing good to say of him. His teaching was unorthodox and subversive; he openly flouted their own authority, and although he did not actually say he was the Messiah, he took upon himself to revise the law of Moses and to forgive sins—conduct which was plainly blasphemous. What made him dangerous was that he undoubtedly possessed an amazing power, which showed itself in the healing of many who were blind or diseased, in the curing of demoniacs and in the devotion of his followers. The authorities

c

would have suppressed him long before if they had dared or known how, but they had feared the people.   At length, however, one of his own disciples betrayed him and gave them their opportunity.   On the Thursday before the Passover they had arrested Jesus by night in a garden. He had been brought to trial before the High Priest and found guilty of blasphemy.   In the morning, on the day of Preparation for the Sabbath, they had brought him before Pilate, the Roman Governor, and had succeeded in persuading that nervous official that the man, if not himself a political agitator, was at least causing dangerous unrest in Jerusalem.   A section of the mob had been induced to clamour for his death, and Jesus had been crucified.   That should have ended the matter, but it had not.   Strange rumours had been heard in the city that Jesus had risen from the dead and had been seen by his disciples.   The tomb where he had been laid was undoubtedly empty, and although the official story was that his body had been stolen by his disciples, it was not a convincing story, for an armed guard had been posted at the tomb.   The mystery remained.

Now, seven weeks later, these events seemed to most of the pilgrims to be past history, something to recount to the people at home who were eager for news from Jerusalem, but nothing more.   Yet there were some who vividly remembered the man himself and could not rid their minds of the impression he had made on them.   Not all the judicial verdicts in the world could make them think such a man a blasphemer or an impostor.   His words lived on in their thoughts, unforgotten, unforgettable:

" If I by Beelzebub cast out devils, by whom do your sons cast them out?   But if I with the finger of God cast out devils, no doubt the kingdom of God is come upon you. . . . The stone which the builders rejected is become the head of the corner. . . . Except a corn of wheat fall into the ground and die, it abideth alone: but if it die, it bringeth forth much fruit." *

Which was the greater marvel—that this man in whom the spirit of God so evidently dwelt, who spoke with authority, healed the sick, cast out devils, and, as trustworthy witnesses asserted, raised the dead, should end his life in failure and ignominy, or that God should raise up his Chosen from the dead? Even those in whose hearts this question rose shrank from thinking out its far-reaching implications. Instead they waited; waited they hardly knew for what, perhaps for some sign from God which should answer once and for all the question: " Who was this Jesus of Nazareth? "

Early on the morning of Pentecost the streets were already thronged with men and women on their way to the Temple or elsewhere. Suddenly from one house there came a confused sound of many voices, all speaking with what seemed to be a deep and overmastering emotion. Passers-by stopped amazed. The sound grew and continued. Words could be distinguished, yet their meaning remained unintelligible. A crowd collected, and soon they could see men on the flat roof of the house, a place commonly used for prayer, and it was evident that they were in no normal state of mind. Some in the crowd recognized them as Galilæans. As the people stood there looking up and listening to a torrent of words, meaningless to them, a feeling of uneasiness took possession of them. Here was something strange, inexplicable, outside the order of their daily lives. Suddenly a man laughed and shouted loudly that those fellows were drunk—drunk, that was all. It was a comfortingly commonplace explanation, but at that early hour of the morning hardly plausible. Another man voiced the thoughts of many when he answered,

* *Luke* 11. 19, 20 (A.V).   *Matt.* 21. 42 (A.V.).   *John* 12. 24 (A.V.).

" No, this is not drunkenness.   Do you not hear how they speak of things unutterable, of the wonderful works of God? "

There came to the minds of those who stood by how the Spirit of God had entered into the prophets in the days of old; how Ezekiel and Isaiah had seen visions and become spokesmen for the Lord Himself, and Jeremiah had been forced to speak God's message even to a generation that would not listen.   They remembered Elijah prophesying drought, Moses coming down from Mount Sinai to declare the Law, David dancing before the Ark, Saul in a sudden ecstasy leaping and shouting with a band of wandering prophets.   As they stood questioning among themselves and wondering, one of the men on the roof made a sign that he would address them, and they recognized him as Peter, a follower of Jesus.   In Peter's bearing there was a new assurance, a confidence which commanded attention, and the crowd fell silent and gathered closer as he began to speak.*

He told them that Joel's prophecy was being fulfilled before their eyes.   This was the day of which the prophet spoke when he said:

" And it shall come to pass in the last days, saith God, I will pour out of my Spirit upon all flesh; and your sons and your daughters shall prophesy, and your young men shall see visions, and your old men shall dream dreams.

" And on my servants and on my handmaidens I will pour out in those days of my Spirit; and they shall prophesy." †

This, then, was the long-looked-for Day of the Lord, that day when God would visit His people and be present in the midst of them.   The crowd listened awestruck, for God is holy, and only men with clean hands and pure hearts dare face the thought of coming into His presence.

* See *Acts* 2.   † *Acts* 2. 17 (A.V.).

Peter went on to speak to them of Jesus of Nazareth, the Messiah whom they had failed to recognize. Jesus, said Peter, was " a man approved of God among you by miracles and wonders and signs, which God did by him in the midst of you as ye yourselves also know; him, being delivered by the determinate counsel and foreknowledge of God, ye have taken, and by wicked hands have crucified and slain: whom God hath raised up, having loosed the pains of death: because it was not possible that he should be holden of it ". And quoting from the Psalms he proved to them that God had made Jesus, whom they crucified, both Christ and Lord.

As he spoke, fear came upon those who heard him. They sensed that they were in the presence of a power other than the power of man. These were not the words of a Galilæan fisherman, but of one who, like the prophets, like Moses himself, was filled with the Spirit of God. Moses' face was glorified when he came down from Mount Sinai, and so was Peter's, fresh from his baptism of fire and Spirit in the upper room. To those who heard them the truth of his words came home with irresistible conviction, and in a flash they realized their guilt and the terror of their present situation. The Messiah had indeed come, but they had failed to recognize him and had allowed him to be put to death. Turning to St Peter and the other Apostles they said:

" Men and brethren, what shall we do ? "

St Peter replied:

" Repent, and be baptized everyone of you in the name of Jesus Christ for the remission of sins, and ye shall receive the gift of the Holy Ghost. For the promise is unto you and to your children, and to all that are afar off, even as many as the Lord our God shall call." *

* *Acts* 2. 37 (A.V.).

Many of those who heard him stayed, being convinced by what they had seen and heard. These listened to the apostles' teaching and, having been baptized, " they continued steadfastly in the apostles' doctrine and fellowship, and in the breaking of bread and in prayers ". In this manner the Church began her age-long mission of preaching the good news of the risen Christ to the world he came to save.

The Book of the Acts of the Apostles, from which almost all our information about the first days of the Church is derived, is a fine piece of historical writing, in the main reliable, economical, and vivid. But it has the defects which belong to the age when it was composed. There was then no generally recognized system for reckoning dates, and consequently writers tended to be less aware of the time-pattern than are modern historians. After narrating a certain sequence of events, St Luke often goes back several years to trace the beginnings of the next matter with which he wishes to deal. Modern historians perforce do the same, but they indicate the relative dates, which St Luke does not. Consequently the chronology of Acts is puzzling, and has to be understood with the help of the few dates which we can fix from other sources. Moreover, every historian must select what he intends to record, and St Luke omits much which we should dearly like to know. We are not told what happened when those Jewish pilgrims who were baptized at Pentecost returned home. Was it through them that Christianity first reached Alexandria, Asia Minor, and Rome itself? St Luke is not concerned to trace the origin of the Christian communities in Alexandria and Rome; he follows the main line of the Church's development, and ignores the rest. But he does give us vivid pictures of life in the primitive Church, and we can rest assured that these are drawn from conversations that St Luke had with actual witnesses. When St Luke accompanied St Paul to Jerusalem he had ample opportunity to collect material for his history. Much of what he tells us about the first few years he must have learnt from St Philip, one of the Seven, with whom he stayed at Cæsarea.* Acts has been proved to be on the whole a reliable source, but when, as we must, we attempt to read between the lines of St Luke's narrative, we have little to help us except a few references in St Paul's epistles and some doubtful traditions recorded at a much later period. In spite of this deficiency, modern scholars have done much towards reconstructing the history of the primitive Church by piecing together minute scraps of evidence. In the account which follows their conclusions are taken for granted. Those who wish to examine the evidence for themselves should consult the books referred to in the footnotes and reading lists.

The Church was catholic from the beginning. On the first day of her history, the day of Pentecost, men from many lands were added to the number of those who believed in Christ; yet all these men were Jews. This seems a contradiction, but it is true to fact. In the fulness of time, when the Messiah came to his people, they were not merely established in the Promised Land, a compact little nation centred upon the holy city of Jerusalem, they were also scattered abroad among the Gentiles, forming a separate colony in almost every important city of the Roman Empire. These Jews of the Dispersion were allowed to live according to their own faith. They were not forced to take part in heathen worship or to break their ceremonial law by mixing with Gentiles. They lived apart, and met each Sabbath in their synagogues to worship God and to hear the reading of the Law. They formed islands of Judaism in the pagan world. But that was not all. In the first century the Jews were filled with a missionary spirit which they since seem to have lost. They welcomed

* *Acts* 21. 8.

Gentiles at their synagogue services. Indeed, as our Lord said, they would "compass sea and land to make one proselyte".* Many of the more thoughtful among the Gentiles were glad to listen to Jewish teaching. They were ready and willing to believe that one righteous God is the Ruler of the universe, and not a crowd of quarrelsome divinities less moral than their worshippers. But few of those who listened were willing to submit to circumcision and the elaborate requirements of the Jewish Law. Some did go the whole way and become Jews. More were content to worship God and keep the moral requirements of the Law, and these were known as god-fearers.

Had the Jews known the hour of their salvation, it is easy to see how quickly they could have proclaimed the news of the Messiah's coming throughout the civilized world. They were within sight of the goal for which their long history had been but a preparation. One of their prophets foresaw that moment and wrote:

"Behold, thou shalt call a nation that thou knowest not, and nations that knew not thee shall run unto thee because of the Lord thy God, and for the Holy One of Israel; for he hath glorified thee." †

But when the time came, the majority of the Jews rejected their Messiah and refused to play their destined role in history. A few, like the "faithful remnant" of Old Testament times, acknowledged Jesus as the Christ, and through them God's purpose was fulfilled. But in the days immediately succeeding Pentecost it is doubtful whether the apostles themselves had fully realized the magnitude of the task before them. They certainly did not see any incompatibility between faith in Christ and full obedience to the Law of Moses. They worshipped daily in the Temple and taught there. They addressed their message to their fellow Jews,

* *Matt.* 23. 15.   † *Isa.* 55. 5.

to the Jews of Palestine, not those of the Dispersion, and they spoke it in the very citadel of orthodoxy, Jerusalem.

The Sadducees at once showed uncompromising hostility. When St Peter healed the lame man, who lay at the Temple gate, and proclaimed that he had done so in the name of Jesus of Nazareth, the Christ, the priests at once arrested him and St John, who was with him. But at the trial before the Sanhedrin next day, the apostles were merely cautioned not to preach in the name of Jesus, and were allowed to go. Although St Peter and the others continued to preach publicly and to heal many in Christ's name, some time seems to have elapsed before the second arrest. It may be that fear of the people had something to do with this, for crowds flocked to hear the apostles, and brought their sick into the streets to be healed by them. When at last the High Priest and certain of the Sadducees arrested them again and brought them before the Sanhedrin for trial a second time, the court was divided in opinion. The Sadducees wished to condemn the apostles to death, but the Pharisees, led by Gamaliel, favoured tolerance, and won the day. The prisoners were beaten for their contempt of the court's previous injunctions and were set free.

During this first period, when they still hoped to convince even the Jewish religious leaders that Jesus was the Christ, the apostles seem to have concentrated their attention on Jerusalem. It is probable that they also went through the cities of Israel two by two, as they had done when our Lord sent them out on a practice tour during his own ministry. They may well have had in mind the words which he then spoke to them:

" Go not into any way of the Gentiles, and enter not into any city of the Samaritans: but go rather to the lost sheep of the house of Israel." *

* *Matt.* 10. 5–6.

True, their commission was now to preach to all the world, but surely, they must have thought, to Israel first. Throughout this time the apostles and all the believers lived the life of devout Jews. They kept the Law and, when they were in Jerusalem, they worshipped in the Temple. They also met privately for prayer; but there was nothing unorthodox in this, for any twelve Jews might form a synagogue. The only new feature was that when they met they broke bread together in remembrance of our Lord's death and passion, in accordance with the commandment which he gave his disciples on the night that he was betrayed. This act of truly Christian worship was the centre of their life of fellowship, but they did not on that account feel indifferent towards the religious practices in which they had been brought up. On the contrary, their customary Jewish worship meant not less but more to them, now that they knew that the age-long hope of Israel had been fulfilled. So too with their study of the Scriptures, taught by the apostles these first believers learnt to interpret the words of the prophets in the light of Christ's life. They felt themselves to be entering into the promised joy for which all their ancestors, from the patriarchs onwards, had prayed and hoped. Years afterwards, the writer of Hebrews composed a glorious roll-call of Old Testament heroes who had lived and died by faith, and he ended it in these words:

" These all having obtained a good report through faith, received not the promise: God having provided some better thing for us, that they without us should not be made perfect." *

It was this knowledge, that they were the inheritors of God's eternal promise, that filled the first Christians with such overflowing joy. They felt the power of God's Holy Spirit within them; they saw proof of his presence

* *Hebrews* 11. 39–40 (A.V.).

in the miracles of healing which led people to bring their sick out into the streets when they saw St Peter passing by; they had moments of ecstasy when they "spake with tongues", as on the day of Pentecost, or broke out into prophecy. They looked forward confidently to our Lord's return in glory, which they expected at any moment and prayed for constantly.

The life of the primitive Church, in the years that immediately followed our Lord's Ascension, was poetry where ours is prose. They moved to a different rhythm, as people do when they are happily in love. Their standards were not the standards of common sense or of this world at all; to them the world was well lost, for they desired a better country—that is, an heavenly. They did not look forward to long centuries of earthly progress and the slow redemption of all mankind. Instead they eagerly expected the end of the world within the lifetime of their own generation, and they were constantly preparing themselves to play their part in the final act of the great drama: the Day of Judgement and the triumph of Christ and his chosen. Meanwhile their daily lives were altered to conform to this great change of heart. They must still eat and drink, buy and sell; but though they must continue to be in the world for the short time that remained, they need not be of it. They no longer cared about possessions or saving money for the future; instead they sold what they had and laid the money at the apostles' feet, so that the whole brotherhood might share alike and none be rich or poor among them.

" And the multitude of them that believed were of one heart and of one soul; neither said any of them that ought of the things which he possessed was his own: but they had all things in common." *

* *Acts* 4. 32 (A.V.).

That this account is not simply an idealized picture of the Church's earliest days is proved by the recorded exception to the rule: the case of Ananias and Sapphira, who sold their land, but, when they gave the price of it to the apostles, kept back part and pretended they had given all. It was not their meanness so much as their hypocrisy which was felt to be a sin against the Holy Ghost, a betrayal of the divine love which united those who believed in Christ. The detestation felt for that act of deception is a measure of the sincerity of the community as a whole.

Thus for a short time, probably less than three years, the Church grew steadily, undisturbed by persecution and untroubled by dissension. To an outside observer it might have seemed that the followers of Jesus formed a harmless sect, which would retain its peculiarities for a while and then be reabsorbed into orthodox Judaism and speedily forgotten. A crisis was needed to reveal the true nature of the new faith, and that crisis came in an unexpected way, through the Greek-speaking Jews in Jerusalem, Hellenists as they were called.

There was always a number of these Jews of the Dispersion resident in the holy city. Young men from far-off cities came there to sit at the feet of famous rabbis and learn from them the interpretation of the Law. The synagogues of every province in the Roman Empire sent their representatives to deliver the money which they had collected for the upkeep of the Temple. Jews from all over the world visited Jerusalem for longer or shorter periods, and for a variety of reasons, as is always the case with a capital city. But these Jews from abroad did not mix easily with those who were natives of Jerusalem. Instead they tended to group together according to the districts from which they came. Thus there was a synagogue of the Cyrenians, another of the Alexandrians, another of the Libertines, freedmen from Rome. In many ways Hellenists differed from the stricter Jews. Their normal language was Greek, not Aramaic. They even studied the Scriptures in Greek, in the famous translation known as the Septuagint. Their whole outlook was cosmopolitan, as well as Jewish. Pharisees and other orthodox Jews, and more especially those of Jerusalem, viewed them with distrust. They suspected them of being contaminated by their intercourse with Gentiles, of having sold their birth-right for a mess of pottage. They dubbed them Hellenists, implying that they were more Greek than Jewish, and they mistrusted them accordingly.

It is easy to attribute their attitude to jealousy and narrow-mindedness, but there was more behind it than that. Throughout their history the Jews had been a small nation surrounded by alien and heathen civilizations. They had gone into exile in Babylonia and had emerged again, their faith intact and purified. Alexander's successors had fought for their land, and under Hellenistic rulers Greek cities had grown up in their midst. Hellenistic civilization, with all its attractiveness, its vice, and its paganism, penetrated the Holy Land itself. In defence the Jews built a protective barrier out of the custom of circumcision, the observance of the Sabbath, and the elaboration of the Law, especially the food rules. Behind this barrier they kept their living treasure, their faith in one God, the Holy One of Israel, and preserved it undefiled. But when the day for attack came, when the Jews should have carried their faith forward into the pagan world, most of them clung to their defences and would not venture out. Their mistrust of the Hellenists was part of their mistrust of the new forward movement for which the time was ripe, but for which they were not ready.

The young Church from the beginning contained Hellenists as well as Palestinian Jews. Some of those Hellenists who joined the Church at Pentecost returned to their homes soon afterwards, but others remained in Jerusalem. Sooner or later the tension between the Hellenists and the Palestinian Jews was bound to make itself felt within the Church. The incident which provoked the actual conflict was trivial in itself, and no one would have suspected that great events would follow from it.

The apostles were faced one day with a domestic crisis. By then the Church was quite a large community. It is doubtful whether all property was still held in common, but certainly there was a common fund from which the apostles supplied food to those in need, especially to widows. The trouble occurred when the Hellenists found that their widows were being neglected in the daily ministration. They complained to the apostles, who thereupon appointed from their number seven men to attend to the needs of their fellow Hellenists, St Stephen being one of those appointed. No action can have seemed less likely to interest the outside world and to provoke persecution. But the Seven were men of character, and they were not simply almoners, but preachers as well. St Stephen made a point of speaking in the synagogues of the Hellenist Jews, and his teaching was far more offensive to Jewish prejudices than that of the apostles had hitherto been.

St Stephen outraged Jewish patriotism by showing from the Old Testament that God had spoken to the patriarchs, not only in the Holy Land, but also in Mesopotamia, Haran, Egypt, Midian, and the wilderness. He attacked the exaggerated devotion to the Temple by showing that it had not been in existence in the great days of the deliverance from Egypt and the entry into the Promised Land, and by reminding them that " the Most High dwelleth not in houses made with hands ". He showed that the rejection of Jesus Christ was the culmination of the nation's continual rejection of the deliverers sent by God, from Moses onwards. Such teaching meant open war. St Stephen was at once engaged in a series of acrimonious debates, and we are told that he often silenced his opponents with his inspired replies. One of his most dangerous adversaries was a young man from Tarsus called Saul, who had come to Jerusalem to study the Law. Although he was proud of the Gentile city where he had been brought up and of his rights as a Roman citizen, Saul was no " Hellenist " in his sympathies, but a Pharisee of the Pharisees. St Stephen's teaching aroused in him a burning indignation, and from what we know of his character, we can be fairly sure that he was one of those who brought St Stephen to trial.

St Stephen was brought before the Sanhedrin on the charge of blasphemy against Moses and against God. His masterly speech, quoted in the seventh chapter of Acts, is not a defence, but a summary of his teaching, a speech for the prosecution with his accusers in the dock. Before he had finished, his hearers, overmastered by their anger, dragged him out of the court and illegally stoned him to death. Saul stood by watching, keeping guard over their clothes.

" And there arose on that day a great persecution against the church which was in Jerusalem; and they were all scattered abroad throughout the regions of Judæa and Samaria, except the apostles." *

The first brief period of peace had ended. It had seemed for a time that Christianity could be contained within the framework of Judaism. The apostles them-selves were Palestinian Jews, reluctant to break with the traditions of a lifetime and subconsciously influenced by the environment of their earlier years. St Peter had been brought up by the lake of Galilee, which in his day was ringed with cities. Professor Adam Smith has described her coasts in the time of our Lord:

* *Acts* 8. 2 (A.V.).

" Greek architecture hung its magnificence over her simple life: Herod's castle, temple and theatres in Tiberias; the bath-houses at Hammath; a hippodrome at Taricheæ; and, farther back from the shore, the high-stacked houses of Hippos; the amphitheatre in Gadara, looking up the lake with the Acropolis above it, and the paved street with its triumphal archway; the great Greek villas on the heights about Gadara; with a Roman camp or two, high enough up the slopes to catch the western breeze, and daily sending its troops to relieve guard in the cities." *

On the occasions when business took St Peter to one of these Greek cities, he would see temples and amphitheatres, statues of gods and goddesses, and image-sellers hawking their wares. To him it would be a City of Destruction whose very stones expressed the idolatrous thoughts of its inhabitants. He felt no desire to convert these people. They were unclean, and his duty was to avoid them as far as circumstances would permit. South of the Lake of Galilee lay the Decapolis, whose ten or more Greek cities were combined in an anti-Semitic league. The Jews hated these cities one and all, and the apostles were not immune from the prejudices of their race. Our Lord himself during his ministry had shunned the way of the Gentiles, and at the time he had bidden his disciples to do the same. His message was to be given first to God's Chosen People, and then through them to the world. There was thus a real danger that the apostles might fail to realize that the first stage had already ended and that it was time to move forward to the next. Professor W. M. Ramsay in his great book *St Paul the Traveller* has made a telling comment on this first period in the history of the Church:

" The Primitive Church had clung to Jerusalem, and lived there in a state of simplicity and almost community of goods, which was an interesting phase of society, but was quite opposed

* *The Historical Geography of the Holy Land*, p. 460.

to the spirit in which Jesus said ' Go ye into all the world and preach the Gospel to the whole creation.' For a time it seemed that the religion of Christ was stagnating into a sociological experiment." *

St Stephen's dynamic preaching brought all danger of stagnation to an end. He and the other Hellenists brought into the Church and into their interpretation of Christianity a liberalism which shocked orthodox Jews and frightened them into acts of persecution. St Stephen's martyrdom bore witness to the heroic aspect of the Church's calling. Like his Master, he prayed as he was dying, for the men who were murdering him and, having commended his spirit to Jesus, he fell asleep. In what better way could he have declared the Church's faith in Christ and the redemptive character of her work?

ANCHOR AND FISHES
Early Christian Symbol of
Hope in Christ
(*From the Catacombs*)

BOOKS FOR FURTHER READING

Commentary and notes in the Clarendon Bible edition of *Acts*.
St Paul the Traveller and Roman Citizen, by W. M. Ramsay.
Historical Geography of the Holy Land, by George Adam Smith, Chapter XXVIII, " The Greek Cities of the Decapolis ".
From Jesus to Paul, by Joseph Klausner, Ph.D. Chapters 2 and 3, on " The Jews of the Dispersion " and on " Proselytes and God-fearers ". A book written from the Jewish standpoint.

* *St Paul the Traveller and Roman Citizen*, by W. M. Ramsay. Chapter 3, p. 42.

D

CHAPTER II

To Antioch and Beyond: The Gospel
Versus the Law

THE persecution which followed the martyrdom of St
Stephen was the first severe trial which the Church had
to endure. It was a time of terror, when men and women
were dragged from their houses to prison, and the most
relentless among their persecutors was the young Pharisee,
Saul. All the leading Christians, except the apostles, left
Jerusalem and scattered to various places in Syria and the
neighbouring provinces. To those who experienced it
this time must have seemed one of calamity. In fact it was
the beginning of a new stage in the Church's growth, for
the effect of persecution was like that of water poured on
blazing oil: it caused the flames to spread. The Hellenist
Christians returned to their home-towns in Phœnicia,
Cyprus, Syria, and elsewhere and carried the Gospel with
them. These missionaries brought their message only to
their fellow Jews, for they, like the apostles, believed that
they were sent first, at least, to " the lost sheep of the house
of Israel ".* But St Luke, the Gentile historian of those
early days, is interested in tracing the growth of the Christian
community from a Jewish sect to a universal Church, and
he sees in this scattering of believers the first step towards
expansion. His account makes it plain that the Church
grew, not as the result of deliberate planning, but as all
living things grow, in accordance with its own inner
spirit. Men made decisions the full force of which they

* *Matt.* 10. 6. *Acts* 11. 19.

40

hardly understood. They took actions which were to
change the course of history, but whose results were hidden
from them. At times they were impelled to behave in a
way contrary to their traditions and upbringing. But
although they were often unaware of the full significance
of their own actions, they knew that they were inspired
and guided by the Spirit who came upon them at Pentecost.

The first step beyond the bounds of Judaism was taken
by St Philip, one of the Seven, when after the martyrdom
of St Stephen he went on a preaching tour in Samaria.
The Samaritans were not, strictly speaking, Gentiles, but
neither could they be reckoned among the Jews. While
accepting the Law of Moses, they had separated themselves
from orthodox Jews by setting up a temple of their own
and refusing to come up to Jerusalem to worship. The
quarrel had the bitterness of a family feud, and the ill-
feeling that perpetuated it can be measured by the astonish-
ment of the Samaritan woman whom our Lord asked for a
drink of water. Jews did not willingly speak to Samaritans,
much less ask for favours from them. Yet St Philip brought
the Samaritans the good news that Christ had come, and
many heard him with joy and believed.

It is not certain that the city where St Philip preached
was the old northern capital of Samaria itself. Sebaste, as
it was called in his day, had been rebuilt by Pompey and
thoroughly Romanized. The population was more Hellenist than Samaritan, and it seems on the whole more
probable that the reading " a town of Samaria " is correct,
and that Sebaste is not the town intended. Evidently St
Philip's preaching took the place by storm. Numbers were
baptized and many sick persons were restored to health of
body and mind amid general rejoicing. When the news
reached Jerusalem, the apostles sent St Peter and St John
to Samaria to examine this new venture. They, as the
accounts in Acts records:

" when they were come down, prayed for them that they might receive the Holy Ghost:

" For as yet he was fallen upon none of them: only they had been baptized into the name of the Lord Jesus.

" Then laid they their hands on them, and they received the Holy Ghost." *

The experience of Pentecost was repeated, and this time among the Samaritans.   The divine power, which had come upon the apostles, now came to these new converts through the sacramental action of the laying-on of hands. This is the first Confirmation of which we have any record, and it is not possible to be sure from Acts that baptism was always followed by the laying-on of hands in these earliest years.   But it would seem that it was the practice of the primitive Church to send an apostle, or some other man of authority, to any place where men had recently heard the Gospel.   St Barnabas was sent to Antioch in this way a few years later.†   The laying-on of hands after baptism certainly did become the normal practice at a very early period.‡   Thus the organization of the Church grew slowly and naturally, as the inevitable expression of the Spirit who united its many members into one body.

The mysterious ways of God cause much perplexity to those tidy souls who wish to fit the whole universe into a pattern of their own devising.   To such men Church history must be peculiarly exasperating, for the Spirit, like the wind, blows where it listeth, and the history of the Church is the record, not of orderly progress, but of disconcertingly unexpected acts of God.   The conversion of St Paul is such an act.   To an attentive reader of the New Testament, the quiet expansion of the Church under the leadership of St Peter follows as a natural sequel to the Gospel story.   But the transformation of Saul, the perse-

* *Acts* 8. 15–17.   † *Acts* 11. 22.
‡ *Hebrews* 6. 2; see also *Acts* 19. 6.

cutor, into St Paul, the Apostle, is unforeseen and startling. The addition of a man of genius to the leaders of the apostolic Church alters the whole preconceived pattern. It is St Paul, and not St Peter, who is the chief agent in freeing Christianity from the limitations of Judaism, and in spreading the faith to the western limits of the world. To anyone accustomed to distinguish between romances and records of fact, this life-like quality of unexpectedness reinforces all the other proofs of the verisimilitude of the New Testament.

Saul, armed with letters from the High Priest, empowering him to arrest Christians, was hastening to Damascus, accompanied by some of the Temple guard, when he experienced the vision which converted him. Three accounts of this vision are given in Acts.* They differ in presentation, for two are reports of St Paul's own speeches, but they agree in stressing the objective character of the experience. According to St Paul's narratives, the whole company saw a light from heaven and fell to the earth in fear, though he alone understood the voice which spoke out of that brightness. Modern critics who attempt to explain the vision as purely subjective—a product of subconscious pondering of St Stephen's arguments—fail to account for St Paul's conviction that he had seen the risen Christ. It was upon this vision that he based his claim to be an apostle, one sent out into the world to bear witness to Christ's resurrection. Writing to convince the Galatians that the Gospel he had presented to them was of God, he said of this experience:

" I certify you, brethren, that the gospel which was preached of me is not after man. For I neither received it of man, neither was I taught it, but by the revelation of Jesus Christ." †

To the Corinthians he says the same thing. After enumerating the post-resurrection appearances of Christ, he adds:

* *Acts* 9. 1–19; 22. 3–17; 26. 9–19.   † *Gal.* 1. 11–12 (A.V.).

" And last of all he was seen of me also, as of one born out of due time. For I am the least of the apostles, that am not meet to be called an apostle, because I persecuted the church of God. But by the grace of God I am what I am." *

St Paul reached Damascus blind and shaken, convinced that he had seen Jesus, the risen Christ, the Son of God. There he was sought out by Ananias, one of the Christians whom he had come to persecute; his sight was restored and he was baptized. By his own account in his letter to the Galatians, we know that he spent some time in the Arabian desert, and then returned to Damascus and preached there until, as we learn from Acts, he was forced to flee for his life, and only escaped because friends lowered him over the city wall by night in a basket.†

Damascus lies on the edge of the barren Arabian desert, and from remotest times caravans have passed that way linking Palestine and the Mediterranean with Babylon, Assyria, and the more distant East. Had his upbringing been different, St Paul might have gone east when he was driven from Damascus, and have spread the Christian faith in India and China; but he was a man of Tarsus, a citizen of the Roman Empire, and his thoughts turned west, not east. He returned to Jerusalem. By then it was three years after his conversion, but he was still remembered as Saul, the persecutor. The church at Jerusalem was at first afraid to receive him, until St Barnabas stood sponsor for him. The friendship between the two men may already have been of long standing; at any rate, St Barnabas knew about St Paul's conversion and what he had suffered for the name of Christ in Damascus, and his testimony convinced the brethren. Of the apostles, only St Peter and St James, the Lord's brother, were at that time in Jerusalem. St Paul conferred with them, and preached

* 1 Cor. 15. 8–10 (A.V.).
† Acts 9. 10–30; 22. 11–16. Gal. 1. 17. 2 Cor. 11. 32–33.

boldly in the synagogues; but soon his arguments with the Hellenist Jews provoked such fierce resentment that the brethren hurried him down to Cæsarea, and sent him by ship to Tarsus, to save his life. For the next few years he seems to have lived quietly in Cilicia, his native province.*

It must have been in about A.D. 41—some ten years after the martyrdom of St Stephen and six or seven years after the retirement of St Paul to Cilicia—that persecution again fell upon the church in Jerusalem. Herod Agrippa had received the title of king in A.D. 37, and in A.D. 41 Claudius granted him Samaria and Judæa, in addition to his other territories.† On his arrival in Jerusalem, he showed much zeal for the Law and delighted in offering the prescribed daily sacrifices. As part of the same policy, he revived the persecution of the Christians by beheading St James, the brother of St John. Finding this action popular, he arrested St Peter also, intending to bring him to trial when the feast of the Passover was ended. But in the brief intervening period the prisoner mysteriously escaped.

St Luke's account of St Peter's miraculous deliverance from prison is unusually vivid, and it has been suggested that he heard the story from St Peter himself, and also from Rhoda, the maidservant, who left St Peter standing at the door in danger of his life, while she rushed to tell the others who was there. After that, St Peter is not heard of again in Jerusalem until A.D. 46, the year of the famine. The persecution ended with Herod's death in A.D. 44, and any time after that it would have been safe for St Peter to return.

* *Gal.* I. 18–24. *Acts* 9. 26–30; 22. 17–21. The accounts of the Jerusalem visit in Acts and Galatians do not exactly tally, but the inconsistencies are not serious. See Clarendon Bible, *Acts*, p. 174, or, for a fuller account, Knox: *St Paul and the Church of Jerusalem*, pp. 102–105 and notes.

† For a fuller account of these events see W. L. Knox, *St Paul and the Church of Jerusalem*, pp. 167 f.

We are not told where he went in the meantime, but it has been plausibly conjectured that this was the occasion when he paid his first visit to Rome. A.D. 42 is the date given by Eusebius for St Peter's arrival in Rome, and there is also an early tradition that, in his parting instructions, our Lord told the apostles to make Jerusalem their head-quarters for twelve years, and then go among the Gentiles. Whether our Lord said anything of the kind we cannot tell, but the tradition may be founded on the fact that about this time the apostles did undertake evangelistic work farther afield.

From this time on, St James, the Lord's brother, not St Peter, is always mentioned as the head of the church in Jerusalem. Unfortunately we have hardly any trust-worthy information about the missionary work of the various apostles. That St Peter went to Rome is well attested both by literary and monumental evidence. St John's work in and about Ephesus has the support of early tradition. But of the other apostles, the only one whose sphere of work is known is St Thomas. According to the Gnostic *Acts of St Thomas*, the apostles cast lots for the districts to which they should go, and India fell to the lot of St Thomas. This might be dismissed as a romantic legend, but some of the details of the account given of his travels have been checked and shown to be authentic. In the first century A.D., there was a trade route between Alexandria and India. The traveller would go by boat up the Nile to Andrapolis, then he would proceed by land to a port on the Red Sea, and take ship from there to the mouth of the Indus. The Acts mention that St Thomas stayed en route at Andrapolis, and they give the name of the king at whose court St Thomas was received on arrival. This king was called Gundaphorus, and he is known to have reigned in the Punjab until about A.D. 50, when his kingdom was invaded. The ancient church of Southern India claims that St Thomas founded it about A.D. 52, and this date seems reasonable, if St Thomas had to flee from the Punjab when his protector was defeated two years earlier.

The expansion of the Church has an inner as well as an outward history, and in this phase the inner history is that of a great struggle between those who would confine faith in Christ within the limits of Judaism, and those who would preach him also to the Gentiles. In this struggle St James played the part of a peace-maker. He himself was an orthodox Jew. He kept the Law and was constant in worship at the Temple, so much so that he had a reputation for piety among Jews as well as among Christians. A second-century Jewish Christian wrote a striking description of him:

" He used to enter alone into the Temple and be found kneeling and praying for forgiveness for the people, so that his knees grew hard like a camel's because of his constant kneeling and asking forgiveness for the people."

Although the epistle attributed to him in the New Testament was probably written by an anonymous author some years after St James's martyrdom, its Jewish trend of thought is quite in character. To St James fell the difficult task of attempting to reconcile the orthodox Jews within the Church with those who would admit the Gentiles.

It was not in Jerusalem, but in Antioch, that men first began to preach Christ to the Gentiles. Nicolas, one of the Seven, was a proselyte of Antioch. In the persecution that followed St Stephen's martyrdom, he would naturally return home to Antioch, and other Christians must have joined him almost immediately. There they preached in the synagogues, and soon made converts among the Jews. There was a large Jewish quarter in Antioch, but the place itself was Greek in origin and thoroughly pagan in character. Officials knew it as the seat of the imperial legate for Syria–Cilicia–Phœnice, and as the Roman military base for wars in the east. But travellers knew it as a vast pleasure city, famous for its night life, its illuminations, its dancing-girls and shows, and above all for the groves " of Daphne by Orontes ", where priestesses and slave-girls by the hundred were dedicated to the orgiastic worship of Apollo. A few miles away lay Seleucia, not only a harbour for traders, but also a Roman naval base, and trade routes from the Euphrates and distant Asia made Antioch the gateway between East and West. In Jerusalem it might be possible for a Jew to keep apart from Gentiles; in Antioch it was not. Even in the synagogues there were God-fearers: Gentiles who were attracted to Judaism, but who had not accepted all the Law. Nicolas himself was a proselyte.

It was several years after the martyrdom of St Stephen that the decisive step was taken. Then the church at Jerusalem was startled by the news that some " men of Cyprus and Cyrene, when they were come to Antioch, spake unto the Greeks also, preaching the Lord Jesus ".* On hearing this, the church chose St Barnabas, and sent him to Antioch to deal with the situation in whatever way the Spirit might guide him. No mention is made of the apostles, and it is probable that this happened after they had left Jerusalem and not very long after St Peter's escape. The choice of St Barnabas was a very happy one. He was himself a Hellenist Jew from Cyprus, and would not share the prejudices of the narrow Pharisaical party within the Church. On the other hand, he had been with the apostles from the earliest days, and could speak with authority. From the first he made a deep impression on the young community in Antioch, " for he was a good man, and full of the Holy Ghost and of faith: and much people was added unto the Lord ". But the largeness of his mind appears most strikingly in his recognition of a man greater than himself. He had not been long at Antioch before he went to Tarsus to seek St Paul, whom he brought back

* *Acts* 11. 20; see also 4. 36.

with him, and the two worked together in Antioch for over
a year. In that city, which was a meeting-place of East
and West, Jews and Gentiles met together in their daily
business, and it was impossible to preserve the social barrier
between them as strictly as in Jerusalem. St Paul and St
Barnabas accepted the situation which they found there.
They continued to receive Gentiles into the Church without
demanding that they should first be circumcised, and the
Christian community increased and prospered. From a
tiny handful of believers it grew large enough to attract
attention. The pagan population, noted for its ready wit,
dubbed them " Christians ", and the nickname stuck.

The little we know about the church at Antioch suggests
that it was organized on rather different lines from the
mother church in Jerusalem. There was no single leader
at its head, nor was there a council of elders. Instead, the
church of Antioch was ruled by prophets and teachers, of
whom the chief were Barnabas, Symeon Niger, Lucius of
Cyrene, Manæn, and Saul.* Lucius must have been one
of the men from Cyprus and Cyrene who first preached the
Gospel to the Gentiles, and Symeon may well have been
another. Manæn was a man of high social position. He
is described as Herod's foster-brother, having been educated
with him at Rome. The use of the term " prophet "
shows how conscious the Antiochene church was of its
dependence on the inspiration of the Holy Spirit. One of
the earliest actions taken by the church of Antioch was
prompted by a prophet, and it had important results.
Agabus, a prophet from Jerusalem, gave warning of
approaching famine, and Christians at Antioch at once
began to collect money for future relief work. Food was
scarce in Palestine in A.D. 45, and famine conditions prevailed in A.D. 46. This must, therefore, have been the
year in which St Paul and St Barnabas set out to carry

* *Acts* 13. 1.

relief to Christians in Jerusalem from those in Antioch. The action was in accordance with the spirit of Christian love and fellowship, which had led the first Christians in Jerusalem to share their goods. It showed plainly that the expansion of the Church had caused no breach in her unity. But if, as seems most probable,* this is the visit alluded to by St Paul in his letter to the Galatians, when he says that in fourteen years he went up again to Jerusalem " by revelation " with Barnabas and Titus, then the visit is important for another reason also. For St Paul took the opportunity to explain to those who were " reputed to be pillars " at Jerusalem what he and St Barnabas had been teaching the Gentiles of Antioch. Already men, whom St Paul describes as " false brethren ", were objecting to the practice of admitting Gentiles into the Church without compelling them to accept Judaism first. St Peter and St John were back in Jerusalem at this time, as well as St James, for after the death of Herod in A.D. 44, the Church was enjoying an interval of peace. St Paul talked the matter over privately with the apostles, and they agreed that he and St Barnabas had been called to work among the Gentiles, while their own mission was primarily to the Jews. Confirmed and encouraged by the apostles' approval, St Paul and St Barnabas returned to Antioch, taking John Mark with them, and shortly afterwards the church of Antioch was guided by the Holy Spirit to send them out on the first great missionary journey to the Gentiles. Accompanied by St Mark, they went down to the nearby port of Seleucia and took ship for Cyprus, the island where St Barnabas was born.

Of the three men who embarked at Seleucia, probably only St Paul realized to the full the significance of the new

---

* *Gal.* 2. 1–10. For the identification of St Paul's visits to Jerusalem mentioned in *Galatians* with those described in *Acts* see Clarendon Bible *Acts*, note on Chapter 11. 30.

undertaking. Years before,* on his first visit to Jerusalem after his conversion, he had fallen into a trance while praying in the Temple, and had heard the voice of God bidding him go as an apostle to the Gentiles. Since then he had thought long and deeply about the relation between the old dispensation and the new. He knew from his own experience that obedience to the law of Moses could not set a man free from the bondage of sin, or enable him to " live unto God "; only faith in Christ could do that. Already he saw the Law, not as the irrevocable ordinance of God, but as a schoolmaster sent to prepare men for Christ. He could foresee a time when Jews who were Christians would realize that they had entered into their inheritance, and, as sons of God, need be under the tutelage of the Law no longer. As for Gentile converts, he could see no reason for imposing upon them the restrictions of the Jewish Law. He went out from Antioch prepared to preach Christ to the whole world, to the Jews first, and afterwards to the Gentiles. It is doubtful whether either of the others saw plainly all that was implicit in this new venture, but St Paul unquestionably did.

St Luke narrates the events of that momentous journey without comment, but evidently the mission was sent in the first place to the Jews of the Dispersion. Throughout Cyprus the three preached in the synagogues, and St Barnabas and St Paul continued to observe this rule in Asia Minor, only turning to the Gentiles when rejected by the Jews. When the work in Cyprus was ended, St Mark left them and returned to Jerusalem, where he probably rejoined St Peter. No reason is given for St Mark's departure, but we know that St Paul felt bitterly about it, and it may be that St Mark took fright when he realized the

* *Acts* 22. 17–21. It has been doubted whether the visit to Jerusalem referred to in this passage was the first after St Paul's conversion, though it appears to be so.

revolutionary nature of St Paul's ideas, and would not associate himself with the enterprise. However that may be, as St Paul and St Barnabas continued their missionary journey through southern Galatia, they met with fierce opposition from the Jewish communities in city after city, as soon as the nature of their teaching became thoroughly known. Before they arrived back in Antioch they had suffered much persecution at the hands of the Jews, and in spite of it had founded a church in every place where they had preached. No doubt some members of these new Christian communities were Jews, others had been prose-lytes, but the majority were Gentiles, uncircumcised and uninstructed in the Law. All ranked equally as Christians.

" There is neither Jew nor Greek, there is neither bond nor free, there is neither male nor female: for ye are all one in Christ Jesus." *

So St Paul wrote to them after his return home, and his practice made the full force of what he preached apparent to the world.

Meanwhile,† an event in Cæsarea had made the question of the admission of the Gentiles into the Church a matter of burning importance to Christians in Jerusalem. St Peter was making a tour of the Christian communities in Samaria and Judæa, and in the course of it he came to the port of Joppa, where he lodged in the house of Simon, the tanner, on the sea-front. The churches in this coastal region had been founded by St Philip some years before. Most of them were in mere villages, for at this period there were in the whole of that inhospitable stretch of coast only two ports—Joppa and Cæsarea. Joppa was as Jewish

* *Gal.* 3. 28 (A.V.).

† This incident is not placed in its correct chronological position in *Acts.* The Roman garrison to which the centurion Cornelius belonged was not stationed at Cæsarea until after the death of Herod Agrippa in A.D. 44, yet at the time of St Peter's visit Cornelius seems to have already been there some time. See Clarendon *Acts*, p. 176.

as Cæsarea was Roman, and the contrast between the two places is significant in view of what happened. Joppa had been won for the Jews by Simon Maccabeus, and was prized as their first and only harbour. The non-Jewish part of the population disliked the strict enforcement of the Mosaic Law and the banishment of their familiar gods. They often revolted, and in Pompey's time secured the city's freedom, but Cæsar handed Joppa back to the Jews, and from then on it became a centre of Jewish fanaticism and intrigue.

From the flat roof of Simon the tanner's house, St Peter could look down on the narrow streets of the old town, where foreign sailors and merchants rubbed shoulders with Jewish zealots, while here and there a Pharisee picked his careful way through the throng, avoiding defiling contacts as best he could. Before St Peter lay the harbour crowded with shipping, and snatches of sea-shanties mingled with a medley of shouts and strange oaths came to him on the wind. Far out to sea, the sail of a great Roman galley caught his eye, and for a moment his thoughts followed her course across the Mediterranean to Ostia, the port of Rome itself.* It was the sixth hour, and indoors the women were preparing dinner. The fresh sea air had made St Peter hungry, and a whiff from the kitchen set him thinking wistfully of food. With an effort he recollected himself and composed his mind for prayer. The sounds from the harbour and the street faded from his consciousness, and as he prayed he fell into a trance. It seemed to him that the heaven opened, and a great sheet, like the sail of a boat, descended from it, containing all kinds of clean and unclean beasts and birds and creeping things. At the same time a voice said: " Rise, Peter, kill and eat." But Peter, in his hunger, would not be tempted to break the ceremonial law, and he answered: " Not so, Lord; for I have never eaten anything that is common and unclean." Then a voice

* *Acts* 10.

said: " What God hath cleansed, make not thou common,"
and after three repetitions of these words the sheet was
drawn up again into heaven.

St Peter came to himself, and was still pondering on the
meaning of this vision, when he heard visitors at the gate,
and on going down he found a Roman soldier and two
household servants who had been sent to him by Cornelius,
a centurion of the Italian cohort at Cæsarea, to ask him to
come and tell him the good news he had from God. In
obedience to the vision, St Peter went, although to accept
Gentile hospitality was contrary to all he had been taught
to think right. He and his escort travelled some thirty
odd miles along the flat coast road before they reached
Cæsarea. The city, when they came to it, was as Roman
as its name. It was quite new, having been built only a
few years before by Herod. Even from a distance they
could see the outline of the pagan temple which, being on
raised ground, dominated the city. Near it was a theatre,
and a little farther on an amphitheatre, so designed that the
audience watching the games looked out across the harbour
to the sea. St Peter had been to Cæsarea before, on visits
to St Philip, whose home was there, and he hardly spared a
glance for its palaces and temples; but when the great
harbour came in sight, there stirred in him a little of the
old wonder and excitement with which he, a simple fisherman from Galilee, had first gazed at that great engineering
feat. The huge anchorage was artificial, being protected
by a breakwater 200 feet wide, reinforced at the entrance
by turrets. Rome's sea-power was very evident at
Cæsarea. As if to emphasize the fact, two statues, one
of Augustus and the other of Rome, looked out over the
harbour from the temple high above.

Even in this pagan stronghold there was a Jewish quarter,
and Cornelius, the centurion who had summoned St Peter,
was one of those who frequently went there to listen on a

sabbath day to the teaching in the synagogue. Cornelius was not a proselyte. He had not been circumcised nor did he keep the ceremonial requirements of the Law. But he was a " God-fearer ". He was attracted by the Jewish belief in one God, and by the high moral standard of their religion. He and those of his household met regularly for prayer, and it was while he was praying that he saw a vision of an angel, who bade him send to Joppa for St Peter. His mind was thus already prepared, and even as St Peter spoke to them he and many of his household believed. Before they could be baptized, the gift of the Holy Spirit came upon them, and they began to " speak with tongues " and praise God, as the apostles had done at Pentecost.

" Here, in a Roman soldier's house, in face of the only great port broken westward through Israel's stormy coast, the Gentile Pentecost took place and ' on the Gentiles was poured out the gift of the Holy Ghost '." *

The importance of what had happened was fully appreciated by the church at Jerusalem. On his return, St Peter had to face severe criticism for his action at Cæsarea. He had eaten with men who were uncircumcised, and had received them into the Church. St Peter's account of his vision, and of the outpouring of the Holy Spirit upon Cornelius and his household silenced the objectors. But although they " glorified God, saying, Then to the Gentiles also hath God granted repentance unto life ",† yet they did not all accept in principle the admission of Gentiles into the Church. On the contrary, certain of the stricter Jews among them consulted together how best to stop this drift from Judaism, which they so much deplored. They had heard, possibly through St Mark, of St Paul's unorthodox

* *The Historical Geography of the Holy Land*, by George Adam Smith, chapter 7. The preceding account of Joppa and Cæsarea is based on his vivid description of these places.

† *Acts* 11. 18.

E

attitude to the Law, and after the incident at Cæsarea they saw reason to fear that neither St Peter nor St James would make a stand against him. They decided to take action on their own account, and, without consulting the leaders of the Church, they sent out missionaries of their own to Antioch, Galatia, and elsewhere, to teach Gentile converts the importance of observing the Law and to persuade them to be circumcised. Before their arrangements were complete, St Paul and St Barnabas arrived back in Antioch from their first missionary journey, and were welcomed with joy by the church which had sent them out.

The church in Antioch evidently gave full approval to the action St Paul and St Barnabas had taken in freely admitting Gentiles into the Church. After their return both men appear to have resumed their former positions in the church, and no doubt undertook evangelistic work in the neighbourhood. A little later, St Peter arrived there to pay a visit of some length. He found that in Antioch Gentiles who had been converted to Christianity were on an equal footing with their Jewish brethren. St Peter raised no objection, and himself sat down to table with the Gentile Christians. It was at this point that the Judaizing missionaries arrived from Jerusalem. They claimed to speak for St James, and they took St Peter and the other leaders to task for defiling themselves by eating with men who were uncircumcised. They insisted that all Gentiles ought to accept the Law and be circumcised before being baptized as Christians. In spite of his recent experience at Cæsarea, St Peter was impressed by their arguments. He was not a man of learning, like St Paul, and he believed without thinking out clearly all the implications of his faith. After all, our Lord himself had fulfilled the requirements of the Law during his earthly life, save when its restrictions transgressed the higher law of love. It is perhaps not surprising that St Peter felt doubtful as to which was the right course. In his uncertainty, he withdrew from Gentile contacts and would no longer eat with brethren who were uncircumcised. Others followed his example, including even St Barnabas. St Paul stood alone, but utterly convinced of the truth which he had seen.

As St Paul wrote afterwards to the Galatians, he withstood Peter to his face because he was to blame. He remonstrated with him publicly, saying that they themselves, though they were Jews, had found salvation through Christ, not through the Law; how, then, dare they impose the bondage of the Law on men who had already found freedom from sin through faith in Christ? That St Peter was convinced we know, because he adopted this very same argument himself, when the question was eventually brought before the council of the whole Church.

This council, which ranks as the first of the great œcumenical, or general, councils of the Church, was held in Jerusalem about the year A.D. 49. The question to be decided was a momentous one, for the free admission of Gentiles meant on the one hand breaking with Judaism, and on the other the establishment of Christianity as a world religion in its own right.* St James presided, and the council apparently consisted of the apostles and elders. St Peter spoke in favour of admitting Gentiles into the Church without compelling them to keep the Law of Moses. He urged that God had shown this to be right when (at Cæsarea) He bestowed on Gentiles the gift of the Holy Spirit. St Paul and St Barnabas then confirmed what St Peter had said, " declaring what miracles and wonders God had wrought among the Gentiles by them ". Finally, St James summed up the matter: St Peter had shown that God himself had called the Gentiles to serve him, and the prophets had foretold that this would happen;

* *Acts* 15. See also Clarendon Bible *Acts*, Essay C, " The Decree of Acts XV and its Results ".

therefore he recommended that no pressure should be put upon the Gentiles to keep the Law of Moses, but simply to refrain from abominations—that is, from idolatry, from fornication, and from blood. This was agreed unanimously, and men were chosen to accompany the Antiochene delegation home and bring the Church's decision with them in writing. Up to a point, the report of the proceedings of this council reads like a summary of a modern conference; but what modern conference has dared to say of its findings, " It seemed good to the Holy Ghost and to us "? He who would be present in imagination at that council should re-read St Paul's letter to the Galatians. There he will find the passionate conviction, the more-than-prophetic inspiration which won the day:

" I through the law am dead to the law, that I might live unto God. I am crucified with Christ: nevertheless I live; yet not I, but Christ liveth in me: and the life which I now live in the flesh I live by the faith of the Son of God, who loved me and gave himself for me. I do not frustrate the grace of God: for if righteousness come by the law, then Christ is dead in vain." *

By the decision taken at the Council of Jerusalem, the Church made ready to fulfil her Lord's command to " make disciples of all the nations ".

BOOKS FOR FURTHER READING

The Earlier Epistles of St Paul, by Kirsopp Lake, especially Chapter 2 on the Judaistic controversy, and Chapter 5 on the Epistle to the Galatians.

Acts and *Galatians* in the Clarendon Bible.

In the Steps of St Paul, by H. V. Morton. Excellent description of ancient Antioch.

The Church in Rome in the First Century, by G. Edmundsen. Lecture 2, on the movements of St Peter.

St Paul and the Church of Jerusalem, by W. L. Knox. A valuable book for reference.

* *Gal.* 2. 19–21 (A.V.).

CHAPTER III

Into the Pagan World

THERE is a work called *The Acts of Paul and Thecla*, written probably towards the end of the second century, which contains much pious romancing with a grain or two of genuine tradition hidden in the chaff. One of these grains is the record of an incident in St Paul's first missionary journey, an incident not recorded by St Luke. Legendary details have been added to the story in the century or so which passed between the event and our recorded version of it, but some of the details appear to be authentic, and the most interesting of them all is a vivid and unflattering description of St Paul's personal appearance.

A man named Onesiphorus, who lived at Iconium, heard of St Paul and desired to listen to his teaching, so when the news reached him that St Paul had been forced to flee from Antioch and was coming to his town, he went along the road to meet him and invite him to his house. He stood there looking at the faces of the passers-by until at last he saw a man who he realized must be St Paul:

" a man little of stature, thin-haired upon the head, crooked in legs, of good state of body, with eyebrows joining and nose somewhat hooked, full of grace: for sometimes he appeared like a man and sometimes he had the face of an angel."

We should probably have thought this man an insignificant little Jew if we had met him in the flesh, but, knowing him through St Luke's record and his own letters, we recognize him for what he is: one of the greatest figures in history.

In the centuries which have passed between his day and ours, his voice has never been silent, for his epistles are constantly read aloud in the churches, and no single generation has succeeded in absorbing the full significance of his thought. There is always more to be discovered. But it was as a man of action that his contemporaries must have seen him, as he tirelessly and indomitably fulfilled his mission of preaching to the Gentiles. What that task involved he himself has told in his second epistle to the Corinthians:

" Of the Jews five times received I forty stripes save one. Thrice was I beaten with rods, once was I stoned, thrice I suffered shipwreck, a night and a day have I been in the deep; in journeyings often, in perils of rivers, in perils of robbers, in perils from my countrymen, in perils from the Gentiles, in perils in the city, in perils in the wilderness, in perils in the sea, in perils among false brethren; in labour and travail, in watchings often, in hunger and thirst, in fastings often, in cold and nakedness. Beside those things that are without, there is that which presseth upon me daily, anxiety for all the churches." *

St Luke's account of St Paul's three missionary journeys in Asia Minor and Greece is too familiar to need re-telling, nor have we any material with which to supplement it except St Paul's letters. Here we are chiefly concerned with the impact of St Paul's teaching upon pagan society, and with the life of the earliest Gentile Christians. That being so, certain questions are bound to occur to us. How did this wandering Jewish preacher impress the Roman officials, the university lecturers, the shopkeepers, artisans and slave labourers, the rich merchants and their wives, and the rest of those who made up the population of such thriving cities as Ephesus, Athens, Corinth, and Pisidian Antioch? Who were the first Gentile Christians? Were

* 2 *Cor.* 11. 24–28.

they rich or poor, slaves or free men? What change did their new faith make in their lives? What happened when they met for prayer and how were the churches organized? By studying the Acts and the Epistles it is possible to answer these questions at least in part.

Only by inference from the facts we have can we guess the impression St Paul made upon his pagan listeners, but we are not left in doubt as to the impression pagan society made upon St Paul. His enemies accused him of being a Hellenist, of being willing to lower the Jewish standard of righteousness in order to admit Gentiles into the Church. Nothing could have been said that was farther from the truth or that revealed a more superficial estimate of St Paul. Born and brought up in Tarsus, just such a pagan city as we have visited in imagination, St Paul had no illusions about the Gentiles. As a Roman citizen he was a member of a society from which, as a Jew, he stood in a sense apart. In the university at Tarsus he had listened to the rhetorical speeches and interminable debates of men who by their wisdom knew not God; he had watched the athletes straining in the race to win a perishable crown of laurel; he had not mixed with the Gentiles, yet he had found opportunity to observe their way of life; he had recognized that among these men, who knew not the Law, some " by patient continuance in well-doing " sought " for glory and honour and immortality ", but he saw that most were sunk in superstition and idolatry, worshipping gods in human and even in animal form, and shamelessly indulging in unnatural vice.

" And even as they refused to have God in their knowledge, God gave them up unto a reprobate mind, to do those things which are not fitting; being filled with all unrighteousness, wickedness, covetousness, maliciousness; full of envy, murder, strife, deceit, malignity; whisperers, backbiters, hateful to God, insolent, haughty, boastful, inventors of evil things, disobedient to parents, without understanding, covenant-breakers, without natural affection, unmerciful: " *

There is no more terrible indictment of a corrupt society than this, St Paul's considered verdict upon paganism. As a Jew he had been content in his younger days to keep himself free from the pollution of the Gentiles' sins, but as an ambassador for Christ he brought a message of salvation to this mortally sick world. St Paul believed that " God was in Christ reconciling the world unto himself, not imputing their trespasses unto them ", and his message was of reconciliation with God, not by obedience to the Law, but through faith in Jesus Christ.

If St Paul saw the pagan world through Jewish eyes, it is equally true that to the Gentiles he at first appeared simply as a Jew. Were we to seek St Paul in that typical pagan city where we wandered for a day, we should most likely find him, not in the Forum, nor even speaking at a street corner, but in the Jewish quarter, preaching in the synagogue. With the contradictoriness which distinguishes life from theory, the most striking feature of St Paul's mission to the Gentiles, as recorded in Acts, is his persistent policy of speaking first to the Jews. In spite of bitter Jewish hostility, in spite of being beaten, stoned, hauled before Roman magistrates by his own countrymen again and again, St Paul still seeks out the synagogue in each city that he visits and preaches there until driven from its doors. This practice was, no doubt, that of the whole apostolic Church, and may have been enjoined upon St Paul at the Council of Jerusalem. But it was also in accordance with his own belief that the Gospel is " the power of God unto salvation to every one that believeth; to the Jew first, and also to the Greek ", and the outcome of his passionate love for his own people, for whose sake he

* *Rom.* I. 28–30.

declares he could even wish himself " anathema from Christ ".*

If we could be present in the synagogue on the sabbath day just after St Paul's arrival in our city, we should see him, at the appropriate moment, take a roll either of the Law or of the prophets, and, having read a passage, sit down to expound it, as any distinguished visitor might do, or else stand up to speak at the invitation of the rulers of the synagogue. Sitting among the proselytes and God-fearers, or among the women in a place apart behind a screen, we should notice the deepening attention of his audience. As he passes from his summary of God's former dealings with the Jews to his announcement that the promised Messiah has actually come, we should see a stir among the congregation, followed by much greater excitement, exchange of glances, muttered comments, suppressed attempts at interruption, when he goes on to describe Christ's death at the hands of the Jews in Jerusalem and the proofs of his resurrection. And finally as he ends his speech we should hear him say:

" Be it known unto you therefore, brethren, that through this man is proclaimed unto you remission of sins: and by him every one that believeth is justified from all things, from which ye could not be justified by the law of Moses ",†

and already the opposition on the part of at least a section of the orthodox Jews would be plain, and so would the enthusiasm of most of his Gentile listeners. We should hear the God-fearers saying on their way out that this was what they had been longing for: an opportunity to become reconciled to God without submitting to circumcision and the full burden of the Jewish Law. We might also see a couple of Jewish elders taking counsel together as to how this dangerous man should be suppressed.

* *Rom.* 9. 3.   † *Acts* 13. 13–end.   Quoted verses 38–39.

It is vitally important to realize that willy-nilly the synagogue prepared the way for the church. Each synagogue had its circle of proselytes, men and women who had turned from paganism to the extent of worshipping God and attempting to obey the moral precepts of the Mosaic Law, though most of them were not willing to become practising Jews. These were the Gentiles who first heard and welcomed the Gospel. They were familiar with the Old Testament, with the prophetic books as well as with the Law. They believed in one God, maker of heaven and earth, and they knew that he is righteous. They were already conscious of their own sin and the evil of the world about them, and were seeking a way of salvation. They found that way in Christ. The first small groups of believers in Ephesus, Corinth, Athens, and other pagan cities must have included a high proportion of Jews and proselytes already trained in Judaism.* In consequence these churches contained a number of believers who were capable of understanding St Paul's teaching, without grossly distorting it, as converts from paganism were liable to do. Moreover, they inherited the Old Testament Scriptures and much of the synagogue's great tradition of worship.

How did St Paul impress the great majority of pagans, those who regarded the Jews with indifference or with active dislike and never darkened a synagogue's doors? Was there anything in their philosophy or in their religious experience which would enable them to understand and welcome the Gospel? There are a few incidents among those recorded by St Luke which are especially revealing. Throughout Acts he shows the Græco-Roman authorities, the proconsuls, and the Greek city rulers, as fair in their treatment of St Paul. For the most part, they protect him against mob violence, although some of them regard him

* See *Acts* 17. 4, 11–12; 19. 10.

as a trouble-maker and are eager to move him on to another city. They plainly treat him as a wandering Jewish preacher whose only title to respect is the rather surprising fact of his Roman citizenship. His message does not interest them. The exception is Sergius Paulus, the pro-consul in Cyprus, who summons St Paul and St Barnabas into his presence, so that he may hear the new doctrine that they are teaching. The most significant feature in the story is not the interest displayed by the proconsul, but the presence of Elymas, "the sorcerer", among his retinue. Elymas was a Jew, and his surname was Bar-Jesus. To describe him as a sorcerer is misleading, for the English word suggests a wicked fairy-tale character, very different from the kind of person meant by the Greek word "magus". The astrologer whom we met when we lunched with Sentius was a "magus", and, though he may have been something of a charlatan, he would have scorned to practise black magic. The magi, who were often to be met with in the Roman Empire, especially in the eastern provinces, claimed to possess the wisdom of the East, which originated in Persia. Some magi were actually Persians, others were Jews or Syrians, who had learnt how to read the stars, cast horoscopes, and foretell the future. All were part of that great influx of new ideas and new cults from the East into the Græco-Roman world, which had outgrown its own crude polytheism and was seeking some more satisfying religion to take its place. Professor Cumont in his fascinating book, *The Oriental Religions in Roman Paganism*, has described this invasion in all its aspects, and speaking of the spread of astrology he says:

" At first aristocratic—for to obtain an exact horoscope is a complicated operation and a consultation is expensive—this Asiatic divination quickly became popular, especially in the urban centres, where swarmed the slaves from the Levant. The learned astrologers of the observatories had their quack brethren who told fortunes at the corner of the crossroads or in the farm yards." *

The more aristocratic astrologers, like the three magi who brought gifts to the infant Christ, were accustomed to the courts of princes, and Bar-Jesus, whom we find in attendance on the proconsul, was evidently of this class. To Sergius Paulus, a " man of understanding ", eager to hear about God, Bar-Jesus seemed as promising a guide as St Paul. If some of the more intelligent pagans were prepared to listen to St Paul's teaching with an open mind, their minds were equally open to the theories of the astrologers and to the emotional appeal of the mystery cults. St Paul's contest with Bar-Jesus is repeated in St Peter's longer conflict with Simon Magus, for astrology in the first century was by no means a negligible opponent to the spread of the Christian faith.

What of the philosophers? Were they more ready than less educated men to recognize the truth, being free from superstition? Once, but as far as we know once only, did St Paul's audience consist entirely of the intelligentzia. That was in Athens, when certain Epicurean and Stoic philosophers seized upon him when he was speaking in the market-place and carried him off to the Areopagus, where they insisted that he should explain to them the new doctrine which he was proclaiming. In a few words St Luke conveys the intellectual pride, the restless curiosity, the sceptical mocking laughter of that university audience:

" And some said, What would this babbler say? other some, He seemeth to be a setter forth of strange gods. . . .

" (Now all the Athenians and the strangers sojourning there spent their time in nothing else, but either to tell or to hear some new thing.) . . .

* *Les Religions Orientales*, by F. Cumont, p. 199.

" Now when they heard of the resurrection of the dead, some mocked; but others said, We will hear thee concerning this yet again.

" Thus Paul went out from among them." *

St Paul's own comment on that scene is to be found in his first epistle to the Corinthians:

" For seeing that in the wisdom of God the world through its wisdom knew not God, it was God's good pleasure through the foolishness of the preaching to save them that believe. Seeing that Jews ask for signs, and Greeks seek after wisdom: but we preach Christ crucified, unto Jews a stumbling-block, and unto Gentiles foolishness; but unto them that are called, both Jews and Greeks, Christ the power of God, and the wisdom of God." †

After his experience at Athens, St Paul abandoned all attempt at persuasive eloquence or the appeal of human learning and determined not to know anything " save Jesus Christ, and him crucified ". But though, as St Paul tells us, there were " not many wise after the flesh, not many mighty, not many noble " among the first converts to Christianity, we must not go to the other extreme and assume that they were drawn only from the poor, from the illiterate, and from slaves. The Gentiles who listened to St Paul when he spoke in the market-place or in a hired lecture hall must have included all sorts and conditions of men. Just as people of every class and of very varied degrees of intellectual attainment listen to broadcast talks today, so did their first-century counterparts flock to hear the travelling teachers and philosophers with which the ancient world abounded. Men of every rank were growing dissatisfied with the traditional forms of Græco-Roman religion, which belonged to an earlier, less self-conscious phase in human development. They were seeking some

* Acts 17. 18, 21, 32–33.   † 1 Cor. 1. 21–24.

basis for a personal faith. Much of the old ritual was connected with seedtime and harvest, and was designed to promote the fertility of flocks and fields. It was full of meaning for a countryman, but the city-dwellers found that it did not touch their daily lives and personal concerns in the same way. Devotion to the household gods and ancestor-worship had also formed part of the old Roman religion; but the importance of family life had declined, and the strength of this cult had declined with it. There remained the deification of the State; but the Roman Empire had deprived innumerable city-states of their independence. Men retained their affection for their native city, but their local patriotism was inevitably diminished. Nor was the worship of the deified Emperor a satisfactory substitute for that of local divinities like Athena. Within the larger unity of the Empire, city communities lost much of their earlier sanctity, and men began to think of themselves as individuals and as men of the world, rather than as citizens whose lives were bound up with the welfare of their native place. To satisfy their new aspirations they turned to the philosophers, to the adepts of the oriental mystery religions with their message of individual salvation, and to the astrologers and the sorcerers, who appeared to offer them means by which they might become masters of their fates.

There can be little doubt that for men of this period the Eastern mystery-cults afforded the most intense religious experiences of any in the whole range of paganism. Though nothing is said in Acts about these cults, there is plenty of evidence in St Paul's epistles that he was familiar with their main features, and that some of the first Gentile believers had previously been initiated into them. In recent years a good deal has been discovered, and much more has been written, about these mystery religions. Some scholars have made the resemblances between their ritual and that of the Church appear far closer and more important than they really are. From our point of view the most interesting thing about them is that they exploited a need which they were unable to satisfy, and so indirectly prepared the way for Christianity. The Mysteries were many—Cybele, Isis, Osiris, Orpheus, Adonis, Mithra, and many others; all had their enthusiastic devotees, but the promise they held out was the same: the initiate would be delivered from the power of evil and assured of immortality. This harmonized well with the current philosophical conception of the human soul as a spirit imprisoned in a body. It was generally believed that matter was evil, and that to escape from it, and from the control which the dæmons ruling the seven planets exerted over the material world, was the necessary preliminary to the immortal life which was proper to the soul. The mystery religions professed to achieve this for the chosen few who were initiated into them, by means of elaborate ritual designed to unite the devotee to the god or goddess concerned. Being in origin fertility cults, their whole worship revolved round the death and resurrection of the god, a deification of the fertility of nature, which seems to die away in the autumn, only to revive again next spring. Having once been united with the god, the initiate was believed to share this power of resurrection, and was assured that after death he would be exalted above the planets.

Time has swept away the Mysteries, leaving behind only a few scanty records, in which allusions to their central rites are discreetly veiled. But in their day their impressive ceremonial made them familiar to thousands who were not among their votaries. Their public rites were dramatic enough. Early in March the worshippers of Isis passed in procession through many a Mediterranean city to launch their sacred vessel on the sea. As they wound their way through the streets, white-robed women scattered flowers and perfume, a band of torch-bearers followed, then a choir of young men singing a hymn to the accompaniment of flutes and pipes, next a host of tonsured, linen-clad initiates, and lastly the gorgeously robed priests, carrying the sacred symbols. Arrived at the shore, they launched their sacred boat with solemn chants and prayers, and watched it sail out to sea, bearing the petitions of the faithful with it. In November the procession set out again, this time in grief, with women wailing for the dead Osiris, only to return at length in joy, announcing his recovery with ecstatic dances and songs. Other mystery cults had similar rites, and, not only the initiates, but half the city would turn out to accompany these processions, to join the Bacchic orgies on the hills, or to witness the ceremonies at Eleusis.

If the public ritual was impressive, the secret rites of initiation were far more so. Only a few were thought worthy to be admitted to the innermost mysteries, and these were selected by the priests. The neophyte first passed through a period of probation. He underwent ritual cleansing with water. He was instructed by the priests in divine secrets which he must on no account reveal. He abstained from all rich food, especially wine and flesh, and avoided sexual intercourse for a certain length of time. When the day of his initiation arrived he was in a state of intense expectancy, which was heightened by a mass meeting in the temple. Then, at nightfall, the actual initiatory ceremonies began. They took place in secret, at first in utter darkness, and then in flashes of brilliant light. The impression they left is well conveyed in the guarded description by Apuleius:

" I drew nigh to the confines of death, and having trodden the threshold of Proserpine, I was borne through all the elements and returned to earth again; I saw the sun gleaming with bright splendour at dead of night; I approached the gods above and the gods below, and worshipped them face to face."

Such an experience was intoxicating, but, like other forms of intoxication, it was followed by a depressing reaction. When the initiate returned to normal life, he found his problems and anxieties as real as ever, and the planets were unpropitious just as often as they had been before he became a companion of the gods. The memory of what he had felt remained to haunt him with a dream of bliss unrealized. The Mysteries appealed to man's sense of wonder, his inexhaustible curiosity about the nature of the universe, his desire to fathom its inmost secrets. But the promised revelation never came. During his initiation the worshipper felt himself to be on the brink of great discoveries, much as a man may do under the influence of a drug which over-stimulates his brain. But when the experience had passed he was left with little which he could grasp with his reason. The myths of Isis, Bacchus, and Osiris might, or might not, have some eternal significance, but they certainly were not records of historical facts. For this reason, the Mysteries encouraged a form of religious sensationalism, and many were initiated into one cult after another in search of a satisfaction which always eluded them. It was surely for men who had known this craving, and who still suffered from the effects of it, that St Paul wrote:

" And if I have the gift of prophecy, and know all mysteries and all knowledge; and if I have all faith, so as to remove mountains, but have not love, I am nothing."

In Christianity the initiate of the mysteries found reality in place of dreams: God incarnate in an actual human life; Christ, instead of a mythical divinity; the Holy Spirit within him, in place of religious emotionalism. Looking back at the time when he had listened to the siren voices of the Mysteries, he might have said with Comus:

F

" Yet they in pleasing slumber lulled the sense
        And in sweet madness robbed it of itself ;
        But such a sacred, and home-felt delight,
        Such sober certainty of waking bliss
        I never heard till now."

Our records show that St Paul found scepticism and
intellectual vanity among the philosophers, worldly indifference among the rich, superstition and sensationalism
among the religious.   Surely, then, it was the poor, the
slaves, the working-class people who welcomed the Gospel?
Yes and no.   Some of the poor, certainly, became Christians; but others were as prejudiced, as worldly, and as
grossly superstitious as any of those who lacked the advantage of poverty.   One of the chief characters in the
Acts is the mob—that fickle, brutal, turbulent element in
the population of the Græco-Roman cities, which occasioned anxiety to all their governors.   Again and again
we read that the Jews stirred up the mob to attack St Paul
and his companions.*   In these cases the pretext was
usually the rumour that the apostles were atheists and
trouble-makers.   But when the populace at Ephesus rose
and staged a demonstration against St Paul and his associates in the local theatre, the instigators were not Jews, but
the silver-smiths who made shrines of Diana, and who saw
their trade threatened by the spread of Christianity.   For
two hours the mob shouted, " Great is Diana of the Ephesians! ", and were with difficulty quieted in the end by the
town clerk.†   A like motive of self-interest occasioned the
riot at Philippi.‡   One other incident sheds some light on
the populace at Ephesus, a city destined to be one of the
great centres of the early Church.   Certain Jewish exorcists
were in the habit of attempting the cure of lunacy by the

* *Acts* 14. 2–6, 19; 17. 5–6, 13.
    † Scenes in Ephesus: *Acts* 19. 8–end.
    ‡ At Philippi: *Acts* 16. 16–34.

use of magic. Some of these added the name of Jesus to the list of names they conjured with:

"And the evil spirit answered and said unto them, Jesus I know, and Paul I know; but who are ye?

"And the man in whom the evil spirit was leaped on them, and mastered both of them, and prevailed against them, so that they fled out of that house naked and wounded."

As a result many gave up the magical arts which they had practised:

"Many also of them that had believed came, confessing, and declaring their deeds. And not a few of them that practised curious arts brought their books together, and burned them in the sight of all: and they counted the price of them, and found it fifty thousand pieces of silver."

A few ancient magical books have survived to our own day, and a strange, unintelligible hotch-potch their incantations appear to us to be. But in the first century the practice of magic was no laughing matter. The old country magic of charms and love-philtres had become a stronger and more horrible thing with the spread of Persian dualism. Given that there are two ultimate forces in the world, an evil as well as a good, it is possible for men to set themselves to propitiate the evil principle and the demons that are part of it. This the sorcerers attempted to do, and in their devil-worship took over rites long since abandoned by the more civilized forms of paganism, including human sacrifice. Many of the magical practices were abhorrent to all decent human feeling, and sorcery was a crime punishable by death under Roman law. Yet in Ephesus, and in other cities, too, magic was secretly practised, and we can see from this passage that Jews as well as Gentiles dabbled in it, and some of the first Christians were guilty of continuing to indulge in it.

If Christians did not realize that magic, even of a fairly harmless type, was incompatible with their new faith, was their conversion real at all? If, as St Paul's epistles show, some of them continued to go to heathen feasts, were grossly selfish, even during the Lord's Supper, and condoned a case of incest in their midst, how were they better than pagans? No member of our own generation of Christians can feel himself entitled to throw stones at his brethren of the first or any subsequent century. If their behaviour did not always square with their profession, neither does ours. In attempting to picture what life was like in those first Christian communities founded by St Paul, it is easier, as we read through his letters, to pick out those features with which he found fault: the noisy, disorderly assemblies at Corinth; the "busybodies" at Thessalonica who would meddle with anything rather than do honest work; the quarrels of Euodia and Syntyche at Philippi. But to do so is to produce a caricature, and not a portrait. These were the blemishes of a church life incomparably richer in every essential than that which most of us experience today. We have but to turn to St Paul's catalogue of the gifts of the Spirit in his first epistle to the Corinthians to realize this:

"Now there are diversities of gifts, but the same Spirit. . . . For to one is given through the Spirit the word of wisdom; and to another the word of knowledge, according to the same Spirit: to another faith, in the same Spirit; and to another gifts of healings, in the one Spirit; and to another workings of miracles; and to another prophecy; and to another discernings of spirits: to another divers kinds of tongues; and to another the interpretation of tongues: but all these worketh the one and the same Spirit, dividing to each one severally even as he will." *

The list is compiled not from theory, but from observation.

* 1 *Cor.* 12. 4, 8–11.

If church assemblies at Corinth were disorderly, it was because members were bubbling over with inspiration, and could hardly wait their turn to speak. If we could be present at one of these gatherings, the spontaneous outbursts of prayer and praise, the ecstatic speech, the talk of miracles performed in the Name of the Lord, would be so unlike all that we are used to—the regular, orderly service, the surpliced choir, the decorous, unemotional congregation—that we should be tempted to dismiss it as " a revivalist meeting ", forgetting to ask what was reviving. If we could stay longer, and come to know the brethren better, our bewilderment at the outward signs of the Spirit would be lost in our amazement at the love which was transforming their lives. In spite of divisons and bickerings, which marred Christian life at Corinth and elsewhere, a new-born love for God was finding expression in love for one another. St Paul wrote to the Thessalonians:

" Concerning love of the brethren ye have no need that one write unto you: for ye yourselves are taught of God to love one another; for indeed ye do it toward all the brethren which are in all Macedonia." *

This " love of the brethren " found expression in works of charity, in the original meaning of that once lovely word. Hospitality, the care of orphans and provision for widows, visiting the sick, the collection of money for the needy brethren in Jerusalem—these were among the commonest forms their charity took. In this respect the Christian churches differed markedly from their pagan counterparts, the burial clubs. There, when gifts were made, they were distributed according to rank, not according to need, the man of highest rank receiving most, as we saw at the Neptune Club. The burial money was not a gift at all, but the payment of an insurance policy. To pagans the

* 1 *Thess.* 4. 9–10.

most impressive thing about the Christians was the love they had for one another.

There is one short letter by St Paul which has been preserved and incorporated in the New Testament almost, it would seem, by a miracle; for the letter has nothing to say about doctrine or about church affairs. It is simply a private letter from St Paul to Philemon, a wealthy Christian of Colossæ, asking him to receive back his run-away slave, Onesimus. In the famous thirteenth chapter of his first epistle to the Corinthians, St Paul has described the greatest of all the gifts of the Spirit—charity. In his letter to Philemon he has unconsciously shown us charity in action. There are no fine phrases about the equality of man or the iniquity of slavery as an institution. St Paul simply asks Philemon to receive back his slave Onesimus. He does not bid him free his slave, but rather welcome him as " a brother beloved ", just as he would welcome St Paul. Given the spirit in which that letter was written, slavery becomes impossible, for you cannot treat a person as a chattel if you love him. Unfortunately we have proved the converse true, too. Given the will to power and the desire to exploit people as though they were possessions, liberty is impossible, even if it be the legal right of every man according to the statute book.

Looking back down the centuries at these first beginnings, it is obvious to us that St Paul and the other apostles were building a world-wide Church which would outlast the Roman Empire and other empires after it. To St Paul and his contemporaries, this was by no means obvious. They looked, rather, for the immediate return of the Lord in glory, and they prayed daily for his coming. The evils of this world seemed to them relatively unimportant, for they were soon to be abolished. St Paul, writing to reassure the Thessalonians about the fate of the faithful dead, voices the hope they all shared:

" For this we say unto you by the word of the Lord, that we that are alive, that are left unto the coming of the Lord, shall in no wise precede them that are fallen asleep. For the Lord himself shall descend from heaven, with a shout, with the voice of the archangel, and with the trump of God: and the dead in Christ shall rise first: then we that are alive, that are left, shall together with them be caught up in the clouds, to meet the Lord in the air: and so shall we ever be with the Lord. Wherefore comfort one another with these words." *

With this expectation constantly in mind, the early Church was not preoccupied with organization. St Paul appointed elders to take charge of each church that he founded, and from the beginning the churches were in constant communication with each other by means of delegates and letters. The custom of collecting money to send to the church at Jerusalem was a means by which the churches expressed their unity, the outward and visible sign of an inward invisible love. We twentieth-century people, with our passion for planning, cannot but be struck by the fact that the pioneers of the Church relied so much on the guidance of the Holy Spirit. As a result, the organization of the early Church remained flexible, capable of adaptation to altered circumstances and of a growth the first Christians did not foresee. St Paul, bidding farewell to the elders of the church of Ephesus, as he set out for Jerusalem with the intention of going from there to Rome, seems to have had a premonition of the imprisonment that awaited him:

" And now, behold, I go bound in the spirit unto Jerusalem, not knowing the things that shall befall me there: save that the Holy Ghost testifieth unto me in every city, saying that bonds and afflictions abide me." †

It was a premonition which the event amply justified. Yet because the plan on which the Church was built was not

* 1 Thess. 4. 15–18.   † Acts 20. 22–23.

man-made, human opposition was unable to frustrate it. St Paul reached Rome, in spite of enemies, in spite of shipwreck; yet he arrived not as a free man, but as a prisoner.

SYMBOLIC SHIP FROM THE CATACOMBS

BOOKS FOR FURTHER READING

Roman Society from Nero to Marcus Aurelius, by Samuel Dill, especially chapters two and three.

The Pagan Background of Early Christianity, by W. R. Halliday.

The Church and the Roman Empire, by W. M. Ramsay. Account of St Paul in Asia Minor, and *The Acts of Paul and Thecla*.

Les Réligions Orientales, by F. Cumont.

Documents Illustrative of the History of the Church, ed. by B. J. Kidd, Vol. I, No. 35, " The Mysteries of Isis," from Apuleius.

CHAPTER IV

Rome: the Apostles and Nero

WE would give much for a document of equal authority
with Acts, covering the foundation of the church of
Rome and the later life of St Peter, but no such book has
survived, if, indeed, it ever existed. Instead we have to
piece together fragments of evidence, and our ignorance is
such that it is possible for some Protestant scholars to deny
that St Peter ever reached Rome at all, while Roman
Catholics are unshakably convinced that he was the first
bishop of that supremely important see. Supremely important it certainly was as long as Rome remained the
capital of the Empire. It was said that all roads led to
Rome, and that was true metaphorically as well as literally.
From all parts of the world men came there on imperial
business, for trade, in hope of advancement, with the
army, as teachers of philosophy, as priests of new cults, or,
like St Paul, as prisoners to be judged by Cæsar. Others
were brought there as slaves, having been captured in war
or bought in the market, and many of these eventually
became freedmen and were added to the city's cosmopolitan
population. Once Christianity had spread beyond Palestine, it was bound to reach Rome in a very short time, and
the church established there could not fail to play an important part in spreading the faith. Language was no
barrier, for Greek was as commonly heard as Latin in the
streets of Rome, and the Hellenist Jews and the first Gentile
converts were all Greek-speaking.

The very word " Rome " calls up to the mind's eye a

picture of magnificence, of wide streets and triumphal arches, temples, amphitheatres, and the great basilicæ surrounding the Forum. The picture is true, but it is a half truth. Rome was far more like its modern counterparts than were most ancient cities. Building land was at a premium and the population was housed in tall tenement blocks which rose precariously, several stories high, on inadequate foundations. Magnificent public buildings contrasted painfully with squalid slums. Great aqueducts brought a plentiful supply of water to the city, but the tenement-dweller, who had to buy his water from the *aquarii*, the slave water-carriers, could not afford to waste the precious stuff in washing the floor of his flat. Rome's huge drains are the admiration of archæologists, but no public drainage system served the poorer houses, as the passer-by sometimes learnt to his cost. Under such conditions dirt and disease were inevitable. Rents were extortionate and tenants relied on sub-letting to meet part of the cost. Thus the ground floor of a building might belong to a well-to-do man, while several poor families shared the garrets. At the opposite end of the social scale were the imperial palaces, where thousands of slaves were employed, and the lavish establishments of the Roman nobility.

If we were seeking for the earliest Christians in this great ant-heap of a city, we should naturally cross to the far bank of the Tiber and begin our inquiries in the Jewish colony which had long been established there. In the apostles' time it was already a century old. In 63 B.C., when Pompey captured Jerusalem, he brought back to Rome a large number of Jews as slaves. Their refusal to conform to Gentile ways made them awkward members of any household and most of them were soon manumitted. They formed the nucleus of the colony which soon grew, especially after Julius Cæsar granted the Jews extensive privileges, including the right to worship in their own way. Edmundsen has described this Jewish settlement for us from his knowledge of contemporary sources:

" A large proportion of these Roman Jews were very poor, living in rags and squalor, making a precarious livelihood as hawkers, pedlars, and dealers in second-hand goods.   Above these were then, as now, the moneylenders, larger traders, and shopkeepers, and at the head the wealthy financiers." *

We do not know who were the first Christian missionaries to reach Rome.   Possibly they were some of the Jewish pilgrims converted at Jerusalem during Pentecost, who afterwards returned home, bringing the Gospel with them; perhaps some of them were traders from Palestine.   Their names are lost to us, unless Andronicus and Junias were among them, whom St Paul mentions in his letter to the Romans as his kinsmen and fellow prisoners, " who are of note among the apostles, who have been in Christ before me ".   However that may be, by A.D. 50 Christians were sufficiently numerous in Rome to attract the attention of the Roman authorities.   In that year riots broke out in the Jewish quarter, and all that the magistrates who investigated the matter could discover was that the trouble was due to a certain " Chrestus ".   " Chrestus " represents a normal Roman mispronunciation of " Christus ", a mistake which was still common more than a century later and there can be little doubt that the rioting was due to the resentment which orthodox Jews felt at the spread of Christian teaching.   Suetonius, who is our authority for this incident, simply records that " the Jews who were continually rioting at the instigation of Chrestus he (Claudius) expelled from Rome ".   (" Judæos impulsore Chresto assidue tumultuantes Roma expulit."—Suet. Claudius 25.)   No details are given, but remembering the trouble which the Jews in Asia Minor stirred up for St Paul, it is not hard to

* *The Church in Rome*, by G. Edmundsen, p. 6.

imagine what happened in Rome. We can picture the angry scenes in the synagogues, the campaign of rumour-mongering against the Christians, the public disturbance skilfully fomented, the accusations of treason brought against the Christians during the subsequent inquiry. It is not clear whether all Jews were expelled from Rome for a time in consequence of these disorders or only those accused of subversive tendencies, that is the Christians. But as the Roman authorities had not yet realized that the Christians were a separate sect, the order was probably general.

Among those expelled from Rome at this time were a Jewish tent-maker and his wife, who settled in Corinth and continued their trade there. They had not been there long, when St Paul arrived on his first visit to the place and at once made friends with them. St Luke gives us the facts very briefly:

"And he (Paul) found a certain Jew named Aquila, a man of Pontus by race, lately come from Italy, with his wife Priscilla, because Claudius had commanded all the Jews to depart from Rome: and he came unto them; and because he was of the same trade, he abode with them, and they wrought; for by their trade they were tentmakers." *

No mention is made of the conversion of these two, who were to play an important part in St Paul's life and in the early Church, and it is reasonable to assume that they were Christians before they ever met St Paul. Indeed, it is probable that their house in Rome had been a meeting-place for Christians before they were forced to leave. It certainly was when they returned to Rome after the death of Claudius, for St Paul in his epistle to the Romans sends greetings to his two friends and also to "the church that is in their house". † The site of that house has been identified,

* *Acts* 18. 2–3.   † *Rom.* 16. 4–5.

probably correctly, with that on which the church of St Prisca now stands. Near the church a house of the Republican period has been excavated; this would have been nearly a century old at the time when Aquila and Prisca lived there or close by.

St Paul's letter to the Romans was written from Corinth at the time when he was planning to visit Rome on his way to Spain, after taking the churches' contributions to Jerusalem and delivering them in person. Scholars are generally agreed that this letter was written about A.D. 57, and we know from Acts that St Paul was prevented from carrying out his plan. He was arrested in Jerusalem, owing to the animosity of the Jews, and eventually reached Rome as a prisoner three years later. From his letter we can gather some impression of the Christian community to which it is addressed, but only with difficulty, for St Paul is concerned with the unchanging truth of God's dealings with man, rather than with those accidents of place and time which differentiate one generation from another. The centuries which have passed between his day and ours are of little consequence when he writes and we read:

" God commendeth his own love towards us, in that, while we were yet sinners, Christ died for us." *

and

" Now if we be dead with Christ, we believe that we shall also live with him:
" Knowing that Christ being raised from the dead dieth no more; death hath no more dominion over him.
" For in that he died, he died unto sin once: but in that he liveth, he liveth unto God." †

Plainly these first Christians in Rome were as capable of thinking out the implications of their faith as any generation

* *Rom.* 5. 8.   † *Rom.* 6. 8–10 (A.V.).

since, and St Paul treated them accordingly. Those who
expect to find in primitive Christianity a simple religion,
free from the difficult dogmas of the Church, must look
elsewhere than here for their evidence, though this is one
of the earliest Christian documents we possess. To hold
any but a rudimentary religious faith and yet be uncon-
cerned about such problems as the existence of evil and the
relation of man's free will to God's omnipotence, a man
must either be content to worship with his heart and not
his head, or else be the inheritor of a long-accepted tradition
of Church teaching. These Roman Christians had no
such tradition. Some of them were Jews who found that
their faith in Christ was not compatible with strict ad-
herence to Judaism. Others were Gentiles who in becoming Christians had altered their whole outlook on life. In
this great epistle, St Paul stated some of the doctrines
fundamental to the Christian faith, and applied them to
the problems of the day; in so doing he helped to form a
new tradition, the tradition of Christian dogmatic teaching
which we have inherited. But here we are concerned, not
with the thoughts of St Paul, which are familiar to all who
read the New Testament, but with the almost unknown
community to which he wrote. What does his letter tell
us about the forgotten beginnings of the church of Rome?

Naturally enough, since St Paul was writing for his own
contemporaries, to whom the facts were familiar, and not
for us, there is no statement in his letter about the origin of
the church of Rome or about St Peter's connection with it.
St Peter is not mentioned by name from first to last. But
that does not mean more than that St Peter was known to
be absent from Rome at the time when St Paul wrote,
otherwise his name would, of course, have been included in
the salutations. In one place St Paul does seem to imply
that the church at Rome was founded by another, for he
writes:

" From Jerusalem, and round about even unto Illyricum, I have fully preached the gospel of Christ; yea, making it my aim so to preach the gospel, not where Christ was already named, that I might not build upon another man's foundation; but, as it is written,

> They shall see, to whom no tidings of him came,
> And they who have not heard shall understand.

Wherefore also I was hindered these many times from coming to you."

He goes on to say that he is planning a visit to Spain and that he hopes to see them on the way. Now it is highly probable that the founder to whom St Paul alludes was an apostle, a man whose authority St Paul recognized as being equal to his own, else he would hardly have been so scrupulous. There is a strong and early tradition that this man was St Peter. Our evidence for the tradition is material as well as written, for St Peter and St Paul are represented together on early medallions and similar finds, suggesting that they were regarded, as early as the second century, as of equal importance in the history of the Roman church. The traditional belief that St Peter was the founder is also in accordance with what we know of the organization of the early Church. When the apostles heard that Samaria had received the word of God, they sent St Peter and St John to confirm the newly baptized. A little later St Barnabas was sent by the church of Jerusalem to the newly founded church of Antioch. What more inherently probable than that when the apostles heard that Christianity had spread to Rome they should send St Peter there at the first opportunity? His first visit may well have been, as Edmundsen supposes, in A.D. 42 after his escape from prison in Jerusalem. If so, he was back in Jerusalem in A.D. 46 at the time of the famine, and was afterwards in Antioch for a time, and almost certainly visited Corinth. But if St Peter led a roving life, going from church to church and taking his wife with him,* that does not disprove his connection with the church of Rome. He was not continually resident there, but he may well have exercised a controlling influence.

On the other hand, there is nothing in St Paul's letter to suggest that the Roman Christians formed a single body led by a bishop or even by a council of elders. On the contrary, in his concluding salutations St Paul mentions five distinct groups of believers: the church in the house of Prisca and Aquila, those of the households of Aristobulus and Narcissus, the brethren with Asyncritus and his friends, and the saints with Philologus and Nereus. Evidently at this time there were five congregations of Christians in Rome, and it is worth noting that whereas St Paul writes to the " church of God " at Corinth, to the church of the Thessalonians and the churches of Galatia, and mentions the bishops and deacons at Philippi, he addresses his letter to the Romans to " all that are in Rome, beloved of God, called to be saints ", and makes no mention of either elders or deacons. Probably each of the five groups which St Paul mentions had its own leaders, and, though they would all respect the apostolic authority of St Peter, there is nothing to show that he had in fact appointed elders or organized the church.

Evidently the Christians in Rome in the earliest period met for the most part in private houses. Those who gathered in the house of Prisca and Aquila would many of them be Jewish, but probably the majority in the other groups were Gentiles. This must certainly have been the case with those of the households of Aristobulus and Narcissus. Narcissus was dead by the time this letter was written. He had been a wealthy freedman, a favourite of the Emperor Claudius, and when suspicion fell on him and he was executed, his slaves became part of the vast imperial house-

* 1 *Cor.* 9. 5.

hold, but evidently retained their old distinguishing name. Some scholars think that the same was true of the household of Aristobulus. In any case, the Christians in both these groups would be slaves, Greek-speaking Gentiles for the most part, some of them employed in menial work, but others well-educated men filling clerical posts, the equivalent of our modern civil servants. In recent years what has been identified as an early Christian sanctuary has been found within the precincts of the first-century imperial palace on the Palatine. We have therefore concrete evidence for the supposition that Christians of Cæsar's household met together for worship and formed one of the several congregations of the church of Rome.

In spite of its unusually long list of salutations, St Paul's epistle to the Romans tells us disappointingly little about the church to which it is addressed. The last chapter of Acts, in which St Paul's arrival in Rome as a prisoner is described, is even less enlightening. St Luke describes how he and St Paul were welcomed by the Christians at Puteoli, where they stayed for a week before continuing their journey to Rome. Evidently the news of their coming went ahead of them, for the brethren came out to meet them. Some were waiting at Appii Forum, a town forty miles from Rome, and others were ready to greet them at the Three Taverns, some ten miles nearer the city. St Luke records St Paul's joy at this welcome: " he thanked God and took courage". And then with the words, " When we entered Rome, Paul was suffered to abide by himself with the soldier that guarded him ", St Luke ends his personal narrative. The last fourteen verses of the book are written in the third person, and they add little except a puzzling account of St Paul's interview with the leading Jews in Rome. The strangest thing about it is that the Jews appear to be quite ignorant of the existence of a Christian community in Rome, and that is barely credible,

G

however ingeniously one may try to explain it.   Probably
the incident was one which St Luke had from hearsay, not
from personal experience, and it has been somewhat
garbled in the telling.   All that we can reasonably conclude
is that St Paul made an independent approach to the Jews in
Rome and, when they rejected his message, spent his time
during his enforced stay in the city in preaching the Gospel
to all who cared to come to him in his own hired lodging.
We have no certain knowledge of what happened at the
end of the two years that he stayed in Rome, but according
to tradition he was released, and carried out his project of
visiting Spain.

There must have been a decade during which the church
in Rome enjoyed comparative peace and grew steadily.   It
was in A.D. 50 that Prisca and Aquila had to flee to Corinth,
and in A.D. 64 the most terrible of the early persecutions fell
upon the church.   About the intervening years we know
very little; but it would seem that Christianity gained
converts among all classes of society.   In A.D. 50 a Roman
lady of rank, Pomponia Græcina, was accused of being
addicted to a foreign superstition.   She was tried by her
husband, Aulus Plautius, in accordance with Roman law,
and was judged innocent.   The discovery that her family
tomb later became an early Christian burial-place confirms
the suspicion that she was a Christian.   To this period, too,
must belong the contest between St Peter and Simon
Magus which caught the imagination of succeeding generations, and so gave rise to a host of legends.   As told by
Eusebius, the fourth-century historian, the story is credible
enough, and Eusebius was relying on an early authority,
the second-century apologist, Justin Martyr.   Simon was
a native of Samaria, and in his own city he had gained a
reputation, not merely as an astrologer, or wise man, but
as a worker of wonders and one inspired by God.   When
St Philip came to Samaria preaching Christ, Simon was

attracted by the miracles of healing and other signs, and, professing himself to be a believer, he was baptized.   His real motive for seeking baptism became plain when St Peter arrived in Samaria to confirm those who believed.   After prayer and the laying-on of hands, the power of the Holy Spirit came upon the newly confirmed and Simon approached St Peter and offered him money saying:

" Give me also this power, that on whomsoever I lay my hands, he may receive the Holy Ghost."

Evidently Simon Magus saw in this new religion a means to attain his own ambition, which was to make a reputation and a fortune as a religious leader and a semi-divine person. St Peter rejected Simon's proposal with horror and warned him to repent, to which Simon Magus replied:

" Pray ye for me to the Lord, that none of the things which ye have spoken come upon me." *

His later behaviour shows plainly that this piously meek answer was due to nothing better than a superstitious fear of being cursed.   Most successful charlatans arrived in Rome sooner or later, and Simon Magus was no exception. According to Justin, Simon appeared there, claiming to be God and accompanied by a former prostitute from Tyre, named Helen, who was supposed to be an incarnation of divine thought proceeding from him.   This precious pair reaped a harvest from the superstitious and the gullible, many of whom were to be found in the capital, and no doubt Simon was disconcerted when his old opponent, St Peter, arrived on the scene and convinced many of the fraudulent nature of Simon's claims.   Eusebius writes as though St Peter utterly defeated his opponent, as indeed he may have done. But the battle between Christianity and the form of super- stition which Simon Magus represented had only begun and was to be bitterly contested for several generations.

* *Acts* 8. 9–24.

According to Eusebius, there was an important sequel to this contest between St Peter and Simon Magus. The Christians in Rome became increasingly anxious to possess a record of St Peter's teaching to which they could refer in cases of controversy, and they urged his companion, St Mark, to undertake the work. The result was the Gospel according to St Mark, which was approved by St Peter and was thenceforth read aloud in the churches. Eusebius quotes St Clement of Alexandria as his authority for this statement, but another early father, St Irenæus, says that St Mark's Gospel was written after the deaths of St Peter and St Paul. Most scholars think the later date the more probable, and agree that it was written after the persecution in A.D. 64 and before the fall of Jerusalem in A.D. 70. But, of course, it is by no means impossible that a first draft of the Gospel was made in St Peter's lifetime, even if the Gospel as we have it is five or ten years later.

For the first thirty years or so of her life, the Church was not subject to persecution by the State. Roman officials did not recognize that Christianity was a new religion, but thought it a form of Judaism. Naturally the Jews who rejected Christ were extremely unwilling to allow the Christians to shelter behind the privileges which had been granted to Judaism. The populace in Rome, as in the cities of Asia and Greece, was ignorant, excitable and quick to adopt a prejudice. St Luke has shown in Acts that in the eastern provinces the Jews and other interested persons found it easy to stir up popular opposition to St Paul. Rumours became widespread in Rome also that the Christians were a dangerous secret society, that they practised obscene rites and feasted on children. Whether these rumours originated in Jewish jealousy we do not know, but some of the early apologists thought so. This was the state of affairs in A.D. 64, when the great fire which occurred in July brought upon the Christians the first official persecution.

The fire broke out in some shops at the end of the Great Circus and spread rapidly. It lasted nine days, and totally destroyed the houses in three out of the fourteen districts of Rome, and left only a few half-ruined buildings standing in seven of the others. It is estimated that nearly half a million people were left homeless. This immense damage was only possible because the huge tenement blocks, which housed most of the population, were flimsily built of brick and timber. The flames easily leapt the narrow streets from one high building to another, and attempts at fighting the fire proved futile. The Emperor Nero behaved admirably in his efforts to relieve the distress occasioned by this great disaster. He opened to the public various buildings and grounds, including his own gardens, and built shelters for the homeless. He also bought up corn and sold it to the destitute at a low rate, thereby instituting what amounted to price control of essential commodities and preventing famine. Yet, in spite of this, he gained no popularity. Rumours spread throughout the city that the fire was not accidental, but had been caused by incendiaries acting on the orders of the Emperor himself. Nero's love of display was well known, and his action in appropriating a huge site in the devastated area for a new imperial palace must have confirmed the suspicion that he had staged the fire, so that he might have an opportunity to carry into effect his plans for the rebuilding of Rome. The rumours were persistent, and the strength of popular feeling alarmed the Emperor. What followed is best told in the words of Tacitus:

" But neither man's efforts to give relief, nor the largesse of the prince, nor the propitiations of the gods were able to dissipate belief in the sinister report that the fire had been ordered. Wherefore to efface the rumour, Nero contrived that accusations should be brought against a set of people hated for their abominations, whom the populace called Christians, and subjected them to the most exquisite torments.   The author of this name, one Christus, had in the reign of Tiberius been executed by the procurator Pontius Pilatus; and the pernicious superstition, though repressed for the moment, began to break out afresh, not only in Judæa, the origin of that evil, but also in Rome, where all things horrible and shameful from every quarter collect together and are practised.   Those therefore who confessed were first brought to trial, afterwards by the information derived from them, an immense multitude were joined with them, not so much for the crime of incendiarism, as for hatred of the human race.   To their deaths mockeries were added, so that covered by the skins of wild beasts they were torn to pieces by dogs and perished or were affixed to crosses set on fire and, when day had fallen, were burnt so as to serve as an illumination for the night.   Nero had offered his gardens for the spectacle, and was exhibiting a public show in the circus.   He mingled with the people in the dress of a charioteer, standing in a car. Hence compassion began to arise, although towards criminals deserving the extremest forms of punishment, on the ground that they were destroyed not for the public good but to gratify a single man's savage cruelty." *

Even to us of the twentieth century, made callous or indifferent by countless stories of atrocities, the scene in the Vatican Gardens is one of fantastic horror.   Indeed it may be that we understand it better than our forefathers could, who lived in a happier age.   To them such a monstrous exhibition of human cruelty seemed remote, a barbarity of a far-off time.   To us it is real and credible in all its loathsome details.   We, too, have seen tyranny in action, and we know how essential a scapegoat is to a régime of that kind.   Persecution of some minority within the nation provides a necessary outlet for the suppressed feelings of resentment against the Government, resentment which might otherwise break out in revolution. If the tyrant is deified, then someone must play the part of the devil and take the blame for whatever goes wrong.

* Tacitus, *Annales* XV, xliv.

Hence Hitler's Jewish pogroms, and hence Nero's persecution of the Church. There is no reason to think that much effort was made to convict Christians of arson. The vast majority suffered on the general charge of being " enemies of the human race ". From then on until the reign of Constantine, Christians were always liable to persecution for the mere confession of their faith. The great number of those who were arrested and died as martyrs proves conclusively that Christianity had already taken a deep hold in Rome. Nor could persecution stamp it out. When the horrible games were over the Christians who survived collected what remained of the martyrs' bodies and gave them burial in the cemetery on the other side of the road, where some one of their number owned a tomb. Now the magnificent church of St Peter extends across the site of that cemetery and over part of the arena itself; so thousands worship where the first martyrs died. " Semen est sanguis Christianorum." *

It is unlikely that St Paul was in Rome at the time of this sudden persecution. St Peter may have been, but if so he seems to have survived the first attack. If the epistle known as I Peter be accepted as authentic, then it must have been written near the end of his life, when the persecution showed signs of spreading to the provinces.† The letter is addressed to Christians in Asia Minor, and in the closing verses, which appear to have been in St Peter's own handwriting, there is a salutation from the church " that is in Babylon ", a figurative expression for the church of Rome. Reading this letter carries us back into those days of trial and courage, of constant danger and immortal hope:

* " The blood of Christians is seed." Tertullian.
† The authorship of I *Peter* has been the subject of much dispute, but on the whole the reasons for believing that the epistle was written by St Peter outweigh those against its authenticity. See *The New Testament: A Reader's Guide*, by C. A. Alington, p. 18.

" Ye are an elect race, a royal priesthood, a holy nation, a people for God's own possession, that ye may shew forth the excellencies of him who called you out of darkness into his marvellous light."

" And who is he that will harm you, if ye be zealous of that which is good? But and if ye should suffer for righteousness' sake, blessed are ye: and fear not their fear, neither be troubled."

" Forasmuch then as Christ suffered in the flesh, arm ye yourselves also with the same mind." *

Even from stray sentences like these the glory of that first time of testing still shines out. There is no fanaticism here. Christians are counselled to be obedient to all proper authorities, not provocative, but ready to give a reasoned defence of their faith if questioned. It is a sensible and sober letter, but written within sight of a better country. St Peter speaks as though from the border of eternity, not because he foresees his own death, though he may well have done, but because he believes the end of the world to be at hand. Later generations have, for the most part, lost this sense of urgency and of imminent judgement, and with it they have lost some of the eagerness of St Peter's hope and the exultant quality of his courage.

There is no reasonable doubt that both St Peter and St Paul were martyred at Rome. The tradition is early and widespread, literary evidence confirms it and archæological evidence is overwhelmingly in its favour. But little more than the bare fact is definitely known. It is almost certain that St Peter was crucified, for at the end of St John's Gospel, which must have been written after St Peter's martyrdom, there is an allusion to the nature of his death:

" Verily, verily, I say unto thee, When thou wast young, thou girdedst thyself, and walkedst whither thou wouldest; but when thou shalt be old, thou shalt stretch forth thy hands, and another shall gird thee, and carry thee whither thou wouldest not.

* I *Peter* 2. 9; 3. 13, 14; 4. 1.

" Now this he spake, signifying by what manner of death he should glorify God." *

According to Tertullian, St Paul was beheaded as became his rank as a Roman citizen, and this is inherently probable. But as to the exact date of their deaths and as to whether both suffered on the same day or no, evidence is insufficient for an absolute decision. Considering the wholesale destruction of Christian documents at a later period, the lack of a well-authenticated account of the apostles' fate is not surprising. All we have left are some chance allusions in early writings and a mass of later legends of little historical value. One legend, however, will always be remembered in connection with the death of St Peter, whether it can be proved to be based on fact or not. This is the famous " Quo Vadis? " legend, which tells how, during the persecution when the Roman police were searching for St Peter, the brethren came to him and begged him to go into temporary hiding for their sakes:

" And he obeyed the brethren's voice and went forth alone, saying: Let none of you come forth with me, but I will go forth alone, having changed the fashion of mine apparel. And as he went forth of the city, he saw the Lord entering into Rome. And when he saw him, he said: Lord whither goest thou thus? And the Lord said unto him: I go into Rome to be crucified. And Peter said unto him: Lord, art thou being crucified again? He said unto him: Yea, Peter, I am being crucified again. And Peter came to himself: and having beheld the Lord ascending into heaven, he returned to Rome, rejoicing and glorifying the Lord, for that he said: I am being crucified: the which was about to befall Peter." †

If the personal messages in what are known as the Pastoral Epistles are accepted as having been written by

* *John* 21. 18–19.
† *Acts of Peter*, section XXXV, in *The Apocryphal New Testament*, translated by M. R. James.

St Paul at this period, then we can form some idea of his life during the last few months when he was awaiting the trial which resulted in his execution. The Second Epistle to Timothy shows us St Paul alone, except for his faithful friend and doctor, St Luke. He complains of desertion even by members of the Church, and begs Timothy to come to him before the winter and bring St Mark with him, and also a cloak and some books. But although St Paul anticipates a long imprisonment, he has no doubt that his trial will result in his condemnation. The confidence with which he waits for death is characteristic:

" I am already being offered, and the time of my departure is come. I have fought the good fight, I have finished the course, I have kept the faith; henceforth there is laid up for me the crown of righteousness, which the Lord, the righteous judge, shall give to me at that day: and not only to me, but also to all them that have loved his appearing." *

With the deaths of St Peter and St Paul, the first, the apostolic, period of the Church's history was practically

BRONZE MEDAL FROM THE VATICAN LIBRARY SHOWING THE HEADS OF ST PETER AND ST PAUL. 2ND CENTURY.

ended. St John alone of the great apostles is believed to have lived on to extreme old age in Ephesus. Elsewhere the successors of the apostles faced the task of preserving the apostolic teaching and strengthening the organization

* 2 *Tim.* 4. 6–8.

of the Church to meet the constant danger of persecution. It is to this second generation, the disciples of the apostles, and to St John, that we owe the greater part of the New Testament.

BOOKS FOR FURTHER READING

The Church in Rome in the First Century, by G. Edmundsen.
Documents Illustrative of the History of the Church, ed. by B. J. Kidd, vol. i.

CHAPTER V

CHRISTENDOM: THE NEW TESTAMENT IN WRITING

UNDER the leadership of the apostles the Church
had grown like the mustard seed in the parable.
Already at the time of the martyrdom of St Peter and St
Paul, her branches had spread far and wide throughout the
civilized world. There were Christians in Rome itself, in
many cities in Asia Minor and Greece, in Alexandria, in
Syria, Persia and the remote, almost fabulous land known
as India. The churches that were within the Roman Empire, where travel was easy, were in constant communication
with each other, as we can see by the letters preserved in
the New Testament. The letters of the apostles, especially
those of St Paul, were copied, and became the common
property of all the churches. They were read aloud at the
time of prayer, and were the earliest distinctively Christian
Scriptures which the Church possessed. Another bond
which the churches had in common was the collection of
alms for the poor in the mother church at Jerusalem. This
was a matter in which sentiment played a strong part,
especially for Jewish Christians, who were accustomed to
paying the Jewish temple tax. The apostolic Church was
not a highly organized body, and there is no evidence that
St James, as head of the church at Jerusalem, made any
attempt to control the more distant churches, at least after
the admission of Gentiles had been agreed on at the apostolic
Council about the year A.D. 47. But Jerusalem remained,
nevertheless, the only visible centre the primitive Church
possessed.

The close of the apostolic period was a time of calamity and terror, when Christians, reading the signs of the times, lived in constant expectation of the end of the world. St James, the Lord's brother, was martyred in Jerusalem in A.D. 62. Two years later came the horror of the Neronian persecution, in which both St Peter and St Paul were killed. Of all the apostles, probably St John was now the only survivor. There followed Vespasian's campaign against the Jews, when the Christians, forewarned, fled from Jerusalem to Pella, and from there watched the fulfilment of Christ's prophetic grief over the city. In A.D. 70 Jerusalem fell to Titus. The Temple was burnt and the city was levelled to the ground. In ten years the Church had lost all her great leaders, except St John, and her natural centre, the city where Jesus had taught and died and risen again, had been destroyed and utterly laid waste. That the Church survived as a unity is, in no figurative sense, a miracle, for it was the work of the Holy Spirit within her.

Instead of disintegrating, the Church at the close of the apostolic period began a new and vitally important phase in her history. She set herself to record and transmit in writing the teaching which the apostles had given by word of mouth. She built up an organization capable of withstanding attacks from without, and she maintained the true faith in spite of insidious attacks from within. This is the more remarkable because there was at this time no one centre from which her leaders could direct the Church's development. The day of Jerusalem was over; the day of Rome had not yet come. Instead the leadership quite naturally fell to the churches that were established in cities of political importance, especially to the churches of apostolic foundation. Antioch, Ephesus, Rome, Corinth, and Cæsarea all exercised authority in their respective localities, and the church of Alexandria, though with less claim than the others to apostolic authority, inevitably became influential also. Each locality made its own contribution to the record of apostolic teaching and to the life of the whole Church. Thus it comes about that we have four Gospels instead of only one in the canon of the New Testament, while similar differences in the forms of prayer used in the various local centres have enriched the Church's liturgy. In this chapter we shall make a rapid tour of Christendom and try to form some idea of the contribution each locality was making to the Church as a whole in the closing decades of the first century.

Jerusalem and Cæsarea.

The last glimpse we have in Acts of the church of Jerusalem is during St Paul's final visit there.* At that time St James, the Lord's brother, was its head, and the breach with Judaism had not yet occurred. The church was organized like a synagogue, with a council of elders, and its members were practising Jews, only distinguished from other Jews by certain Christian practices and by their belief that the Messiah had actually come in the Person of Jesus Christ. Exaggerated rumours of St Paul's hostility to the Law had reached Jerusalem. It was generally believed that he had encouraged Jews of the Dispersion to abandon the Law and leave their children uncircumcised. Jewish resentment ran so high that his life was not safe in the city. The feeling against St Paul was strong within the church as well as without, and St James had to act as peace-maker. He and the elders welcomed St Paul cordially and approved his work among the Gentiles, but they urged him to give the lie to the current rumours by an outward sign of his own personal obedience to the Law. This St Paul was willing to do, but Jewish hatred of him

* *Acts* 21.

was too strong to be checked, and would have led to his death, had he not been arrested by the Roman authorities, and so saved from mob violence.

As long as he lived, St James by his tact and moderation succeeded in preventing the Jewish Christians from dissociating themselves from the Gentile Church. But in A.D. 62 Festus, the Roman procurator, died, and in the interval before his successor could arrive the Jewish High Priest seized his opportunity and put St James to death. Shortly afterwards the Jewish insurrection against Rome broke out, and the Christian Jews, under the leadership of Symeon, one of the Lord's kinsmen, withdrew to Pella. There they lived in virtual isolation. The Jews resented their desertion of the national cause at a moment of such dire crisis, and the destruction of the Temple broke the last link that bound the Judaizing Christians to their fellow Jews. Yet the breach with Judaism did not lead them to a closer union with the rest of Christendom. Instead they remained in a backwater, preserving a form of Christianity which the rest of the Church had outgrown. They continued to observe the Law, and they especially venerated St James, ranking him above all the apostles. The extremists among them went much farther in the direction of Judaism, and denied the divinity of our Lord while declaring him to be the Messiah. These, the descendants of the Judaizers of the apostolic Church, preserved their hatred of St Paul, and regarded him as anathema and the whole Gentile Church as a mistake.

One would naturally expect that the church of Jerusalem would make a great contribution towards the written record of our Lord's earthly life, his passion, and resurrection. It has been suggested that a collection of testimonies, which appears to have been one of the documents used by the writer of Matthew, originated in Jerusalem; but this cannot be proved. This book, now no longer in existence, must have been a collection of passages from the Old Testament, which Christian preachers could use to show that Jesus was indeed the Messiah. St Peter's speeches, as quoted in Acts, perfectly illustrate this method of preaching. Passages were chosen to emphasize the main features of the Christian message: our Lord's descent from David, his redeeming death and his resurrection. Thus the collection as a whole would form an epitome of the Gospel. Apart from this, the church of Jerusalem cannot be credited with any contribution to the New Testament except the epistles of St James and St Jude. Critics doubt that the epistle of St James is really by our Lord's brother. They incline to think it rather later in date. But it certainly expresses admirably the patient forbearance and practical goodness which St James showed in his life, and also that stress on the need for good works, as well as faith, which might be expected from one who was noted for his keeping of the Law. The letter by St Jude may be by the brother of St James or else by an early bishop. It shows one of the dangers that beset the Church from within, both in Palestine and elsewhere, in the second generation of Christians. Some men attempted to abuse the Pauline doctrine of freedom from the Law, behaving as though Christian liberty were an excuse for licentiousness. St Jude's letter is a call to order, not in the name of the Law, but in the strength of Jesus Christ.

Nothing written by the church at Pella has found its way into the New Testament canon, but a gospel did originate there, fragments of which survive. It was known as *The Gospel of the Hebrews*, and one passage which we still have describes how our risen Lord appeared to St James. *The Gospel of the Hebrews* is nearer to St Matthew's Gospel than to any other, but evidently it was coloured by the peculiar beliefs of some of the Jewish Christians. It emphasized the part played by St James in the apostolic

Church, and put into our Lord's mouth such strange expressions as this:

" Just now my mother, the Holy Spirit, took me by one of my hairs and bore me up on to the great mountain Tabor."

The Gospel of the Hebrews was popular in Syria, and was known and used in Egypt also, but it failed, no doubt for good reasons, to be accepted as part of the New Testament.

The church of Cæsarea was from the beginning a Gentile, not a Jewish community; for the place was a great Roman port and trading centre. It was to Cæsarea that St Peter was summoned from Joppa to convert the centurion Cornelius, and so to open the door of the Church to Gentiles. There St Philip the Evangelist made his home, and it was in his house that St Paul and St Luke were made welcome when St Paul was on his way to Jerusalem for the last time.* When St Paul was brought back to Cæsarea from Jerusalem as a prisoner, St Luke undoubtedly came, too, for he especially mentions that St Paul's friends were allowed to minister to him. During the many hours which he must have spent in the company of St Philip and his four prophetic daughters, St Luke collected a good deal of the material which he afterwards incorporated into his Gospel and into Acts. St Philip could tell him a great deal about the earliest days of the Church, about St Stephen, and about his own missionary work in Samaria and elsewhere; he may also have been able to speak from personal recollection of our Lord. It is possible that it was St Philip who told St Luke the parable of the good Samaritan.

Antioch.

The church of Antioch, as we see it in Acts, was half Jewish and half Gentile. From the first its attitude was liberal. It was the base from which St Paul set out on his

* *Acts* 21. 8

H

great missionary journeys, and it is evident that he had the support of the Antiochene church in his free admission of Gentiles. In those early days the leaders at Antioch were prophets and teachers, and there is no mention of a council of elders, such as we find at Jerusalem. But by the beginning of the second century Antioch had come into line with other churches and had a bishop at its head, who traced his succession from St Peter, with elders and deacons under him. It is not difficult to guess what had happened. In the enthusiasm of the first few years, the Christians at Antioch relied on the guidance and inspiration of the Holy Spirit. Under the influence of St Paul and St Barnabas, and visited at intervals by St Peter, the church went from strength to strength. But, when the apostles were no longer at hand, and men who claimed to be inspired taught doctrines very different from theirs, the need for regular clergy became imperative.

We know the name of one of these false teachers: he was Menander of Capparatea in Samaria, a follower of Simon Magus who fell foul of St Peter by attempting to buy the Holy Ghost for money. If Menander's ideas were anything like Simon's—and presumably they were—they were very far indeed from the truth. According to Simon, the Supreme Power had a female counterpart, his Thought, who produced the angels. The angels refused to accept their proper position as creatures, and in turn created the world. Having done so, they imprisoned the First Thought in a succession of female forms. Among other manifestations, she was said to have appeared as Helen of Troy, and Simon claimed that in his own day she was disguised in the body of a certain prostitute from Tyre whom he led about with him. The dangerous point for the Church in all this nonsense was that Simon had accepted the Christian belief in the Incarnation and had worked it into his scheme. He taught that the Supreme Power also had taken a variety of forms in the course of history and had eventually appeared as Jesus, seeming to be a man, but not being truly human or really suffering at all. The aim of the Supreme Power in doing this was supposed to be to release his First Thought from the power of the angels.

Neither in Antioch nor elsewhere could the Church allow men to put forward doctrines of this kind and call them the Christian faith. The Church always maintained that God, and not some inferior angel, was the Creator of the world. She was equally firm in her assertion that Jesus Christ was a real man and did actually suffer death upon the cross. Individual Christians, however, could easily be confused and misled by a clever speaker who claimed to be inspired. There were two obvious remedies. One was to discourage unauthorized people from holding forth in Christian assemblies and to appoint sincere and knowledgeable men to teach the people. Another was to provide an authoritative written account of our Lord's life and teaching which could be read aloud when Christians met for prayer. In due course the Syrian churches, led by Antioch, did both.

Among the early Christian books, not included in the New Testament, which have survived to the present day, is one called the *Didache* or *The Teaching of the Twelve Apostles*. It is a church manual: the kind of book which Christian teachers would use when preparing candidates for baptism and which would be a guide for those concerned with church government. Most critics agree that it comes from Syria and, though its date is not certain, it reflects a primitive state of affairs which could hardly have persisted into the second century, unless in some remote country district. Evidently, when the *Didache* was written, many country places had no resident clergy, and wandering prophets went from village to village conducting services, exhorting the people and living on charity.   It is plain from the *Didache* that many of these travelling prophets were frauds, for Christians are warned not to give hospitality to a prophet for more than two days unless he be willing to settle among them, in which case he would presumably become their parish priest, for a prophet could celebrate the Eucharist.   They are also to beware of those who teach false doctrines, and the wise caution is added:

" But whosoever shall say in a spirit ' Give me money, or something else,' you shall not listen to him; but if he tell you to give on behalf of others in want, let none judge him." *

The prophets must have been very like the friars of a later period; and in their case, too, men of the second or third generation abused their privileges, so that the whole order gradually fell into disrepute.   The *Didache* mentions bishops and deacons as well as prophets, and it plainly depicts a transition stage when prophets were beginning to lose the confidence of the people and were being gradually replaced by resident clergy.   Indeed, it has been suggested that one of the main purposes of the *Didache* was " to secure that the resident ministers shall no longer be treated as of subordinate importance ", and " to create, wherever it did not yet exist, a resident ministry of episcopi and deacons ".†

The *Didache* gives detailed instructions for the behaviour of a Christian community, and from it we can tell how worship was conducted in an early Syrian church.   But with that we shall be concerned in a later chapter.   The first part of the little tract deals with morals.   It is called the " Two Ways ", and follows a pattern already familiar to both Jewish and Hellenistic writers.   The instructions are a blend of the Sermon on the Mount with the Ten

* *Didache*, xi. 12.
† *The Primitive Church*, by B. H. Streeter, p. 150.

Commandments, and particular stress is laid on sins to which those for whom the book was written were especially prone. These were a fondness for dabbling in magic and an excessive desire for money. The latter is a temptation common in any age, but the first-century Syrian was in exceptional danger where magic was concerned, for the country was overrun by sages and magicians from Persia, seeking to persuade men of the efficacy of their arts. Catechumens needed a special warning:

" My child, regard not omens, for this leads to idolatry; neither be an enchanter, nor an astrologer, nor a magician, neither wish to see these things, for from them all is idolatry engendered." *

The book ends with a comment on the signs of the times and the imminence of the Day of Judgement. Looking round him, the writer saw corrupters and false prophets; lawlessness was increasing and many were losing their faith. Undismayed, he predicted that these evils heralded the final fiery trial of mankind before the coming of the Lord. We know now that man's testing time was not to end so soon. But the passage of time, which has falsified the writer's prophecy, has left untarnished his ever-present awareness of God's judgement upon sin and his unconquerable hope.

In this time of doubt and lawlessness, when heresies multiplied and authority was hard to find, the first need was for regular clergy and properly organized church government. But the second necessity was equally vital, and that was a written record of the Gospel. Without it, the apostles' teaching might have been distorted in passing from mouth to mouth. For Antioch and for the Syrian church as a whole, this need was supplied by the Gospel according to St Matthew. Scholars think it likely that

* *Didache*, iii. 4.

this gospel was composed not in Antioch itself but farther east, where such traditions as that of the visit of the Magi were probably current. Beyond the Roman province of Syria lay Mesopotamia, and both there and in North Syria the Jews of the dispersion were extremely numerous. In Acts we are told that " Parthians and Medes and Elamites and dwellers in Mesopotamia " were among those who witnessed the outpouring of the Holy Spirit at Pentecost, and there is reason to believe that Christianity spread to these regions at an early date. Whoever composed St Matthew's Gospel—and it was almost certainly not the apostle Matthew—the book is thoroughly Jewish in tone. The writer was evidently trained in Rabbinical methods of argument, and loved to quote proof texts and to assemble his material in groups of five, in imitation of the five-fold division of the Pentateuch, or in sevens and tens. But he did not have any sympathy with the Sadducees and Pharisees of Jerusalem, and one of his aims was to show that, led by them, Judaism had failed and the Christian Church had inherited the promises made by God to Israel. Like the writer of the *Didache*, the composer of this gospel was much concerned with the need for order in the Church. He stressed the authority of St Peter and the qualities required in an apostle or missionary. He had the same awareness of the evils of the time and the same conviction that the Last Judgement was at hand. In collecting his material, he made use of St Mark's Gospel and also of a collection of our Lord's sayings, known to the critics as Q, already in existence at Antioch, and possibly composed there. It was small wonder that his gospel became widely popular and was soon recognized as *the* gospel by the church of Antioch. It included all that people valued in earlier writings; it was perfectly adapted to the needs of the time; and it was especially suitable for reading aloud in church services.

Ephesus.

When St Paul bade farewell to the elders of Ephesus on his last journey to Jerusalem, he left behind him a church that was already well established and capable of giving a lead to the other churches of Asia. The elders, whom he had appointed there and in other places in Asia Minor and Greece, had the alternative name of bishops and, in the absence of the apostles, they were entrusted with full charge of their respective churches. Whether one of them was appointed as president or whether they took it in turns to preside at the celebration of the Eucharist, we do not know. " One bishop, one church " was not an accurate description until rather later. Monarchical bishops were not needed as long as the apostles were still alive.

If we could accept the Pastoral Epistles at their face value, we could rest assured that St Paul's farewell to the elders at Ephesus was not final, that he was acquitted at his trial in Rome and returned to see once more his beloved churches in Asia Minor and Greece. But a strong case can be made out for supposing that these epistles are not by St Paul, but were composed towards the end of the first century by someone much concerned about church government, who believed he was setting forth St Paul's views. The literary dishonesty of such a proceeding would not have been apparent to a writer of this period. His aim was to offer sound counsel to those on whom the weight of responsibility fell, and, if he could claim apostolic authority for his words, so much the better. Neither the style nor the theology of the main body of these letters is distinctively Pauline, but scraps of genuine letters of his have been incorporated, most of them personal messages torn from their contexts.

Even though we cannot feel convinced that 1 and 2 Timothy and Titus are genuine letters, or, for the most part, written by St Paul, still we can be sure that they are early Christian documents and that they give a true picture of conditions in Asia towards the end of the first century. As in Syria, false teachers were giving much trouble. There were some of Jewish origin who wasted men's time with " foolish questionings and genealogies and strifes and fightings about the law ". Others, probably Greeks, professed to be philosophers, denied the resurrection of the body and went to extremes either of asceticism or of licentiousness. A lively picture is given of them:

" For these are they that creep into houses, and take captive silly women laden with sins, led away by divers lusts, ever learning, and never able to come to the knowledge of the truth." *

Other pen portraits are to be found in the Pastoral Epistles: the bishop who could not keep his own children in order, and so could not be expected to control a church; the young widows who had a gay time and went gossiping from house to house while drawing money from charitable funds; married women who came flaunting to church in rich clothes, their hair braided and adorned with gold and pearls. The general impression is of a church at peace, troubled by worldliness and heresy within, but not by persecution from without.

The churches of Asia were not left to fend for themselves without apostolic guidance after St Paul's departure. St Peter may have visited them occasionally. The fact that his first epistle is addressed to " the elect who are sojourners of the Dispersion in Pontus, Galatia, Cappadocia, Asia, and Bithynia " suggests that he may have taken a particular interest in the Jewish converts there. But the apostle who exercised a formative influence on the churches of Asia was St John.

* 2 *Tim.* 3. 6–7.

Controversy has raged over the Johannine problem and, unless fresh evidence can be discovered, certainty is beyond our reach. The matter is complicated by the presence of two, probably three, important leaders of the name of John in the Asian church at about the same time. Differences of style make it as certain as anything in literary criticism can be that the Fourth Gospel and the Book of Revelation are not by the same man. To distinguish him, the author of Revelation has been dubbed John the Seer. There is a strong tradition that St John the apostle was for a long time in charge of the church of Ephesus, and died in that place at last in extreme old age. But there is also mention of a certain John the Elder, who was a disciple of the Lord, but not an apostle; he, too, was a man of authority in the Ephesian church. Some scholars have attempted to simplify matters by denying that St John the apostle was ever in Ephesus and putting all mention of him down to confusion with John the Elder. There is a tradition that St John was martyred with his brother St James, but it comes from a late source and is quite untrustworthy. Our chief, but not our only authority for St John the apostle's life in Ephesus is St Irenæus, who as a young man listened eagerly to St Polycarp, the aged bishop of Smyrna, as he retailed to his disciples all that he had heard from the lips of the apostle John himself. It is hard to see how either St Irenæus or St Polycarp could have been mistaken in a matter of such importance. Certainly the churches of Asia claimed apostolic authority for certain practices in which they differed from Rome, and their claim passed unchallenged in the second century. References in the early Fathers show that it was the common belief of the Church that St John the apostle had governed the church of Ephesus until his death. We can feel reasonably safe in accepting the evidence of St Irenæus and believing what he has to tell us about St John.

False teachers, not unlike those denounced in the Pastoral Epistles, were troubling the church of Ephesus when St John first took charge there. The most popular among them was a certain Cerinthus. His ideas resembled in some respects those of Simon Magus and Menander, but he made no supernatural claims for himself. He taught that the God of the Jews, who gave the Law to Moses, was only an angel, the Supreme God having no interest in so low a matter. Jesus, he asserted, was the son of Joseph and Mary, an ordinary man upon whom the Holy Spirit came at his baptism, leaving him again before his crucifixion. He looked forward to a millennium of feasting, drinking, and marrying; his ideas were therefore hardly calculated to encourage his followers in sober living. St John abominated the man's teaching and all his works. One day, as St Polycarp was wont to tell, St John entered the public baths, but before he had had time to undress he perceived that Cerinthus was there. At that, without waiting to bathe, he ran from the bath-house, crying to those who were with him: " Let us flee, lest even the bath-house fall, because Cerinthus, the enemy of the truth, is within." There spoke the man who, in his youth, would have called down fire upon a Samaritan village and whom Christ nicknamed " Son of Thunder "!

St John did not confine his activities to Ephesus. He toured the neighbouring churches, ordaining bishops and supervising their work. The organization of the Church owed much to him. Early in the second century we find that each of the churches in this area has its bishop, with elders and deacons serving under him. One of the stories told of St John, preserved for us by St Clement of Alexandria, is that while touring the churches St John commended a young man to the care of a certain bishop, and, returning that way some years later, heard to his distress that the young man had run away, joined a band of brigands in the hills, and become their captain. At this St John exclaimed:

"'I left a fine keeper of a brother's soul! But let a horse now be got ready and someone to guide me on my way.'

"He rode as he was, away from the church, and coming to the country, was taken prisoner by the outguard of the banditti. He neither attempted, however, to flee, nor refused to be taken; but cried out 'For this very purpose am I come; conduct me to your captain.'

"He, in the mean time, stood waiting, armed as he was. But as he recognized John advancing towards him, overcome with shame he turned about to flee. The apostle, however, pursued him with all his might, forgetful of his age, and crying out, 'Why dost thou fly, my son, from me, thy father; thy defence-less, aged father? Have compassion on me, my son; fear not. Thou still hast hope of life. I will intercede with Christ for thee. Should it be necessary, I will cheerfully suffer death for thee, as Christ for us. I will give my life for thine. Stay; believe Christ hath sent me.'

"Hearing this, he at first stopped with downcast looks. Then threw away his arms; then trembling lamented bitterly, and embracing the old man as he came up, attempted to plead for himself with his lamentations, as much as he was able. . . . The apostle pledging himself, and solemnly assuring him that he had found pardon for him in his prayers at the hands of Christ, conducted him back again to the church. Then suppli-cating with frequent prayers, contending with constant fastings, and softening down his mind with various consolatory declara-tions, he did not leave him, as it is said, until he had restored him to the church." *

In the Apocryphal *Acts of St John* many other anecdotes are told of the apostle, but these are obvious legends and quite incredible. One example will suffice. Once, while St John was visiting the churches, it is recorded that he and his disciples came to a deserted inn and decided to spend the

* Quoted by Eusebius: *Ecclesiastical History*, Bk. III, ch. 23.

night there. But the bed upon inspection proved to be infested with bugs, whom St John thereupon addressed:

" ' I say unto you, O bugs, behave yourselves, one and all, and leave your abode for the night and remain quiet in the one place, and keep your distance from the servants of God.' "

On the following morning, when his disciples arrived, they saw a great number of bugs standing at the door of the house. Then St John

" sat up on the bed and looked at them, and said,
" ' Since ye have well behaved yourselves in hearkening to my rebuke, come into your place.'
" And when he had said this and risen from the bed, the bugs running from the door hasted to the bed and climbed up by the legs thereof and disappeared into the joints." *

It may well have been during the period of unrest which culminated in the Roman campaign against the Jews that several leading figures in the early Church left Palestine and settled in Asia Minor, to the great benefit of the churches there. St Philip and at least three of his four prophetic daughters moved from Cæsarea to Hierapolis, a place not far from Colossæ. John the Elder, who was a disciple of the Lord, though not one of the Twelve, apparently settled at Ephesus. According to a document called " The Apostolic Constitutions ", he succeeded St John the apostle as bishop, and he was certainly regarded as an authority on our Lord's life and teaching. Another disciple of our Lord, the Elder Aristion (or Ariston), became bishop of Smyrna. Thus there was gathered round St John a group of men who had themselves both seen and heard the Lord. From this school of Christian thought came the Fourth Gospel, the epistles of St John, and the Apocalypse.

On the face of it, the authorship of the Fourth Gospel

* *Acts of St John.* *Apocryphal New Testament*, by M. R. James, p. 60 ff.

presents no problem. The last verse but one, evidently by a different hand, reads:

" This is the disciple which beareth witness of these things, and wrote these things: and we know that his witness is true."

The disciple referred to is the beloved disciple, St John the apostle, who is not mentioned by name in the Fourth Gospel. But the majority of modern scholars doubt that the matter is quite so simple. Would St John describe himself as " the disciple whom Jesus loved "? If the author of the gospel is the author also of the three epistles, 1, 2, and 3 John—and their style seems to bear this out *— then why does he call himself " the Elder "? The title of apostle would have carried more weight. The theory which best accounts for all the facts is that summarized by Dr Temple in the preface to his great book, *Readings in St John's Gospel*:

" The view which now seems to me to do fullest justice to the evidence is that the writer—the Evangelist—is John the Elder, who was an intimate disciple of John the Apostle; that he records the teaching of that Apostle with great fidelity; that the Apostle is the ' Witness ', to whom reference is sometimes made, and is also the ' disciple whom Jesus loved '."

We can imagine the circle at Ephesus: St John himself, an old man, but as active in mind as ever; John the Elder, his friend and disciple, upon whom falls an increasing amount of the administrative work of the church; the other elders of the church of Ephesus and young men, like Polycarp, in deacon's orders, eager to listen and destined, some of them, to become bishops themselves in a few years time. Upon this day, it may be, St Philip has arrived from Hierapolis, bringing with him the manuscript of a new

* Not all scholars are agreed on this point, but see *The New Testament: A Reader's Guide*, by C. A. Alington, xxv, " The Epistles of John ".

gospel, written by his friend St Luke. When the reading of it is finished, a silence falls. St John's thoughts are far away, for he is living again the days when he knew the Lord in the flesh. St Philip looks inquiringly at John the Elder.

"Your friend, the doctor, has written his book beautifully," says the Elder thoughtfully, "and I can see that he did not waste his time when he stayed with you at Cæsarea. Some of what he records he must have learnt at Antioch, but for the order of events he depended on Mark. Do you not think so?" he adds, looking at St John.

St John nods his agreement: "Luke wasn't there," he says, "neither was Mark. How could they know?"

John the Elder turns back to St Philip:

"Mark, you know, acted as interpreter for Peter, and he wrote down accurately everything that he remembered, without, however, recording in order what was either said or done by Christ. For neither did he hear the Lord, nor did he follow him, but afterwards, as I said, attended Peter, who adapted his instructions to the need of his hearers but had no design of giving a connected account." *

"I see," says St Philip, "what Mark set down is quite true but not always in the right order, and Luke has copied him in that. Sir," he goes on, looking earnestly at St John, "will not you set down in writing your memories of the Lord, so that we may be sure of the truth, and our children after us?"

But St John, owing to his age, shrinks from undertaking so great a work, and he only yields to the pressure put upon him by all present when John the Elder promises to write the book, if the apostle will tell him what to say.

In some such fashion, it appears, the Church gained one

* This paragraph is quoted almost verbatim from the report of John the Elder's words given by Papias, and quoted in Eusebius, op. cit., III, 39.

of her greatest treasures, the Gospel according to St John.
But the book was not written simply to supplement St
Mark's Gospel and to correct his chronology. Its purpose
is plainly stated at what was once the end of the book,
before the addition of the last chapter:

" Many other signs therefore did Jesus in the presence of the
disciples, which are not written in this book:
" But these are written, that ye may believe that Jesus is the
Christ, the Son of God; and that believing ye may have life in
his name."

It is the witness of one who knew Jesus in the flesh to the
Church's faith that Christ is truly man and truly God. In
the face of would-be philosophers, who endeavoured to
persuade people that Christ was not really human at all,
and of Jews, who denied that he was the Messiah, St John's
Gospel proclaimed the truth that he is the Word of God
and that " the Word became flesh and dwelt among us ".

Revelation is a mysterious book, intentionally mysterious.
All we know for certain about the author is that his name
was John, and that he was well known in the churches of
Asia. The tradition that he was St John the Apostle is
very early, for Justin Martyr mentions it in A.D. 136.

" I John," writes the author of the Apocalypse, " your brother
and partaker with you in the tribulation and kingdom and
patience which are in Jesus, was in the isle that is called Patmos,
for the word of God and the testimony of Jesus."

He was writing during a time of persecution, probably in
the reign of Domitian, and he foresaw far more severe
trials in the immediate future, for which he wanted his
fellow Christians to be prepared. Towards the end of
Domitian's reign, the Emperor's growing tyranny, combined with his understanding of mass psychology, led him
to give strong official support to the practice of Emperor-
worship, already popular in Asia. It must have been at

this time that refusal to worship the Emperor became a treasonable offence. It should not be difficult for us to imagine the position in which these first-century Christians found themselves, for we, too, live in an age of excessive State control, and have seen in other countries the struggle between the demands of the State and those of Christ upon the individual conscience reach the final extremity of active persecution.

" The imperial cult brought to its sharpest expression the inherent difference between Paganism and Christianity. Cæsar was the embodiment of all material forces—pride, wealth, the glory of the world: were these things to be worshipped? were they to be regarded as the highest good? "*

To that question Christians could but answer, " No. Jesus Christ and he only is our Lord." The Apocalypse was written that men might have the necessary courage and determination to make that answer, and to hold to it even to the death. No wonder it is often obscure, with topical allusions cloaked beneath its symbolism; for the writer was advocating treason, and its earliest readers discussed the book secretly, and hoped that if it were found in their possession their enemies might fail to understand its purport. Nero, the first persecutor of the Church, was rumoured to be still alive and in hiding. The evil which he symbolized was certainly still powerful in the world. John gave warning that the forces of evil would have their hour, and that persecution would become far more intense. In Hebrew, each letter of the alphabet has a numerical value, and the letters which spell the name of Nero add up to 666, the number of the beast.†

* Prof. E. F. Scott: Essay on " The Opposition to Cæsar Worship " in *Church History*, Vol. II, No. 2. American Society of Church History.

† This is the most probable of the many interpretations which have been suggested.

"Here is wisdom," writes John, giving his readers a hint. "He that hath understanding, let him count the number of the beast; for it is the number of a man: and his number is Six hundred and sixty and six." *

He spares his readers nothing. He depicts for them the winepress of the wrath of God, plague succeeding plague, as evil is let loose to work its own destruction. In this vision of judgement, the worshippers of the beast, the children of this world, are seen to be perishing, while the servants of God are entering into eternal life. "Write," says a voice from heaven, "Blessed are the dead which die in the Lord from henceforth." And John sees them as a great multitude, which no man could number, standing before the throne of God, arrayed in white robes and with palms of victory in their hands. He looks forward with the perfect confidence of faith to the establishment of the Kingdom of God. The Empire of Rome will pass away; the Empire of Christ will endure for ever.

"And I saw the holy city, new Jerusalem, coming down out of heaven from God, made ready as a bride adorned for her husband. And I heard a great voice out of the throne saying, Behold, the tabernacle of God is with men, and he shall dwell with them, and they shall be his peoples, and God himself shall be with them, and be their God: and he shall wipe away every tear from their eyes; and death shall be no more; neither shall there be mourning, nor crying, nor pain, any more: the first things are passed away."

The book of Revelation is a "mystery", for it speaks in symbols of things divine, which pass human understanding. But things divine are not remote from daily life, rather they are the heart of it, therefore this book was and is a firebrand which kindles men to revolt against the powers of evil and inflames them with longing for that perfect society which John describes as a city, the City of

* *Rev.* 13. 18.

I

God. It was written for Christians not unlike ourselves. In the churches of John's day there were patient, hard-working, faithful men, who yet had lost their first enthusiasm; he had met some of them at Ephesus. There were others, especially at Pergamum and Thyatira, who had let themselves listen to popular teachers who encouraged them in sexual indulgence and in accepting the standards of the world. At Sardis the church seemed dead. The Laodiceans were well-to-do, complacent, indifferent, not the stuff of which martyrs are made. Yet in all these churches, as well as in faithful Smyrna and Philadelphia, there were men who heard the voice of God speaking to them in John's Revelation, and who answered with their lives.

" The kingdom of heaven is like unto leaven, which a woman took, and hid in three measures of meal, till it was all leavened."

Corinth.

No church is better known to us through the epistles of St Paul than is that of Corinth. Composed mainly of Gentiles, drawing its members from the population of a thriving port, the church of Corinth was subject to numerous temptations. Its members were lively, intelligent, full of enthusiasm; many of them were gifted by the Spirit with unusual powers; but they had little self-control or sense of discipline. They were given to forming factions, some saying they were of Paul's party, others of Apollos', others of Peter's. They were litigious, unruly, and apt to be noisy and disorderly even during the Lord's Supper. Living among pagans, they easily fell to the moral level of those around them, and indulged in sensual sins or continued idolatrous practices. It was a church with great possibilities, but with many inner weaknesses. Presumably Timothy and Titus, St Paul's deputies, exercised some authority over the Greek churches after his departure, but

all record of the years immediately following has been lost.
Fortunately we have a letter written by the church of Rome
to the church of Corinth about the last decade of the first
century. It is known as the first epistle of Clement, for
it is traditionally supposed to have been written by Clement,
the third in the succession of Roman bishops.

The opening paragraphs of the letter explain themselves:

" The Church of God which sojourns in Rome to the Church
of God which sojourns in Corinth, to those who are called and
sanctified by the will of God through our Lord Jesus Christ.
Grace and peace from God Almighty be multiplied to you
through Jesus Christ.

" Owing to the sudden and repeated misfortunes and calamities which have befallen us, we consider that our attention has
been somewhat delayed in turning to the questions disputed
among you, beloved, and especially the abominable and unholy
sedition, alien and foreign to the elect of God, which a few rash
and self-willed persons have made blaze up to such a frenzy
that your name, venerable and famous, and worthy as it is of
all men's love, has been much slandered."

The writer goes on to speak of the high reputation of the
Corinthian church, and to deplore the recent disturbances
there, in which some of the younger men had revolted
against the authority of the elders and had ejected them
from office. The church of Rome is characteristically
shocked at such revolutionary behaviour, so alien to her
own sense of order and discipline. A large part of the
long letter sent by Rome to her erring sister church consists of examples of obedience drawn from the Old Testament and a homily on the Christian virtues, especially the
virtue of humility. The church of Corinth is urged to
repent and to reinstate the deprived elders. The serious-
ness of her offence in allowing them to be degraded from
office without just cause is made plain by a statement of the

apostolic origin of the episcopate. The terms "bishop" and "presbyter" are used interchangeably, and evidently both churches were still governed by a number of presbyter-bishops. The day of the single monarchical bishop had not yet come in most places, though in Syria about this time St Ignatius was successfully establishing himself in that position. About the authority of these presbyter-bishops, however, there is no question. The church of Rome is emphatic on that subject:

"The apostles received the Gospel for us from the Lord Jesus Christ," she writes, "Jesus Christ was sent from God. The Christ therefore is from God and the apostles from Christ. . . . They preached from district to district, and from city to city, and they appointed their first converts, testing them by the Spirit, to be bishops and deacons of the future believers."

She continues:

"Our apostles also knew through our Lord Jesus Christ that there would be strife for the title of bishop. For this cause, therefore, since they had received perfect foreknowledge, they appointed those who have been already mentioned, and afterwards added the codicil that if they should fall asleep, other approved men should succeed to their ministry. We consider therefore that it is not just to remove from their ministry those who were appointed by them, or later on by other eminent men, with the consent of the whole Church, and have ministered to the flock of Christ without blame, humbly, peaceably, and disinterestedly, and for many years have received a universally favourable testimony."

We do not know what response was made by the church of Corinth, but as the letter was treasured and read aloud at service-time for many years afterwards, it is probable that she accepted the admonition and put her house in order. Unfortunately, little else is known about any of the churches in Greece before the second century. As to their contribution to the New Testament, there is no book

which unquestionably comes from the Corinthian or any
other of the Greek churches. But it is highly probable
that the Gospel used in these churches was that according
to St Luke and, if so, Acts must be assigned to the same
region. St Luke's ability to write good Greek, and the
great interest he shows in the spread of Christianity to
the Gentiles, would naturally commend his books to the
Greek churches. Moreover, he is closely linked with the
church of Philippi. According to tradition, St Luke's
birthplace was Antioch, and he was probably one of the
earliest Gentile converts to Christianity. But at the time
of St Paul's second missionary journey, St Luke seems to
have been living at Philippi, probably practising as a doctor
there. Professor Ramsay has suggested that St Luke was
the man from Macedonia whom St Paul saw in a dream
beseeching him for help. It is certainly at this point in
Acts that St Luke begins to use the first person, which
shows that he actually took part in the events which he
describes. St Luke was with St. Paul during his mission
in Philippi, and then he remained behind while St Paul
went on to further work in Greece and Asia Minor. Judging from the passages in Acts which are written in the first
person, it was not until St Paul was about to set out on his
last journey to Jerusalem that St Luke rejoined him, presumably as the delegate of the Philippian church.* Whether
he returned there after his long stay in Rome with St Paul
we do not know, but certainly copies of his writings, his
Gospel and Acts, must have reached Philippi and been
treasured there. It is hard to imagine Acts being written
anywhere else than in a Greek seaport, preferably Corinth.
It smells of the sea, and is as full of navigational details as
if it had been written by a retired Liverpool merchant.
St Luke collected much of his material elsewhere, but the
character of his writings is that of the Greek churches.

* *Acts* 16. 9 to end, and 20. 1–6.

Rome.

To contemporaries, it must have seemed impossible that the church in Rome could survive the persecution under Nero. Hundreds of its most devoted members lost their lives, among them the two great apostles, St Peter and St Paul. Those who survived and remained steadfast were left without the leaders upon whom they had depended, and were safe only so long as they could avoid attracting the attention of the authorities. But the church survived and flourished. Probably St Mark had already recorded a good deal of St Peter's teaching during the apostle's lifetime. After St Peter's death, he completed his work, and soon the Gospel according to St Mark, the earliest of all the Gospels, was being read aloud whenever the Roman Christians gathered together for worship. Thus the written word insured that the apostle's message should still be heard, though his living voice had been stilled.

For leaders, the Roman church had a body of elders who had been ordained by the apostles. One of these elders, or presbyter-bishops—for the names seem to have been interchangeable—must have been chosen as president and, according to the earliest lists of Roman bishops, his name was Linus. Whether he had been designated by St Peter as his successor, or was ordained by his fellow presbyter-bishops, or was elected by the whole Church, we cannot tell from the evidence we have. There is certainly no indication that he wielded exceptional power or was regarded as the head of the whole Church. On the contrary, the earliest surviving letter from the Roman church, 1 Clement, makes no mention of a bishop, but is simply addressed to the church of Corinth in the name of the church of Rome. This letter is usually dated about A.D. 96, or even later, because Clement, who according to tradition was the writer, did not become bishop of Rome until

A.D. 92. But the evidence of the letter itself points to an earlier date. Giving examples of the harm done through jealousy, the writer speaks of the apostles:

" But, to cease from the examples of old time, let us come to those who contended in the days nearest to us; let us take the noble examples of our own generation. Through jealousy and envy the greatest and most righteous pillars of the Church were persecuted and contended unto death."

He goes on to recount the deaths of St Peter and St Paul and the other martyrdoms of Nero's time, speaking as though these were recent events, not, as they would be in A.D. 96, thirty years old. Again he writes as though daily sacrifice were still being offered in Jerusalem, which could not be the case after the destruction of the Temple in A.D. 70. Therefore it may be that this letter was written only a few years after the terrible events of A.D. 65, at a time when Clement was not yet bishop, but was dealing with the Roman church's correspondence as secretary to the elders. In any case, the letter gives us an impression of the Roman church at the end of the first century. Already the Roman church stands out as an upholder of apostolic tradition and of order and discipline against those who would attempt revolutionary innovations. The Corinthians are urged to restore their ejected elders to office, and the appeal is made to them on the authority of the Old Testament, of Christ's example, of the ways of the Creator, of the teaching of St Paul. Nowhere is it suggested that the Roman church has the right to dictate to that of Corinth. The letter is tactfully worded:

" We are not only writing these things to you, beloved, for your admonition, but also to remind ourselves; for we are in the same arena, and the same struggle is before us."

The letter reveals the qualities which fitted the Roman church for leadership: steadfastness, faithfulness to tradition, respect for authority, a sense of order, a sane and balanced judgement. It shows a sober, cheerful determination which no persecution could subdue.

Most of the letter consists of exhortations and quotations from the Old Testament and was so highly valued in the early Church that it was often quoted as Scripture. But to modern readers the most interesting things in it are a couple of chance allusions to events of the day. Besides the disorders at Corinth, which are the subject of the letter, the writer mentions, in passing, the martyrdoms under Nero and says:

" Through jealousy women were persecuted as Danaids and Dircæ, suffering terrible and unholy indignities; they stedfastly finished the course of faith, and received a noble reward, weak in the body though they were."

For a moment we can see the arena where, in a loathsome theatrical performance, a Christian girl is forced to play the part of Dirce in the final scene when she is dragged to death by a bull. Again, giving examples of love, the writer mentions actions in their own way no less heroic:

" We know that many among ourselves have given themselves to bondage that they might ransom others. Many have delivered themselves to slavery, and provided food for others with the price they received for themselves."

Such was the quality of Christian faith and Christian love in first-century Rome. The few other facts that are known about the Roman church at this period will be mentioned in the seventh chapter, which deals with the catacombs.

Alexandria.

Alexandria is hardly mentioned in the New Testament. Apollos, the learned Jew who became a fellow-worker with Priscilla and Aquila, came from there, but when he reached Ephesus he was not a Christian, but a follower of St John the Baptist. However, it cannot have been long before Christianity reached that great city with its large and influential Jewish colony. According to tradition, St Mark was the founder of the church of Alexandria, and his cousin St Barnabas helped in the work. Although it had not the prestige of being founded by either St Peter or St Paul, the church of Alexandria was plainly destined to become one of the leading churches in Christendom. Alexandria, a crucible where ideas from East and West amalgamated, had already produced a great Jewish thinker, Philo, who was a contemporary of our Lord. He was a resident of the Jewish colony, but he was also an eager student of Greek thought. The university of Alexandria, with its world-famous library, was an intellectual centre for the whole Roman Empire, and at this time was more important than the university of Athens, the old home of philosophy. It was not Stoicism, but Platonism, that was expounded most persuasively in the lecture-rooms at Alexandria. Philo became a convinced Platonist, but he remained a devout Jew. He set himself the task of proving that the truths of Greek philosophy were expressed in a different way in the Old Testament. The difficulties of his undertaking might well have been too much for him, had it not been that allegorical interpretation was in vogue, both among Greek and among Jewish Rabbinical writers. Philo honestly believed that by looking for hidden meanings in the Old Testament he was revealing its divine message, and not, as modern readers would think, merely distorting its true, literal sense. He was confirmed in this opinion by his acceptance of Plato's doctrine of Ideas. Plato held that all earthly things are poor imitations of their heavenly counterparts, the eternal types which exist in the mind of God. On this view, it is the eternal Idea which is important, and not its earthly shadow. Greatest of all these Ideas, according to Philo, is the Idea of the whole of creation, as it exists in God's mind, and this he called the Logos.   St John was thinking on the same lines when he began his Gospel by saying:

" In the beginning was the Word, and the Word was with God, and the Word was God."

But St John has gone a step farther than Philo.   For him the Word is a Person, God's Eternal Son, the Christ.*

Although in the coming years the church of Alexandria was to contribute much to the intellectual life of the Church, her share in the writing of the New Testament is small. The New Testament is above all the record of the teaching of the apostles, and Alexandria, unlike Antioch, Ephesus, and Rome, had not heard the Gospel from the lips of the apostles themselves.   A version called the " Gospel according to the Egyptians " did circulate locally, but it was later rejected by the Church as a whole as being heretical.   Only a few fragments of it have survived.   One New Testament book, however, is thought by many scholars to have been written by someone connected with the Alexandrian church, and that is the Epistle to the Hebrews.   Neither the style nor the ideas are those of St Paul, and the tradition which attributes the book to him is not reliable.   The Alexandrian church thought highly of it, and continued to quote it as Scripture, but the name of its author is unknown.   Origen, the great third-century Christian scholar, is quoted as saying: " Who wrote the Epistle God only knows certainly ", and there the question must be left.†   But of its connection with Alexandria the book speaks for itself.   The writer, whether he was an Alexandrine or not, had learnt to think in types—thus Melchizedek, priest of God Most High, is a forerunner of Christ, our great High Priest, and the sacrifices ordained

* For Philo and his ideas see the introduction to Hebrews in the Clarendon Bible.
† Eusebius: op. cit. vi. 25.

by the Law of Moses foreshadow Christ's one sufficient sacrifice upon the cross.   Above all, he found in Philo's blend of Greek and Hebrew thought concepts through which he could express his own full conviction of Christ's divinity.   He does not actually speak of Christ as the Word, or Logos, but he sees him as the end and the beginning of all things, one with God as radiance is one with the light it shines from, and as a seal's impression is one with the seal:

" God, having of old time spoken unto the fathers in the prophets by divers portions and in divers manners, hath at the end of these days spoken unto us in his Son, whom he appointed heir of all things, through whom also he made the worlds; who being the effulgence of his glory, and the very image of his substance, and upholding all things by the word of his power, when he had made purification of sins, sat down on the right hand of the Majesty on high." *

Among the books which, like 1 *Clement*, were occasionally quoted as Scripture and were included by some churches in the New Testament, is a treatise called *The Epistle of Barnabas*.   It almost certainly originated in the church of Alexandria, and there is no likelihood whatever that it was written by St Barnabas.   It was not written until after A.D. 70, when the Temple was destroyed, and it may be considerably later.   Most of the book is concerned with proving that the Christians, not the Jews, are the inheritors of God's promises.   It is indeed a tract against Judaism, and its method of argument is not very convincing to present day readers.   One extract will suffice:

" Learn fully then, children of love, concerning all things, for Abraham, who first circumcised, did so looking forward in the spirit to Jesus, and had received the doctrines of three letters. For it says, ' And Abraham circumcised from his household eighteen men and three hundred '.   What then was the know-

* *Hebrews* 1. 1–3.

ledge that was given to him? Notice that he first mentions the eighteen, and after a pause the three hundred. The eighteen is I (= ten) and H (= 8)—you have Jesus—and because the cross was destined to have grace in the T he says 'and three hundred'. So he indicates Jesus in the two letters and the cross in the other."

The explanation of this extraordinary passage lies in the fact that, in Greek, numerals are expressed in letters. I H are the first letters of the Greek for Jesus and the symbol for 300 is T.

Perhaps this piece of allegorizing is not much more far-fetched than the treatment of the scanty Old Testament references to Melchizedek in Hebrews:

" For this Melchizedek, king of Salem, priest of God Most High, who met Abraham returning from the slaughter of the kings, and blessed him, to whom also Abraham divided a tenth part of all (being first, by interpretation, King of righteousness, and then also King of Salem, which is, King of Peace; without father, without mother, without genealogy, having neither beginning of days nor end of life, but made like unto the Son of God), abideth a priest continually." *

Thus Melchizedek is shown to be a prototype of Christ, and the analogy is worked out in detail in the verses that follow. In modern historical criticism there is no place for this method of interpreting the Bible at all, either for the numerals of Barnabas or for the symbolism of Hebrews. But no one who has read the two books in their entirety can fail to be thankful for the spiritual discernment of those who included the Epistle to the Hebrews in the New Testament and rejected the Epistle of Barnabas. The Epistle of Barnabas was a tract for the times and nothing more. But in Hebrews the method of argument is of little consequence compared with the inspiration behind it, for truth looks

* *Hebrews* 7. 1–3.

lovely even in old fashioned clothes. In a flash we pass
from mystifying exegesis to revelation, as when the writer
says of Christ:

> " ' Thou art a priest for ever
>   After the order of Melchizedek.'

" Who in the days of his flesh, having offered up prayers and
supplications with strong crying and tears unto him that was
able to save him from death, and having been heard for his godly
fear, though he was a Son, yet learned obedience by the things
which he suffered; and having been made perfect, he became
unto all them that obey him the author of eternal salvation;
named of God a high priest after the order of Melchizedek." *

In that difficult but glorious book surely the church of
Alexandria made her first great contribution to Christian
thought.

BOOKS FOR FURTHER READING

The Four Gospels, by B. H. Streeter.
Introductions to the individual Gospels in the Clarendon Bible.
The Gospels, by B. K. Rattey: an easier book than Streeter's.
Introduction to the New Testament, by F. Bertram Clogg.
The New Testament: a Reader's Guide, by C. A. Alington.
The Apostolic Preaching and Its Developments, by Prof. C. H. Dodd.
Archæology and the New Testament, by Stephen Caiger, B.D., sections
    viii and ix.
The Archeology of Palestine, by W. F. Albright.   Chapter XI.

* *Hebrews* 5. 6–10.

CHAPTER VI

ASIA MINOR: THE NOBLE ARMY OF MARTYRS

IN the flickering heat of late July or early August about the year A.D. 110, a cloud of dust on the road from Ephesus to Smyrna showed where a party of travellers was moving. There were ten of them, all men. In their dress they were in no way remarkable, but three out of the number were bishops, two were priests, and two were deacons; for these were the delegates sent by the Christians of Ephesus, Magnesia, and Tralles to greet Ignatius, Bishop of Antioch, at Smyrna on his way to Rome and martyrdom.

About the same time St Ignatius himself and his Roman guards (his ten leopards, as he called them) were nearing Smyrna after their long journey by land from Antioch. Half dazed from weariness and heat, St Ignatius found his thoughts swinging like a pendulum between the two ends of this interminable road: the church he had left behind him at Antioch, and the ultimate trial that awaited him in the arena at Rome. For years the church at Antioch had been in his charge. Antioch, the city where St Paul and St Barnabas had taught, the church which had sent the apostle of the Gentiles out on his first missionary journey; it had been a heavy responsibility. Conscious that he was the successor of the apostles, St Ignatius was also conscious of his weakness as a man. He had struggled to preserve his church from heresy and lack of discipline, which threatened to destroy it body and soul; but, looking back over his life's work, he could not comfort himself with the thought that he had succeeded. At that very moment the community he loved was undergoing the test of persecution and he, its leader, was far away.   Would the laity in such a time of terror remain faithful?   Would they continue to obey their priests and deacons?   Would the clergy themselves stand together?   Fears constantly assailed him.   In the time of the apostles the church at Antioch had been led by prophets and teachers,* but afterwards it had come into line with other Christian communities with a bishop as its head, presbyters (or priests) under him, and deacons as the third and lowest order.   St Ignatius was utterly convinced that this three-fold hierarchy had been ordained by the apostles.   Certainly St Paul had appointed presbyters in the churches which he founded.   These had been known indifferently as presbyters and as *episkopoi* or bishops, but they resembled the order of bishops, as St Ignatius knew it, only in name.   He and his fellow bishops had succeeded to the authority, not of this second order, but of the apostles themselves.   They were men, like St Timothy, appointed to the apostolic work of the care and administration of the churches.   It was for them to ordain presbyters and deacons, and no one had the right to question their authority.   But men did question it.   Presbyters did not always obey their bishop.   The laity allowed themselves to be led away by false teachers or split into factions for merely personal reasons.   Wandering prophets, professing to be inspired, were often a disturbing influence in the church.   St Ignatius gave them no encouragement, and when he spoke, as he sometimes did, of " the divine prophets ", it was to the prophets of the Old Testament that he referred.†   During his episcopate, St Ignatius had had to assert his authority continually, not from love of power, but because he saw that only if they were united could the

---

* *Acts* 13. 1.

† *St Ignatius to the Magnesians*, 8. 2; and *to the Philadelphians*, 2. Translated in *Apostolic Fathers*, by Lightfoot, vol. 2, Sec. 1. 5.

scattered Christian communities survive. Now, on his way to end his life in the glory of martyrdom, his chief concern was still the Church's needs and the dangers that beset her.

Evening came on, and the guards with their prisoners camped by the wayside. After the evening meal one of the soldiers produced a lyre from the baggage and began to play. The others gathered round and sang ballads from their native land and the popular songs of the day. St Ignatius listened, and his cares fell from him. The voices singing in unison brought him a sudden vision of the Church united in her praise of God. Writing to the church at Ephesus a short while afterwards, he said:

" Do ye, each and all of you, form yourselves into a chorus, that being harmonious in concord and taking the key-note of God ye may in unison sing with one voice through Jesus Christ unto the Father, that he may both hear you and acknowledge you by your good deeds to be members of his Son." *

At last the singing ceased; the guards turned in to sleep and all was silent. St Ignatius, his anxieties forgotten, meditated lovingly upon the life of Jesus Christ his Lord, upon his acts, upon his words, upon his silences.

" Now there is one teacher, who spake and it came to pass," he wrote later, " yea and even the things he hath done in silence are worthy of the Father. He that truly possesseth the word of Jesus is able also to hearken unto his silence, that he may be perfect."

In awe he thought of the hidden mysteries which were wrought in the silence of God, but which now must be shouted to the world. Especially he thought of the virginity of Mary and her child-bearing. Looking up, he saw a bright star which reminded him of the star that had shone over the stable at Bethlehem. It seemed to him that it was shining now above all the stars; its light was unutterable; its strangeness amazed him; and as he gazed the

* St Ignatius to the Ephesians, paragraph 4.

rest of the constellations with the sun and moon formed themselves into a chorus about the star. Thus listening to the music of the spheres he fell asleep.*

Next morning early the march was resumed. By noon they were passing through mountainous country, with Mount Olympus in the distance. Away to their right lay the ancient city of Nymphaion, where castle walls and rock-cut tombs of remote antiquity told of a day when Smyrna was not built and Homer had not sung. A few miles farther on they reached the top of the pass and, looking down, saw Smyrna in the distance, her temples gleaming white beside the blue waters of the gulf. As they neared the city the traffic became thicker, and at one point they had to wait to let a religious procession go by. First came the priestess and the members of the guild of initiates, carrying the image in its shrine, and after them flocked the devotees, mostly women. They were all dressed in their holiday clothes and they laughed and sang, enjoying their outing. St Ignatius, as he watched them, thought of his own second name, Theophorus. He too was a " God-bearer ", but he carried his god, not in his hands, but in his heart. The procession left the road and slowly wound its way uphill to the Metroon, the temple of the great mother goddess, who had been worshipped in that region from time immemorial. Some of her rites were performed in a near-by valley, and there, centuries later, Christian women would still come to consecrate their babies, blessing them in the name of St Anna, the mother of the mother of God. But on that sun-soaked afternoon when St Ignatius entered Smyrna, the day when paganism would be driven underground, to reappear in strange disguises, was still far off. Paganism was the established order and appeared unshakable. Everywhere he looked he could see temples. The east gate of the city, through which they were about to

* *St Ignatius to the Ephesians*, paragraphs 15 and 19.

K

enter, was protected by the shrine of Apollo Aguieus, the guardian of the highways. To the south, near the Stadion, stood the Temple of Dionysos, from which, in time of festival, initiates would lead the populace to wild orgies on the hills. Above, on the summit of Mt Pagos, stood the Nemeseion, dedicated to the avenging fates, its graceful entrance columns shaded by a plane-tree, at the foot of which bubbled a sacred spring. All these were without the walls, and so was the fine colonnade devoted to the genius of Homer, who was worshipped there. The towers of the city walls were themselves shrines. One was dedicated to Artemis, another to Leto, others to Heracles and to the Heavenly Twins. The walls thus made a magic circle round the city. But St Ignatius entered unafraid, for he knew that "every sorcery and every spell was dissolved . . . when God appeared in the likeness of man unto newness of everlasting life ".

Smyrna was famous for its beauty, even among travellers familiar with the splendours of many ancient cities. But St Ignatius hardly noticed the long, straight streets, paved with stone and adorned with statues of emperors and famous benefactors. He passed indifferently the great temple erected to Tiberius, the theatre, the baths, the public library, the schools of Rhetoric and Medicine, the altar to Zeus the Saviour in the market-place. Neither the grandeur nor the paganism of the city impressed him. He took both for granted, and his thoughts were concentrated on the hope of being once more among friends. There was a Christian community at Smyrna, and he knew that Bishop Polycarp would visit him at the earliest possible opportunity; representatives from neighbouring churches might be there, too, for the unity of the Christian Church was consciously felt in those early days of persecution. A little while and the weariness of his journey was forgotten in the joy of being welcomed by the brethren.

During the days that followed, St Ignatius conferred often with his fellow bishops. They were glad to bring their difficulties to him, for he was older than most of them and could give them advice based on years of experience. In the evenings, after they had gone, St Ignatius pondered over what they had told him, relating, in his practical way, each man to his problem. There was Polybius, the bishop of the Trallians, a big, quiet man with the heart of a child. He had given a good account of his people's steadfastness, " the result of his own sound teaching, but he is too humble to see that ", St Ignatius thought. His trouble was with discipline; people presumed on his quiet manner, and the gentleness which made him loath to deal severely with offenders. Onesimus, the Ephesian bishop, was a man of a different stamp. There was no disobedience in his church, and when heretical teachers had come he had shown himself to be a stout defender of the faith. His people were fortunate to have such a bishop. The other two were younger men. St Ignatius had liked the way the presbyters from Magnesia treated their bishop, with genuine respect and yet with a kind of protective affection. Damas was having trouble in securing united public worship in his church, but, with the support of his presbyters, St Ignatius believed he would succeed. Polycarp, the Bishop of Smyrna, was rather older; he was nearly forty. He had been much concerned to find that false ideas about the person of Christ were gaining acceptance among his people. St Ignatius was convinced that Polycarp dealt with the spread of heresy in quite the wrong way. He was too fond of scholars and of secular learning. It was no use arguing with these specious false teachers. He himself had learnt not to. They only led you into a trap, and made the truth appear less reasonable than their own plausible doctrines. The only way to bring such pestilent fellows into subjection was to stand firm, like an anvil, and reply to all their blows with an unyielding assertion of the true faith. And so, resolving to put this plainly to Polycarp in the morning, St Ignatius would drop off to sleep.

Many other visitors came, too, both the delegates from the more distant churches and Christians from Smyrna. He quickly realized that his approaching martyrdom already invested him with far greater authority than he had ever exerted before. As far as he personally was concerned, he saw in the honour which men now paid him a temptation to be resisted (" they that say these things are a scourge to me "), but he grasped the opportunity which this prestige afforded him to put the coping-stone on his life's work. The bishops from all the distant churches urged him to give them some written words which they might take back to their people. With the help of Burrhus, a deacon from Ephesus, who acted as his scribe, St Ignatius wrote letters to the Ephesians, the Philadelphians, the Magnesians, and the Trallians. Later in his journey he wrote to the Smyrnæans and to their bishop, Polycarp. To all he urged the vital necessity of unity and of obedience to the bishops and clergy.

" I advise you," he wrote to the Magnesians, " be ye zealous to do all things in godly concord, the bishop presiding after the likeness of God and the presbyters after the likeness of the council of the apostles, with the deacons also who are most dear to me, having been entrusted with the diaconate of Jesus Christ, who was with the Father before the worlds and appeared at the end of time."

Some of the bishops must have complained to him of irregularities in public worship, of men who took it upon themselves to celebrate the Eucharist without being ordained, and so he writes:

" Let that be held a valid eucharist which is under the bishop or one to whom he shall have committed it."

And again:

"Let no man be deceived. If any one be not within the precinct of the altar, he lacketh the bread of God."

The Eucharist, the central act of Christian worship, which united all believers into one body in Christ, must be administered by those ordained to do so, lest the Church should cease to be one and become many.

With equal earnestness he pleaded with those to whom he wrote to remain steadfast in the faith. The danger from Judaizers—those who would fetter Christianity with the Mosaic law—was nearly over. That battle had been won by St Paul, though St Ignatius still finds it necessary to say: "It is monstrous to talk of Jesus Christ and to practise Judaism." But another and more subtle heresy was being industriously spread throughout Asia Minor. Certain teachers, familiar with current philosophical ideas, were professing themselves to be Christians while denying that Jesus Christ was ever truly man or really suffered. They held that God was impassible, having neither parts nor passions, and they argued that if Christ were God he could not have suffered and died on the cross. Furthermore, they despised the body as being of the nature of matter and, in their view, the very opposite of spirit. They would not believe that God, who is Spirit, would humble himself to enter our human flesh in the person of Jesus Christ. So they asserted that Christ only *seemed* to be a man, and from this their particular error came to be called "docetism" (from Gk *dokeo*, I seem). St Ignatius saw, as St John had done before him, that this false teaching denied the central truth of Christianity, and in his letters he constantly warns the churches to have nothing to do with men who spread such poison. He does not argue; he is content to reaffirm the true faith. Christ, he says, is

"truly of the race of David according to the flesh, but Son of

God by the Divine will and power, truly born of a virgin and baptized by John . . . truly nailed up in the flesh for our sakes under Pontius Pilate."

And then he points out that errors in belief inevitably result in evil conduct. Those who despise the body care nothing for the bodily needs of their fellow men; those who deny the humanity of Christ cannot receive the sacrament.

"Mark ye those who hold strange doctrine touching the grace of Jesus Christ which came to us, how that they are contrary to the mind of God. They have no care for love, none for the widow, none for the orphan, none for the afflicted, none for the prisoner, none for the hungry and thirsty. They abstain from eucharist and prayer, because they allow not that the eucharist is the flesh of our Saviour Jesus Christ, which flesh suffered for our sins, and which the Father of his goodness raised up."

Of the ordeal which awaits him St Ignatius says little, save to ask for their prayers. "Though I desire to suffer," he writes, "yet I know not whether I am worthy." The thought that he is following in the footsteps of St Paul both inspires and humbles him. He writes as one keyed up to a moment of great endeavour:

"Near to the sword, near to God; in company with wild beasts, in company with God. Only let it be in the name of Jesus Christ, so that we may suffer together in him."
"My spirit is offered up for you, not only now, but also when I shall attain unto God."

An opportunity occurred to send a letter to Rome, and St Ignatius gladly seized the chance. Delegates from Antioch would already have reached Rome and have told the church there of the fate in store for him. Some of the Roman Christians were men of high position, and he feared lest they might use their influence to procure a mitigation of his sentence.

" I dread your very love," he writes, " lest it do me an injury. . . . For neither shall I myself ever find an opportunity such as this to attain unto God, nor can ye, if ye be silent, win credit of any nobler work. For, if ye be silent and leave me alone, I am a word of God; but if ye desire my flesh, then shall I be again a mere cry."

He breaks out into passionate pleading:

" I exhort you, be ye not an ' unseasonable kindness ' to me. Let me be given to the wild beasts, for through them I can attain unto God. I am God's wheat, and I am ground by the teeth of wild beasts that I may be found pure bread. . . . Bestow not on the world one who desireth to be God's, neither allure him with material things. Suffer me to receive the pure light. When I am come thither, then shall I be a man. Permit me to be an imitator of the passion of my God."

Some modern critics have regarded such passages as signs of hysteria. They see St Ignatius as a neurotic with an unhealthy passion for martyrdom. But, in thus dismissing him, they disregard his statesman-like grasp of the Church's condition and her needs. The Church of his day had need of martyrs. They ignore the saint's deep devotion to his Saviour, Jesus Christ. They forget that St Ignatius was not an Englishman and had never been taught that it is bad form to give unfettered expression to one's feelings.

By the end of August, St Ignatius and his guards had left Smyrna for Troas. There they delayed some days waiting for a ship. A deacon from Cilicia called Philo, and a certain Rhaius Agathopus from Syria, caught up with the party and brought good news to St Ignatius. The persecution was ended and the church at Antioch was at peace. With a mind at ease and full of thankfulness, St Ignatius employed the time in writing to the Philadelphians, whom he had visited before reaching Smyrna, and to the Smyrnæans and their bishop Polycarp. He urged both churches to send specially elected envoys to Antioch to congratulate the Christian community upon its recent deliverance. It was by such means that the different members of the Church expressed their unity. He also asked Bishop Polycarp to make copies of his letters and circulate them to the churches he had been unable to visit. His letter to the Philadelphians shows him in fighting form, contending to the last against heresy and schism. The church at Philadelphia contained an unusually large proportion of Jewish converts, and, during his visit there, St Ignatius had argued vigorously against some among them who propounded Judaism, and would not accept any part of Christian teaching which they could not confirm by reference to the Old Testament. He recalls part of the discussion in his letter:

" I heard certain persons saying, ' If I find it not in the charters, I believe it not in the Gospel.' And when I said to them ' It is written ', they answered me ' That is the question '. But as for me my charter is Jesus Christ, the inviolable charter is his cross and his death and his resurrection, and faith through him."

Already, at the time St Ignatius wrote, the danger that Christianity would be absorbed into Judaism was over, but the Church had still to define her attitude to the Old Testament, and the tendency to appeal to the letter rather than to the spirit of Scripture was to be a recurrent weakness appearing in different forms down the ages.

As St Ignatius was finishing his letter to Polycarp, word came that the ship which was to take them across to Neapolis in Greece had docked, and he must have sailed very soon afterwards. Apparently the party landed at Neapolis, took the land route across Greece, crossed the Adriatic to Brundusium, and then travelled up via Appia to Rome. At the beginning of this second half of their journey they passed through Philippi, and St Ignatius was eagerly greeted by the Philippian church. He had no time to write letters—

the stay may only have been for a night—but he urged the Philippians to send words of encouragement to his beloved church of Antioch. This they did, and sent their letter with a covering note to Polycarp at Smyrna, asking him to forward it by the messenger he was sending to Antioch, and also to send them copies of the letters which St Ignatius wrote to the churches. Polycarp did so, and we have his reply, in which he asks the Philippians to send on to him any reliable news they hear about St Ignatius. And that is the last we know of him, for the accounts which have come down to us of the martyrdom of St Ignatius are late and quite unreliable. There can be no doubt, however, that he met the death he desired in the arena in Rome.

In the letters of St Ignatius we see the persecutions of the Christians from the point of view of one of the sufferers. In the correspondence between the younger Pliny and the Emperor Trajan, we are fortunate enough to have a record of the official standpoint at almost exactly the same period. About A.D. 112 Pliny was appointed governor of Bithynia, a province in the north of Asia Minor, with instructions to restore order. Previous governors had been slack and many regulations had fallen into abeyance. Pliny, a lawyer by profession, was determined that the law should be strictly enforced. His letter enables us to picture the state of affairs which he found on his arrival. Christianity was so wide-spread, both in town and country, that the pagan temples were almost deserted; very few sacrifices were being offered, and festivals passed without the customary celebrations. Business interests were seriously affected; Pliny particularly mentions the sale of sacred cattle for the sacrifices. On the arrival of the new governor, a number of prominent Christians were denounced, probably by those to whom the spread of the new faith meant financial ruin. On his own showing, Pliny had had no previous experience of trying Christians, and it would seem that such trials were judged, not according to written statutes, with which Pliny would of course have been familiar, but by case law.   However, Pliny was well aware that there was ample precedent for condemning all who professed to be Christians, for from the time of Nero onwards Christians had been classed with atheists and sorcerers as sacrilegious persons and enemies of the human race.   He therefore questioned the accused and when, under threat of death, they affirmed thrice over that they were Christians, he sent the provincials among them to execution, and sent those who were Roman citizens to Rome for trial.

But this was only a beginning.   Accusations poured in, and an unsigned paper denouncing a large number of people by name was sent to him.   Pliny found that those who now came before him fell into three groups.   Some denied the charge, and proved their innocence by offering incense before the statues of the gods and of the deified Emperor, and by cursing the name of Christ.   These Pliny acquitted. Others persisted in affirming their Christianity, in spite of threats, and these he thought deserved to be punished for their obstinacy, if for no other crime.   But there remained a third group consisting of men and women who confessed that they had been Christians, three, five, some even twenty-five years previously.   These were now willing to recant, but Pliny was not sure whether he could rightly pardon them.   If Christians were indeed guilty of the atrocious crimes popularly attributed to them—incest, cannibalism, and the like—then recantation would not clear them in the eyes of the law.   Pliny proceeded to investigate the whole matter.   He questioned the prisoners closely about their beliefs and practices.   Two slave-women, who were deaconesses, he examined under torture.   To his surprise, he could discover nothing criminal, or even harmful, in the practices of this " depraved superstition ".   The Christians were in the habit of meeting for worship before dawn on a fixed day (presumably Sunday). They first sang an antiphonal chant to Christ, as " to a god ", and then they bound themselves by a *sacramentum* never to commit theft, fraud, adultery, or any other breach of faith. Later in the day, they met again for a common meal of ordinary, harmless food; but this habit they had discontinued, since Pliny had enforced an order rendering such social club-meetings illegal.

At this point in his investigations Pliny became seriously troubled. If he acted in strict accordance with established legal precedents, he would have to execute hundreds, per-haps thousands of harmless people, whose only fault was their persistence in their own peculiar superstition. As the measures already taken against the Christians had resulted in a revival of pagan practices, and a consequent improve-ment in the trades dependent on them, such drastic action seemed hardly necessary. In a very carefully worded letter, Pliny put the facts before the Emperor and asked for his guidance. He especially desired to know whether the admission that he was a Christian were in itself enough to condemn a man to death, without any proof of crime. His letter is an extremely tactful plea for permission to use greater leniency than was compatible with strict enforce-ment of the existing law.

Trajan replied with equal caution. He praised Pliny for his correct procedure, and stated that no hard-and-fast rule could be made in such cases. He said that Christians were not to be hunted out, but those who were denounced must be tried, and punished if they were found guilty. Those who recanted were to be pardoned, whatever their past history. Anonymous accusations were to be alto-gether disregarded. As Christian apologists were later to point out, this reply was not logically sound. Christianity was treated as a crime, which, if proved against a man, must be punished; yet these " criminals " were to be ignored, unless forced on the governor's notice by informers. Trajan was not prepared to break with the legal tradition established by his predecessors, but he wished to modify the law in favour of the Christians by allowing it to be administered leniently. The correspondence between Trajan and Pliny was published, and this rescript of Trajan's gave the Church a period of comparative peace.

But Christians were in danger, not only from police measures on the part of the Roman authorities, but also from mob violence. Inclined to stir up trouble whenever an opportunity occurred, the populace, ignorant, excitable, and credulous, hated what it did not understand. Wild stories were circulated about the Christians: they were atheists who would destroy the world with fire; they feasted secretly on the bodies of children; they practised incestuous rites. From time to time, alarmed by some natural calamity such as an earthquake, or angry at a slump in trade, the mob would clamour for vengeance on the Christians, and the governor would be faced with a very difficult situation. Some such events lie behind the letter which Trajan's successor, the Emperor Hadrian, wrote to Minucius Fundanus, proconsul of Asia, about A.D. 125. He was dealing with a report sent to him by the predecessor of Fundanus, Q. Licinius Silvanus Granianus, about some disturbance in which a public outcry was made against the Christians. The Emperor, in his reply, demands that a proper inquiry be made, "lest the inoffensive should be disturbed, while slanderous informers are afforded an opportunity of practising their vile trade". He continues:

"Now, if our subjects of the provinces are able to sustain by evidence their charges against the Christians, so as to answer before a court of justice, I have no objection to their taking this course. But I do not allow them to have recourse to mere clamorous demands and outcries to this end."

He instructs Fundanus to judge all such charges according
to the law, and concludes:

" On the other hand, I emphatically insist on this, that if any
one demand a writ of summons against any of these Christians,
merely as a slanderous accusation, you proceed against that man
with heavier penalties, in proportion to the gravity of his
offence ".*

Christians were still outlaws, but under Trajan and Hadrian
persecution was discouraged and mob violence and malicious
informers discountenanced.

It is natural enough that the few contemporary documents, which have survived from this early period, should
record the martyrdoms of Christians rather than their daily
lives. Yet it is clear that persecution was sporadic, and
seldom lasted long. Christians might at any time be denounced, tried, and summarily executed, but for the most
part they lived quietly among their heathen neighbours and
were able to assemble for worship undisturbed. And even
while Christians were being persecuted in one city, in
another they would be at peace. Tantalizingly slight as
the evidence is, we can picture from it the ordinary life of
the Church. To the Roman authorities the Church was a
secret society, potentially dangerous, and, reading the letters
of St Ignatius, we can see that from their point of view they
were right. In each city, Christians formed an organized
body under the leadership of their bishop. The city would
include within its jurisdiction a large tract of the country
surrounding it, and the church in that city would do the
same. Each bishop had under him a number of presbyters
whom he could depute to take his place, and these men would
conduct the worship of groups of Christians in outlying
places. Pliny particularly mentions that in Bithynia
Christianity was widespread in the country, as well as in

* Translated in *Documents of the Christian Church*, edited by
Henry Bettenson, World's Classics, p. 9.

the towns. In addition to the presbyters, there were deacons whose especial task it was to carry out the corporate acts of mercy which were an essential part of Christian life. They cared for widows and orphans, tended the sick, and visited prisoners. More alarming to the authorities than its local strength was the Church's unity. The churches in different cities were in constant touch by envoy and by letter. News spread rapidly from one to another. Leading Christians travelled to meet each other, and the churches in the cities through which they passed rejoiced to show them hospitality. To be a Christian was to be a member of the Church, the body of Christ, not merely of the particular community at Ephesus, Smyrna, Rome, or wherever else you chanced to live. The secret of this unity, which baffled the policing methods of the Empire, lay in the Church's worship. The binding act, which Pliny described as a *sacramentum* or oath, and about which he was certainly given little information, can have been none other than the celebration of Holy Communion. We know from St Ignatius how that central act of Christian worship was regarded:

"Assemble yourselves together", he wrote to the Ephesians, "breaking one bread, which is the medicine of immortality and the antidote that we should not die, but live for ever in Jesus Christ."

By this act, Christians were united to one another in Christ their Lord. The Agape, or Love Feast, which by now took place later in the day, was a natural expression of their fellowship, but not essential to it. At one meeting or the other, perhaps at both, passages would be read aloud from St Paul's epistles, from the Gospels (in Asia Minor the best loved would be the Gospel according to St John), and from the letters of other apostles, saints, and martyrs. Thus all the churches shared the same faith, with only slight local variations in emphasis or interpretation. The letters of St Ignatius are full of echoes of St Paul's epistles, which he probably knew by heart, and the only letter by St Polycarp which we have shows his familiarity with New Testament writings.

The life and death of St Polycarp perfectly illustrate the conditions under which Christians lived in the first half of the second century, for his long, quiet working life ended in sudden, unexpected martyrdom. An excellent contemporary account of his death has survived, but what we know of his life is pieced together from fragments of early writings embedded in the fourth-century church history by Eusebius, and a *Life of Polycarp*, probably written nearly a century after his martyrdom by Pionius, who was himself martyred at Smyrna in A.D. 250. The *Life* contains stories about St Polycarp which have lost nothing in the telling, but the main outlines of it are neither marvellous nor improbable. According to Pionius, Polycarp was a slave-boy of Christian parentage, who was brought to Smyrna from the East, probably from Syria, and was then bought by a wealthy Christian lady called Kallisto. Pionius attributes this, not to coincidence, but to a heaven-sent dream; it may equally well have been due to Christian fellowship and the excellent system of communication between the churches. The boy showed himself to be trustworthy, and in course of time was made steward over the lady's household. Eventually, on her death, Polycarp inherited her estate and took his place in Smyrna as a wealthy freedman. Whether this romantic story be true or not, Polycarp was certainly a man of means in later life. In either case, a far more important fact about his younger days is recorded by his pupil, Irenæus, who says that Polycarp " not only had been made a disciple by apostles, and had associated with many who had seen the Lord, but was also appointed by apostles bishop in the church at Smyrna ", and he recalls how St Polycarp used to speak of his personal recollections of St John. St Polycarp was a man called to high office, destined to be a leading figure in the Church, but many humbler Christians of his day had also seen the apostles face to face. Old men would describe to their grandchildren how St Paul had fired them with his own enthusiasm, when they first heard him, and, when a passage from one of the Gospels was read, they would comment afterwards, " Yes, that is just what happened. I heard it myself from the lips of John the apostle." Alike to St Polycarp and to the people he led, the authority of the apostles was present in the living tradition of the Church, as well as in the New Testament writings. Questions of faith, of conduct, and of ceremonial were all judged by the same test: was the decision in accordance with the teaching of the apostles?

Before many years had passed, St Polycarp had come to be regarded as an authority on all such questions. This was partly due to his own strong faith and sound judgement, and partly to his personal knowledge of St John. Neighbouring churches would consult him over their problems, and at one time a large number of the letters which he had written were in general circulation. Only one of these has come down to us, and that is one addressed to the Philippian church a short time after the death of St Ignatius. The Philippians had written to St Polycarp in great distress because one of their presbyters had embezzled church funds, with his wife aiding and abetting him. Evidently stern measures were at once taken against the erring elder, for St Polycarp writes of the need, not of punishment, but of bringing the sinner to repentance:

" I am exceedingly grieved, brother ", he writes, " about that man and his wife: may the Lord give them true repentance. So be yourselves moderate in this and count not such persons as enemies, but recall them as frail and erring members, in order that ye may save the body of you all. "

Such patience and forbearance must have enabled St Polycarp himself to build the church in Smyrna into a strong, united body during his long episcopate, and, by the avoidance of unnecessary friction, must have done much to preserve his church from persecution. But there was one matter over which St Polycarp was neither patient nor forbearing, and that was the corruption of the faith by false teachers.

" Let us be zealots for the good ", he writes, " refraining from offences and from false brothers and from those who bear the Lord's name in hypocrisy, who mislead empty men. For ' everyone who does not acknowledge that Jesus Christ is come in the flesh is antichrist '; and whoever does not acknowledge the testimony of the cross is of the devil; and whoever perverts the Lord's oracles to his own lusts, and says there is neither resurrection nor judgement, he is the first-born of Satan."

St Polycarp could tolerate heresy as little as a doctor can tolerate cancer, and for the same reason : the disease would destroy the body whose health was his care. It was therefore quite in character that when the heretic, Marcion, came to Smyrna and sought for recognition, St Polycarp should have replied, as he is said to have done, " I recognize thee; I recognize the first-born of Satan! "

Half a century later, Irenæus, writing to a friend who had adopted false ideas about the nature of evil, recalled the days when they had both belonged to the group of eager young men who listened to St Polycarp in his old age.

" For I clearly remember the events of that time ", he writes, " so that I can even tell the place where the blessed Polycarp used to sit and discourse, and his goings out and in, and the manner of his life, and the appearance of his body, and the discourse which he used to deliver to the multitude, and how he used to describe his intercourse with John and with others who had seen the Lord; and as he remembered their words, and what were the things he had heard from them about the Lord

L

and about his miracles and about his teaching—as having received (the facts) from the eye-witnesses of the life of the Word, Polycarp used to describe all things in conformity with the Scriptures. To these things even then, through the mercy of God bestowed upon me, did I eagerly listen, making memorial of them, not on paper, but in my heart. And by the grace of God I always ruminate genuinely on them: and I can testify before God that, if that blessed and apostolic elder had heard any such thing (as thou sayest now) he would have shouted out, and stopped his ears, and, saying according to his custom, ' O good God, to what times hast thou kept me that I should endure this!' would have fled from the place where sitting or standing he had heard such words ".

At the age of eighty-five, St Polycarp, as the loved and honoured representative of the churches of Asia, undertook the long journey to Rome, in the hope of settling a question which was causing friction and ill-will within the Church. It was a matter neither of faith nor of morals, but of custom. Christians in Rome and other western churches were in the habit of celebrating Easter on the Sunday following the Passover, which falls on the fourteenth Nisan, the first month in the Jewish calendar. Christians in the East, especially in the province of Asia, celebrated Christ's triumphant act of redemption on Passover Eve, whatever day of the week that might be. The dissension which resulted from this comparatively trivial matter came to be known as the Paschal Controversy, and those who followed the Eastern custom were known as Quartodecimans, because they kept Easter on the fourteenth day of the month. Feeling had not yet become embittered on the subject, when St Polycarp set out for Rome in an attempt to end the dispute for ever. Anicetus, the newly consecrated Bishop of Rome, was equally anxious to reach a settlement. But although the two bishops conferred together with the greatest amity, neither was able to convince the other. Each claimed apostolic authority for the custom of his own

locality, probably with justice. Anicetus held that the
Western practice was that of St Peter and St Paul; St
Polycarp affirmed from his personal knowledge that the
Eastern tradition was derived from St John. To show
that no breach of Christian fellowship was involved in this
difference of observance, Bishop Anicetus invited St
Polycarp to preside at a celebration of the Eucharist before
his departure from Rome.

St Polycarp returned home and spent the winter months
in peace. He was a very old man now, much loved and
honoured, and he could look back on a long life of quiet,
constructive work. Then, suddenly, like a storm out of a
summer sky, persecution came upon the church of Smyrna.
The League of the Hellenes, an association of the leading
cities of Asia, celebrated an annual festival, the games being
held at each of the four chief cities in turn. In February
A.D. 156, the League Festival was being held at Smyrna.
The city was crowded with holiday-makers from all parts
of the province, and the Stadion, where the contests took
place, was packed with shouting spectators day after day.
The proceedings opened with a loyal demonstration of
devotion to the Emperor: an admirable opportunity for an
outcry against the Christians, especially as those who bore
them ill-will in Smyrna were reinforced by others from
neighbouring cities. Accusations were made, and a
number of Christians were arrested, among them several
from Philadelphia. In the excitement that followed, a
Phrygian Christian named Quintus voluntarily gave himself up, and persuaded others to follow his example. The
arrested men were all removed to prison, pending their
trial on the following day, and the church of Smyrna had a
few hours' respite in which to decide how best to meet the
crisis. The elders and most of the laity disapproved of
the behaviour of Quintus and his companions. No man,
they felt, had the right to snatch at martyrdom; it was for

God to choose who should suffer for his name. With this St Polycarp entirely agreed, but, when the elders urged him to leave the city at once, he strongly opposed the idea. Without wishing to court martyrdom, he desired to remain with his people in the hour of danger. At length, however, his protests were overborne, and he left for a farm in the country, accompanied by a few attendants. On his arrival, he spent a long time in prayer, and afterwards he told his companions that he was sure he would be burnt alive, for during his prayers he had fallen into a trance and seen his pillow set on fire.

On the following morning, people flocked to the Stadion even earlier than usual to obtain good seats for what they anticipated would be an exceptionally thrilling spectacle. The Proconsul, L. Statius Quadratus, who was representing the Emperor Antoninus Pius at the Festival, in due course took his place, and the Christians were brought before him for trial. He was anxious to avoid bloodshed if possible, partly because he was a just man, and partly because he sensed the excitement of the crowd and knew the danger of it. He therefore did his utmost to persuade the prisoners to recant, and, when his words had no effect, he ordered them to be scourged and threatened with hot irons. Several gave way under this treatment, and made the required sacrifice before the statue of the Emperor, but others remained firm. At last the Proconsul gave the order that they should be thrown to the beasts. The warders withdrew from the arena, and the doors of the cages were opened. Quintus had endured everything up to this point, but when he saw the lions coming his nerve broke and he fled to the exit from the arena, crying that he would sacrifice and recant. The rest met their deaths with fortitude, especially a young lad named Germanicus, while the crowd howled, "Away with the Christians!" Then a new cry was taken up: "Where is Polycarp?" "Hunt out Polycarp!" The Proconsul made a gesture to command silence; but the mob had been blooded, and could no longer be controlled. As the yells for Polycarp became louder and more insistent, the officer of the peace, a man named Herod, came forward and offered to have him fetched. Herod knew well enough where to look, for his own aunt had been a prominent Christian. It was illegal to hunt out a Christian against whom no formal charge had been preferred, but the Proconsul was too much afraid of the anger of the mob to insist on strict legality. He gave his consent, and Herod at once detailed a posse of armed police to search for Polycarp on his country estate.

The search-party reached the place in the late afternoon, but found St Polycarp gone, for he had been warned in time, and had fled to another farm. The police then seized two slave-boys and tortured them, until one of them consented to guide them to his master's hiding-place. It was late in the evening when they reached the cottage where St Polycarp was, and the old man was upstairs in bed. He had been told that his pursuers were drawing near, but had refused to flee further, saying: "The will of God be done." When he heard the police arrive he came down to greet them, and ordered his servants to provide them with a plentiful supper. Then he asked for time to pray, which was granted him. Rather than travel in the dark, his guards decided to wait until the following day, and it was nearly noon on a Saturday morning when the party reached the gates of Smyrna. There they were met by the Chief Constable Herod and his father. These insisted that St Polycarp should dismount from his ass and sit with them in their carriage. As they drove with him to the Stadion they urged him to recant saying:

"Now what harm is there in saying 'Lord Cæsar' and in offering incense, and so on, and thus saving thyself?"

To this St Polycarp made no reply, and when they pressed him for an answer, simply said: " I do not intend to do what you advise." At this they lost patience with him and, having reached the stadium, they pushed him so roughly from the carriage that the old man grazed his shin. Paying no heed to his hurt, St Polycarp walked straight on with his guards into the stadium, and, at the sight of him, the crowd sent up a deafening shout, so that the place was in a tumult.

The games were over for the day, and St Polycarp was led at once before the Proconsul, who put him through the usual form of examination. When St Polycarp had said who he was and had declared himself to be a Christian, the Proconsul tried to persuade him, saying: " Have respect to thine age. Swear by the genius of Cæsar. Repent! Say, ' Away with the atheists.' " At that St Polycarp, who had been silent, cast his eyes around the packed benches of the amphitheatre, and, pointing to the mob, he said, " Away with the atheists! " The Proconsul persisted and said, " Swear, and I will release thee; curse Christ ". St Polycarp answered: " Eighty and six years have I served him, and he hath done me no wrong; how then can I blaspheme my King who saved me? " Pressed again to take the oath, St Polycarp offered to instruct the Proconsul in the Christian doctrine if he would allow him sufficient time. " Persuade the people ", said the Proconsul grimly, for his voice could hardly be heard among their angry shouts.

" Thee I had deemed worthy of discourse ", St Polycarp replied, " for we are taught to render to authorities and the powers ordained of God honour as is fitting. But I deem not this mob worthy that I should defend myself before them."

When persuasion proved futile, the Proconsul resorted to threats, with as little success. At last he gave up the attempt, and sent his herald to proclaim three times in the middle of the arena, " Polycarp hath confessed himself to be a Christian." A roar from the crowd greeted this announcement, and immediately the people began to clamour for a lion to be loosed on Polycarp. Their spokesman pressed their demand upon the Asiarch who had charge of the festival arrangements.

" This man ", they said, " is the teacher of Asia, the father of the Christians, the destroyer of our gods, that teacheth many not to sacrifice nor worship."

The Asiarch, however, refused their request on the grounds that the games had ended at mid-day and it was not lawful for him to loose a lion afterwards. Not to be baulked, the mob then shouted that Polycarp should be burnt alive and, without waiting for the authorities, some of the crowd rushed out of the stadium and seized whatever timber they could lay hands on at the workshops and baths which were nearby. Although it was the sabbath, the Jews, who were bitterly hostile to the spread of Christianity, joined eagerly in the work. Hurrying back to the stadium with piles of faggots, the men began to build a pyre, urged on by howls of satisfaction from the mob. Meanwhile the ring-leaders seized St Polycarp, ordered him to strip, and were about to nail him to the stake when he cried out:

" Let me be as I am. He that granted me to endure the fire will grant me also to remain at the pyre unmoved, without being secured with nails."

At that, they let the nails alone and contented themselves with binding his arms. St Polycarp looked up to heaven and gave thanks to God as the executioners set a light to the pyre. The flames blazed up, but the wind blew them away from the martyr's body and carried them in an arc over his head. The lynching party, impatient to make an end of him and perhaps afraid of interference, called to a slaughterer, employed to butcher wounded animals in the arena, and he quickly killed St Polycarp with a stab of his knife.

With the death of St Polycarp the persecution ended for that time. The mob would not allow the Christians to take the martyr's body for burial until it had been reduced to ashes; but with that their outburst of savagery spent itself. The Christians collected his ashes and buried them with honour. A short while afterwards, at the request of some brethren in Phrygia, the secretary of the church of Smyrna and one of the elders wrote an account of St Polycarp's martyrdom and addressed it in the form of a letter, not only to the church at Philomelium, but to " all the communities of the holy and catholic Church in every place ". The account was circulated widely, and fortunately has been preserved to our own time. The Church, both at Smyrna and elsewhere, afterwards kept the anniversary of St Polycarp's martyrdom as a joyful festival " for the commemoration of those that have already fought in the contest, and for the training and preparation of those that shall do so hereafter ".

SYMBOLIC PALM AND CROWN
FROM THE CATACOMBS

BOOKS FOR FURTHER READING

Documents of the Christian Church (World's Classics). Pliny-Trajan Correspondence and the Martyrdom of Polycarp.

Documents illustrative of the History of the Church, ed. by B. J. Kidd, vol. i. Pliny-Trajan Correspondence and also extracts from letters of St Ignatius.

Letters of St Ignatius, translated in J. B. Lightfoot's *Apostolic Fathers*.

Ancient Smyrna, by C. J. Cadoux.

CHAPTER VII

ROME: AN UNDERGROUND MOVEMENT

OUTSIDE the city of ancient Rome lay the city of the dead. No burials were allowed within the walls, but along the Appian Way, the Via Labicana, the Nomentan Way, and the other great roads leading to the city, stood lines of tombs: elaborately adorned burial-places belonging to noble families, columbaria, where trade guilds housed the ashes of their dead members, burial chapels, private monuments. Many of the epitaphs begged the attention of the passer-by; some craved a libation for the dead:

" Stop, traveller, who passest by on the Flaminian Way; pause and read and read again ! "
" Mix, drink and give to me."
" Traveller, curse me not as you pass, for I am in darkness and cannot answer."

Others offered cynical advice:

" Fortune makes many promises but keeps none of them; live for the present hour, since nothing else is really yours."

More appealed to the reader's pity:

" Our hope was in our boy: now all is mourning."
" Here I lie, unhappy girl, in darkness."

But there were no signposts pointing the way to the vast labyrinth of underground passages where the Christians laid their dead. The catacombs, as they are called today, were constructed during the centuries of persecution when Christians were not anxious to draw attention to themselves. The catacombs were not secret hiding-places, for all burial-places had to be officially registered, and the authori-

ties must at all times have been fully aware of their existence. But once the right to bury his dead in a certain plot of ground had been granted to any individual or corporate body, that piece of land was sacred in the eyes of Roman law, and any outsiders who attempted to interfere with it were liable to be charged with sacrilege and severely punished. By cutting out passages through the soft rock with niches at the sides, and here and there rock-hewn chambers, Christians constructed a network which, in the course of centuries, became a veritable underground city, a city of the dead.   It has been estimated that the Catacomb of Callistus alone contains 587 miles of passages, and the total extent of all the catacombs has not yet been explored. Some of them are like mines, with galleries cut one below the other, four or even five tiers deep, the lower levels being the more recent.

In exploring the past, the hardest thing of all is to re-discover the thoughts and feelings of ordinary, undistinguished men and women.   Only a small minority in any age leaves a written record for posterity, and those who do are usually the learned or the especially gifted.   The early Christians are no exception to the rule.   But, for once, fate has been kind.   The catacombs have preserved for later generations the hopes, longings, joys, and sorrows of the Roman Christians of the first four centuries.   Elaborate paintings, rudely cut epitaphs, often ill-spelt and un-grammatical, symbols drawn by men who could not write, carved sarcophagi: all these remain to tell a story which even the early Fathers left untold.

There is a description of the catacombs by a Christian poet, Prudentius, who wrote in Latin during the fourth century, when the Church was no longer persecuted:

" Among the orchards, hard by the City walls, there is a deep crypt, with dark recesses.   A steep path with winding stairs leads down through dim turnings, and the daylight from the mouth of the cavern somewhat illumines the first part of the way. As you advance the darkness grows more intense until you meet openings, cut in the roof above, which bring the bright rays of the sun into the crypt. Although the galleries twisting this way and that form narrow chambers, with recesses in deep gloom, yet some light finds its way through the pierced vaulting into the crypts below.''

The light-shafts which he describes, however, were not part of the original design, but were added after the peace of Constantine, when Christianity was officially recognized and the catacombs became places of pilgrimage. Before that, the dark, tomb-lined corridors and tiny rock-hewn chambers were lit by lamps attached to the walls. The sconces where they used to hang can still be seen. Yet the catacombs were far from being dreary places. What light there was fell upon gaily painted walls, where birds fluttered among luxuriant vine-branches, the blessed feasted in paradise, and the Good Shepherd piped light-hearted ditties to his happy sheep.

Parts of the oldest catacombs date from the end of the first century, and these tell a somewhat surprising story. The frescoed walls and ceilings of the earliest vaults are bright with festoons and garlands, with cupids, doves, and flowers. Here a peacock preens himself, and there a sea-horse prances. There is little that is specifically Christian about the decoration, save for representations of the Good Shepherd and of a couple of familiar Old Testament characters: Daniel in the lions' den and Noah in his ark. It would seem that the decorators themselves must have been pagans, and their Christian employers must have chosen the most inoffensive subjects from their stock designs, avoiding all that savoured too much of idolatry. These vaults, then, are proof that before the end of the first century, Romans of wealth and high position had secretly joined the Christian Church, for slaves and free men of a humble position could not have constructed the catacombs at all or borne the expense of such lavish decoration. All the evidence goes to show that, in spite of persecution, Christianity was spreading through all classes of society. Discoveries in the catacombs have strengthened the case for detecting Christian influence in certain happenings described in guarded terms by ancient historians. The most important is the trial of Flavia Domitilla and her husband in A.D. 95.

Flavia Domitilla was a great lady in the days of Domitian. Her husband, Flavius Clemens, was related to the Emperor, and their two sons, Vespasianus and Domitianus, had been named as his heirs. But, in the last year of Domitian's reign, the Emperor, in a fit of sudden suspicion, had Flavius Clemens and his wife tried on a charge of atheism and Jewish practices. Clemens was executed, and Domitilla was exiled to a lonely island. The discovery that one of the oldest catacombs, part of which dates from the first century, was built on an estate that once belonged to the Flavian family, and contains tombs of Flavia Domitilla's relatives and dependents, has confirmed the supposition that Domitilla was a Christian, and her husband at least a sympathizer with the new faith. Since the profession of Christianity involved the refusal to worship pagan gods, it was tantamount to atheism in Roman eyes, and many Christians were condemned on that charge. It is very probable that the catacomb which bears her name was begun by Flavia Domitilla as a resting-place for the Christian members of her own household, many of whom would be slaves. It is characteristic that here and throughout the catacombs the epitaphs hardly ever make mention of rank or any social distinction. True to St Paul's teaching, these early believers recognized that in Christ there is no difference between the slave and the free man. Conspicuous in this particular catacomb is a slab with the single word:

Ampliatus. Judging from the number of graves clustered about this tomb, it must have been accounted an honour to be buried near to it. The tomb is certainly very early, and it may be that of Amplias, whom St Paul greeted in his letter to the Romans.* Some of the slaves in the great Roman households were loved and trusted family servants, who had the ear of both master and mistress and had much to do with bringing up the children. If Ampliatus occupied such a position in Domitilla's household, it is not so difficult to imagine how a high-born Roman lady came to be an adherent of a despised and persecuted religion.

The austere morals of the Roman Republic did not survive unchanged into the Empire. Fashionable society in Rome in the first and second centuries was as pleasure-loving, as idle, and as gay as in any other period of civilized prosperity. No wonder the earliest converts to Christianity among the patricians gained the reputation of being either melancholy or indolent. There was much in which they could not or would not join: feasting that was revolting in its excess, cruel and murderous shows in the arena, ceremonies involving pagan sacrifices. Inevitably they stood apart, withdrawn as far as possible from a world which had a different standard of values from that which they were learning from Christ. Pomponia Græcina, the wife of Aulus Plautius, the general who conquered Britain, gained this reputation for melancholy as early as A.D. 57, when she was charged with practising a foreign superstition, and was tried and acquitted by her husband. In the catacomb of Callistus there is a very early crypt, and among its second-century graves are several belonging to Pomponia's family, including one inscription to a certain Pomponius Græcinus, probably a descendant. One of the oldest catacombs, that of St Priscilla, was the burial place of the Acilian family. How many other Romans of rank were

* *Rom.* 16. 8 (A.V.).

converted to Christianity at the end of the first and early in the second century is not known, though a thorough exploration of the catacombs may yet reveal more names. Their influence was not sufficient to save the Church from persecution, but their wealth enabled them to provide their fellow Christians with places where they could meet for worship above ground and also with catacombs for their dead.

The painting of frescoes needs professional skill, but anyone can scratch a design upon soft rock, or, if he can write, engrave a name. Some of the most touching records in the catacombs are those which illiterate Christians made for themselves, or for their nearest relatives. On one grave-slab a carpenter has drawn his set of tools, and a mason has been employed afterwards to add the inscription:

BAVTO ET MAXIMA SE VIVI FECERVNT

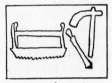

" To Bautus and Maxima.   They
made this during their lifetime."

On another there is a picture of a vine-dresser with his wine-cask beside him and an inscription put up by his brothers:

" To Guadentius.   His brothers made this.
He lived twenty-eight years, eight months,
seventeen days."

Often a symbol is drawn to represent a name.   Dracontius is depicted as a dragon.   A girl called Navira has a ship on her grave-slab, with the following inscription:

" Navira in peace; a sweet soul, who lived sixteen years and five months; a soul sweet as honey: this epitaph was made by her parents.   The sign, a ship."

Most pathetic of all is the drawing of a little pig accompanied by the words:

PORCELLA HIC DORMIT IN P.
Q. VIXIT ANN. III. M. X. D. XIII

" Here sleeps Porcella in peace.   She lived three years, ten months, and thirteen days."

But sad as the parents of Porcella must have been to lose their " piglet ", there is no hint here or elsewhere in the catacombs of the despair and bitter, unavailing grief which inspired so many pagan epitaphs.   The earliest Christian inscriptions are brief, sometimes consisting simply of a name.   But where a few words are added, they are words of hope and confidence:

In peace,
Mayest thou live among the saints ;
Refresh thyself among the holy spirits ;
Mayest thou live in God ;
Peace be with thee ;
In Christ.

These are some of the expressions most often used.   But symbols which convey the same ideas are more common than words upon the earliest graves, for symbols have the advantage of being intelligible even to those who cannot read.

" The hope which is set before us : which hope we have as an anchor of the soul, both sure and steadfast ", wrote the author of Hebrews, and the Roman Christians loved to carve an anchor on their tombs as a symbol of their sure hope in Christ.   The cross they never used.   Their sign for Christ was not the emblem of his Passion, but the fish, an anagram of his name in Greek.   The Greek word for a fish, ΙΧΘΥΣ (ichthus) begins with I for Jesus and X, that is Ch, for Christ, and the rest of the letters were interpreted as a summary of the creed.

I Jesus
X Christ
Θ God (Theos)
Υ Son (Uios)
Σ Saviour (soter)

SYMBOLIC FISH, FROM THE CATACOMBS

Often the anchor and the fish are found together, thus making a complete picture statement of hope in Christ. The thought that the departed soul is happy with the blessed in paradise is also expressed in picture form.   The soul is represented as a dove, with a spray of palm in her beak to symbolize the joy and triumph of heaven.

PAX

SYMBOLIC DOVE, FROM THE CATACOMBS

The very names of those buried in the catacombs speak of their faith.   Elpis and Spes, the Greek and Latin forms of Hope, Philumena or Beloved, Felicitas or Happiness,

M

Urania or Heavenly, are among the names on the earliest graves. The names recorded were, of course, " Christian names ", names given at baptism and chosen to express the character of the new life into which the convert from paganism was entering. Agape, " Love "; Anastasia, " Resurrection "; Peregrinus, " Pilgrim "; Gaudiosa, " Rejoicing "; Eirene, " Peace "; Innocentia, " Innocence "; Benignus, " Kind "; Ingenua, " Sincere "—these names and many more like them are found on the inscriptions. Sometimes a comment is added:

> " Simplicia who was rightly so-called."
> " Here lies Verus, who ever spoke verity."

Some used a phrase as a name: Deus Dedit, " God gave "; Theotokos, " God-born "; Deo Gratia, " Thanks to God ". Others called themselves Renatus, " Born again "; Redemptus, " Redeemed "; Sozomene, " Saved ". Our Puritan forbears, with their love for such names as Patience, Perseverance, Praise-God, and More-Fruit, cannot have known how closely they were following primitive Christian custom, for the catacombs then had not been properly explored. The enthusiasm of conversion in both cases produced the same effect. The early Christians, however, did not share the Puritan passion for names from the Old Testament. The only Scriptural names which occur at all are from the New Testament: Peter, Stephen, Paul, Elizabeth, and, rarely, Mary.

From the middle of the second century onwards, the decoration of the catacombs becomes more explicitly Christian. The frescoes still occasionally show devices borrowed from paganism, but their chief themes are drawn from the Church's faith. The grave-slabs, too, show scenes from the Bible as well as Christian symbols. Probably by this time it was possible to find craftsmen who were themselves believers and were capable of developing a truly Christian art. Also, the Church had had time to overcome her initial prejudice against graven images—a prejudice inherited from Judaism. Various aspects of the Christian faith appeal to men of different centuries and of different national traditions, for none are able to grasp the whole truth in its fullness. The art of the catacombs illustrates the faith of Roman Christians in the first four centuries, and for most of that time Christians were members of a persecuted community, always in danger, often suffering for their religion. Yet the dominant note of the paintings in the catacombs is that of joy. Even the sufferings of our Lord are not depicted during the earlier centuries, still less those of the martyrs. The favourite mode of representing our Lord is not as Christ upon the Cross, nor as the Babe in the Virgin's arms, nor even as the Lord in Glory, but as the Good Shepherd, carrying a lost sheep upon his shoulder. Paradise, a place of birds and flowers, where, in the presence of their Shepherd, the chosen flock feeds for ever in green pastures beside the waters of comfort: this scene appears again and again. The banquet scenes, of which there are several, are less easy to interpret. Do they also represent the joys of heaven? Are they pictures of the funeral feasts which certainly did take place in the catacombs? Are they representations of the Agape, the Christian Love Feast, or of the Eucharist? The exact intention of the artist may be uncertain in a particular case, but these are not entirely separate conceptions, for the idea of joy and fellowship in Christ is at the heart of all of them. In this fellowship, the living believers and the blessed dead are united. The epitaphs as well as the frescoes bear witness to the early Christians' firm belief in this communion of saints. A typical epitaph is: " Januaria, mayest thou be well refreshed, and pray for us," in which the living and the dead are bound together by their prayers.

Only a limited selection of Bible scenes is represented on

the grave-slabs and frescoes of the catacombs in the second century. Jonah and the whale, Noah in his ark, Moses striking the rock, the sacrifice of Isaac, the three Hebrew children in the burning fiery furnace, and the story of Susanna are the favourite Old Testament subjects. From the New Testament, the Adoration of the Magi, the raising of Lazarus, the miracle of the multiplication of the loaves and fishes, and some of the miracles of healing are depicted. The choice at first sight seems arbitrary, but the explanation lies in the fact that these scenes are prayers in picture form. An early Christian prayer for the dying which has come down to us in a fourth-century manuscript runs as follows:

" Lord, deliver his soul, as thou didst deliver
    Enoch and Elijah from the death common to mankind,
    Noah from the deluge,
    Abraham from the city of Ur of the Chaldees,
    Job from his calamities,
    Isaac from being sacrificed by the hand of his father Abraham,
    Lot from Sodom and from fire,
    Moses from the hand of Pharaoh, king of Egypt,
    Daniel from the lions' den,
    The three children from the fire of the furnace and from the
        hand of the wicked king,
    Susanna from an imaginary crime,
    David from the hand of Saul and the hand of Goliath,
    Peter and Paul from prison,
    And as thou didst deliver the blesséd Thecla, thy virgin and
        martyr, from atrocious torments, so deign to receive the
        soul of thy servant, so that he may rejoice with thee in
        heavenly bliss."

As it stands, this prayer is no doubt later than the second century, but there is good reason to believe that similar prayers were used from the earliest times. In the letter sent by the Roman church to the church of Corinth at the end of the first century, Clement gives the following list of those to whom God accorded pardon in answer to prayer: Noah, Abraham, Lot, Job, Moses, Daniel, the three young Hebrews, and Jonah. It is no mere coincidence that these are the characters most frequently represented in the catacombs. The thought common to all the scenes is that of deliverance:

" Did not the Lord deliver Daniel, deliver Daniel, deliver Daniel?
Did not the Lord deliver Daniel?
Then why not every man? "

The modern American negroes in this, as in others of their spirituals, are very close to the thoughts and feelings of the

THE STORY OF JONAH

early Church. The decorations of the catacombs represent the prayers and songs of deliverance which were constantly

upon the lips of Christians in the first two or three centuries.   They thought of themselves as the inheritors of
the promises which God had made to Israel.   They were
the new Israel, and it was natural to them to find in the Old
Testament types and examples of the deliverance from sin,
and from the powers of evil, which they themselves had
found in Christ.

Subjects chosen from the New Testament are not common
before the third century, with the exception of the few
named above.   Of these, the raising of Lazarus and the
miracles of healing are clearly meant to illustrate the saving
power of Christ.   The Adoration of the Magi is probably
intended to symbolize the salvation of the Gentiles, and
there can be little doubt that the miracle of the loaves and
fishes typifies the Eucharist.

What was the importance of the catacombs in the life of
second-century Roman Christians?   Were they simply
burial-places, or were they places of refuge in times of persecution?   Did members of the Church meet secretly for
worship in these dark vaults below the surface of the
ground?   So far, exploration has revealed no chamber in
the catacombs large enough for congregational worship,
and no indication that they were ever inhabited by refugees.
People may have hidden in them now and again and left
no trace behind, but the sheltering of fugitives was not one
of the uses intended by those who constructed these
labyrinthine cemeteries.   Nevertheless, the catacombs were
much more than mere burial-places.   Pagan custom coun-
tenanced the celebration of feasts in commemoration of the
dead, and the Christians seized upon this for the opportunity it afforded them of meeting for worship without
incurring the suspicion of the Roman authorities.   Persecution was sporadic during the second century, and it must
often have been possible for Christians to meet for worship
above ground.   But it would seem that they felt it wise to

conduct their secret mysteries in the seclusion of the cata-combs, where they were safe from interruption. Baptisms took place there, and so did the instruction of catechumens. Small groups of Christians gathered in the vaults for the Agape, or Love Feast, and there, too, the Eucharist was celebrated. Owing to the restricted space, only a few could be present, but it was the custom in the early Church to carry the consecrated elements to those unable to attend. One of the early martyrs met his death in this way, for, as he was carrying the Sacrament through the streets of Rome in the early morning, he was set upon by a hostile crowd and died in the attempt to save the sacred elements from pollution. The favourite symbol for Christ, the fish, is often associated with bread and wine in the paintings and drawings of the catacombs. Very likely the miracle of the loaves and fishes, and the meal of fish which the risen Lord prepared for his disciples by the Sea of Galilee, were in the minds of those who traced these symbols; but the mystery they were expressing was the mystery of the Eucharist, which they were always careful to hide from pagan eyes.

EUCHARISTIC SYMBOL. FISH WITH A BASKET OF LOAVES

In several of the catacombs, fonts have been found, and in at least one case the basin is fed by living water from a stream. Baptism in running water was preferred in the early Church, and the underground streams in the cata-combs supplied just what was needed. Pictures and sym-bols of baptism are not uncommon, and among the epitaphs there are some to neophytes, Christians recently baptized.

In spite of the fact that none of the chambers is large

enough to serve the purpose of a church, there can be no doubt that the catacombs were of great importance to Christians in second-century Rome. At the entrance to each of these subterranean places, there was a door-keeper to prevent unbelievers from entering. Once within, secrecy was assured. It is not hard to imagine the impression which would be made upon a convert from paganism, undergoing instruction, as he was led past the door-keeper, down a rock-cut staircase, along dimly lit, tomb-lined passages, to a small chamber where the class was assembling for instruction. On the walls he would see symbolic pictures, intelligible only to the instructed believer. Nearby, it might be that the Eucharist was being celebrated, a mystery from which the unbaptized were rigidly excluded. The darkness and the terrors of the pagan mystery cults were artificially contrived to stimulate the emotions, but there was nothing theatrical or unreal about the catacombs. He must have been conscious of the solemnity of what he was doing, aware of the dangers he was about to face in joining a persecuted community, and aware also that he was compassed about with a cloud of witnesses, the men and women whose memorials he could see around him. To the confirmed Christians, the catacombs were a place of sanctuary, free from pagan interference and hallowed by the bodies of the saints. There they could draw strength from their fellowship with the Church triumphant. Leaving behind them for a while the anxieties and evils of the world, they could taste in anticipation the joys of paradise, and lift their hearts in thanksgiving to their Saviour, their Good Shepherd, Jesus Christ.

The Shepherd of Hermas.

In the first half of the second century, a book was written in Rome which was read with great enjoyment by many of those who now lie buried in the catacombs. Fortunately, copies of this book have survived to the present day.   Its name is *The Shepherd of Hermas*, and it has some of the qualities of *Piers Plowman* and *Pilgrim's Progress*, though not their literary greatness.   The book consists of a series of visions or allegories which depict the state of the church of Rome at the time it was written.   The opening paragraph will convey, better than any description, the attractiveness of the book and the freshness of its style:

" He who brought me up sold me to a certain Rhoda at Rome.   After many years I made her acquaintance again, and began to love her as a sister.   After some time I saw her bathing in the river Tiber, and gave her my hand and helped her out of the river.   When I saw her beauty I reflected in my heart and said: ' I should be happy if I had a wife of such beauty and character '.   This was my only thought, and no other, no, not one.   After some time, while I was going to Cumæ, and glorifying the creation of God for its greatness and splendour and might, as I walked along I became sleepy.   And a spirit seized me and took me away through a certain pathless district, through which a man could not walk, but the ground was precipitous and broken up by the streams of water.   So I crossed that river, and came to the level ground and knelt down and began to pray to the Lord and to confess my sins.   Now while I was praying the Heaven was opened, and I saw that woman whom I had desired greeting me out of Heaven and saying, ' Hail, Hermas '.   And I looked at her, and said to her: ' Lady, what are you doing here?' "

Being questioned, the lady explains to Hermas that she has been taken up into Heaven to accuse him of his sins, especially the sin of having harboured an evil desire and to urge him to repent.   At that Hermas is taken aback and says to himself:

" If this sin is recorded against me, how shall I be saved? Or how shall I propitiate God for my completed sins?   Or with what words shall I beseech the Lord to be forgiving unto me?"

This introduces the main theme of the book, which is the possibility of obtaining forgiveness for sins committed after baptism. Many early Christians believed, not only that baptism cleansed them from their sins, but also that after baptism they were capable of living sinless lives and that there was no further hope of forgiveness should they fall from grace. This view was widely held, and as a result some fell into despair and, having sinned after baptism, made no further attempt to amend their lives, but went from bad to worse. Others put off baptism as long as possible, so that they might have a chance of forgiveness before they died. *The Shepherd of Hermas* was written to urge men to repent, and to assure them that after baptism they had one, but only one, further opportunity for forgiveness.

For the modern reader, the book's chief interest lies in the picture it gives of life in the early Church. Hermas is deeply concerned at the worldliness of some Christians. He continually warns them of the disastrous consequences of being " double-minded ", that is of failing to serve God whole-heartedly. In one vision, an ancient lady, whom Hermas recognizes to be the Church, shows him " a great tower being built on the water with shining square stones ". The lower part of the tower is built of stones taken from the sea, and these fit together so perfectly that no joins can be seen. But around the base of the tower lie many stones rejected by the builders, some of them rotten, some cracked, and some so round that they are unsuitable for building. Immediately, Hermas pesters the ancient lady for an explanation of this vision. She is anxious to hurry away, but yields to his persistence, saying:

" You will not cease asking for revelations, for you are shameless." She then tells him that the tower is built on water, because men are saved by the water of baptism. The stones in the lower courses are the apostles and their immediate successors; those brought from the sea are they who have suffered for the name of the Lord. These fit together perfectly, for they lived at peace with one another. The rotten stones are the apostates who have forsaken the faith. Those which are cracked are they who bear malice in their hearts against each other.

" ' But who, lady,' " says Hermas, " ' are the white and round ones, which do not fit into the building? '

" She answered and said to me, ' How long will you be stupid and foolish, and ask everything and understand nothing? These are they which have faith, but have also the riches of this world. When persecution comes, because of their wealth and business they deny their Lord '.

" And I answered and said to her, ' Lady, but then when will they be useful for the building? '

" ' When ', she said, ' their wealth, which leads their souls astray, shall be cut off from them, then they will be useful to God. For just as the round stone cannot become square, unless something be cut off and taken away from it, so too they who have riches in this world cannot be useful to God unless their wealth be cut away from them.' "

A similar lesson is taught him later in the book by the Angel of Repentance, who is called the Shepherd. One day, while he is walking in the country, Hermas notices a vine growing on an elm tree. The shepherd appears to him and points out that if the vine were left to spread along the ground, it would bear little fruit and that that little would be rotten. When supported on the elm, however, it bears beautiful grapes. He continues:

" ' This parable, therefore, applies to the servants of God, to the poor, and to the rich.'

" ' How, sir? ' said I, ' let me know.'

" ' Listen,' said he, ' the rich man has much wealth, but he is poor as touching the Lord, being busied about his riches, and his intercession and confession towards the Lord is very small, and that which he has is weak and small, and has no other power.   But when the rich man rests upon the poor, and gives him what he needs, he believes that what he does to the poor man can find a reward with God, because the poor is rich in intercession and confession, and his intercession has great power with God.' "

The catacombs, surely, are the proof that the Angel's counsel did not pass unheeded.   There, in the vaults provided originally by a few wealthy Christians, are thousands of humble graves, and on many of them prayers and expressions of trust and faith in God can still be seen.

But there was another side to the life of the Roman church in the second century.   Persecution was a constant danger and Hermas was well aware of it.

" The fourth vision which I saw, brethren," he writes, " was a type of the persecution which is to come.   I was going into the country by the Via Campana.   The place is about ten furlongs from the public road, and is easily reached.   As I walked by myself I besought the Lord to complete the revelations and visions which he had shown me by his holy Church, to make me strong and give repentance to his servants who had been offended, ' to glorify his great and glorious name ' because he had thought me worthy to show me his wonders. And while I was glorifying him and giving him thanks an answer came to me as an echo of my voice, ' Do not be double-minded, Hermas '.   I began to reason in myself, and to say, ' In what ways can I be double-minded after being given such a foundation by the Lord, and having seen his glorious deeds ? '   And I approached a little further, brethren, and behold, I saw dust reaching as it were up to heaven, and I began to say to myself, ' Are cattle coming and raising dust ? ' and it was about a furlong away from me.   When the dust grew greater and greater I supposed that it was some portent.   The sun shone out a little, and lo ! I saw a great beast like some Leviathan, and fiery locusts were going out of his mouth.   The beast was in size about a hundred feet and its head was like a piece of pottery. And I began to weep and to pray the Lord to rescue me from it, and I remembered the word which I had heard, ' Do not be

double-minded, Hermas '.   Thus, brethren, being clothed in
the faith of the Lord and remembering the great things which
he had taught me, I took courage and faced the beast.   And as
the beast came on with a rush it was as though it could destroy
a city.   I came near to it, and the Leviathan for all its size
stretched itself out on the ground, and put forth nothing except
its tongue, and did not move at all until I had passed by."

The joyfulness, which is so conspicuous in the frescoes
of the catacombs, is characteristic of Hermas also.   The
old woman, clothed in shining garments, who represents
the Church, describes him as patient, and good-tempered,
and always laughing.   Later in the book, three dispositions
are especially condemned as inimical to the presence of the
Holy Spirit; they are double-mindedness, a grieving spirit,
and ill temper.   Being double-minded is best defined as
the opposite of being single-minded.   It implies the
absence of wholehearted devotion, too much interest in
worldly concerns, and a tendency to doubt and question in
matters of faith.   A gloomy, mournful disposition is condemned, because it " wears out the Holy Spirit ", who
petitions to be withdrawn from dwelling with such a man.

" Put on, therefore, joyfulness ", says the Shepherd, " which
always has favour with God and is acceptable to him, and
flourish in it; for every joyful man does good deeds, and has
good thoughts, and despises grief."

As for ill-temper, this is inseparable from grief and
double-mindedness.   For Hermas has in mind the man or
woman who is " made bitter out of nothing, because of
daily business or of food or some trifle, or about some
friend, or about giving and receiving, or about some such
foolish matters ".   And, as he wisely says:

" Ill temper is first foolish, frivolous, and silly; then from
silliness comes bitterness, from bitterness wrath, from wrath
rage, and from rage fury; then fury, being compounded of
such great evils, becomes great and inexpiable sin."

The temper which he commends is that of joyfulness and long-suffering, for " long-suffering is great and mighty and has steadfast power and prospers in great breadth, is joyful, glad, without care, ' glorifying the Lord at every time ', has nothing bitter in itself, but remains ever meek and gentle ".

There was a rigorist element in the second-century Church which was opposed to the spirit of Hermas and of the artists of the catacombs, patient, good-tempered, and always laughing. The rigorists believed that there was no hope whatever for those who sinned after their baptism, and they condemned *The Shepherd of Hermas* for its lax teaching. Those who loved to adorn their burying-places with pictures of the Good Shepherd were on the side of Hermas. They delighted to remember the joy there is among the angels in heaven over one sinner that repenteth. They not only depicted the Good Shepherd with a lost sheep upon his shoulder, on at least one occasion they showed him carrying a goat. Matthew Arnold has summarized this conflict in a poem:

> " ' He saves the sheep, the goats he doth not save! '
> So rang Tertullian's sentence, on the side
> Of that unpitying Phrygian sect which cried:
> ' Him can no fount of fresh forgiveness lave,

> " ' Who sins, once washed by the baptismal wave! '
> So spake the fierce Tertullian. But she sigh'd,
> The infant Church; of love she felt the tide
> Stream on her from her Lord's yet recent grave.

> " And then she smiled, and in the Catacombs,
> With eyes suffused but heart inspired true,
> On those walls subterranean, where she hid

> " Her head in ignominy, death and tombs,
> She her Good Shepherd's hasty image drew;
> And on his shoulders, not a lamb, a kid."

BOOKS FOR FURTHER READING

Early Christians in Rome, by H. D. M. Spence-Jones.

Epitaphs of the Catacombs, by J. S. Northcote.

The Catacombs of Rome, by W. H. Withrow.

Christian Inscriptions in Ancient Rome: Their Message for Today, by H. E. Fox. A short book which is easy to read.

L'Art Chrétien Primitif, by Marcel Laurent.

Roma Sottereana: an Account of the Roman Catacombs, by J. S. Northcote and W. S. Brownlow. 2 volumes. A useful reference book.

A translation of *The Shepherd of Hermas* will be found in J. B. Lightfoot's *Apostolic Fathers*.

CHAPTER VIII

Enemies within the Gates

" From all false doctrine, heresy, and schism. . . . Good Lord
deliver us."—Litany.

Part 1. *Superstition and the Gnostic Heresy*

THOSE who cannot read or write love to hear and re-
tell stories, and the more marvellous the stories are,
the better they like them. The early Christians were no
exception to the general rule in this respect. Besides the
Gospel narratives, which they heard in church, and the
account of the doings of the apostles given in Acts, they
knew many legends about Christ and his apostles, and
these, as they were handed on by word of mouth, lost
nothing in the telling. Fortunately, many of these legends
were eventually written down, some as early as the second
century, some later. It is thus possible for us in the twentieth century to listen to the tales which delighted alike the
simple and the superstitious among the early believers.
After doing so, it is much easier to enter into the mind of
an ordinary second-century Christian, to see the temptations
which beset him and the difficulties which hindered him
from apprehending the truth. Such a man was brought
up in pagan surroundings, and was neither better educated
nor more intelligent than his heathen neighbours. He had
a thirst for signs and wonders which the miracles of the
New Testament only partially satisfied. The Gospels,
Acts, and Epistles, now collected together under the title
of *The Apocryphal New Testament*, were written partly in

response to this demand for more miraculous tales about Christ and his apostles, and partly to popularize their authors' views. In due course, the Church rejected these books as uninspired and, in some cases, positively harmful. But, except where a writer was endeavouring to spread heretical opinions, the purpose of those who composed the books was pious enough. Their fault was in not being satisfied with the truth. The tremendous mysteries of the Incarnation and the Atonement were not enough for them. They must needs seek out lesser marvels, without inquiring whether these miracles had really taken place.

Among the most popular stories were legends of our Lord's childhood, and of the birth and upbringing of his mother, Mary. *The Book of James*, or *Protoevangelium* as it is sometimes called, describes the miraculous birth of Mary and her upbringing in the Temple; her betrothal to Joseph, a widower with sons by a previous marriage; the annunciation; the birth of Christ and the massacre of the Innocents. The writer's chief intention is to emphasize the virginity of Mary, and the account of the Nativity is altered to introduce a sceptical midwife, whose hand is withered in punishment of her unbelief in Mary's virginity and healed again by touching the holy Babe. *The Gospel of Thomas* is intended to fill another gap in the New Testament by supplying stories of the childhood of Jesus. Unhappily, most of the stories are not only manifestly false, but repulsive as well. Jesus is shown as possessed of miraculous powers which he uses indiscriminately and often vindictively, cursing and striking dead those who offend him. The most appealing tale is that which describes how the child Jesus, at play on the Sabbath modelling clay sparrows, was reproved by his father Joseph for breaking the Law. In answer, the child clapped his hands and cried to the sparrows: " Go! " whereat they all flew up and went away chirping.

N

Plainly, such stories could do great mischief by giving a false conception of our Lord's character and by undermining belief in his humanity. Other stories of a like nature were told about the apostles. A whole cycle of tales centred on St Peter has been preserved in *The Recognitions of Clement* and *The Acts of Peter*. The Clementine story is a popular romance of lost relatives finally reunited. This has been attached to the names of Clement and St Peter in just the same way that anecdotes today are attached to any appropriate public figure, regardless of their actual origin. *The Acts of Peter* is chiefly concerned with the conflict between St Peter and Simon Magus in Rome. This may have a foundation in fact, but most of the details are pure fantasy, as will be seen from a summary of the opening sections.

St Paul having sailed on a missionary journey to Spain, the church in Rome is left without a leader, and when Simon Magus makes a spectacular entry by flying through the air over the city gate, even the brethren are impressed, and many of them become his followers. The faithful remnant thereupon send a deputation to Jerusalem to beg St Peter to come to their aid, which he does at once, fasting during the whole voyage, and miraculously converting the captain of the ship *en route*. On his arrival in Rome, St Peter first makes a lengthy speech in the synagogue and then, being told that Marcellus, formerly a benefactor of the Christians, is now the chief patron of Simon Magus, he proceeds to Marcellus's house. There he is refused admission by the porter, who tells him that Simon Magus has bidden him say he is out whenever St Peter calls, either by night or day. At that St Peter looses the chained watch-dog and commands the animal to announce his presence to Simon. The dog thereupon receives a human voice and, running into the house, delivers St Peter's message to the astonished magician. Not content with repeating what he has been told, the intelligent animal rebukes Simon Magus at some length, and then runs back to St Peter and falls dead at his feet. Marcellus repents, and the multitude, much impressed, characteristically asks for more signs, which St Peter willingly provides.

There follow several other improving episodes in the contest between Simon Magus and St Peter, ending in the defeat of the magician. Finally, there is an account of St Peter's martyrdom. This is prefaced by the lovely " Quo Vadis? " story, which is told with a beauty and simplicity which suggest an early source. The rest is in a different, more homiletic vein. Having arrived at the scene of his martyrdom, St Peter discourses for some time on the meaning of the cross, and then begs the executioners to crucify him upside down. This being done, St Peter delivers a sermon on the allegorical meaning of his request, and, after a protracted thanksgiving, expires.

From her earliest years, the Church has had to wrestle with credulity and superstition in her own members, as well as in the world without. She has done so down the ages with varying success. The books now included in *The Apocryphal New Testament* failed from the start to obtain recognition. Bishops would not allow them to be read in church, and in some cases emphatically condemned them. But people continued to read and enjoy them. Many thought these tales edifying, and no doubt they served as source-books for homilies in the allegorical style which then was fashionable. The legends embedded in these apocryphal gospels and acts became so much a part of popular piety that they persisted throughout the Middle Ages, as any large collection of paintings by old masters will abundantly show. During the Reformation, a large part of the Church disencumbered herself of these legends and of the beliefs built upon them, basing her faith on the sound foundation of the New Testament alone; but the

Roman Catholic Church continues to give them a large measure of credence, even to the present day.

The credulity of the ignorant was not the worst danger the Church had to face within her own ranks. The speculations of the intelligent were an even greater threat to truth, for there were men who claimed to be more enlightened than their fellow-Christians, and who did not hesitate to distort the teaching of the apostles to suit their own theories. Such men came to be known as Gnostics, from the Greek word, γνῶσις, which means knowledge. They all had certain ideas in common, but Gnosticism is extraordinarily difficult to define, for the term includes a number of different schools of thought, some claiming to be Christian, others almost wholly pagan. The second century within the Roman Empire resembled our own era in one respect: improved communications had drawn men from distant lands together, so that East and West had mingled. One result was that instead of remaining faithful to their own religious and philosophical traditions, men attempted to assimilate all the strange and often conflicting ideas which came their way, and to blend them into a whole. Many men thought at that time, as some do today, that there is some truth in all religions and that a synthesis of them all is the ideal solution. The Gnostics within the Church were those who had seized upon Christianity as an important ingredient in the mixture, and who were bent on harmonizing its doctrines with the ideas about God and about the universe which they had derived from other sources.

From Greek philosophy, more especially from the Neo-Platonists, the Gnostics had learnt to conceive of God as the Absolute, incomprehensible, immaterial, impassible, a spiritual Being definable only by negatives. Along with this belief went the view that matter is evil and that the perfecting of the soul consists in setting itself free from the bondage of the body. From Zoroastrianism, the religion of Persia, came dualism: the belief that this world is a battle-ground for two opposing forces, good and evil, light and darkness. Matter was identified with evil, and many Gnostics found it impossible to believe that God is the Creator of the material world. Those of them who were most imbued with Eastern ideas usually ascribed the creation of the world to an evil angel, the Demiurge, and regarded Christ as the redeemer sent by the Supreme God to save the elect from bondage to the Demiurge and to render them truly spiritual. Some even went so far as to regard the God of the Old Testament as the devil, and to worship his adversary, the Serpent. The members of this peculiar sect were known as Ophites, or Naassenes. Their serpent cult was a continuation of the pagan serpent-worship, which was especially widespread in Asia Minor, and it was so obviously incompatible with Christianity that the Ophites soon became an obscure sect, a curiosity rather than a menace. But the idea that the God of the Old Testament was an evil, tyrannical being persisted, and appeared again in various forms.

Even those Gnostics who allowed that God was the ultimate source of the creation interposed a series of intermediaries between the Absolute and the material world. It was inconceivable to them that God could be directly responsible for the creation of the physical universe. Instead, they imagined a succession of emanations, each less purely spiritual than its predecessor, the lowest and grossest of which created the world. Their speculations sound fantastic to a modern reader, unaccustomed to expressing abstract thought in an allegorical form, but the problems they were trying to solve were real enough. Given on the one hand that God is perfect Love, and on the other that he is the active cause of whatever he permits, then it is not unreasonable to ask: " How can he be the Creator of this world, where sin and death and pain are all too evident?"

Again, there are passages in the Old Testament which show Jehovah as jealous and vindictive, demanding the destruction of those who offend him, even unwittingly. These are hard to reconcile with the doctrine that God is Love, except on the theory of progressive revelation, which required more historical knowledge than the second-century thinkers possessed.

It would seem, on the face of it, that Gnosticism could only affect a small minority of the more learned and highly educated within the Church. But this was not the case. Only a few could understand the philosophical conceptions which underlay the various Gnostic systems, but many were attracted by the mysterious language in which they were expressed, and the notion of being one of the elect appealed to that deadliest of human weaknesses, spiritual pride. The followers of the great Gnostic thinkers popularized their ideas in various ways, including the composition of hymns. One such hymn has been preserved in the apocryphal *Acts of John*, and there is no denying that it has a beauty of its own. It is attributed to Christ, who is supposed to have taught it to his disciples on the eve of his crucifixion:

" He bade us therefore make as it were a ring, holding one another's hands, and himself standing in the midst he said: Answer Amen unto me. He began then to sing an hymn and to say:

Glory be to thee, Father.
And we, going about in a ring, answered him: Amen.
Glory be to thee, Word: Glory be to thee, Grace. Amen.
Glory be to thee, Spirit: Glory be to thee, Holy One: Glory be to thy glory. Amen.
We praise thee, O Father; we give thanks to thee, O Light, wherein darkness dwelleth not. Amen.
Now whereas we give thanks, I say:
I would be saved, and I would save. Amen.
I would be loosed, and I would loose. Amen.

I would be wounded, and I would wound. Amen.
I would be born, and I would bear. Amen.
I would eat, and I would be eaten. Amen.
I would hear, and I would be heard. Amen.
I would be thought, being wholly thought. Amen.
I would be washed, and I would wash. Amen.
Grace danceth. I would pipe; dance ye all. Amen.
I would mourn: lament ye all. Amen.
The number eight singeth praises with us. Amen.
The number twelve danceth on high. Amen.
The Whole on high hath part in our dancing. Amen.
Whoso danceth not, knoweth not what cometh to pass.
      Amen.
I would flee, and I would stay. Amen.
I would adorn, and I would be adorned. Amen.
I would be united, and I would unite. Amen.
A house I have not, and I have houses. Amen.
A place I have not, and I have places. Amen.
A temple I have not, and I have temples. Amen.
A lamp am I to thee that beholdest me. Amen.
A mirror am I to thee that perceivest me. Amen.
A door am I to thee that knockest at me. Amen.
A way am I to thee a wayfarer. Amen.
Now answer thou unto my dancing.
Behold thyself in me who speak, and seeing what I do, keep
      silence about my mysteries.

It is not hard to imagine the ritual that accompanied this
hymn or to guess its emotional appeal, but only an outline
of the system of Valentinus, the greatest of the Gnostics,
can make it at all intelligible.

Gnosticism was a product of the spirit of the age, and its
adherents were to be found in all parts of the Empire, but
there were local variations. Egyptian Gnostics were deeply
influenced by Greek thought; those in Asia Minor went to
extremes of asceticism or of licence; those in Syria accepted
the Persian doctrine of dualism. Valentinus studied in
Alexandria, but about A.D. 140 he settled in Rome and began
to expound his ideas there. He imagined the Fullness

(*Pleroma*) of the Godhead as being composed of thirty
æons, or attributes, which he grouped in pairs, one of each
pair being thought of, as in a sense, male, the other female.
From each pair of *æons* others emanated.   His theory is
roughly represented by the following scheme:

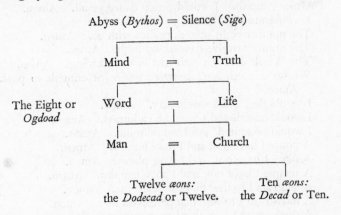

Abyss (*Bythos*) = Silence (*Sige*)

The Eight or *Ogdoad*

Mind   =   Truth

Word   =   Life

Man   =   Church

Twelve *æons*:
the *Dodecad* or Twelve.

Ten *æons*:
the *Decad* or Ten.

Thus, in the hymn quoted above, the number eight is the
ogdoad, the first eight attributes of God.   The number
twelve is the *dodecad*, and the Whole is the *Pleroma* of thirty
æons, all of which are imagined as moving together in a
mystic dance.

According to Valentinus, the creation of the world was
in this wise: Sophia or Wisdom, the youngest and lowest
of the *æons*, desired to know the depths of God's Being.
She soared up through the *Pleroma* towards the Abyss,
only to fall back in sorrow and despair at her utter inability
to achieve her desire.   From this sorrow Achamoth, a
lower form of Wisdom, was born.   Achamoth also
yearned to reach upwards, but was barred from entering
the *Pleroma* by Stauros, the Cross.   Out of Achamoth's
grief was born Demiurgos, the creator of the material
universe.   To redeem the confusion caused by Sophia,

two other Eternities were brought into being, Christ and the Holy Spirit, composed of the best of all the rest. Christ came down to Achamoth and comforted her, before returning to the *Pleroma*, thus affording mankind the possibility of redemption. Valentinus and his followers taught that there are three types of men: spiritual men, derived from Christ and the Lower Wisdom; psychic men, who drew their being from Wisdom and the Demiurge; and carnal men, the offspring of the Demiurge alone. This was a deplorable distinction, for it led some to believe that they were inherently different from their fellows. Those who flattered themselves that they were spiritual believed that they were bound to be saved whatever they did, while carnal men were as certainly damned. Psychic men could be saved, but they could never reach the heights of which spiritual men were capable.

The worst of all the bad effects which Gnostic ideas had upon ordinary Christians was to make them doubt the humanity of our Lord. Today, it is only too easy to find people who doubt our Lord's divinity, but few, if any, question that he lived a truly human life, if they admit the evidence for his existence. In the first and second centuries, when men were accustomed to the pagan myths of gods and dæmons assuming human form, it was not at all difficult to persuade them that Christ only appeared to be a man, but was not truly human at all. That the Word should be made flesh was a thought abhorrent to the Gnostics, with their hatred of matter. They pictured Christ as a Divine Being having only the semblance of a man, with none of the usual human limitations, and incapable of suffering hunger, weariness, or pain. This view of Christ's Person is known as Docetism, and it was alarmingly prevalent in the first and second centuries. The emphasis on our Lord's humanity in the fourth Gospel is especially strong, as an answer to this heresy. St Ignatius on his way to martyrdom finds it necessary to write to the Trallians to stop their ears when godless men assert that Christ "suffered in phantom only". A number of the apocryphal Gospels and Acts, written during the second century or even later, must have done much harm by popularizing false ideas about our Lord, and by making his sacrifice on Calvary seem mere play-acting. Naturally, most of these books have failed to survive, for those in authority in the Church did their best to discourage their flock from reading them, and time also has taken a heavy toll. A few pages remain of " The Gospel of Peter ", and these contain an account of our Lord's Crucifixion, based on the four Gospels, but with some significant alterations. When our Lord is crucified, it is said, " He kept silence, as one feeling no pain ", and his death is described in the following words: " And the Lord cried out aloud saying: My power, my power, thou hast forsaken me. And when he had so said, he was taken up."

The *Acts of John*, which contain the Gnostic hymn quoted above, also provide a fair sample of the portrait of Christ which such teachers presented to their people. The apostle John is represented as recounting to his disciples his personal recollections of the Lord. He describes how, when Christ first called his brother James and himself by the Sea of Galilee, James saw a child standing on the shore, while he saw a comely young man. Again when they had landed, James saw a youth whose beard was newly come, but he saw a man with a thick, flowing beard, rather bald on the head. At this they were naturally perplexed, and the writer continues:

" Yet unto me there then appeared this yet more wonderful thing; for I would try to see him privily, and I never at any time saw his eyes closing, but only open. And oft-times he would appear to me as a small man and uncomely, and then again as one reaching unto heaven."

The impression of a supernatural being, masquerading in human form, is confirmed by a distorted account of the Transfiguration.

"Again in like manner he bringeth us three up into the mountain, saying: Come ye with me. And we went again: and we saw him at a distance praying. I, therefore, because he loved me, drew nigh unto him softly, as though he could not see me, and stood looking upon his hinder parts: and I saw that he was not in any way clad with garments, but was seen of us naked, and not in any wise as a man, and that his feet were whiter than any snow, so that the earth there was lighted up by his feet, and that his head touched the heaven."

The Crucifixion is dealt with in the following fashion:

"Thus, my beloved, having danced with us the Lord went forth, and we as men gone astray or dazed with sleep fled this way and that. I, then, when I saw him suffer, did not even abide by his suffering, but fled into the Mount of Olives, weeping at that which had befallen. And when he was crucified on the Friday, at the sixth hour of the day, darkness came upon all the earth. And my Lord standing in the midst of the cave and enlightening it said: John, unto the multitude below in Jerusalem I am being crucified and pierced with lances and reeds, and gall and vinegar is given me to drink. But unto thee I speak, and what I speak hear thou."

There follows a long discourse in which Christ explains to St John the meaning of the Cross. The gist of it is summed up in the words:

"Care not therefore for the many, and them that are outside the mystery despise: for know thou that I am wholly with the Father, and the Father with me. . . . Thou hearest that I suffered, yet I did not suffer: that I suffered not, yet did I suffer; that I was pierced, yet I was not smitten; hanged, and I was not hanged; that blood flowed from me, and it flowed not: and, in a word, what they say of me, that befell me not, but what they say not, that did I suffer."

194   LIFE IN THE EARLY CHURCH

Such passages make it plain why it was that the Church
had to win her fight against Gnosticism, if the Christian
faith was to survive.

Not all the ideas of the Gnostics were absurd, even from
a twentieth-century standpoint.   There was much that was
reasonable and true in their criticism of the Old Testament,
and this made the false conclusions they reached all the
more dangerous.   The chief protagonist in the attack on
the Old Testament was a man called Marcion, a well-to-do
ship-owner, from Pontus in Asia Minor, whose father was
a bishop.   Marcion arrived in Rome about A.D. 138, and
at first there seems to have been no question of his orthodoxy.   He presented the church in Rome with a sum
amounting to £2,000 in modern money, a gift which was
later returned to him when he was excommunicated for
heresy.   Marcion seems to have been a practical man with
no taste for fantastic theories, but, unfortunately, he came
under the influence of a disciple of Cerdon, a Syrian Gnostic,
who taught that the God of the Old Testament was quite a
different Being from the God Christians worshipped.
Marcion firmly believed in a personal and loving God and,
after carefully studying the Old Testament, he came to the
conclusion that Cerdon was right.   Jehovah, the stern law-
giver, the just and jealous God, was not identical with
the God revealed in Christ.   Nor was Christ himself the
Messiah foretold by the prophets.   Christ was sent by the
true God, who was revealed in him for the first time.
There was no continuity between the Old Testament and
the New, for the former was inspired by the Demiurge, the
latter by the true God.   Had Marcion had more knowledge
of history, he could have found a solution of his difficulties
in the idea of progressive revelation, but he was a man of
his time, and not in any way a profound or original thinker.
Faced with a complicated problem, he attempted to solve
it by cutting the knot.   His Biblical criticism reached con-

clusions more extreme than those of any modern scholar. He rejected the whole of the Old Testament, and then turned his attention to the New Testament books. These did not suit his theories either, for Christ was shown as the long-expected Messiah. Marcion therefore rejected all but St Luke's Gospel and the Pauline Epistles. Even in these he made some cuts and alterations, for he objected to the story of Christ's birth as too humiliating. " Away with that poor inn," he is reported to have said, " those mean swaddling clothes and that rough stable." But the Crucifixion he believed in, as the proof of God's love for man.

After he had been excommunicated, Marcion became the founder of a sect. He assumed the authority of a bishop and founded churches modelled on orthodox lines. His followers not only accepted his peculiar ideas, they also adopted a much more ascetic way of life than ordinary Christians followed. They went so far as to think that both marriage and the eating of meat were sinful, and they used water instead of wine when celebrating the Eucharist. Dreary as their practices sound, the Marcionites succeeded in spreading their churches throughout the Empire, and it was not until the sixth century that the sect finally died out.

Another attempt to prune and revise the New Testament was made towards the end of the second century by a Christian writer, called Tatian, who had become influenced by heretical ideas. His revision was not nearly so extreme as that of Marcion. He simply produced a harmony of the four Gospels, known as the " Diatessaron ", using extracts from each to form a single narrative, and omitting passages of which he did not approve. His book was popular in the East and, when it was translated into Latin, it enjoyed a vogue in the West as well. Fortunately, orthodox bishops discouraged the use of it, and the people themselves generally preferred the Gospel they were used to, whether it were

Matthew or Mark, Luke or John; otherwise we might by now have nothing but Tatian's "Diatessaron" in their place.

During the second century and the beginning of the third, the Church met the Gnostic attack and defeated it on all fronts. Irenæus in the West, Tertullian in North Africa, Clement and Origen in Alexandria, all in their various ways defended the apostolic tradition and attacked the Gnostics either with reasoned arguments or with ridicule. Tertullian had no use at all for their fanciful theories, but St Clement of Alexandria met them on their own ground. He claimed that the orthodox Christian was the true Gnostic, and he attempted in his own writings to harmonize Greek with Christian thought. He was not entirely successful. Now and again his Christian Gnosis slithered some way down the slippery descent to Docetism; yet he never let go his grasp of Christian truth. He probably did more to save those with leanings towards Gnosticism from falling into its more serious errors than did Tertullian with his mocking laughter. St Irenæus found the best answer of all, which was to examine the authority of the canonical Gospels and Church tradition on which orthodox Christians based their beliefs. "That which purifies us is trial, and trial is by what is contrary." The Church became aware of the full meaning of her faith by being forced to defend it against error; she defined the canon of the Scriptures in answer to those who would have robbed her of them; against those who claimed to be "spiritual", she maintained that salvation is equally available for all; she unwaveringly affirmed the full humanity of Jesus Christ, her Lord, excommunicating those of her members who denied it.

Some account of the chief defenders of the faith will be given in later chapters. It now remains to consider a movement which, though not heretical, caused the Church both trouble and loss.

Part 2. The Montanist Schism

The cities along the coasts of Asia Minor were in constant touch with the rest of the civilized world, but inland,
up in the mountain villages, away from the main trade
routes, wild, orgiastic forms of religion flourished.   There,
too, Christianity was spreading, but it was apt to assume
some of the characteristics of the paganism it displaced.
About the middle of the second century, a pagan priest
called Montanus, who lived in a village on the border between Mysia and Phrygia, was converted to Christianity.
Soon afterwards he startled the neighbourhood by falling
into an ecstasy and proclaiming himself to be a prophet,
the mouthpiece of God.   " I am come neither as an angel,
nor ambassador," he announced, " but as God the Father."
He also claimed to be the voice of the Paraclete.   Naturally
this amazing revelation was received with caution by the
more sober and thoughtful Christians, but some readily
believed that this was the beginning of a new outpouring of
the Holy Spirit, greater even than that at Pentecost.   Many
became devoted adherents of Montanus, and among them
were two women, Prisca and Maximilla, who left their
husbands and joined him.

As the movement spread, and its fanatical and ecstatic
character became more obvious, synods of the local clergy
and of the faithful were called to consider the whole matter.
These concluded that Montanus and his followers were
inspired, not by the Holy Spirit, but by demons.   They
proposed to exorcise both Prisca and Maximilla, but the
prophetesses refused their offer with indignation.   The
Montanists were pained by this treatment, but they were
undaunted.   Maximilla complained:

" I am driven away from the sheep like a wolf, though I am
no wolf but Word and Spirit and Power."

The Montanists gave out that their mission was to inaugu-
rate the reign of the Holy Spirit, and they withdrew to two
villages in Phrygia, Pepuza, and Tymion, the nearest places
to the spot where, they said, the New Jerusalem would
descend to earth from heaven at Christ's Second Coming.
There they attempted to institute a reign of saints, while
waiting for the Second Advent. Enthusiasts sold their
possessions, abandoned their families, and came to join them.
The " New Jerusalem " became a place of pilgrimage and,
far from dying out, Montanism began to attract sympathizers
from other provinces of the Empire.

The Church was reluctant to excommunicate the Montanists, whose fault lay in unbalanced enthusiasm rather than
in heresy. But their outrageous claims could not be allowed
to pass. In A.D. 172, the church in Asia Minor formally
condemned the movement, and this decision was later confirmed by the church of Rome. In spite of many efforts on
the part of their supporters, the Montanists failed to secure
a reversal of this verdict. In Asia Minor, its first home,
Montanism degenerated after the deaths of its founders.
But in Africa it captured the imagination of Tertullian, one
of the ablest controversial writers among the early Fathers.
The rest of its history therefore belongs to a later chapter.
But here it is mentioned only in order to record that Montanism, even in its earlier phase, was more important than
its absurdities suggest. It was a protest against the laxity
which Gnosticism had produced in some sections of the
Church. Those tinged with Gnosticism saw no reason
why they should die for their faith, nor even why they
should utterly condemn pagan practices. The wild zeal
of the Montanists was a popular reaction against the barren
intellectualism and the spirit of compromise, which were
undermining Christian faith and practice.

BOOKS FOR FURTHER READING

The Apocryphal New Testament, translated by M. R. James.
Studies in the Life of the Early Church, by F. J. Foakes-Jackson.
History of the Church to A.D. 461, by B. J. Kidd, Vol. I—the relevant
    chapters.
Early Church History to A.D. 313, by H. M. Gwatkin.

CHAPTER IX

PAGAN ATTACK AND CHRISTIAN DEFENCE: THE APOLOGISTS

DURING the first half of the second century, the Roman Empire was exceptionally well-governed, and was consequently strong enough to maintain peace. Trajan, in whose reign the century opened, extended the frontiers of the Empire by conquering Dacia, now known as Roumania, and, by so doing, thrust back the barbarians who threatened to push across the Danube into Roman territory. He then attempted to realize his dream of a great empire in the East, and he conducted a successful war against the Parthians beyond the Euphrates. But a rebellion in his rear compelled him to retreat, and in A.D. 117 he died, worn out and disappointed. His successor, Hadrian, was a sounder statesman. He consolidated the Empire by strengthening its defences and perfecting the organization of the army. Behind such fortifications as the great wall, which he built right across the north of Britain, the civilian population lived in security. In A.D. 138 Antoninus Pius succeeded Hadrian, and he also was a just, good ruler; but he was not vigorous enough in his measures against the barbarian hordes that were constantly pressing against the outer defences of the Empire. Disaster came, not in his time, but under the next Emperor, Marcus Aurelius (A.D. 161–180). In A.D. 161, the Parthians gave trouble. After a four years' war against them, Marcus Aurelius secured his eastern frontier, but the returning troops brought a terrible plague back with them, which decimated the population of Italy. At this moment of

weakness, the Germanic barbarians broke through the
northern defences and poured down into Italy. By an
immense effort, Marcus Aurelius drove them back, but the
period of security was over.

It is against this background that the history of the
Church in the second century must be seen, if it is to be
fully understood. During the whole of this time, Christianity was prohibited upon pain of death, but the earlier
Emperors were not active persecutors.* Initiative in the
matter was left to the local authorities, the governors of
provinces and the like, and the general ruling was that any
who were accused of being Christians must be tried and, if
guilty, condemned, but that Christians should not be
hunted out. Persecution was therefore local and sporadic.
But when danger threatened the Empire in the latter half
of the century, civil disobedience could not be tolerated.
Refusal to worship the Emperor was tantamount to treason,
and it is not surprising that under Marcus Aurelius the
measures taken against the Christians were more severe and
actual persecution more frequent. Public opinion, among
the educated and the uneducated alike, supported this
increased sternness towards a sect which was thought to be
sapping the Empire's morale.

The Christians, on their side, did not suffer in complete
silence. There were educated men among them capable of
both lecturing and writing in defence of their beliefs and
conduct, and this they felt it their duty to do, especially as
they knew that their condemnation was unjust. From the
time of Hadrian down to the end of the century, a number
of " Apologies " were written in defence of Christianity,
addressed in most cases to the reigning Emperor. Of these,
several have survived, but others are known only from
quotations in Eusebius or references elsewhere. Controversial pamphlets of a bygone age usually make dull read-

* See Chapter VI, pp. 143–7 for the policy of Trajan and Hadrian.

ing.   Even if the subject-matter is still of vital interest, the
arguments which appeal to one generation seldom appeal to
another, born several centuries later.   To a certain extent,
this is true of the second-century Apologies.   It would be
tedious to recapitulate their arguments in detail.   Some of
their favourite lines of approach, such as the proof from
prophecy, are unconvincing to modern readers, and it is
impossible at this date to say what influence they had upon
those to whom they were addressed.   But in so far as the
Apologies reveal the thoughts and lives of the men who
wrote them, they are of lasting interest.   It must have taken
no small degree of courage to write an open letter addressed
to the Emperor on behalf of a prohibited religion; yet,
although written by men in danger of death, these Apologies
are never subservient in tone; instead, they present the case
for Christianity with dignity and force, sometimes becoming
daringly outspoken in their denunciation of idolatry.
Indeed, the last of the second-century Apologies, written
by Tertullian, a brilliant North African lawyer, is apologetic
in one sense only, for it is a slashing attack upon the enemies
of the faith.

In A.D. 126, Hadrian visited Athens and was initiated into
the Eleusinian mysteries.   It is said to have been on this
occasion that a Christian teacher called Quadratus, a man of
influence in his locality, presented the Emperor with a
written defence of the Christian faith.   This, the earliest of
the Apologies, has now been lost, save for a fragment which
Eusebius quotes, to the effect that proof of our Lord's
miracles long remained in the persons whom he healed,
some of whom had survived until the writer's own day.   A
philosopher, called Aristides, also petitioned Hadrian on
behalf of his fellow-Christians.   His Apology, long believed to be lost, was rediscovered at the end of the nine-
teenth century.   He pleaded the innocency of the Christian
way of life, and claimed that the Christians are " they who,

more than all the nations on earth, have found the truth. For they know God, the Creator and Fashioner of all things through the only-begotten Son and the Holy Spirit; and beside him they worship no other God." Whether Hadrian was influenced by these petitions or not, we have no means of telling. He was certainly no persecutor. The attitude he adopted is made plain in his letter to Minucius Fundanus, Proconsul of Asia. In it, he insists that Christians must be fairly tried, but he does not relax existing regulations against them.

Justin Martyr may fairly stand as the representative of all the Apologists. His writings belong to the reign of Hadrian's successor, Antoninus Pius, but not only his written work but his whole life is characteristic of this phase of Christian defence. He was born of heathen parents in the Greek city of Neapolis in Samaria, and he was given a Greek education. It was not until many years later that he first read the Jewish Scriptures in a Greek translation. Considered apart from Christianity, the second century was an age which offered a man of good social position a comfortable life, and a fair degree of culture, but little that was inspiring. Art was at a low ebb; the drama was debased; literature was almost devoid of great writers, and the spirit of scientific inquiry was practically dead. Philosophy was no longer producing great original thinkers, like Plato and Aristotle, but instead a multitude of lesser men disputed endlessly over the merits of their rival schools of thought. Patriotism, during this period of security, was a sentiment proper to a law-abiding citizen, not a call to heroism, and pagan religion was unsatisfying, both intellectually and morally, to most thinking men. Justin, like many other educated men of his day, was aware that his life lacked the motive power of any great ideal, and he sought satisfaction in philosophy. In his *Dialogue with Trypho*, he has given his own account of his researches.

" Being at first desirous of personally conversing with one of these men ", he writes, " I surrendered myself to a certain Stoic; and, having spent a considerable time with him, when I had not acquired any further knowledge of God (for he did not know himself, and said such instruction was unnecessary), I left him and betook myself to another, who was called a Peripatetic, and as he fancied, shrewd. And this man, after having entertained me for the first few days, requested me to settle the fee, in order that our intercourse might not be unprofitable. Him, too, for this reason I abandoned, believing him to be no philosopher at all. But when my soul was eagerly desirous to hear the peculiar and choice philosophy, I came to a Pythagorean, very celebrated—a man who thought much of his own wisdom. And then, when I had an interview with him, willing to become his hearer and disciple, he said, ' What then? Are you acquainted with music, astronomy, and geometry? Do you expect to perceive any of those things which conduce to a happy life, if you have not been first informed on those points which wean the soul from sensible objects, and render it fitted for objects which appertain to the mind?' " *

Sadly dashed by this reception, Justin admitted his ignorance, and went away to think the matter over. He decided that it would take too long, were he to attempt to make good the deficiencies of his earlier education, and he reluctantly gave up the notion of becoming a Pythagorean. Finally it occurred to him to join the Platonists, and at last he achieved a measure of success.

" I thereupon spent as much of my time as possible with one who had lately settled in our city—a sagacious man, holding a high position among the Platonists—and I progressed, and made the greatest improvements daily. And the perception of immaterial things quite overpowered me, and the contemplation of ideas furnished my mind with wings, so that in a little while I supposed that I had become wise; and such was my stupidity, I expected forthwith to look upon God, for this is the end of Plato's philosophy."

* *Dialogue with Trypho*, Chapter 2. Ante-Nicene Christian Library, Vol. 2.

It was while he was in this frame of mind that he one day felt a longing for solitude, and set out for a quiet place which he often visited, where the fields came down to the sea. Usually he could count on being alone in such a retired spot, and he was surprised to find that an old man, " by no means contemptible in appearance ", was following him at a little distance. Presently they fell into conversation. The old man declared that he was searching for some members of his household about whom he felt concern. He was, in fact, a Christian, but of this Justin was not at first aware. The two were soon deep in the kind of discussion which Justin loved, the old man attacking and Justin earnestly defending the claim that through philosophy men could learn the truth about God. At last the old man boldly referred Justin to the writings of the prophets, " men more ancient than all those who are esteemed philosophers, both righteous and beloved of God, who spoke by the Divine Spirit, and foretold events which would take place, and which are now taking place ". Justin was deeply impressed, and listened with attention to what the old man told him both about the prophets and about Christ, the Son of God whom they foretold. Finally they parted, the old man's last words to Justin being:

" Pray that, above all things, the gates of light may be opened to you; for these things cannot be perceived or understood by all, but only by the man to whom God and his Christ have imparted wisdom."

This was the turning point in Justin's life. He did not see the old man again, but he followed his advice and studied the Scriptures. He had already been impressed by the fortitude with which Christian martyrs met their death. His conversion was partly the result of intellectual conviction, partly it was due to the impression made upon him by the lives of those Christians with whom he came in contact.

When he became a Christian, Justin did not change his manner of life. He continued to wear a well-worn cloak, the outward sign of his calling as a philosopher, for to him the Christian faith was the true philosophy, the reward of his long search for truth. His conversion probably took place in Ephesus, and it was there that he was first led into controversy in defence of his beliefs. He has himself described how he was accosted by a Jew called Trypho, who hailed him as a philosopher and drew him into argument. The *Dialogue with Trypho* is a lengthy presentation of the Christian case against Judaism. Trypho may be an imaginary character, for the natural setting and the dialogue form are clearly modelled upon the Platonic dialogues. But if Justin is not recalling an actual incident, he is representing one that was typical both of his time and of his own life. The intellectual life of the day was centred in the lecture-rooms, which were to be found in every great city. There, philosophers of every school of thought expounded their ideas to all who cared to listen, and among them Christians, like Justin, found an opportunity to preach the Gospel to those who were seeking for knowledge. Discussions with the Jews can seldom have been as dispassionate as that described in the " Dialogue with Trypho ", for at that time Jewish hatred of Christianity often gave rise to acts of persecution, and Christians in return spoke and wrote bitterly about the Jews. But Trypho is depicted by Justin as a very civil antagonist, as well as an able one. At some points the Jew certainly had the better of the argument. His knowledge of Hebrew enabled him to detect the fallacy in the interpretation which Christian preachers put upon certain passages in Old Testament prophecy. He knew, for example, that the word mistranslated " a virgin " in Isaiah's prophecy, " Behold, a virgin shall conceive and bear a son ",* really meant a young woman, and was no

* *Isa.* 7. 14.

argument for or against our Lord's virgin birth. However, as so often happens in these discussions, neither opponent convinced the other, but they parted with expressions of mutual esteem.

From Ephesus, Justin went to Rome, and in that he was following the usual custom of philosophers, for they were wont to travel from city to city, speaking in lecture-rooms or receiving private pupils. In Rome, Justin taught those who chose to come to him at his lodgings, and he also disputed in public with some of the pagan philosophers. His first " Apology ", addressed to the Emperor Antoninus Pius, his natural and adopted sons, the sacred Senate and the whole Roman people, was written about A.D. 148, and, from that time onwards, Justin must have been a marked man. His " Apology " is a demand for justice and for an investigation into the charges commonly laid against Christians. He vigorously rebuts the charge of atheism, asserting that the supposed gods are really demons and were exposed as such by Socrates, the great philosopher who was stupidly condemned on the very same charge of atheism. He later describes Christian life and worship, in order to show the utter absurdity of the popular accusations, saying all he possibly can without revealing the inmost secrets to the profane, and he outlines the Christian faith. Throughout he writes as a Greek and a philosopher. To him, Greek philosophy, like Hebrew prophecy, was a preparation for the coming of Christ. It was a partial, imperfect expression of the Word of God, an anticipation of the perfect revelation in Christ:

" We have been taught that Christ is the first-born of God, and we have declared above that he is the Word of whom every race of men were partakers; and those who lived reasonably are Christians, even though they have been thought atheists; as among the Greeks, Socrates and Heraclitus, and men like them; and among the barbarians, Abraham, and Ananias, and Azarias, and Misael, and Elias, and many others whose actions and names we now decline to recount, because we know it would be tedious." *

But though he writes as a philosopher, he pretends to no secret knowledge, as the Gnostics did; on the contrary, it is his boast that:

" Among us these things can be heard and learned from persons who do not even know the forms of the letters, who are uneducated and barbarous in speech, though wise and believing in mind." †

Justin was thus the spokesman for the ordinary Christian to the men of his own day, and it is not as a philosopher, but as a Christian martyr that he is still remembered.

To be a Christian Apologist in the second century was to court danger. No harm seems to have befallen Justin on account of the petition which he presented to the Emperor, but he soon made a personal enemy by his arguments with the pagan philosophers in Rome. A certain cynic, called Crescens, whom he had often refuted, plotted to bring about his death and that of his disciple Tatian. This he could have done without much difficulty by denouncing them both as Christians, but Justin was warned in time and escaped, probably by leaving Rome. Before he went, he addressed a strong protest to the Roman citizens against what seemed to him a particularly flagrant miscarriage of justice. A Christian woman, who had long endured the shame of living with a vicious heathen husband, at length abandoned all hope of reforming him and divorced him, as she was legally entitled to do. The man determined to be revenged on her, and denounced her as a Christian. She then appealed to the Emperor for time to settle her affairs,

* Justin: *First Apology*, Chapter XLVI.
† Idem, ibid., Chapter LX.

which was granted, and her former husband, in his impatience, went to work to secure the death of the teacher who had converted her, a certain Ptolemæus, who was in prison on account of his faith. His scheme succeeded. Ptolemæus was asked one question only: was he a Christian? He confessed that he was, and was at once condemned to death. Another Christian called Lucius rose in court to protest against this summary procedure and the injustice of condemning a man who was guilty of no crime. Urbicus, the prefect who was trying the case, merely replied: " You also seem to me to be such an one ". To which Lucius answered: " Most certainly I am ", and was condemned to death on the spot. A second protester shared the same fate.

About ten years after these events, Justin was again living in Rome and teaching all who would come to him in his private lodgings. Marcus Aurelius had succeeded Antoninus Pius as Emperor, and was engaged in a war with the Parthians, in defence of his eastern frontier. In consequence of the danger that threatened the Empire, stricter measures were taken against all those whose loyalty was in doubt, including the Christians, and Justin, with six others, was arrested and brought to trial before Rusticus, the prefect of Rome. An account of his trial has fortunately been preserved. Unlike most of the later Acts of the Martyrs, it is matter-of-fact and reliable, containing no romantic or miraculous additions. The prefect turned first to the most important prisoner, and ordered Justin to obey the Emperor, in other words to offer sacrifice. This Justin refused to do in the Name of Jesus Christ. He was then asked what doctrines he professed, to which he replied:

" I have endeavoured to learn all doctrines; but I have acquiesced at last in the true doctrines, those namely of the Christians, even though they do not please those who hold false opinions."

Rusticus next demanded to know where the Christians assembled.   Justin refused to name any place but his own lodgings, " above one Martinus, at the Timiotinian bath ", where he was in the habit of teaching all who came to him. Rusticus then questioned the other prisoners, one of whom was a woman.   All confessed that they were Christians. Rusticus demanded: " Did Justin make you Christians? " * At least three of them claimed that their parents had taught them to be Christians.

" Pæon: ' From our parents we received this good confession.'

" Euelpistus: ' I willingly heard the words of Justin.   But from my parents also I learned to be a Christian.'

" Rusticus: ' Where are your parents? '

" Euelpistus: ' In Cappadocia.'

" Hierax: ' Christ is our true father, and faith in him is our mother; and my earthly parents died; and I, when I was driven from Iconium in Phrygia, came here.' "

The prefect then turned upon Justin and demanded whether he really supposed that if he was scourged and beheaded he would " ascend into heaven to receive some recompense ".

" Justin said, ' I do not suppose it, but I know and am fully persuaded of it '."

The prefect gave them all a final opportunity to obey the Emperor by sacrificing to the gods, and, when they all refused, he condemned them to be scourged and beheaded.

" The holy martyrs having glorified God, and having gone forth to the accustomed place, were beheaded, and perfected their testimony in the confession of the Saviour.   And some of the faithful having secretly removed their bodies, laid them in a suitable place, the grace of our Lord Jesus Christ having wrought along with them, to whom be glory for ever and ever."

* The Martyrdom of Justin and Others, A-N.C.L., Vol. II.

Of the Christians who suffered with Justin, one was a
" servant of Cæsar ", another, Liberianus, was probably a
freedman. It is unlikely that any one of them could have
written a reasoned " Apology " for his faith. Yet these
ordinary unlearned men and women, who composed the
majority of every congregation, had their part to play in
the defence of Christianity. In time of persecution, any
one of them might be called on to answer for his faith in a
court of law, and his steadfastness would be more convincing than any argument he could bring forward. Christians were well aware of this, and they were aware, too, that
those who are unaccustomed to law-courts can easily be
shaken and confused by clever questioning. To meet this
danger, something not unlike a training for martyrdom was
evolved by the early Church. Christians were instructed
what answers they should give in court, and were schooled
in their behaviour. They were encouraged to endure hardship and to look upon suffering as a privilege. The " Acts
of the Martyrs ", the letters which St Ignatius wrote on his
way to the lions, and passages from the New Testament
foretelling persecution, were frequently read aloud to the
congregation. Martyrs were venerated, and to be buried
near the tomb of one of them was accounted a great honour.
Confessors, those who had been imprisoned or had suffered
for their faith in other ways, were treated with deep respect.
Christians in prison were visited and encouraged by their
fellow believers, and were urged to be steadfast to the end.
Before long, the veneration of martyrs and confessors was
to lead to abuses, but in the second century the fostering of
the spirit of martyrdom was an essential part of the Church's
defence against persecution by the State. Justin, Apologist
and Martyr, typifies both lines of defence, word and deed,
learned argument and courageous endurance. Neither
would have been complete without the other.

The Apologies were intended to influence, not only

the Emperors, but educated opinion generally. Some, like the " Epistle to Diognetus ", were addressed to intelligent pagan inquirers. The majority of educated men at this time were not prepared to give Christianity a sympathetic hearing, but even those most strongly prejudiced against the new religion were compelled to take it more seriously when it was defended by such men as Aristides, Justin, Athenagoras (an Athenian scholar), and Apollonius, who was renowned for his culture and philosophy. Fragments have survived of a lengthy and brilliant attack on Christianity, written towards the end of the second century by a pagan called Celsus. Celsus regarded Christianity as subversive, a threat to the inner security of the Empire. His book, which was entitled *The True Word*, was intended as a counterblast to Christian propaganda, and it certainly must have afforded considerable entertainment to those who shared his opinions, for his style is both vigorous and biting. He said what outraged pagans were doubtless in the habit of saying whenever Christianity was mentioned, but he said it better and more pungently.

Celsus was equally disgusted by the ignorance and by the vulgarity displayed by the adherents of this new cult. " They always bring in their ' Do not examine but believe ' and ' Thy faith shall save thee ' ", he writes, and he quotes the Christians as saying : " ' Let no cultured person draw near, none wise, none sensible ; for all that kind of thing we count evil ; but if any man is ignorant, if any is wanting in sense and culture, if any is a fool, let him come boldly.' " He follows this up by describing the insidious methods by which Christians spread their faith.

" We see, indeed," he writes, " in private houses, workers in wool and leather, and fullers, and persons of the most uninstructed and rustic character, not venturing to utter a word in the presence of their elders and wiser masters ; but when they get hold of the children privately, and certain women as ignorant as themselves, they pour forth wonderful statements to the effect that they ought not to give heed to their father and to their teachers, but should obey them; that the former are foolish and stupid, and neither know nor can perform anything that is really good, being preoccupied with empty trifles; that they alone know how men ought to live, and that, if the children obey them, they will both be happy themselves, and will make their home happy also." *

It is impossible to doubt that Celsus is here describing a scene which he actually witnessed. Such scenes must often have been enacted in wealthy households where Christian slaves and servile workers were employed. They account for the rapidity with which Christianity spread to some of the noblest families in Rome, and they account, too, for some of the bitterness felt towards Christians by pagans, who resented what they regarded as the corruption of their children. A religion which welcomed slaves, ignorant men, and sinners, offended the sense of decency in Celsus and his like—in other words, it hurt their pride.

As to Christian teaching, that seems to Celsus just the absurd kind of doctrine which might be expected from such ignoramuses. Its root fault, in his opinion, is that it gives man an importance in the universe which he does not possess. The whole universe is the work of God, and he does not care for one part of it more than for another. " In no way is man better in God's sight than ants and bees ", says Celsus. The Christians and the Jews in their churches and synagogues are " like a swarm of bats—or ants, creeping out of their nest—or frogs, holding a symposium round a swamp—or worms in conventicle in a corner of the mud —debating which of them are the more sinful, and saying, ' God reveals all things to us beforehand and gives us warning; he forsakes the whole universe and the course of the

* A.-N.C.L., xxiii, 136 seq. Quoted by Kidd, *Documents Illustrative of the History of the Church*, Vol. I, No. 61.

heavenly spheres, and all this great earth he neglects, to dwell with us alone; to us alone he despatches heralds, and never ceases to send and to seek how we may dwell with him forever ' ".* The conception of God as the Father who cares for all his creatures and loves individual men and women is unthinkable to Celsus, and he dismisses it as childish folly. As for the Incarnation, that strikes him as being equally absurd, but even more revolting. He conceives of God as being perfectly good, perfectly beautiful, and perfectly happy. Any change could only be for the worse, and therefore God is by definition incapable of change. Celsus knows about the life of Jesus and its poverty; its many humiliations and sufferings confirms him in his opinion. He classes the miracles with the wonders performed by mountebanks in the streets. He utterly denies the fact of the resurrection. His explanation of Christian belief in it has been echoed by many later sceptics:

" Do you imagine . . . that while alive he was of no assistance to himself, but that when he was dead he rose again, and showed the marks of his punishment, and how his hands were pierced with nails: who beheld this? A half-frantic woman, as you state, and some other one, perhaps, of those who were engaged in the same system of delusion, who had either dreamed so, owing to a peculiar state of mind, or under the influence of a wandering imagination had formed to himself an appearance according to his own wishes, which has been the case with numberless individuals; or, which is most probable, one who desired to impress others with this portent, and by such a falsehood to furnish an occasion to impostors like himself." †

Celsus completes his indictment by some acid comments on Christian disunion. " Faction ", he says, " is their

* *Conflict of Religions in Early Roman Empire*, by T. R. Glover, Chapter VIII.

† A.-N.C.L., xxiii, 58.   Kidd: op. cit. No. 60.

keynote, taken from the Jews at first; and faction splits them up into innumerable sects beside the ' great church '. They all say, ' Believe if you wish to be saved, or else depart ', but how is a man to know which to adhere to? Should he toss for it ? "

The attitude of Celsus towards Christianity is surprisingly modern. But scepticism, like faith, is to be found in many ages in various guises. It is most prevalent among those who have cultivated their intellects by abstract thinking and by the learning that can be acquired through books, to the neglect of other channels of experience. In the civilized Græco-Roman world, it was quite as common as it is today. Celsus, for all his acute intelligence, had a fatal blind spot. He could study the life of Christ with attention, and yet assert that Jesus was a mere impostor, a charlatan. He was presumably equally blind in judging the characters of the Christians whom he actually met. Upon men such as Celsus, neither the arguments of the Apologists, nor the courage of the martyrs, made any impression.

The civilization of Christian Europe was born of the union of two great traditions: Greek thought and Hebrew religion. The two are so different, in some respects so opposed, that even to-day it is possible to distinguish the two chief strains in our diverse inheritance, and to say: " This we owe to the classics and that to the Old Testament." In the second century, the Christian Apologists championed revealed religion, foreshadowed in the prophets and realized in Christ, and some of them were prepared to reject the wisdom of the Greeks as being mere foolishness in the eyes of God. But others, like Justin Martyr, or Apollonius, the Christian philosopher martyred in the reign of Commodus, believed that truth is one, and were convinced that there was no real opposition between philosophy and revealed religion. It would have been as hard for them to abandon the conclusions of the philosophers as it would be

P

for a modern scholar to reject the methods and findings of science.   Their aim was to show that Christianity and philosophy were two aspects of the same Truth, and they wished to achieve a harmony of the two traditions.   In this they only partially succeeded.

Of the Christians who, carried away by their enthusiasm, poured scorn not only on the idolatrous character of pagan religion, but on pagan learning as well, the ablest was Tatian, a man apt to carry all his ideas to extremes.   By birth an Assyrian, he was converted to Christianity by studying the Scriptures, and was for a time a pupil of Justin Martyr in Rome.   He had none of the gentleness and moderation of his master, nor was his judgement so sound. He later fell into heresy and returned to the East, where the work for which he is best known, his *Diatessaron*,* enjoyed great popularity.   But it was while he was still an orthodox member of the Church that he wrote his *Oratio adversus Græcos* or *Oration Against the Greeks*, in which he mocked at Greek culture, identified the pagan gods with demons, and claimed that the Old Testament was superior to all the literature of Greece, on account of its greater antiquity as well as its inspiration.   In the course of this argument, he describes his own conversion.   He tells how, having sampled all that pagan religion had to offer, its mysteries, its sacrifices, its superstitious rites, he sought to discover the truth in solitude.   He continues:

" And while I was giving my most earnest attention to the matter, I happened to meet with certain barbaric writings, too old to be compared with the opinions of the Greeks, and too divine to be compared with their errors; and I was led to put faith in these by the unpretending cast of the language, the in-artificial characters of the writers, the foreknowledge displayed of future events, the excellent quality of the precepts, and the declaration of the government of the universe as centred in one

* See Chapter VIII, p. 195.

Being. And my soul being taught of God, I discerned that the former class of writings lead to condemnation, but that these put an end to the slavery that is in the world, and rescue us from a multiplicity of rulers and ten thousand tyrants, while they give us, not indeed what we had not before received, but what we had received but were prevented by error from retaining." *

The influence of those " barbaric writings ", which we call the Old Testament, was indeed remarkable. Justin Martyr, Tatian, Athenagoras, and Theophilus, the author of *To Autolycus*, all by their own admission owed their conversion to the impression made on them by reading the Old Testament. Fortunately, most of them did not, like Tatian, at once jettison all that they had previously learned from Greek philosophy. Had they done so, their attempts to win for Christianity a favourable hearing among educated people would have been foredoomed to failure, and Christian thought would ultimately have been seriously impoverished.

Towards the close of the second century Christianity gained some new defenders in a group of young and able Roman lawyers. One of them, Tertullian, came from North Africa, and his *Apology* will be considered along with his other writings in a later chapter. Another, Minucius Felix, wrote a dialogue called *Octavius*, which is utterly unlike Tertullian's *Apology* in character and very like it in some of its arguments, for *Octavius* also is a defence of Christianity. That one borrowed ideas from the other seems almost certain, but whether they were personally known to each other is not sure. Tertullian's *Apology* is a torrent of forensic eloquence, while the dialogue by Minucius is as lovely and untroubled as were the still waters of the psalmist.

The *Octavius* is written in memory of a friend. Minu-

* Tatian: *Oratio adversus Graecos*, xxix. Kidd: op. cit., No. 50.

cius and Octavius were friends from boyhood; both were practising lawyers; both were converted to Christianity. The Dialogue records one singularly happy incident in a short holiday which the two friends spent together by the sea at Ostia. One year, towards the end of summer, Octavius came up to Rome on business, and at once sought out Minucius. For two days they talked, trying to make up for the time during which they had been separated, and then, as it was vacation and legal work was slack on account of the vintage, they decided to go to Ostia, a seaside resort fifteen miles from Rome, and enjoy the sea-bathing together. There they fell in with Cæcilius Natalis, a friend of theirs who was still a pagan, and the three joined forces. Minucius recounts what followed:

" One morning at dawn we happened to be walking along the bank of the Tiber towards the sea; the gentle breeze invigorated our limbs and the walk over the sand, as it yielded beneath our soft tread, was especially delightful. Cæcilius noticed an image of Serapis and, after the custom of the superstitious vulgar, put his hand to his mouth and kissed it.

" Thereupon Octavius said: ' Brother Marcus, it is unworthy of an honest man to leave one who in and out of the house is your constant companion, in such blind and vulgar ignorance. On a fine day like this, how can you allow him to do homage to stones, even though they are fashioned in the likeness of the gods, anointed with oil, and crowned with garlands? You must be aware that the shame of his error will recoil as much upon you as upon him.'

" While Octavius was speaking, we were half-way between Ostia and the sea, and were already nearing the open beach, where the gentle waves, which laved the furthest stretch of sands, extended, and as it were laid it out for a promenade. The sea is always restless, even when the winds are still, and although it did not reach the shore in white, foaming waves, we were highly delighted to see it curling and winding round and about our feet, when we dipped them at the water's edge. . . .

" In this manner we walked on slowly and quietly along the

shore of the gently winding beach, beguiling the way with conversation, which turned upon Octavius's account of his voyage."

The three friends paused to watch some small boys playing " ducks and drakes " with flat shells collected from the beach. Both Octavius and Marcus Minucius enjoyed the unself-conscious movements of the children and their eagerness over their game; but Cæcilius remained indifferent, silent, and aloof. At last Minucius inquired into the cause of his unusual solemnity. Cæcilius replied that he had been hurt by the way in which Octavius had attempted to score a point against him indirectly, through blaming Minucius. In return, he challenged Octavius to a serious scientific discussion of their religious differences and proposed that Minucius should act as umpire. This was readily agreed to by the others, and the three settled themselves comfortably on a breakwater, with Minucius seated in the middle to keep the two disputants apart.

Cæcilius, having been trained in rhetoric, as were all educated men of his day, embarked upon a lengthy attack on Christianity, first denying on philosophic grounds its fundamental doctrine of the benevolence of the Creator and then repeating all the usual slanders against Christians. He first adopted the position of the Sceptics: that real knowledge is unattainable and man should recognize his own ignorance. He felt it as a grievance that " certain people— people, too, ignorant of learning, unlettered, and unacquainted even with the meanest arts—should pronounce definitely upon the universe ", pretending to a knowledge which philosophers did not possess. He then toyed with the Epicurean conception of the universe as a " fortuitous concourse of atoms ". He made great play with the disasters of nature to prove that the conception of a beneficent Creator is not borne out by the facts. Shifting his ground, he spoke in defence of the traditional Roman religion, alleging that the victories of Roman arms proved the value of the rites they practised, and justified their reliance on augury. He then poured scorn on the enemies of the gods: " certain fellows belonging to a party whose case is hopeless, proscribed and desperate ". He described them as a number of ignorant men and credulous women, dragged from the lowest dregs of the population. " It is a people that lurks in darkness and shuns the light, silent in public, talkative in corners," he said. He represented them as members of a vicious secret society which should be utterly rooted out, and he repeated the usual scandalous charges that Christians indulged in abominable rites which included human sacrifice and incestuous orgies. He mocked at their belief in the resurrection of the body and the vain courage which their faith inspired. Finally, he quoted with approbation the opinion of Hiero, who, when asked what he thought about the gods, said: " The more carefully and deliberately I examine the matter, the more obscure does the truth appear." Suspension of judgement was the only course for a wise man.

Satisfied that he had made a good debating speech, Cæcilius sat down, well pleased with himself, and his good temper quite restored. Octavius then began his reply and answered him point by point. He insisted that sneers at Christian poverty were irrelevant, as a theory should be judged on its merits and not according to the social position of its supporters. He defended man's right to exercise his reason on all matters, even the highest. He claimed that, to the unbiased observer, the universe did present an appearance of order and purposeful arrangement which could best be explained by the hypothesis of a benevolent Creator. One instance that he gave comes home. " God takes thought not only for the universe but for each of its parts," he said. " Britain lacks sunshine, but is refreshed by the warmth of the sea that surrounds it." He gave arguments for the unity of God, and called in evidence not only the poets and philosophers, but the common people as well, for he said: " When the common people stretch out their hands to heaven, they say nothing but ' God ' and ' God is great ' or ' God is true ', ' if God grant '." He then attacked the absurdities of pagan religion; the myths of the gods, the irrationality of image-worship, the animal cults, the superstitious rites. He attributed augury to the work of demons and asserted that " the Romans owed their greatness, not to piety but to sacrilege that went unpunished ". " All the territory that the Romans now hold, cultivate, and occupy has been acquired by barefaced theft; the temples have all been built with the proceeds of the spoils of war, the destruction of cities, the murder of priests, the plundering of the gods."

Turning to the slanders against Christians, Octavius said that he, too, had believed them before his conversion, without attempting to verify them. As an advocate, he had undertaken the defence of criminals, but had thought that Christians did not deserve a hearing. " Sometimes, out of pity for them," he said, " we treated them with even greater cruelty, torturing them to force them to deny their faith, so as to save their lives." He utterly denied the abominable accusations against the Christians, saying that only minds steeped in idolatry could even have thought of them. He answered the objections levelled against the doctrine of the resurrection of the body and of judgement to come, saying that as man was originally made by God, so he can be re-made by him. In nature, he found a foreshadowing of the resurrection. " Flowers die and revive . . . the body also has its spring, which we must wait for." The charge that most Christians were paupers, he said, was no shame, but a glory. " Who can be poor if he wants nothing, if he does not long for what is another's, if he is rich in God ? " As to the tribulations which Christians endured, these were not a proof that their God could not help them, but were a discipline by which God purified them, like gold in a furnace. " We do not show our wisdom in our dress but in our heart "; he concluded, " we do not proclaim great things but live them; and are proud of having obtained what philosophers have sought with their utmost efforts but have failed to find."

When Octavius had finished, a silence fell, which was broken by Cæcilius, who congratulated Octavius and joyfully admitted his own defeat. He said that he only waited for further instruction before becoming a Christian himself, and the three friends left the sea-shore together, united in a single happiness.*

During the centuries of persecution, Christians were given little opportunity to defend themselves in courts of law, yet the defence of Christianity was maintained unceasingly. Apologists petitioning the Emperor, philosophers lecturing to their students, martyrs enduring torture for their faith, slaves secretly instructing their masters' children, friends on holiday arguing together, all played their part, and, in spite of persecution, in spite of unpopularity, in spite of malicious lies, the number of Christians steadily increased. " We are but of yesterday," wrote Tertullian triumphantly in his *Apology* at the end of the second century, " yet we have filled all that is yours, cities, islands, fortified towns, country towns, centres of meeting, even camps, tribes, classes of public attendants, the palace, the senate, the forum; we have left you only your temples." Tertullian was an orator. The victory he was celebrating was not yet complete—far from it—but the spirit that made victory possible was there.

* *The Octavius of Minucius Felix*, trans. J. H. Freese, Translations of Christian Literature Series, S.P.C.K.

BOOKS FOR FURTHER READING

Christian Apologetics of the Second Century, by Philip Carrington. S.P.C.K. 1921.

Conflict of Religions in the Ancient World, by T. R. Glover.

The Octavius of Minucius Felix, trans, J. H. Freese, M.A.   Translations of Christian Literature, S.P.C.K.

Documents Illustrative of the History of the Church, ed. B. J. Kidd. S.P.C.K.

No. 24. Quadratus.

   „   26. Aristides.

   „   29. " Epistle to Diognetus ".

   „   39–49. Justin Martyr.

   „   50. Tatian.

   „   58–59. Athenagoras.

   „   60–61. Celsus.

   „   66. Minucius Felix.

CHAPTER X

The Christian Mystery: Worship in the Early Church

"AS to the main questions, in regard to Providence and God I accept your belief"; exclaimed the pagan Cæcilius, convinced by the arguments of his Christian friend, Octavius, "I recognize the purity of your sect, which is henceforth my own." At this point, the dialogue comes to a satisfactory conclusion, but the conversion of Cæcilius was not concluded; it had only begun. Before he could be admitted to full membership of the Christian Church, he must pass through a period of instruction and probation as a catechumen, and then be baptized. Until after his baptism, he would be rigidly excluded from the mystery of Christian worship, though he might attend meetings of the Church which were held for instruction in the Scriptures, as well as the special instruction given to the catechumens. It was this extreme secrecy which lent colour to the popular rumours of scandalous orgies and murderous rites perpetrated by the Christians behind locked doors. Used as we are to public worship which is open to all, nothing would seem easier than to have given the lie to all these malicious absurdities by admitting any who cared to come to Christian services. But, in the early centuries, this was unthinkable. The early Christians were aware, as we are not, of their separation from the world "which knew not God". They were surrounded, not by people nominally Christian, but by people frankly heathen. They were God's Chosen People, his Redeemed, and corporately

THE ATRIUM OF A ROMAN HOUSE

they were the Body of Christ, continuing his redemptive work in the world. Especially was this so when they met for prayer and for the celebration of the Eucharist. The worshipping Church prayed in the name of Christ, as very members incorporate in his mystical Body, and therefore no one who had not been made a member of that Body by baptism could take part.

If we follow Cæcilius in imagination through his catechumenate, his baptism, and his initiation into the mystery of Christian worship, we shall be able to form a fairly clear idea of the practice of the Church in the second and third centuries, when the forms of her services had already become established in general outline.

For the next couple of weeks after the momentous conversation on the sea-shore at Ostia, Cæcilius was frequently in the company of his two Christian friends. All three had returned to Rome, and in their leisure time, after their legal business was finished, both Minucius Felix and Octavius gladly gave him further instruction. All that he learnt confirmed Cæcilius in his determination to become a Christian, and he begged his friends to take him with them to the Christian meeting-place on the following Sunday. This they agreed to do, but they warned him that he would have to leave after the first part of the service was over.

It was nearly an hour before the dawn of Sunday morning when Octavius and Minucius called for him. The three friends moved quietly along the dark streets of Rome, through which the market-carts, prohibited in daytime, were still busily rumbling. His two friends led Cæcilius by a devious route, taking every precaution to see that they were not followed, and brought him at last to the side door of a very large house, which belonged to one of the noblest families in Rome. Minucius, knowing the prearranged signal, knocked on the door, which was opened immediately. The deacon who guarded it recognized Minucius and Octavius, and gave them a friendly greeting; but he looked curiously at Cæcilius.

" Who is the third ? " he said.

" An honest inquirer," replied Minucius. " I vouch for him."

" And so do I," said Octavius.

" Pass in," said the door-keeper, " I am satisfied.'

As the three friends entered, they saw that many of the faithful had arrived before them. Already more than a hundred men and women had assembled, and others were arriving by different entrances in twos and threes. They stood chatting together in little groups, waiting until it should be time for the meeting to begin. Octavius and Minucius took the opportunity to lead Cæcilius forward and present him to the bishop and the presbyters, who were already assembled in the *tablinum*, an inner sanctum raised a couple of steps above the level of the main hall. The hall itself—or *atrium*, to give it its Roman name *—was of palatial dimensions. Pillars supported the roof, and in the centre was the usual *impluvium*, or rain-water tank, open to the sky. This tank was occasionally used for baptisms. The dais on which the bishop's throne was placed was at the end of the hall farthest from the entrance, and immediately below, at the foot of the steps that led to it, was a large stone table known as the *cartibulum*. In heathen households, the ancestral shrine and the sacred hearth with its undying fire stood in the *tablinum*, and there all important family rites were celebrated. A few changes had sufficed to adapt the whole lay-out to the needs of the Christian Church. The pagan shrine had been removed; the bishop had taken the place usually occupied by the head of the family; the *cartibulum* served as a communion table; the spacious *atrium* provided ample room for the congregation.

As the time for the commencement of the service approached, a deacon led Cæcilius to the back of the hall, where a number of catechumens and some pagan inquirers like himself were gathered, while Octavius and Minucius took their places among the congregation of the faithful. The pillars supporting the roof divided the hall into aisles, and the men stood on one side, the women on the other, all facing the dais. The bishop seated himself on his throne, which was draped in white linen, and the presbyters took their places in a semi-circle round him. Two of the deacons stood one on either side of the bishop's throne, and these now signed to the congregation to be silent. In the hush that followed, the bishop gave the customary greeting: " Peace be unto you," and the people replied: " And with thy spirit."

A lectern had been placed at the foot of the steps leading to the dais, and from there a reader began to intone a lesson from the Old Testament, enunciating the words clearly so

* See the account of the merchant's house in the Introduction.

that everyone could hear.   The lesson that morning happened to be from Exodus, and told of the gift of manna to
the children of Israel wandering in the wilderness.   When
it was finished, a soloist standing on the steps of the dais
began an elaborate rendering of psalm 107 (A.V.):

" O give thanks unto the Lord for he is good : for his mercy
endureth for ever. . . .
" They wandered in the wilderness in a solitary way : they
found no city to dwell in.
" Hungry and thirsty, their soul fainted in them.
" Then they cried unto the Lord in their trouble and he delivered them out of their distresses."

" Oh that men would praise the Lord for his goodness ",
sang the church in unison, with a heart-felt sincerity which
was new to Cæcilius.   After a short reading from one of
St Paul's letters and another psalm, a passage from St
Matthew's Gospel followed—the feeding of the five thousand.   Then the bishop, still seated, began to preach.   He
expounded to the assembled church the meaning of the
Scriptures which had just been read.   He explained that the
deliverance of the children of Israel in the wilderness was
but a type of their own far greater deliverance.   They, too,
had been hungry of soul and about to perish, but Christ had
given them bread from heaven.

" For he satisfieth the longing soul, and filleth the hungry
soul with goodness."

As the bishop ceased speaking, one of the deacons called
out : " Bow down your heads for a blessing, O ye catechumens."
The catechumens and inquirers bowed their heads, and
the bishop, raising his hand, gave them his blessing.
Then the deacons all cried out : " Let the catechumens
depart.   Let no catechumen remain."

And, in another minute, Cæcilius found himself in the street, where the first light of dawn was beginning to appear.

As he made his way home, Cæcilius hardly noticed the streets through which he passed, for his thoughts were concentrated with a longing, which he had not previously experienced, upon that mystery from which he was excluded. Octavius, Minucius, and the others were at that moment receiving the " bread from heaven " of which the bishop had spoken; so much he knew. But the meaning of those words he had yet to understand. He thought over the service to which he had just listened and wondered why it had so deeply moved him. Nothing had been done for effect; there had been no deliberate stimulation of the emotions, as in the pagan mysteries into which he had been initiated. Everyone, even the bishop, had worn ordinary everyday clothes and had behaved in a perfectly natural manner. It was the words themselves, he decided, that had moved him, the words of these wonderful writings that the Christians possessed—that, and the absolute conviction with which the congregation made its responses. He resolved to borrow whatever copies he could obtain of the Scriptures and study them for himself.

In the autumn, Cæcilius was formally admitted to the catechumenate. The early Church did not dismiss the pagan gods as unreal, but thought of them as demons, malicious and fallen spirits who delighted to deceive men into worshipping them. The rite of initiation into the catechumenate therefore included a formulary of exorcism. The presbyter to whom the bishop had delegated this task next signed Cæcilius with the cross on his forehead, and placed a particle of salt in his mouth, saying: " Cæcilius, receive the salt of wisdom . . ." He then stretched his hand over him in prayer, and the rite was ended.

Cæcilius was anxious to be baptized as soon as possible, but he was told that the admission of converts into the

Church took place at Easter, and he must wait until then. Meanwhile, he was given regular instruction together with the other catechumens.

During Lent, this training reached its climax. Those who wished to be baptized at Easter gave in their names, Cæcilius among them. They were then presented to the faithful, who joined in prayer on their behalf and who might, if they saw good reason, object to any of the candidates. This " scrutiny ", as it was called, was repeated on several Sundays, and was accompanied by further attempts to defeat the powers of evil by exorcism. But the most important of the preliminary ceremonies was the *Traditio Symboli*, commonly known as the " Opening of the Ears ". Cæcilius and the other catechumens who were deemed to be ready for baptism, and were hence styled " competents ", presented themselves when the church met for worship on an appointed day in Lent. Then, in the presence of the whole congregation, the Church's creed, her *symbolum* or " pass-word " was solemnly delivered to them. It was the first of many occasions which would serve to remind them that they were henceforth soldiers of Christ, for, from the days of St Paul onwards, the Church used expressions drawn from army life and discipline to convey the need for loyalty and devotion in the service of Christ. All the evidence goes to show that the creed which Cæcilius and the other competents would be taught in Rome in the second century was substantially the same as that which we know as " The Apostles' Creed ". It was a simple statement of belief in God, the Father, Son, and Holy Spirit, and of the main facts about the Lord Jesus Christ. Originally it was expressed in Greek, but later it became the custom to divide the competents according to the language they habitually spoke and to teach the Creed in both Greek and Latin. There is good reason to believe that this Creed, the Church's " pass-word ", goes back in substance to the time of the

Q

apostles, or their immediate successors, having been handed on orally with great care from one generation of Christians to the next. It thus represents a tradition as old as that of the Gospels and of great authority. In some churches, but not in all, it was customary to deliver the four Gospels and the Lord's Prayer to the competents at the same ceremony. The *Traditio Symboli* was completed just before Easter, usually on Maundy Thursday, by the *Redditio Symboli*, when the competents in turn stood up before the congregation, renounced the devil, and declared their faith by repeating the Creed which they had learnt.

At last came the day to which Cæcilius had long been looking forward: the Eve of that Easter Day on which he was to be baptized. He had prepared himself, as he had been told to do, by prayer and fasting, and, not only his sponsors, but the whole church had prayed and fasted for his sake and for that of the other catechumens. Minucius was one of his sponsors, and Octavius, whose home was in the country, had made a special effort to come up to Rome for Easter, so that he could stand sponsor for him as well. In early times and in the country, baptisms often took place out of doors in shallow streams. Christians preferred to use running water, as being a fitter symbol for the living water of baptism. But in Rome and in other great cities, baptism out of doors was clearly impossible, especially in times of persecution. Often the rain-water tank in the *atrium* of the house where the church was accustomed to meet for prayer must have been used for this purpose; but at least as early as the third century Christians began to build baptisteries—special buildings attached to the house-church where they worshipped. One of the earliest of these baptisteries was in the catacombs, and there the font was a basin hollowed out of the rock, fed with running water from a spring.

In the second century, Easter was celebrated as a great

festival of redemption, and in this celebration the baptism of those newly converted had an important place. The whole church, including the catechumens, met on the Saturday night, and kept vigil together until the dawn of Easter morning. Cæcilius and the rest of the competents, who knew that their baptism would take place shortly before dawn, at first found it difficult to fix their attention on the series of readings from the Old Testament, interpersed with chants, with which the intervening time was filled. But, as one passage succeeded another—the Creation, the deliverance of Noah from the Deluge, the sacrifice of Isaac, the safe passage of the children of Israel through the Red Sea, Ezekiel's vision of the dry bones restored to life, Jonah's three days' sojourn in the belly of the whale—Cæcilius became aware that he was watching a great pageant of redemption, scenes from the vast drama of God's dealings with mankind. All these passages were familiar to him now; he had read them for himself; had been instructed in the symbolic meaning of these stories, and had observed them represented with pathetic simplicity upon the grave-stones in the catacombs. He had entered into a great tradition, and was fast making it his own. Much that had at first seemed to him barbarous or childish in this ancient new religion he now saw to be the " foolishness of God ", which is wiser than the wisdom of the philosophers.

The reader closed the book of Exodus, from which he had been reading the account of the origin of the Jewish Passover. The last lesson was from the Gospel of St John, and told of the Crucifixion of our Lord, and then the bishop began his sermon. " Christ our passover is sacrificed for us," he said, quoting from St Paul, " therefore let us keep the feast." His theme was redemption, and much of what he said was addressed especially to those about to be baptized. When he had finished, the candidates and their sponsors withdrew to the room where the baptism was to take place. There the candidates, stripped of their clothes, came forward in turn. In answer to questions from the officiant, Cæcilius affirmed his belief in God, the Father, Son, and Holy Ghost. He then stepped into the shallow basin which served as a font. The officiant poured water over his head three times, saying: " I baptize thee in the Name of the Father, and of the Son, and of the Holy Spirit." After that, his sponsors led him away to clothe him in the white garments which were always worn by neophytes.

In the early Church, it was usual for confirmation to follow immediately after baptism, so Cæcilius and the other neophytes were at once brought before the bishop. The bishop laid his hand on the head of each neophyte, saying: " In the name of the Father, and of the Son, and of the Holy Spirit. Peace be unto thee." Then he anointed him with consecrated oil, called *chrism*, and gave him the kiss of peace. Cæcilius and the others were now full members of the Church and, as such, could join in Christian worship. In a little while they would be making their first communion, for the dawn of Easter morning was approaching. The doors were already shut, and none but the faithful were present, as the bishop summoned the church to prayer. First he guided them in intercession, saying: " Let us pray, my dearly beloved, for the holy Church of God, that our Lord and God would be pleased to keep her in peace, unity, and safety throughout all the world, subjecting unto her principalities and powers, and grant us to live out the days of a peaceful and quiet life in glorifying God the Father Almighty." * Then one of the deacons said: " Let us bow the knee," and all knelt and

* Quoted from *The Shape of the Liturgy* by Dom Gregory Dix. This passage is a translation of the old Roman Good Friday intercessions.

prayed in silence for a while, until told to rise. Lastly, while all stood, the bishop summed up their prayers in a concluding collect. In a similar way, prayers were offered for the civil government, for the sick, and for the newly baptized. When the prayers were completed, the celebration of the Eucharist began. The bishop greeted the people with " Peace be unto you," and all exchanged the kiss of peace with their immediate neighbours. Then two deacons brought a white linen cloth, and spread it over the stone table at the foot of the dais. While they were doing this, others collected the offerings the laity had brought— little loaves of bread and flasks of wine. Cæcilius had been taught what to expect, yet the warmth and friendliness of the Christian greeting took him by surprise. During the months of his training he had come to love these people, and now he was one of them. It was with thankfulness in his heart that he handed to the deacon the offering of bread and wine which he had brought with him, remembering as he did so to pray that God would accept his life to be henceforth a living sacrifice to him. When the deacons had placed the offerings on the altar, the bishop rose from his throne and, stepping down from the dais, stood on the far side of the altar, facing the people, with his presbyters grouped around him. He added his own gift to the offerings on the altar, and then he, together with his presbyters, silently blessed the oblation.

" Lift up your hearts ", he said to the people.

" We lift them up unto the Lord ", the laity replied.

" Let us give thanks unto the Lord ", said the bishop.

" It is meet and right ", answered the congregation.

The bishop began the prayer of consecration, which was not at this time fixed in a set form, but which always followed traditional lines. He gave thanks to God, through Jesus Christ, for the creation of the world through the Word, for the incarnation of the Word, and for the redemption of the world by the Word. Then he recalled Christ's institution of the Eucharist, saying:

" Who, when he was betrayed to voluntary suffering in order that he might abolish death, and rend the bonds of the devil, and tread down hell, and enlighten the righteous, and establish the ordinance and demonstrate the resurrection, taking bread and making Eucharist to thee, said: Take, eat, this is my Body, which is broken for you. Likewise also the cup, saying: This is my Blood which is shed for you.

" When ye do this, ye do my *anamnesis*."

He offered the elements in obedience to Christ's command for the *anamnesis*, or recalling of his death and resurrection, and prayed that all who partook might be made one and be fulfilled by the Holy Spirit, and ended with words of praise, saying:

" Through thy Servant Jesus Christ, through whom honour and glory be unto thee with the Holy Spirit in thy holy Church, now and for ever and world without end."

The laity assented with a loud *Amen*, and the communion followed. The bishop broke some of the consecrated bread and made his own communion, and the presbyters and deacons were the next to communicate. The laity came up to the altar in single file and stood, instead of kneeling, as is the modern custom. For Cæcilius and the rest of the neophytes, this was a very special occasion, their first communion, and for them special provision was made. Besides the chalice of consecrated wine and water, there were two other cups, one filled with water and the other with mingled milk and honey. The water symbolized their purification, the milk and honey signified their entry into the " promised land ". As the bishop gave a fragment of the consecrated bread to Cæcilius he said: " The Bread of heaven in Christ Jesus ", and Cæcilius replied *Amen*.

Then he passed on to where deacons were holding the three chalices, and he received from them in turn the water, the milk and honey, and the Eucharistic wine. Each cup was offered to him in the Name of the Father, Son, and Holy Spirit, and from each he sipped three times. Then he returned to his place.

When all had communicated, the deacons received fragments of the consecrated bread to carry to the sick who were unable to come to make their communion. In Rome, where the Christians were too numerous to meet in one place, it was the custom to send fragments of the bread consecrated at the bishop's Eucharist to be placed in the chalice at any other meeting where the Eucharist was being celebrated. Some of the faithful also received portions of the consecrated bread, which they took home and used to make their own communions privately on the days when the Eucharist was not being celebrated. Finally, when the vessels had been cleansed, one of the deacons said: " Go in peace," and the congregation quietly dispersed.

In the weeks and months which followed, Cæcilius took his part regularly in the worship of the Church. From Easter to Pentecost, he and the other neophytes continued to wear their white robes, for this was kept as a season of continuous festival, an anticipation of the joy of heaven. No other special festivals were held, apart from Easter and Pentecost, but Christians met with unfailing regularity on Sunday mornings, even at the risk of their lives. In Asia Minor, the " birthdays " of martyrs were already being kept with special celebrations of the Eucharist, and by the beginning of the third century the custom spread to North Africa and to Rome. The day of a martyr's death was counted as being his birthday in heaven, and was celebrated accordingly as a festival. The Church on earth, conscious of her union with the Church triumphant in heaven, found this a natural and becoming thing to do. Fasting, on the other hand, was left as a matter of private devotion, and the practice of keeping Lent as a penitential season had not yet developed.

Minucius explained to Cæcilius what was the custom of Christians in their private devotions. Those who could do so prayed at the third, sixth, and ninth hours, as well as at dawn and on going to bed. They kept Wednesday and Friday as " station " days—that is, as fasts—and they said grace before and after meals. Obviously many Christians would find it impossible to observe such a rule of life at all strictly—some were slaves, whose time was not their own. These customs had, in fact, been taken over and adapted from Judaism, and were not considered binding by the Church, but they were the expression of an important truth: that religion is concerned with the whole of life. One way in which Christians showed their consciousness of this was by making the sign of the cross, even over the most trivial acts.

" In our coming in and our going out, when we put on our shoes, when we wash, when we eat, when we kindle the lights, when we sleep, when we sit down, whatever business occupies us, we sign our forehead with the sign of the cross." *

Not long after he had been made a full member of the Church, Cæcilius was invited to an Agape or Love Feast. This was held at a private house, but the meal had a religious character, and would not have been considered in order unless the bishop or his representative was present. In his unregenerate days he had often taken part in pagan feasts which also had a religious character, but this meal was much more sober, more homely and intimate. It was a custom derived from Judaism, and not from paganism. It was sometimes called " The Lord's Supper " and, like the Eucharist, it had its origin in the last meal which the Lord

* Tertullian: *De corona militis.*

ate with his disciples. At some time in the first century, probably within the lifetime of the apostles, the rite especially instituted by our Lord, the Eucharist, was separated from the Agape. The behaviour of Gentile converts at Corinth, who called down upon themselves a rebuke from St Paul for their greed and drunkenness during the Lord's Supper,* suggests the reason for this change. In the second and third centuries, an Agape was usually held at the invitation of some wealthy Christian, who wished to make a feast for the whole community, and especially for its poorer members. Cæcilius was particularly struck by the absence of frivolous conversation. The talk was all on religious matters, and consisted for the most part of questions asked by the guests and answered by the bishop. What pleased Cæcilius most was the wording of the blessing which was said over the bread:

" We give thanks unto thee, our Father, for the life and knowledge, which thou didst make known unto us through Jesus thy servant; to thee be the glory for ever. As this broken bread was scattered upon the tops of the mountains and being gathered became one, so gather thy church from the ends of the earth into thy kingdom; for thine is the glory and the power through Jesus Christ for ever." †

This was not the bread of the Eucharist, the Lord's Body, but it was blessed bread of which only the baptized might eat. Cæcilius rejoiced in the sense of fellowship which this common meal gave him, not only with those immediately around him, but also with other Christians all over the world.

Christian worship in the first three centuries was essentially the same, whether it took place in Rome or in Antioch, in the western provinces or in the east, but it was by no

* I *Cor.* 11. 20–34.
† Given in the *Didache*. But there the distinction between the Agape and the Eucharist is not clearly made.

means uniform. If Cæcilius had travelled widely, as many of his contemporaries did, he would have found the Church wherever he went in the Roman Empire, in Edessa on the eastern frontier, and in barbarous Gaul in the north, as well as in highly civilized Alexandria. In any or all of these places, Christians would have welcomed him as a brother and would have invited him to join with them in the celebration of the Eucharist. As a rule, the service would be in Greek, which was widely spoken in the Roman Empire, especially in the East. Even had he chanced to find his way into a country church in Syria, where the prayers were said in the local dialect, he would still have been able to follow the action of the rite. But he would have noticed striking differences, especially in the prayer offered by the bishop when consecrating the elements. In Alexandria, for instance, he would have found his thoughts carried up to heaven by the glorious words of the Sanctus :

" Holy, holy, holy, Lord of Sabaoth ; full is the heaven and the earth of thy glory.

" Full is the heaven, full also is the earth of thine excellent glory. Lord of powers, fill also this sacrifice with Thy power and thy partaking : For to thee have we offered this living sacrifice, this unbloody oblation."

(The use of the Sanctus was later adopted by other churches, but it is not in the earliest known Roman liturgy.) In Syria, he would have been struck by the absence of the words of institution from the consecration prayer, and by the fact that the prayer was addressed to Christ himself instead of to the Father. He might also have noticed differences of procedure, small in themselves, but destined to have important results. For example, in Syria he would have found that it was usual for people to hand their offerings to a deacon before the service began, instead of presenting them during the service, as was apparently the usual

custom in the West. From that seemingly trivial difference was to grow one of the distinguishing features of
Eastern liturgy, the Great Entrance, when the elements are
carried in and placed upon the altar. In Asia Minor, he
could not have failed to hear much about the Paschal
controversy, the dispute as to the correct date for celebrating Easter, and he would also have been surprised at
the degree of veneration paid to local saints and martyrs,

REPRESENTATION OF THE AGAPE OR LOVE FEAST
(From the Roman Catacombs)

shown in the celebration of their "birthdays". In his
travels he might even have found in certain churches practices which would undoubtedly have been condemned by
his bishop at home, such as the celebration of the Eucharist
with water, instead of wine, from a mistaken kind of asceticism. But this was exceptional; as a rule he would have
found the churches at one in their worship, showing only
the diversity which was consistent with the conception that
they were the several members of one Body.

That there should have been such unity in faith and practice in churches so far apart shows plainly that all had inherited one tradition, the tradition which they derived from the apostles, either directly or at one or two removes. During the second century, when persecution and the lack of any central authority tended to promote local divergences, the essential unity of the Church persisted. The local variations served in the end to enrich the Church's liturgy when the time came for freer intercourse between the churches and for greater uniformity.

Note on Church Buildings and Appointments before Constantine

While Christianity was a persecuted religion, it was plainly impossible for Christians to build churches in which to conduct public worship. All the evidence that remains goes to show that during the first and second centuries Christians met for worship in private houses, and that only in the relatively peaceful periods which preceded the great persecution in the third century did they begin the building of churches. It was very unlikely that any of these early house-churches would survive to show in what setting Christian worship was conducted in the first two and a half centuries, but, by a piece of immense good fortune, one was discovered during the excavations at Dura-Europos in Syria.* There, in what had been an ordinary dwelling-house, was found a Christian chapel, the walls of which were covered with frescoes resembling those in the catacombs. Investigation showed that the chapel was painted at the very beginning of the third century, evidently at a time when it was quite necessary for Christians to keep their place of worship concealed, and that, about thirty years

* *Excavations at Dura-Europas, Fifth Season,* 1931–32, Yale University Press.

later, in A.D. 232, the whole house was altered for use as a church. Presumably the Christian community had grown, and, as the alterations took place during the reign of the tolerant Alexander Severus, there was less need for conceal-ment.

Much the most interesting feature was the painted chapel, which was almost certainly a baptistery. It was a long, narrow room with an arched niche at the farther end. Within the niche was a basin, most probably used as a font for baptisms. The walls of the chapel, the archway, and the niche were all painted. Along the arch ran a pat-tern of grapes, pomegranates, and wheat-stalks, and the pilasters on each side were painted to imitate marble. As he stood in this little baptistery, the Christian would see all around him pictures that spoke to him of his faith. Above the font was the Good Shepherd with his flock, a rescued ram on his shoulder. Just below were Adam and Eve clutching fig-leaves about them, while the serpent slithered off through the grass. On the walls were the three Marys, bearing spices to the tomb of Christ; Christ himself, young and beardless, healing the paralytic; the disciples in a ship upon a stormy sea and Christ, walking on the waves, stretch-ing out his hand to save St Peter, who is represented as having short, curly hair and a beard; the woman of Samaria drawing water from a well, and David slaying Goliath. The rest of the paintings are destroyed, but enough remain to show that Christians in Syria, like those in Rome, loved to represent the Saviour as the Good Shepherd, and to record stories of deliverance upon their walls. The pic-tures are not mere decoration, but sermons in paint which the simplest Christian could understand.

In the first two or three centuries Christian worship must often have been homely and unadorned, but this was due to force of circumstances. There is nothing to show that the majority of early Christians preferred a puritanical plainness. On the contrary, a record of church plate seized during one of the third-century persecutions, and one or two other indications, suggest that Christians equipped their churches as richly as they could. Certainly the chapel at Dura-Europos, with its gaily coloured walls, was as bright as its decorators had power to make it, and even the dark windings of the catacombs were made more cheerful by paintings. Christianity was never " penny plain "; it was " twopence coloured " from the very beginning.

BOOKS FOR FURTHER READING

The Shape of the Liturgy, by Dom Gregory Dix. The previous chapter is, in the main, based on the first eleven chapters of this great study of the development of the Liturgy. Chapter VI of Dom Gregory Dix's book contains a vivid picture of early Christian worship.

Documents Illustrative of the History of the Church, edited B. J. Kidd. Volume I, Numbers 19, 77–79, 92.

Documents of the Christian Church, World's Classics. " The Old Roman Creed," p. 33, and Section vii, " The Church, the Ministry, and the Sacraments," i–iv.

The Excavations of Dura-Europos. Report of Fifth Season, 1931–32. Ed. M. I. Rostovtzeff. Yale Univ. Press. London-Oxford Univ. Press, 1934.

CHAPTER XI

EAST AND WEST: CHRISTIAN MISSIONS IN A
DISRUPTING EMPIRE

ABOUT the year A.D. 140, a group of eager young men,
some hardly more than boys, might have been seen
gathered round their teacher in one of the many colonnades
or porticoes of the beautiful city of Smyrna. The lecturer
was St Polycarp, bishop of Smyrna,* and among the young
men listening to him was a lad called Irenæus, destined to
become a great missionary bishop in the province of Gaul.
St Irenæus became a defender of the faith against the attacks
of heretics, a pioneer in missionary work among the Celts, a
peacemaker maintaining unity within the Church; yet none
of his achievements was of greater importance than the
fact that he, by his own personal experience, linked together
both the East with the West and the days of the apostles
with the third century. As a boy, he drank in all that St
Polycarp could tell him of St John and of others who had
seen the Lord. The bishop, at that time already nearing
seventy years of age, was never tired of recounting all that
he remembered of the apostle and of the apostolic elders,
and St Irenæus, with a boy's retentive memory, stored up
all that he heard. As a man, he defended the orthodox
faith by appealing to the authority of that apostolic tradition which his own life so aptly illustrated.

St Irenæus grew up in what seemed a stable, well-organized
world; but when he died, at the turn of the century, strife
within the Empire and barbarian pressure from without
were already threatening the security of civilized life.

* See B. J. Kidd, op. cit., Vol. I, pp. 60–61.

His boyhood was spent in Asia Minor, and there, in the prosperous Græco-Roman cities, disaster, other than the natural danger of earthquake, seemed as remote to the ordinary citizen as it did to a Londoner in the thirties of this century. Cities vied with one another in the magnificence of their public buildings, in the splendour of their civic festivals, in the number of their schools and lecturers. The government found it necessary to limit the number of town-physicians and teachers that might be appointed in any one city, on account of the adverse effect on tax returns of the excessive expenditure on health services and education. There was no standing army in Asia Minor, except for some troops on the frontier; a small police force was sufficient to keep law and order. Travel was easy and trade flourished. In these conditions, Christianity had spread far and wide in the country as well as in the towns. " The whole country is full of atheists and Christians ", wrote Lucian disgustedly about A.D. 170, and elsewhere, in his satirical account of the adventures of Proteus Peregrinus, he mentioned that Christians from Asia Minor would go in numbers as far afield as Syria to visit and comfort those suffering imprisonment for their faith. During the second century, Asia Minor was, in fact, a Christian stronghold, and the churches there were as important as a centre of the faith as was the church of Rome itself, with its apostolic tradition derived from St Peter and St Paul.

The churches of Asia had an apostolic tradition of their own. Many of them owed their foundation to St Paul, some possessed epistles which he had addressed to them; St Peter had sent them his famous letter, 1 Peter; St Philip and his daughters, together with others who had known the Lord, had settled in their midst; most important of all, St John had made his home in Ephesus and, by his pastoral work and his writings, had stamped his imprint on the character of that church. Already, in the days of St

Polycarp, the churches of Asia had shown their determination to adhere to their own customs, even when these differed inconveniently from those of churches in the West. The controversy over the date of Easter had not been settled, and was to cause further trouble before the end of the century. Meanwhile, in the years from A.D. 160 to 180, the churches of Asia and those of Greece, with which they were in close communion, produced a number of able writers who defended Christianity against the attacks both of pagans and of heretics. Among those whose writings survived, at least to the time when Eusebius composed his *Ecclesiastical History* in the fourth century, were: Melito, bishop of Sardis; Apollinaris, bishop of Hierapolis; Athenagoras of Athens; Rhodo and Musanus. But the most outstanding personality of the period was Dionysius, bishop of Corinth, whose letters to the various churches— to Rome, Athens, Crete, and several places in Asia Minor— were widely read and collected together under the title of *Catholic Epistles.*

During the second century, it was the East rather than the West that supplied the Church with thinkers and apologists. Even Justin Martyr, who wrote and died in Rome, gained his education in the eastern provinces. The churches in the cities of Asia, in Corinth and Athens, and, at the other extreme, in Syrian Antioch, all made their contribution. Theophilus was the first bishop of Antioch, after St Ignatius, to leave his mark on Christian literature, but after him there came several able men who made Antioch a centre of Christian learning. Together with this intellectual activity went practical enterprise as well. The enthusiasm which led to the extravagance of Montanus and his followers * was characteristic of the churches of Asia, and found other and more valuable outlets within the framework of the Church. The very synods which con-

* See Chapter VIII above.

R

demned Montanism are evidence of the high degree of organization which the churches in Asia had achieved, and of the energy of their bishops. The rapid spread of Christianity throughout the province bears witness to their great missionary activity. More striking still is the fact that the church in Gaul almost certainly owed its existence to the Christians of Asia.

The Greeks had been keen traders from very early times, and they established settlements up and down the Mediterranean coasts to serve as trading centres. One of these early Greek colonies was Marseilles, on the southern coast of Gaul. By the second century A.D., the importance of Marseilles had dwindled. The great bulk of the export and import trade of Gaul was now handled by Lyons, a city of Roman foundation, and Arles, the port near the mouth of the Rhone, was growing in importance. But although in the course of centuries one city rose and another declined, the trade connexion between the Greek cities and Gaul remained unbroken. The Hellenistic, Greek-speaking cities of Asia Minor inherited this tradition, and there can be little doubt that St Irenæus, growing up in the thriving commercial city of Smyrna, heard talk of trading ventures in Gaul, and heard travellers' tales from those who had lived for a while in those distant parts and had afterwards returned home. These men would have spoken of the eagerness with which the Gauls were adopting Roman ways, and of the opportunities which were thus afforded to enterprising merchants. Already the country was more than half civilized. The peasants on the great estates, of course, remained poor, illiterate, and Celtic-speaking, but the landowners, the descendants of the tribal chiefs, were showing an astonishing enthusiasm for education. The booksellers in Lyons were doing a thriving business, and there were good openings for teachers and physicians.

There is not enough evidence to show whether the

churches of Asia sent an organized mission to Gaul, or whether Christianity was first brought there by individual Christians with no official status. There is a tradition that St Polycarp sent missionaries to Gaul, and that is by no means incredible, but it cannot be proved. The earliest reliable document relating to the Gaulish church is a letter describing the terrible persecution which was inflicted on the churches of Lyons and Vienne in A.D. 177. When the persecution began, an old man of ninety, St Pothinus, was bishop of Lyons; his name shows that he was of Greek extraction, and, from his great age, it is likely that he had already spent many years in Gaul. One of the martyrs was from Pergamum, another was a physician from Phrygia, and the names of about a third of the rest are Greek. This alone would be enough to indicate that Christians from the eastern provinces formed an important element in the Gallic church; but there is also evidence that the churches of Gaul and of Asia Minor were in close touch with one another. It was to the Christians of Asia and Phrygia that the letter describing the persecution was addressed by the survivors at Vienne and Lyons. Previous to that, some of the Montanists in Asia Minor had appealed to the Christians at Lyons for support. Last, but perhaps not least, of our surviving scraps of evidence, is the fact that the man chosen to succeed the martyred bishop, St Pothinus, was St Irenæus, a Greek by birth and a disciple of St Polycarp.

From the days when St Irenæus was a boy in Smyrna to the time when he became bishop of Lyons hardly anything is known about his life, nor is the chronology of his career at all certain. He apparently went to Rome as a young man, and was there in A.D. 154 or 155, when St Polycarp in his old age visited the Roman bishop, Anicetus. At the time of the persecution at Lyons he was a presbyter of that city, and was sent by the Christians of Gaul to Eleutherus, the bishop of Rome, with letters from the confessors then in prison and with the judgement of the Gallic church on the Montanist question. It may well have been owing to this mission that he did not lose his life in the ruthless persecution which swept away most of the leading Christians in both Lyons and Vienne. As it was, he was spared to undertake the difficult task of reconstruction when the storm of popular fury had subsided.

Our knowledge of the church of Gaul during the first three centuries is like a moonless night. Here and there dim forms appear silhouetted against the stars, but, for the most part, the darkness is impenetrable. A storm comes up, and suddenly the whole scene is lit by lightning flashes, vividly, unforgettably. The storm passes and darkness swallows up the place once more. In the history of the church of Gaul, the letter describing the persecution of Lyons and Vienne in A.D. 177 is the lightning, and what it reveals is terrible—glorious, also, but only to those who can face and bear the terror of it.

In the early summer of A.D. 177, the great provincial city of Lyons presented every outward appearance of security and peaceful civilized life. The streets, the public baths, the market-places, and shops were thronged with people speaking three different languages. Roman citizens attached to the Governor's court, and the soldiers of the city garrison spoke mostly Latin; the merchants, physicians, and teachers from the East were mainly Greek in tongue; the Gauls from all the three imperial Gallic provinces who met at Lyons, their capital city, spoke Celtic in many local dialects. Already preparations were going forward for the great annual event—the meeting of the Gallic Diet on the first of August. This assembly, which had been instituted by the Romans to unite the Gauls and to insure their loyalty, had for its ostensible purpose the public worship of the Emperor and the celebration of sacred games to mark the occasion. But, naturally, much business was conducted at the same time. The delegates, who came from every tribe in Gaul, presented petitions to the Governor, aired their grievances, negotiated deals with the merchants, and took the opportunity to make all their most important purchases of the year.

Normally, the early summer in Lyons was a time of cheerful bustle, in preparation for the business and festivities of August. But in this year of A.D. 177, although trade was as brisk as usual, there was an undercurrent of anxiety which found vent in a crop of unfounded rumours. It was whispered that trouble was brewing on the eastern front, that plague was raging in the cities of North Italy, that the Germani had broken through in several places and were about to invade Italy, Greece, or Gaul itself. All these calamities had, in fact, occurred during the troubled reign of Marcus Aurelius, the reigning Emperor, and the fear of their recurrence made men uneasy and suspicious. Their sense of security had gone. They were in the mood to listen to stories of spies, secret agents, and anarchist plots to destroy the very foundations of law and order. Of all the rumours, the most persistent was that the misfortunes of the Empire were largely due to the wickedness of the Christians. The members of this pernicious sect were said to meet secretly for their murderous and loathsome rites and to be bent on destroying belief in the gods and loyalty to the Emperor, the key-stones of the social order. The Christians in Lyons were a small and by no means powerful body, but recently one or two people of note had joined them. Another group of them was known to exist in the neighbouring town of Vienne, and it was said that their agents were at work, perverting simple people in many towns in Gaul.

Before long the Christians in Lyons were made uncomfortably aware of the state of popular feeling. Their heathen acquaintances shunned them; they were driven from the public baths and from the market-places. Christians who ventured to appear in the streets were jeered, hissed at, and attacked with stones. Soon the mob went further. A number of Christians were seized, haled before the tribune, and, after brief questioning, cast into prison. There they remained until the Governor, who had been away, returned to the city. The Governor on his return showed none of the justice and moderation customary in Roman magistrates. His savage treatment of the prisoners, by which is probably meant his use of torture, provoked remonstrance on the part of a young man of good standing, Vettius Epagathus, a Christian who had not been previously apprehended. He asked that he might be allowed to speak in defence of the accused, but those in the court shouted against him, and the Governor's only answer was to ask whether he were a Christian himself. When he confessed that he was, he shared the fate of the rest.

Ten of the accused Christians gave way under the threat of torture and denied their faith, but the rest held firm. Meanwhile, the arrests continued, and heathen servants belonging to Christian households were seized and brought to court to give evidence against their masters. Some of these slaves, in fear of torture, said whatever was required of them and gave false evidence in support of the scandalous charges against the Christians. This further inflamed public opinion, and the Christians were regarded with abhorrence even by their own relations. Meanwhile the Governor had sent to Rome for instructions as to what he should do with those of the prisoners who were Roman citizens, and he kept all alike in prison, intending to reserve the condemned for the arena at the Festival Games in August. Two of the prisoners in especial were tortured again and again, with every refinement of cruelty. These

EAST AND WEST 253

were Sanctus, a deacon of Vienne, and Blandina, a slave-girl belonging to a Christian mistress. Neither of these would give way or make any reply to their accusers, except the repeated assertion: " I am a Christian." People marvelled that they remained alive after all that they had suffered. By now it was hot July weather, and the atmosphere of the overcrowded jail was stifling and foul. Several of the prisoners died of suffocation or of the ill-treatment they had received. Among the latter was the bishop, Pothinus, a frail old man of ninety, who was beaten unmercifully by the crowd and died two days afterwards.

Even those who had denied their faith gained nothing by their apostasy, for they, too, were imprisoned on the charge of being murderers and scoundrels, because they had taken part in Christian rites. The writers of the letter comment on their wretched condition. " For the burden of the confessors ", they write, " was lightened by the joy of martyrdom, the hope of the promises, their love of Christ, and the Spirit of the Father; but the others were grievously tormented by their conscience, insomuch that their countenances could be clearly distinguished from all the rest as they passed by." During the weeks of imprisonment several of the apostates repented and, encouraged by the confessors, who assured them of God's forgiveness, they reaffirmed their faith in Christ and died at last as martyrs.

The Governor received the Emperor's reply to his request for instructions at the commencement of the festival. The Emperor gave orders that those who recanted should be released, but those who remained obstinate should die, Roman citizens by beheading, and the rest by torture. On the first day of the festival, Maturus, Sanctus, Blandina, and Attalus were put through a round of torments in the arena for the delight of the mob, and those who had previously recanted were given a second hearing. While they were being questioned, a certain physician called Alexander, a Phrygian who had lived a long time in Gaul, stood by the tribunal, and encouraged them to persist in their faith. On being challenged, he confessed to being a Christian, and was forthwith condemned to the wild beasts. Those of the condemned who could claim Roman citizenship were then beheaded, with the exception of Attalus. In his case the Governor yielded to the clamour of the mob and ordered him to be thrown to the beasts, in spite of his Roman citizenship. Maturus and Sanctus had died on the first day in the arena, but Blandina survived, and was reserved for the third day's entertainment. On the second day, Attalus and Alexander were tortured until they died, the culminating cruelty being roasting in an iron chair heated to burning point. On the last day Blandina was forced to witness the sufferings of all the rest, including a fifteen-year-old boy called Ponticus. She encouraged the others, and after enduring every variety of cruelty patiently herself, she was tossed insensible by a bull and died.

Even this orgy of horrors did not satisfy the blood-lust of the mob. They refused burial to the dead, and for days the heads and mangled remains of the martyrs were exhibited to the delight of laughing and jeering crowds. Finally, they burnt all the bodies and flung the ashes into the Rhone, saying; " Now let us see if they will rise again, and if their god can help them and deliver them out of our hands."

So ended the persecution of the Christians at Lyons and Vienne. The survivors, few in number and shaken by their terrible experience, wrote a description of what their church had suffered to their brethren in Asia and in Phrygia. They wrote, not in despair, but in triumph, as men who were recording a costly victory. They thanked God for the constancy of the martyrs, for their courage, and for their humility, which led them to refuse the title of martyrs and ask to be known only as confessors. Their final words about them were: " Victorious in everything, they departed to God. Ever lovers of peace, they also commended peace to us, and, accompanied by peace, journeyed to God, leaving no sorrow to their mother (the Church), no dissension and war to their brethren, but rather joy and peace and concord and love."

On his return from Rome, St Irenæus succeeded St Pothinus as Bishop of Lyons. Unfortunately, very little indeed is known about the church of Gaul before the time of Constantine. Tradition has preserved the memory of several martyrs, but the records about them are comparatively late and must be used with caution. St Epipodius of Lyons and his Greek friend St Alexander were betrayed to the authorities by a servant, either in the autumn of A.D. 177, or in the following year, and it may well be that the persecuting fury of the mob only died down gradually. The surviving Christians must certainly have been in danger for many months after that fatal summer. The story of St Symphorian of Autun suggests that there were at least one or two martyrs farther afield, in parts of Gaul where there were a few Christian missionaries or a handful of believers here and there. St Symphorian is said to have been denounced by the mob as a Christian on a day when the streets were thronged with people engaged in celebrating the festival of Berecynthia, a Celtic goddess. St Symphorian failed to pay the customary reverence to the image which was being carried by in procession, and when accused of being a Christian, unhesitatingly admitted that he was. He was tried before the local magistrate, scourged, and, when unrepentant, was led to execution. His mother seeing him, leant out of the window and cried:

" Oh, my son, my son Symphorian, remember the living God. Be of good courage, my son; today, child, by a happy exchange you will pass away into eternal life."

A reference to these words was incorporated into the

Proper Mass for St Symphorian's day, and has been preserved in the Gothic Missal.

From a few stray references in his own writings, it is plain that St Irenæus was an active missionary bishop and that the church of Gaul prospered during his episcopate. He himself learnt Celtic, and habitually preached to the Gauls in their native language. He even feared that his frequent use of Celtic had had a bad effect upon his Greek style. He certainly won converts. Writing of the apostolic tradition, he says that it is assented to " by those many barbarous tribes who believe in Christ, who have salvation written by the Spirit in their hearts without paper and ink, and diligently keep the old tradition."

Elsewhere, after summarizing the Christian faith in a form nearly resembling the Apostles' Creed, he continues:

" This Kerygma and this faith the Church, although scattered over the whole world, diligently observes, as if it occupied but one house, and believes as if it had but one mind, and preaches and teaches as if it had but one mouth. And although there are many dialects in the world, the meaning of the tradition is one and the same.

" For the same faith is held and handed down by the Churches established in the Germanies, the Spains, among the Celtic tribes, in the East, in Libya, and in the central portions of the world."

It was probably during this period of missionary effort that Christianity reached Britain. Writing about A.D. 208, Tertullian says, with a characteristic rhetorical flourish:

" In all parts of Spain, among the various nations of Gaul, in districts of Britain inaccessible to the Romans, but subdued to Christ, in all these the kingdom and name of Christ are venerated."

There is a touch of exaggeration about Tertullian's statement, but there is no reason to doubt that Christianity did spread from Gaul to Britain about the beginning of the third century. Origen also mentions the British church some twenty years later. But, apart from these two references, nothing is known about Christianity in Britain before the martyrdom of St Alban in the Diocletian persecution. Archæological evidence is also extremely scanty, which suggests that Christians formed a very small minority in Britain before the fourth century. The same is probably true of Gaul. In both countries, dearth of evidence about the early history of the Church has encouraged the growth of legends. One legend has formed round the name of St Joseph of Arimathea, who was believed to have settled in Glastonbury. Another has grown round Lazarus and his sisters, who were thought to have founded the church of Gaul. Others relate visits to Britain of St Paul, and even of the infant Christ. For none of these assertions is there a shred of evidence, and the stories must be classed as pious fictions, born of the desire to establish the antiquity of the churches of Gaul and Britain.

St Irenæus is remembered today chiefly for his writings. Finding that Gnosticism was spreading in his diocese and causing dissension and moral laxity, he composed a great treatise in several books, entitled *Against the Heresies*, in which he exposed the absurdities of Gnosticism and defended the orthodox faith. This work has survived in a crude Latin translation made by a Celtic priest, though all but some fragments of the original Greek version are lost. It is important both for the detailed description of Gnostic beliefs and also for the light it throws on orthodox Christianity at the end of the second century. St Irenæus based his defence of the faith on the Scriptures, and on the unwritten tradition of the Church preserved by means of the episcopate and the creed which converts learnt before being baptized. It is plain from all his writings that in his day men attached great importance to the living witness of the

Church, which we call tradition. This was only natural, when they were still so near to the time of the apostles that they could count the links in the chain of human memory. St Irenæus himself had listened to St Polycarp's personal recollections of St John and others of the first witnesses. Thus, the link of a single life joined him to the apostles. St Irenæus and the Christians who were his contemporaries valued the written record, which they had in the New Testament, but they relied quite as much on oral tradition. They were vividly aware that in their worship, and in many of their customs, they were perpetuating the practice of the apostles and of their first converts. In the unbroken succession of bishops in the great sees, the ordinary Christian, as well as his more learned leaders, found assurance that the Church was truly apostolic. The Church had thus already established three great bulwarks against the encroachments of heresy: the canon of the Scriptures, the apostolic succession of bishops, and the baptismal creed. Two or three books were still sometimes included in the New Testament which have since been definitely excluded from the canon, but St Irenæus is emphatic that " it is impossible that the Gospels should be in number either more or fewer than these "— that is, than our four Gospels, Matthew, Mark, Luke, and John. He is equally confident that the apostolic succession has remained unbroken in all the churches, and he quotes the list of bishops of the church of Rome as an example. His statement of the faith which the Church received from the apostles is substantially the same as the Apostles' Creed. St Irenæus was the first of the early Fathers to show plainly what is meant by the expression, " One Catholic and Apostolic Church ", though the phrase " Catholic Church " had been used even earlier by St Ignatius.

In A.D. 189 Eleutherus, the bishop of Rome, died and

Victor succeeded him. The authority of the church of Rome had been gradually increasing during the second century, partly owing to her position in the capital of the civilized world, and partly owing to the respect which all Christians felt for her great apostolic tradition, derived from St Peter and St Paul. Rome was the only apostolic see in the West, and no other had a doubly-apostolic foundation. Victor determined to exert this authority in a new way and establish the position of the Roman church as the head of the whole of Christendom. In one matter the churches of Asia had hitherto refused to conform to the Roman practice, and this was in the date at which they celebrated Easter. They kept the festival of our Lord's resurrection on the fourteenth day of the first Jewish month, the month called Nisan, the time when Jews begin the celebration of the Passover. The rest of the Church held that Easter ought to be celebrated on a Sunday, and so kept the feast on the Sunday following the 14th Nisan. The difference was inconvenient in practice, and had tended to cause dissension. Victor decided to settle the question once and for all. He circularized the churches, and received satisfactory replies from all except Polycrates, Bishop of Ephesus, who wrote on behalf of the churches of Asia. Polycrates defended the Quarto-deciman practice, as it was called, on the ground that it had the apostolic authority of St John, and he enumerated the apostolic men and their successors who had lived in Asia to prove that his church also could claim the authority of apostolic tradition for her customs. This answer so angered Victor that he took the unprecedented step of excommunicating the churches of Asia.

This high-handed action on the part of the bishop of Rome called forth protests from several bishops, the chief among whom was St Irenæus. Although he agreed with the Roman practice of keeping Easter on a Sunday, he could not consider it justifiable to excommunicate a whole church for a difference of custom in which no heresy was involved. He therefore addressed a strongly worded letter of protest to Bishop Victor, and reminded him that this difference was of long standing, and hitherto had not been allowed to cause discord in the Church. He especially instanced the behaviour of Anicetus, who was bishop of Rome when St Polycarp paid his visit there in A.D. 154. Although Anicetus and St Polycarp discussed the Easter question and were unable to reach any agreement, yet they parted in perfect charity, and " in the church Anicetus yielded the (celebration of the) Eucharist to Polycarp, manifestly out of respect ". Thus St Irenæus, as Eusebius says, lived up to his name, which means " Peacemaker ". The remonstrances of St Irenæus and the other bishops had the desired effect. Victor withdrew his excommunication of the churches of Asia, and in the course of time the Roman practice in the keeping of Easter prevailed without the use of compulsion.

When St Irenæus died, about the close of the century, the church of Gaul was expanding and growing stronger; but the troubles of the third century appear to have nipped it like a frost. In A.D. 193, Gaul supported Clodius Albinus of Britain against the rival and successful candidate for the throne, Septimius Severus. The Gaulish nobles and the chief cities suffered in consequence. The next fifty years were disturbed by frequent civil wars, and the Christians had to endure in addition their full share of the persecutions that afflicted the Church as a whole. Finally, in the latter half of the century, the province was swept by barbarian invasions from across the Rhine. It is therefore not very surprising that little is known of the Gallic church during the third century; rather the wonder is that it survived in face of popular hostility and official repression. Certainly one other determined attempt to evangelize Gaul was made, this time by the Roman church, probably about A.D. 240. Seven bishops were sent as missionaries to some of the leading cities of Gaul; but the terrible Decian persecution which followed ten years later must have undone much of their work.

Meanwhile, in the East, Christianity had already spread beyond the boundaries of the Roman Empire. About the time when St Irenæus was a presbyter in Lyons, Abercius Marcellus, then Bishop of Hieropolis in Phrygia, went on his travels. Carrying with him his precious copy of St Paul's epistles, he journeyed to Rome and, having seen the wonders of that city and the faithful church there, he took ship, presumably, to Antioch, and visited the cities of Syria. Everywhere he found Christians who made him welcome, and his enthusiasm led him across the river Euphrates as far as the city of Nisibis, near the borders of Armenia and Assyria. Returning home at last, he felt that some record should be made of his travels, so he had his epitaph carved in his life-time, and on it he wrote:

" Abercius by name, I am a disciple of the pure Shepherd, who feedeth his flocks of sheep on mountains and plains, who hath great eyes looking on all sides; for he taught me faithful writings. He also sent me to royal Rome to behold it and to see the golden-robed, golden-slippered Queen. And there I saw a people bearing the splendid seal. And I saw the plain of Syria and all the cities, even Nisibis, crossing over the Euphrates. And everywhere I had associates. In company with Paul, I followed, while everywhere faith led the way, and set before me for food the fish of the fountain, mighty and stainless (whom a pure virgin grasped), and gave this to friends to eat always, having good wine and giving the mixed cup with bread. These words I, Abercius, standing by ordered to be inscribed."

In the days of Abercius, Mesopotamia was outside the Roman Empire. An independent king ruled at Edessa, and the language of the country was not Greek, but Syriac, a form of Aramaic. But neither political frontiers nor language differences were sufficient to separate Abercius from his fellow Christians and, as a visiting bishop, he evidently celebrated the Eucharist with them wherever he went.

Little enough is known about the church of Edessa. Many Jews had their home in Edessa, and it is probable that through them the Gospel became known at quite an early date, both there and elsewhere in Mesopotamia. An amazing document exists which purports to be the correspondence between our Lord himself and Abgar, King of Edessa. The oldest manuscript version of it dates from the fourth or fifth century, and it has also been found inscribed on a lintel in Ephesus. The letters of Christ and of King Abgar, who writes inviting Christ to visit him, are, of course, apocryphal, but they bear witness to the belief that the church of Edessa had its origin in the apostolic period. According to the "Doctrine of Addai", in which the whole legend is recorded, our Lord promised to send one of his disciples to King Abgar, and, after the Ascension, Addai, one of the seventy-two, was sent by the apostle Judas Thomas to Edessa, where he lodged with a Jew called Tobias. Through him King Abgar was converted and also many of the Jewish merchants of the city. Actually it was not until A.D. 201 that the royal house became Christian, though Christianity must have reached Edessa early in the second century, if not in the first.

About A.D. 170, just about the time when Abercius must have been enjoying his travels, Tatian * left Rome and returned to his native country, Mesopotamia. He was a man of good education and a pupil of Justin Martyr, but he had fallen under the influence of a Gnostic teacher, and the disapproval which his unorthodox views met with in Rome probably caused his return to the East. There he published in Syriac his famous "Diatessaron", a harmony

* See Chapter VIII, p. 195, for Tatian's *Diatessaron*.

of the four Gospels, which became immensely popular and was used by Syriac-speaking Christians as their "Authorized Version". The effect of this book in spreading Christianity cannot now be estimated, but it must have been considerable.

The church of Edessa, like the church of Gaul, was an outpost of Christianity. Behind it lay the Roman Empire, where, in spite of persecution, the Church was firmly established in all the principal cities. In front lay the old Persian Empire, at that time governed by the Parthians, where the religion of Mazda, with its fire-worship, its dualism, its priestly caste, and its magical rites, was taking on a new lease of life. The northern barbarians might be slow in accepting Christianity and ready enough, on occasion, to join in persecuting the new faith, but the Christians of Edessa were facing a far more serious menace. Early in the third century, a revolution brought the first Sassanid ruler to the throne of Persia, and he was greeted with the title: "The Mazda-servant God Artaxares, king of kings of the Aryans, of divine descent". In the ding-dong struggle between the Roman Empire and the Persians along the line of the Euphrates, the people of Edessa might at any time find themselves the subjects of the Sassanids. From them no toleration of Christianity could be expected, for the priestly caste, the Magi, had attained to new influence under their rule, and would not brook rivals. Apart from political considerations, the Persian religion was in itself a force to contend with. In the form of Mithraism, it was taking a deep hold on the Roman army and was spreading throughout the Empire, even as far as Britain in the remotest West. By the end of the third century, it was to appear in the still more dangerous form of Manicheeism, more dangerous because Mani attempted to find a place for Christ within the scheme of Persian dualism.

In these circumstances, it is no wonder that Christians in

s

Edessa inclined to an ascetic ideal. They were in a lonely outpost where " commandos " were needed. From this came the curious ban on marriage, which was a feature of the church of Edessa. The Sons and Daughters of the Covenant, the initiated, those who were admitted to the sacraments, must be celibate and prepared to devote themselves entirely to God. Other believers might marry and bring up children, but Baptism and Holy Communion were not for them. A similar system prevails in Buddhism and there, too, as in the development of monasticism in the West, asceticism and mysticism are two aspects of one movement, a movement of withdrawal from the world for the purpose of contemplating God. Unfortunately for the church of Edessa, the man who best expressed her aspirations and who roused most popular enthusiasm for Christ was unable to curb his luxuriant imagination, and was ultimately ejected as a heretic. This was Bardaisan, who set the whole city afire with his hymns. Over a century later, an orthodox Christian from Syria visiting Edessa found the people still singing his hymns and persisting in his heresy. Judging from those hymns that have survived, this is not to be wondered at. The famous *Hymn of the Soul* is one of them, and it is among the immortal allegories, simple enough to appeal to any child and profound enough to appeal to every mystic. The story is like a fairy tale. A young Prince, who is still no more than a child in the house of his Father, is sent by his parents on a long and perilous journey to Egypt to bring back a precious pearl. Before he goes, he is stripped of the glorious Robe and Tunic of scarlet which he has worn in his Father's palace, and is clad instead in armour of adamant. He is warned that the pearl is guarded by a mighty serpent, and, on arriving in Egypt, he makes his dwelling near its lair and resolves to seize the pearl as soon as the serpent falls asleep. But, while he is waiting, he makes a friend among the Egyptians

of a boy about his own age, and this friend betrays him.
The Egyptians put magical drugs into his food, and he
forgets his home, forgets the pearl he had come to fetch,
and he serves the Egyptians. Meanwhile, his parents have
not ceased to care for their child. They know of his bondage, and they send a letter to awake him from his dream.

" From thy Father, the King of Kings,—from the Queen, thy
    Mother—
  And from thy Brother,—to thee, our Son in Egypt, be greeting!
  Up and arise from sleep, and hear the words of our Letter!
  Thou art a son of Kings: by whom art thou held in bondage?
  Think of the Pearl for which thou wast sent to sojourn in Egypt.

" Think of thy shining Robe and remember thy glorious Tunic;
  These thou shalt wear when thy name is enrolled in the list of
    heroes,
  And with thy Brother Viceroy thou shalt be in the Kingdom."

This letter, sealed with the King's own seal, flies like an
eagle until it alights beside the exiled Prince in Egypt.
On hearing it speaking in the words of his own country, the
Prince awakes, breaks the seal and reads the letter. At
once he remembers his Royal race and the task on which
he had set out, and he begins to charm the hissing serpent
with the triple Name of his Father, his Brother, and the
Queen his Mother. The serpent falls into a magic sleep,
and the Prince seizes the pearl and returns with joy to his
own country. His Father's letter becomes a light to guide
him on his way and, as he reaches his native country, his
Robe comes to greet him, appearing to be not so much a
garment as his own heavenly counterpart.

" While I gazed it sprang into life as a sentient creature,
  Even as if endowed with speech and hearing I saw it,
  Then I heard the tones of its voice as it cried to the keepers:
  ' He, the Champion, he for whom I was reared by the Father—
  ' Hast thou not marked me, how my stature grew with his labours? ' "

At last, clad in his immortal Robe, the Prince re-enters his Father's palace and takes his place near his throne for ever.

This allegory of the human soul, forgetful of its heavenly home and of its God-appointed task, is as characteristically Eastern as our own *Dream of the Rood* is Saxon. Neither expresses or attempts to express the whole of the Christian faith, and in each that faith is interpreted in the medium of a national tradition. But the people who sang the " Hymn of the Soul " as they went about their work had learnt at least part of the truth which the Church had to teach them, and had made that part their own. In the history of the Church, neither the Christians of Edessa, nor the first missionaries in Gaul played a vitally important role. The main line of development lay elsewhere, and much of their work ended in apparent failure. But even our knowledge of later events does not qualify us to judge the value of their efforts. That is known only to him to whom all hearts are open and from whom no secrets are hid.

BOOKS FOR FURTHER READING

The Origin & Development of the Christian Church in Gaul, by T. Scott Holmes, D.D. Macmillan, 1911. The first four chapters deal with the pre-Constantine period.

The Conversion of Europe, by C. H. Robinson. Part of Chapter IV, England, and part of Chapter VI, France.

Early Eastern Christianity, by F. C. Burkitt, 1904.

The Mission and Expansion of Christianity in the First Three Centuries, by Adolf Harnack, Vol. II.

Documents Illustrative of the History of the Church, Vol. I, ed. B. J. Kidd.

     No. 53 & 54. Dionysius, Bishop of Corinth.

       ,,   68–80. Extracts from the writings of St Irenæus.

       ,,   57. The Epistle of the Gallican Churches, A.D. 177.

       ,,   64. Epitaph of Abercius Marcellus, Bishop of Hieropolis.

History of the Expansion of Christianity, Vol. I, by Prof. K. Latourette.

CHAPTER XII

ALEXANDRIA: CHRISTIANS IN THE UNIVERSITY

TO the majority of Romans in the second century A.D., the name of Alexandria would have evoked first the thought of heavily laden grain-ships, carrying a large share of Egypt's harvest to feed the people of Rome, and then a mental picture of great bales of linen cloth and of papyrus stacked upon the quay-side. Some, who had actually been there, might think instead of the amazement with which they had first beheld the greatest port in the world, when, as their ship sailed in, they had seen the city lying along a narrow strip of land between Lake Mareotis and the sea, with the huge lighthouse, which ranked as one of the seven wonders of the world, guarding her harbours. Comparatively few would think first of her famous university and its unrivalled library. The city itself had this double character. To most of its many inhabitants trade was all important; but in the lecture-rooms, art galleries, and leafy gardens of the Museum, scholars and poets congregated who cared and knew little about commerce. There they discussed philosophy, practised rhetoric, studied the medical theories of Galen, recorded their astronomical observations, or lectured to students on the latest discoveries in mathematics or geography. This aspect of the city's life was inherited from the Greeks through Alexander and his successors, the Ptolemies, who had endowed the university and founded the library. By means of it, the Alexandrine church was enabled to play a vitally important role in the development of Christian thought.

The church of Alexandria is said to have been founded by St Mark, but nothing is known of the first century of its history. It is probable that during this time Christianity was spreading among the merchants and poorer traders, but not among the scholars of the university. However that may be, Alexandrine ideas were influencing Christian thought long before the church there had become at all important. Two out of the five districts into which Alexandria was divided were entirely Jewish and, from the foundation of the city, Jews had enjoyed a privileged position. There the Septuagint, the Greek translation of the Old Testament, was completed in the second century B.C., and there, during the earthly life-time of our Lord, Philo was occupied in the difficult task of harmonizing Greek philosophy with the Hebrew Scriptures. Philo was the ablest and best known of many Alexandrine Jews who, both before his time and afterwards, endeavoured to reconcile Greek ideas with the Mosaic Law. Their allegorical methods of interpreting the Old Testament; their theory that the philosophers had borrowed ideas from the Hebrew Scriptures; above all, their doctrine of the Logos, the Word of God—these were all current among educated Jews of the Dispersion in the first century A.D. and influenced early Christian writers.

It must not be supposed that these Jewish scholars were professors at the Museum. No Jew, however liberal in outlook, could accept an official position in a pagan university, since that would involve him in idolatrous practices. But the resources of the vast libraries of Alexandria were open to them, and no doubt they sometimes listened to pagan lecturers and were stimulated by exchanging ideas with men brought up in a different tradition from their own. To these men the search for truth was more than an intellectual activity, it was an approach to God. Many of them dedicated themselves to this search with a devotion resembling that of Christian hermits at a later period. They handed their property over to their relations and retired to quiet places outside the city, where they devoted themselves all day to the study of the Scriptures and to " allegorizing the law of their fathers ". They used to fast through the day, eating only at night, and they had private chapels in which they worshipped God with prayer and hymn-singing. Naturally, the " Therapeutæ ", as they were called, formed only a tiny minority in the vast Jewish population of Alexandria, but their influence was out of all proportion to their numbers. It was from them, rather than from the pagan philosophers at the university, that Clement, the first great Christian writer at Alexandria, derived his ideas.

Clement was not an Alexandrine by birth. From the few autobiographical allusions in his writings it seems that he was an Athenian. Like Justin Martyr before him, he had an insatiable desire to know the truth, and when the teachers in Athens failed to satisfy him he set out on his travels. He went from Italy to the East, and from Palestine to Egypt. At last, in Alexandria, he found what he was looking for: a teacher who could show him how he might ultimately attain to the vision of God. This teacher was Pantænus, at that time head of the Christian Catechetical School in Alexandria. Very little is known of him. By birth a Sicilian, he was known as the " Sicilian Bee " and his early training was that of a Stoic. He is said to have undertaken missionary work in India, and seems to have survived to the end of the second century. The Catechetical School, destined to become famous for its pioneer work in Christian education, almost certainly began in a humble and quite ordinary way as a school for catechumens. Such schools were a normal feature in all Christian communities. There converts were instructed in the elements of the faith before being admitted to baptism, and there, too, the children of Christian parents were taught, just as

Jewish children were in the schools attached to the synagogues. Christianity had inherited from Judaism this consciousness of the importance of education and, from the first, the teacher was recognized as having a special status in the Church. For, as St Paul wrote to the Corinthians, " God hath set some in the church, first apostles, secondarily prophets, thirdly teachers." * But, hitherto, these schools had been hardly more ambitious in their aims than the modern Sunday School or Confirmation Class, and were not likely to attract intellectual pagans. The transformation of the school at Alexandria into something resembling a Christian college, offering education up to university standard, was due to the genius and personality of three men: Pantænus, Clement, and Origen.

St Clement arrived in Alexandria about A.D. 180, at a time when the Church was enjoying comparative peace. During the next twenty years, he and Pantænus developed the Catechetical School, and the church of Alexandria emerged from its obscurity to occupy a position of importance second only to that of Rome. Just as St Clement had been attracted by the teaching of Pantænus, so other pagan inquirers crowded his own lecture-room. Such men required far more than simple instruction in the Christian faith. What they sought was a statement of the Christian doctrine in the terms used in current philosophical speculation. To this gigantic task St Clement applied himself. He planned a vast work in three parts which, when completed, would cover the whole course of the Catechetical School. The first part was addressed to pagans and was designed as a preparation for baptism. In it the Word of God is thought of as the " Protrepticus ", the Converter of men's souls, and the business of this book is to detach men from their old pagan way of life and from their pagan ideas. The second part was addressed to neophytes—

* I *Cor.* 12. 28 (A.V.).

those recently baptized—and was entitled " The Tutor ". This book was intended as a manual of moral discipline, a handbook of the Christian way of life. The third part was to be addressed to Christians and was to be called " The Doctor ". In it the initiated were to be instructed in all the mysteries of Christian doctrine. Unfortunately, St Clement never completed his design, and it would seem that something other than the sheer magnitude of the task prevented him. He postponed the completion of his great work and began instead a long, rambling compilation which he entitled *Stromateis* or " Carpet-bags ".

For lack of external evidence, the reason for this strange behaviour can only be guessed, but M. de Faye has brilliantly conjectured that strong opposition within the Church itself forced St Clement to pause and to attempt to justify his opinions before proceeding farther. The cause of the opposition is not far to seek. At this time Gnosticism was a serious menace to the Church, and many Christians thought that the only sure defence against it was to shun pagan philosophy altogether and rely on simple faith. A considerable part of the " Miscellanies " or " Carpet-bags " is devoted to a defence of learning and to a portrait of the " true Gnostic ", the Christian who understands his faith and therefore cannot be shaken by false arguments.

" But the multitude ", says St Clement, " are frightened at the Hellenic philosophy, as children are at masks, being afraid lest it lead them astray. But if the faith (for I cannot call it knowledge) which they possess be such as to be dissolved by plausible speech, let it be by all means dissolved, and let them confess that they will not retain the truth." *

In defending philosophy, St Clement was not advocating any particular system, but was affirming that it was the Christian's right, and indeed his duty, to use his reason.

* *Stromateis* or *Miscellanies*, Bk. VI, Chapter 10.

If the use of philosophy were denied to the Christian, then the capacity for abstract thought would be denied to him, too, for no other terms and no other method of reasoning were then available than those of philosophy. The genius of the Hebrew mind had not lain in the direction of abstract thinking, and no substitute could be found in the Scriptures. By his defence of philosophy, St Clement claimed for Christianity the Greek passion for truth as well as the Hebrew passion for righteousness. It is hard now to imagine how Christianity might have developed if he had lost his case.

" Man is made principally for the knowledge of God," St Clement affirmed, " but he also measures land, practises agriculture, and philosophizes." *

Upon this basis and on the assumption that " all things necessary and profitable for life came to us from God, and that philosophy more especially was given to the Greeks, as a covenant peculiar to them ", St Clement developed the Catechetical School. In theory, and perhaps also in practice, the School under his guidance became something in the nature of a Christian college. Among the subjects which he approved for his pupils were harmony, arithmetic, geometry, astronomy, and dialectics. For, he writes:

" He who culls what is useful for the advantage of the catechumens, and especially when they are Greeks (and the earth is the Lord's and the fullness thereof), must not abstain from erudition, like irrational animals; but he must collect as many aids as possible for his hearers. But he must by no means linger over these studies, except solely for the advantage accruing from them; so that, on grasping and obtaining this, he may be able to take his departure home to the true philosophy, which is a strong cable for the soul, providing security for everything."

The aim of St Clement's system of education was the training of the " true Gnostic ". Moral discipline was as

* Ibid., Chapter 8.

important a part of it as was the pursuit of truth, for its ultimate end was not scientific, but religious. " Blessed are the pure in heart for they shall see God " sums up his whole intention. His description of the true Gnostic, therefore, is the description of a man sufficiently purified by self-discipline and suffering to be capable of advancing to the final stage of the whole process, the contemplation of God. The Gnostic's life consists in prayer and converse with God.

" Such an one is persuaded that God is ever beside him, and does not suppose that he is confined in certain places. . . . Holding festival, then, in our whole life, persuaded that God is altogether on every side present, we cultivate our field, praising; we sail the sea, hymning; in all the rest of our conversation we conduct ourselves according to rule. The Gnostic, then, is very closely allied to God, being at once grave and cheerful in all things,—grave on account of the bent of his soul towards the Divinity, and cheerful on account of his consideration of the blessings of humanity which God hath given us." *

St Clement makes it plain that the true Gnostic may be a married man. (Indeed, he appears to consider the married state a severer form of discipline than that of celibacy!) He does not advocate severe asceticism or withdrawal from worldly duties. But St Clement's conception of the nature of God was coloured by his early studies in philosophy. He was profoundly impressed by the transcendence of God and the difference between the Divine nature and the human. Therefore he insisted that God is impassible and that the true Gnostic must become the image of his Creator, passionless and free from all desire. " The Gnostic is temperate and passionless, incapable of being dissolved by pleasures and pains, as they say adamant is by fire." There is a good deal of Stoicism in such an ideal, and it is true that in St Clement's thought

* *Stromateis*, VII, 7.

the Greek elements are not always perfectly fused with the Christian. His outlook was still dominated by the conception of Truth as a mystery hidden from all save a few enlightened souls—a conception which belongs to Gnosticism, but not to Christianity. He found support for this belief in St Paul's words to the Corinthians:

" Howbeit we speak wisdom among them that are perfect; yet not the wisdom of this world, nor of the princes of this world, that come to nought: but we speak the wisdom of God in a mystery, even the hidden wisdom, which God ordained before the world unto our glory."

And again:

" I have fed you with milk, and not with meat: for hitherto ye were not able to bear it, neither yet now are ye able." *

This St Clement interpreted as meaning that only the advanced Christians, the Gnostics among the believers, could be fed on the meat of mystical contemplation. More than that, he believed that there was a secret tradition, derived from the apostles and passed on to those fit to receive it, which the majority of believers could not understand and should not be told. This notion of an inner circle of the initiated was both false and dangerous. So was the over-emphasis which he placed on God's impassibility, for that led him at times perilously close to denying the true humanity of our Lord. But the greatness of his achievement lies in his realization that Greek philosophy could and should be not the rival but the servant of Christian faith. The task he attempted was too great for any one man, and St Clement's mind was allusive rather than logical, but in his pupil, Origen, he trained a greater man than himself, one who could continue where he left off.

For the history of the church in Alexandria, the last two decades of the second century are a twilit period. Pan-

* 1 *Cor.* 2. 6 & 7; 3. 2 (A.V.).

tænus, St Clement, the Catechetical School, and the Alexandrian church itself can be seen as distinct shapes in the half-light, but few details about them can be discerned with any certainty. Then, at the beginning of the third century, the scene suddenly becomes almost as bright as day, but the central figure is no longer St Clement: his place is taken by his pupil Origen.

The Emperor Septimius Severus was not an ardent persecutor, but he viewed with disquiet the increase of Judaism and of Christianity in the provinces. He therefore made an order forbidding the Jews to proselytize, and he later extended it to include Christians also. In effect, this decree bore hardly on converts, and it also encouraged local magistrates to deal rigorously with any Christians who were brought before them. It was in A.D. 203 that persecution began in Alexandria. St Clement, who firmly believed that it was not the part of a true Gnostic to court martyrdom, left Alexandria and never returned. He lived for another ten or twelve years in retirement, probably in Palestine, but hardly anything more is known about him. Pantænus was already dead, and the Catechetical School was left without a master. The whole great enterprise might have come to an end, were it not that a number of young pagans, both men and women, who had become interested in Christianity, were determined that the school should be continued. They looked about for a teacher to whom they could attach themselves, and their choice fell upon a young man of eighteen, the most brilliant of St Clement's pupils, a Christian, and already a notable scholar—Origenes Adamantius.

Origen was the son of Christian parents, and from his earliest years he showed promise of his future greatness. His father, Leonides, sent the boy to the ordinary heathen schools, but he was particular to instruct him in the Scriptures himself. The boy needed no urging to this extra study, but showed extraordinary interest in it, and often asked his father shrewd questions about the meaning of passages which he was learning by heart. Leonides was quite unable to answer these questions himself, and he silenced his son in the traditional way by saying that he must be satisfied with the literal meaning of the text until he was older. But often at night, when the boy was asleep, Leonides would stand by his bedside, dreaming of the great future he was sure Origen would have, and thanking God for giving him such a son. When the persecution began in Alexandria, Leonides was among the first to be arrested. Origen was on fire to share in his father's martyrdom, and his mother was compelled to hide his clothes to prevent him from going out and delivering himself up to the authorities. The most that Origen could do was to write to his father during his imprisonment, which he did. One sentence only of that letter has been preserved, but it is characteristic:

" Take care not to change thy mind on our account."

Leonides was condemned and beheaded. His property was confiscated, and Origen, the eldest son, found himself destitute at the age of seventeen, with his mother and six younger brothers to support. Fortunately, in this emergency a wealthy lady came forward with an offer of help. She installed Origen in her house and, presumably, provided what was necessary for the widow and her orphan children. Origen's temperament, however, was not such as would make life easy for him. His patroness was also aiding a well-known heretic from Antioch, whom she treated as her adopted son, and with this man Origen absolutely refused to consort. Instead he set himself to become independent by taking pupils in literature. In a short time he was earning a good income by giving instruction, not in Christian, but in secular learning.

It was when he was thus engaged, about a year after his

ALEXANDRIA

father's death, that the group of young pagans approached him with the request that he would reopen the Catechetical School for their instruction. Origen saw in this invitation a call to devote himself to God's service, and he responded without reserve. He gave up his secular teaching, sold his extensive library of pagan books, many of them copies made by himself, and with the proceeds bought a small pension which provided him with about sixpence a day. On this he contrived to live in the utmost frugality. He drank no wine, went barefoot, and at night slept on the floor. This austerity was in keeping with the ascetic tendencies of his age. Pagan philosophers and Jewish Therapeutæ showed the same zeal for self-discipline, the same belief that low living and high thinking should go together. His asceticism marked Origen out, not as a Christian, but as a philosopher. It was the outward sign that his mind was fixed on higher things in contempt of bodily needs, and as such it attracted pagan students to his lecture-room. But in one respect Origen went beyond anything that pagan or Christian asceticism demanded or could, indeed, approve. He took in a literal sense the saying in St Matthew's Gospel that " there are eunuchs which made themselves eunuchs for the kingdom of heaven's sake ", and put it in practice upon himself. Afterwards he was to regret this rash action bitterly, but at the time it may even have appeared to him to be expedient, for he was teaching women as well as men, and was anxious to avoid any suspicion of scandal, for the sake of the Church. Demetrius, bishop of the Alexandrine church, watched young Origen's career with interest. He himself was endeavouring, with considerable success, to strengthen the power of the episcopate in Alexandria. He gave the young man his support; deprecated the rash act he had committed, but urged him to devote himself to teaching, and confirmed him as head of the Catechetical School. In this way Demetrius gained a measure of control over the School and hoped that Origen, genius though he was, would remain obedient to his authority.

Origen reopened the Catechetical School in a time of danger. Persecution continued sporadically, and it was particularly directed against recent converts. Prominent among the young pagans who had invited Origen to be their teacher were two brothers, Plutarch and Heraclas. These and several others were converted to Christianity, and not long afterwards Plutarch was arrested, tried, and beheaded. Origen stood beside him throughout, and narrowly escaped being stoned to death by the mob. The activities of the Catechetical School were suspect to the police, and for a time Origen's house was watched by soldiers. He and his pupils met in different places, where and when they could. In all no fewer than seven of Origen's pupils were martyred for their faith at this time, one being a woman. Most of them were recent converts. It was presumably owing to the fact that the persecution was directed especially against converts that Origen himself was not arrested, in spite of his disregard for danger. The persecution died down in time, perhaps owing to a change in the local administration, and Origen continued his work at the Catechetical School without interruption for several years.

At first Origen concentrated his own attention and that of his students on the study of the Scriptures, which he interpreted by the allegorical method then in vogue among pagan commentators on Homer, as well as among Jewish and Christian commentators on the Bible. Language they held to be the expression, the outward sign, of the invisible mystery we call thought. They looked at the universe, and saw everywhere a spiritual order, expressed in a material world. In man they found body, soul, and spirit, united in one being. Similarly in the Scriptures they found three senses, literal, moral, and spiritual, uttered in the same

words.   The literal sense of a passage was, to their thinking,
the least important, and often, of course, this is true.   Poets
of all ages have spoken figuratively, not least in the Bible.
Isaiah's Vineyard of the Lord of Hosts, Ezekiel's Valley of
Dry Bones, our Lord's Sower and his Prodigal Son—
these are all parables, and their true meaning lies in their
application, not in their literal sense.   But there are other
parts of the Bible—the Law and the historical books, for
instance—which are written not as poetry, but as statements
of fact.   To interpret these allegorically was bound to be
misleading.   Thus St Clement understood the distinction
between clean and unclean animals in the Law as symbolic
of the distinction between the divine Church on the one
hand and Jews and heretics on the other.   The Jews are
those who ruminate, but do not part the hoof: that is to
say, they have the oracles of God, but do not have faith in
the Father through the Son.   Heretics are those who part
the hoof, but do not ruminate: in other words, they have
faith, but are incapable of chewing upon the Scriptures.
True Christians, like the clean beasts, both ruminate and
part the hoof: they understand the Scriptures and have
faith in Christ.*   This is ingenious, and it was no innova-
tion to consider the clean and unclean beasts symbolically.
Had not St Peter had a vision of clean and unclean creatures
let down from heaven in a sheet, and understood from it
that he must preach the Gospel to the Gentiles as well as
to the Jews?   But it is a method which is open to abuse,
and it does not readily commend itself to modern readers.
In the days of Origen, however, it had the great advantage
of offering an escape from what was otherwise a painful
dilemma.   Must the Christian accept the whole Bible in its
literal sense as the inspired word of God, or else must he
entirely reject a large part of it, as Marcion and other
heretics had done?   The simpler Christians inclined to the

* Clement: *Stromateis*, Bk. VII, 18.

T

former alternative, but that involved taking at their face value the crude anthropomorphic stories about God which were embedded in the Old Testament. This the more critical and thoughtful Christians could not do, and, since they had not sufficient historical knowledge to arrive at the idea of a progressive revelation, the allegorical method was the best solution open to them.

Many of Origen's students were familiar with the various philosophical theories of the day, and they asked him all manner of questions then being debated in the Schools. Is man's will in any real sense free? What of the origin of the human soul? Was there a time before the world came into being when God was not yet Creator? Are the stars living beings? To these and many other such questions the Church had as yet given no authoritative answer. Origen set himself to study philosophy, so that he might discover how much truth was to be found in it and how far the teaching of the philosophers was consistent with the Christian faith. For this purpose, he not only read widely, but also attended pagan lectures on philosophy at the university. For this he was later criticized by some of the less liberal Christians, and part of a letter he wrote in reply has survived.

" But as I was devoted to the word," he wrote, " and the fame of our proficiency was spreading abroad, there approached me, sometimes heretics, sometimes those conversant with Greek learning, and especially philosophy, and I thought it right to examine both the opinions of the heretics, and also the claim that the philosophers make to speak concerning the truth."

He and Heraclas, the brother of the martyred Plutarch, together attended the lectures of Ammonius Saccas, the Neoplatonic philosopher who began life as a porter, and who numbered among his pupils the ablest men of the day, Plotinus, Longinus, and Origen himself.

The years from A.D. 204 to 215 were for Origen a time of ceaseless activity. During the day he taught relays of pupils, attended the lectures of Ammonius Saccas, and studied Hebrew. At night he worked late, comparing different texts of the Scriptures and studying both Old and New Testaments with unremitting thoroughness. In these formative years his own ideas took shape and found expression in the lectures which he gave to his more advanced students. His *De Principiis* or *First Principles*, written probably between A.D. 219 and 230, sums up what he was in the habit of teaching to those who sought from him a statement of the philosophical implications of the Christian faith. On the basis of the apostolic Doctrine he builds a system of cosmic vastness. In his first book he considers the nature of God; the Trinity; God's eternal activity and the eternal generation of the universe; the creation of rational beings, both men and angels, and their freedom to fall; the nature of the stars; the pre-existence of souls and the final consummation. In the remaining three books he treats of particular questions within this all-embracing outline. Throughout he attempts, as far as is possible, to base his theories on the evidence of Scripture, and he never wittingly teaches anything contrary to the tradition which the Church received from the apostles. Yet, even so, it was inevitable that in venturing to speak of such mysteries as the nature of the Trinity, the origin of the human soul, and the ultimate fate of men and angels, he should sometimes put forward views which the Church afterwards rejected, and sometimes fail to safeguard his statements from misinterpretation. Thus it came about that more than a century after his death he was condemned as a teacher of heresy by men who certainly did not comprehend the greatness of his achievement. For, as Dr Prestige has said:

" In spite of every hostile criticism, the theology of the great doctrinal definitions, which has determined the essential faith of Christendom, grew up out of the vast and systematic discipline which Origen imposed.

" The Church owes it to Origen, first and foremost, that, whenever Christianity is true to itself, it is a rational faith." *

But, while Origen and a small number of other scholars, pagan and Christian alike, were discussing the nature of the universe, collating texts, and lecturing to students, the turbulent populace of Alexandria was very differently employed. Their rioting, sedition, and scurrility exasperated successive Emperors, and in A.D. 215 Caracalla resolved to teach the city a lesson. He visited Alexandria in person and, from a vantage point in the huge temple of Serapis, which dominated the city, he directed an indiscriminate massacre of the population. While the city was in uproar, Origen secretly escaped, and made his way to Palestine, where he was welcomed by his old school-fellow, Alexander, now bishop of Jerusalem, and also by Theoctistus, bishop of Cæsarea. During his visit to Cæsarea both bishops invited him to preach in their presence, despite the fact that he was a layman. Such an action was by no means unprecedented, but when news of it reached bishop Demetrius of Alexandria, he was enraged, and wrote at once to expostulate and to demand that Origen should return. Both Alexander and Theoctistus wrote and quoted the precedents for their action, but Demetrius would not be satisfied. He again demanded that Origen should return, and sent deacons to fetch him. Origen, no doubt realizing that his work at the Catechetical School was at stake, returned and made his peace with Demetrius for the time being. Save for two short visits, one to Rome and the other to Arabia, Origen continued his work in Alexandria with scarcely a break until about A.D. 230.

But although Origen remained head of the Catechetical School until he left Alexandria for ever, yet about the year

* *Fathers and Heretics*, by Dr G. L. Prestige, p. 133.

A.D. 219 he made a revolutionary change, both in the management of the School and in his own way of life. This change came about through the good offices of one of his pupils, a wealthy man named Ambrose whom Origen had converted from Gnosticism to orthodox Christianity. Hitherto, Origen's heavy teaching programme and his voluntary poverty had prevented him from writing, but now Ambrose offered to supply him with a secretarial staff, consisting of seven stenographers, several copyists, and a number of girl amanuenses—the ancient equivalent of typists. The stenographers were to work in relays, one being always ready to take down in shorthand whatever Origen might choose to dictate. With this magnificent equipment, literary work on a large scale became possible. At the same time Origen reorganized the School. He put his old pupil Heraclas in charge of all the elementary work, keeping only the advanced students for himself. By this time the scope of the School had been much enlarged. Origen was wont to instruct promising pupils in geometry, arithmetic, secular philosophy, and other branches of general education, as well as in Christian doctrine and the Scriptures. Even the less able students were urged to improve their general knowledge. There was therefore ample work for a second teacher. Even with Heraclas as an assistant, Origen must have had as busy a life as ever with his literary labours added to his daily lecturing.

Origen had long been collating all the available versions of the Old Testament, and now with the help of his secretaries he published this monumental work. It was known as the " Hexapla ", for the different texts were written side by side in six columns for purposes of comparison. The first column gave the Hebrew text, the second showed the Hebrew text in Greek letters, and the other columns contained different Greek translations. Origen was not an exceptionally acute critic, but by his immense labours he prepared the way for other scholars. At the same time he set himself to the task of supplying the Church with commentaries on the books of both the Old and New Testaments. He began with a commentary on St John's Gospel. This was completed, and he had also dictated much of his commentaries on Genesis and on the Psalms before leaving Alexandria. In addition, he wrote his " First Principles ", a treatise on the Resurrection, a commentary on Lamentations and a book called " Stromateis ". These publications added immensely to his growing fame as a Christian teacher, and his advice was increasingly sought for, even by distant churches. Demetrius, who had devoted his life to the task of strengthening the episcopal power in Alexandria, now found that it was not the bishop of Alexandria who was consulted over questions of doctrine, but the lay teacher, whose authority came not from holy orders but from natural genius. The fact that Origen showed no wish for power and no ambition, save that of searching out the truth, did not lessen the bishop's resentment. It is probable that neither man fully understood the outlook of the other. Origen, absorbed in his lecturing and his literary work, was certainly unaware of the strength of the forces which were massing against him. The large section of the Alexandrine church which had opposed St Clement's attempt to reconcile Christianity with philosophy, viewed Origen's attendance at heathen lectures with strong disapprobation. As " simple " Christians, these men distrusted Origen's ideas without understanding them. Demetrius could therefore count on considerable support for any steps he might take against Origen, and, as events were to show, Heraclas, for reasons now unknown, was prepared to support the bishop against his friend and master.

The events which caused the final breach between Demetrius and Origen are now known only in part. About the year A.D. 230 Origen was invited to go to Greece to deal with a matter of heresy. He left the Catechetical School in the charge of Heraclas, and set out, not by the direct route, but via Palestine. He stayed for some time at Cæsarea, and there he was ordained presbyter by Theoctistus of Cæsarea and Alexander of Jerusalem. Afterwards he went on to Greece and engaged in public disputations with heretics, both at Athens and at Ephesus. Meanwhile, Demetrius had heard of Origen's ordination, and his indignation was unbounded. He summoned a synod of bishops and presbyters in Alexandria, and obtained a verdict of censure on this act of indiscipline. Origen was forbidden to return to Alexandria and deprived of his right to teach there, but the synod refused to degrade him from the priesthood. Demetrius was not satisfied. He called another synod, this time consisting only of bishops whom he had himself appointed, and from them he obtained a verdict of deposition. To Origen the loss of the School to which he had devoted himself, banishment from his native city, and the proof of enmity from men who should have been his friends, combined to make this blow exceptionally cruel; yet he bore it with patience and without recrimination. Rome, always concerned for the maintenance of order and discipline, confirmed Origen's deposition, but the Palestinian bishops and those of Phœnicia, Arabia, and Greece ignored it, and treated him with every honour. Eventually Origen settled in Cæsarea and, by dint of prolonged effort, he not only continued his interrupted literary work, but also gathered fresh pupils and became as great an influence there as he had ever been in Alexandria.

During the remaining years of Origen's life he accomplished a vast amount of literary work, including his book against Celsus and many commentaries and homilies. On several occasions he was summoned to deal with heretics who were disturbing the faith of churches far from Palestine.

At this, or at a somewhat earlier period, he was given an audience by the Empress Mammæa, for his reputation had spread abroad among pagans as well as Christians. At the express desire of the bishops of Cæsarea and Jerusalem he preached regularly for several years, adapting his scholarly style to the needs of the general congregation. Even so his sermons must often have been above the heads of his hearers, for he complains in more than one of his homilies of the difficulty of keeping their attention, and speaks of little knots of people talking at the back of the church and of the ceaseless gossiping of the women. He continued to instruct students, the work which was probably the nearest his heart. One of these students, Gregory, later named Thaumaturgus, on parting with his master, wrote an appreciation of all that Origen had done for him, and this panegyric has fortunately survived. Gregory and his brother Athenodore were young men of heathen parentage who, after their father's death, left their home in Pontus and travelled with the intention of studying Roman Law. Chance, or, as it afterwards seemed to Gregory, God's providence brought them to Cæsarea, where they met Origen. After that the project of studying law was forgotten. They remained his pupils for five years, were converted to Christianity, and on their return to Asia Minor were ordained as bishops. Through them Origen's influence on the churches of Asia Minor went deep and lasted long. Origen gave the two young men a liberal, indeed almost a Socratic education. Gregory remembered with feeling how his master had stripped him of all illusions until he was fully aware of his own ignorance and inadequacy. It was a painful experience but, as he realized afterwards, very salutary. Both Origen's greatness as a teacher, and the love and admiration which his pupils felt for him, are fully revealed in Gregory's panegyric. It shows a side of Origen to which his books hardly do justice, for he was not a stylist, and his writings preserve his thoughts, but little of his personal charm.

About A.D. 236 Origen's friend Ambrose was martyred during a severe local persecution at Cæsarea. Origen was in Cappadocia at the time, where a Christian lady called Juliana gave him hospitality. It was to encourage his friend and the other confessors at Cæsarea that Origen wrote his *Exhortation to Martyrdom*. Some quiet years followed, and then in A.D. 250 the first really systematic attempt to suppress Christianity began at the order of the Emperor Decius. Origen, who of course refused to save himself by sacrificing to heathen gods, was thrown into prison and tortured. Every attempt to break his spirit failed, and at length, after the death of Decius in the following year, he was released. He survived for a couple of years, shattered in health by what he had endured, and died at Tyre, where his tomb was long a place of pilgrimage.

That Origen was a man of genius there can be no doubt at all. His critical labours alone would have sufficed for the life-work of an ordinary scholar. In his vast *Hexapla* and his work on the different manuscripts of the New Testament books he was a pioneer of textual criticism. In addition, he wrote commentaries on almost all the books of the Bible. These were a mine of information for later Christian writers. But his fame, for good and for evil, depends less upon his critical work than upon his original speculations. In his *De Principiis* he outlined a Christian philosophy based upon the Scriptures. It was the first attempt at systematic theology on the part of any Christian writer and, although some of his speculations were daring beyond the reach of sober reason, his thought has the stamp of greatness. As a teacher he must have been unrivalled. If St Clement had dreams of something resembling a Christian university, Origen turned the dreams into reality. The Catechetical School at Alexandria under Origen gave its students a comprehensive education of a very high level, based on Christian, not pagan, principles. Later, the pupils who came to Origen in his exile at Cæsarea found him a university in himself. He was also an able defender of the faith against pagan critics, as he showed in his reply to Celsus, and his whole life's work disproved their contention that Christianity was not intellectually respectable.

A man may be a genius, but have an unlovable personality. It was not so with Origen. He had an infectious enthusiasm for God and for truth, which never deserted him, and attracted to him friends and pupils throughout his life. He had the modesty which so often accompanies true scholarship, and in his middle years he endured enmity and misfortune without showing any sign of bitterness or rancour. In youth he longed for martyrdom, and in age his high courage did not fail him, for he died a confessor, after suffering both imprisonment and torture. His book on prayer reveals the man. A Christian's life, he writes, should be " one great unbroken prayer ". Many lesser men have been accorded the title of " saint ". To Origen it has been denied, partly on account of his breach with his ecclesiastical superiors, partly because some of his ideas, though not heretical in themselves, led to heresy in those who came after him.

Although the church of Alexandria viewed Clement with suspicion and expelled Origen, these two great men determined the character of the contribution which Alexandria was to make to Christendom. Rome placed at the service of the Church her administrative genius; Carthage offered the eloquence of her lawyers and their power of codifying doctrine; Alexandria transferred to Christianity the capacity for abstract thought and the conception of a liberal education which she herself inherited from Greece. In the theological disputes which racked the Church during the third and fourth centuries, Alexandria played an important and on the whole a noble part. Significantly enough, while the rival school of Antioch had a surer grasp of our Lord's humanity, Alexandria had a clearer vision of his divinity. And, if Arius the heretic found support for his errors in a distortion of Origen's teaching, Athanasius, who saved the Church from Arianism, was far closer to his essential meaning and, in effect, continued the great task which Origen had begun of giving a rational exposition of the Church's faith.

BOOKS FOR FURTHER READING

Christian Platonists of Alexandria, by Charles Bigg. Bampton Lectures for 1886.

Fathers and Heretics, by G. L. Prestige. Lecture III. Bampton Lectures for 1940.

Clément d Aléxandrie, par Eugène de Faye. Paris 1898.

Origène, Sa Vie, Son Œuvre, Sa Pensée, par Eugène de Faye. Paris 1923.

Christian Education in the First Four Centuries, by the Rev. L. Miller, M.A.

The Provinces of the Roman Empire from Cæsar to Diocletian, by Theodor Mommsen. Vol. II, Chapter 12.

Ecclesiastical History, by Eusebius. Book VI. (The chief source for the life of Origen.)

Documents Illustrative of the History of the Church, Vol. I, to A.D. 313. Ed. by B. J. Kidd. Nos. 105–115 and 122–130.

The Fathers for English Readers, Clement and Origen.

Clement of Alexandria, by R. B. Tollinton; a standard work.

CHAPTER XIII

CARTHAGE: NORTH AFRICAN MARTYRS AND
TERTULLIAN

ALONG the North African coast, some hundreds of
miles west of Alexandria, lay Carthage, a prosperous
port through which flowed corn, oil, slaves, and cattle from
the fertile parts of Numidia and Mauretania. Then, as
now, the mighty barrier of the Libyan desert separated the
two great African cities more effectually than any sea, and
Carthage looked across to Europe for both trade and culture.
The Carthage of the second century A.D. was not Rome's
ancient rival, but a Roman provincial capital built on the
devastated and abandoned site of Hannibal's city. This
new Carthage was more Roman than the Romans. Greek
might be the language of culture in Alexandria, and even in
Rome itself, but in Carthage Latin was the delight of all
who had any pretensions to literary skill—the writers,
rhetoricians, and lawyers. And so it came about that the
Church learned to express her doctrines in the terms of
Greek philosophy at Alexandria and in terms of Roman
law at Carthage. It would be hard to estimate which
medium was the more important in the development of
Western Christianity.

Of those who first brought Christianity to North Africa
nothing at all is known. Characteristically the first mention of Christians in Carthage is a record of martyrdom.
In the summer of A.D. 180, Namphamo of Madaura suffered
for his faith, and a few days afterwards, in July of the same
year, seven men and five women were brought before the

magistrate, questioned, and, when they declared themselves to be Christians, were immediately executed.   The
report of the trial of these Scillitan martyrs (as they are
called from their native place, Scillium, near Carthage) is a
simple statement of the magistrate's questions and the
prisoners' answers, probably recorded on the spot.   There
can be no doubt of its authenticity.   An extract will best
show its character.

After some preliminary questions the Proconsul Saturninus said to Speratus, one of the accused:

" Do you persist in remaining a Christian?

" Speratus said: I am a Christian.   And with him they all
agreed.

" Saturninus the proconsul said: Will ye have a space to
consider?

" Speratus said: In a matter so straightforward there is no
considering.

" Saturninus the proconsul said: What are the things in your
chest?

" Speratus said: Books and epistles of Paul, a just man.

" Saturninus the proconsul said: Have a delay of thirty days,
and bethink yourselves.

" Speratus said a second time: I am a Christian.   And with
him they all agreed." *

They were then condemned to be executed by the sword,
whereupon they all gave thanks to God and were led out
to their deaths.

The courage and confidence of these men and women,
which impresses a modern reader of this bare report,
impressed eye-witnesses at that and at other similar trials.

" The oftener we are mown down by you, the more in number we grow; the blood of Christians is seed," *wrote Tertullian,
the first great Christian writer of the North African church, at
the close of his Apology.*   " That very obstinacy you rail
against is the preceptress.   For who that contemplates it is not

* *Passio Martyrum Scillitanorum.*   Trans. Kidd, op. cit., No. 67.

excited to inquire what is at the bottom of it? Who, after inquiry, does not embrace our doctrines? and when he has embraced them, desires not to suffer that he may become partaker of the fullness of God's grace, that he may obtain from God complete forgiveness, by giving in exchange his blood?" *

St Clement of Alexandria was drawn to Christianity by his hunger for truth, his longing for the vision of God. Tertullian was attracted by the confidence with which the martyrs faced both life and death, unhampered by guilt or doubt. The reactions of the two men were characteristic both of themselves and of the traditions which they helped to mould. To St Clement, and to the Alexandrine School of thought, Christ was primarily the Word of God, the perfect revelation of the Father. To Tertullian, and to Western Christendom after him, Christ was above all the Redeemer. To the one the Incarnation, to the other the Redemption appealed supremely, though the difference between them was not one of faith, but merely of emphasis. To Tertullian, converted by witnessing the quality of Christian living and Christian dying, religion was not a philosophy, but a way of life. To turn from the writings of St Clement and Origen to those of Tertullian is to pass from the study to the court room; for Tertullian was a lawyer in his pagan days, and in his style he remained a lawyer all his life. He dedicated his rhetoric, his epigrams, his irony, his slashing invective, his ready wit to the service of Christ, but he remained the man that nature and education had made him. His fervour and impatience carried him to extremes, so that he ended his days as a Montanist. But, though he became a schismatic, he rendered the Church an inestimable service. He began the task of formulating Christian doctrine, not in Greek, the language of scholars, but in Latin, the language commonly spoken in the Western world. Ecclesiastical Latin was his gift to the Church.

* Tertullian: *Apologeticum*, Section 50.   Trans. J. E. B. Mayor.

As Dr Glover has said: " He was the first Latin churchman, and his genius helped to shape Latin Christianity."

Tertullian was born in or near Carthage about A.D. 160 of heathen parents. His father was a centurion and, as a soldier's son, the boy grew up with a strong sense of duty and with nothing but contempt for all those who, through cowardice or slackness, fell short of his own ideal. The education he received suited him admirably. At his grammar school he must have studied the Greek as well as the Latin classics, but it was the orators rather than the poets who delighted him. At about fourteen, boys passed on from the grammar school to the college of rhetoric, and there young Tertullian must have thoroughly enjoyed the wit combats and mock debates which were an essential part of the training. He learnt to argue on any theme that might be proposed, and soon he was a master of the art of verbal fencing. He thought of studying medicine, but the attraction of the law-courts was too strong, and it must have seemed to all who knew him that he had a great future before him as an advocate. Here and there in his writings are hints of the life led by the brilliant young lawyer before his conversion. Carthage was more like Antioch than Alexandria in its gaiety and vice. There, soldiers from the great camp at Lambæsis came to enjoy themselves, and sailors from numerous merchant-ships went on shore to taste the pleasures of the port. In later years, Tertullian remembered with horror the popular amusements he had once enjoyed—the racing, the obscene theatrical shows, the games in the arena.

" Seated where there is nothing of God, will one be thinking of his Maker?" *he asked in his treatise on Spectacles.* " Will there be peace in his soul when there is eager strife there for the charioteer? Wrought up into a frenzied excitement, will he learn to be modest? Nay, in the whole thing he will meet with no greater temptation than that gay attiring of the men and

women.   The very intermingling of emotions, the very agree-
ments and disagreements with each other in the bestowing of
their favours, where you have such close communion, blow up
the sparks of passion.   And then there is scarce any other
object in going to the show, but to see and to be seen.   When
a tragic actor is declaiming will one be giving thought to prophetic appeals?   Amid the measures of the effeminate player,
will he call up to himself a psalm?   And when the athletes are
hard at struggle, will he be ready to proclaim that there must
be no striking again?   And with his eye fixed on the bites of
bears, and the sponge-nets of the net-fighters, can he be moved
by compassion?   May God avert from his people any such
passionate eagerness after a cruel enjoyment!''*

It is against that background of unwholesome excitement
—triumphs in the law-courts, varied by visits to the theatre,
the race-course, and the arena—that Tertullian's conversion
and his career as a Christian must be understood.   The
pendulum of his passionate, impatient nature swung from
one extreme to the other, so that he ended his days as a
rigorist.   The turning point was a spectacle, the spectacle
of Christian martyrs in the arena.   Tertullian was not a
philosopher like St Clement.   He professed later to despise
philosophy.   But he had absorbed Stoicism during his
study of the law, and even earlier, in a practical form, he had
learnt it from his soldier father.   Half-consciously his
standard of values had been formed on that pattern, and in
the quiet endurance of the martyrs he saw the realization of
the ideal he most admired.   After that experience he did
not rest until he had himself become a Christian; nor did he
hesitate to abandon his legal career, so that he might be free
from paganism and serve Christ body and soul.   Half-
measures were unthinkable to Tertullian.   The martyrs had
freely given their lives; he, their disciple, would give all he
possessed, and his life, too, if it were required of him.
    The glow of the fire which kindled Tertullian's ardent

* Tertullian: *Of Spectacles*, Sec. 25.   A.-N.C.L.

spirit still warms the pages of that most amazing of all acts of the martyrs, *The Passion of SS. Perpetua and Felicitas* (March 7, A.D. 203). There is an introduction, very probably by the hand of Tertullian himself, a narrative by St Perpetua, and another by St Saturus of their experiences in prison, and, finally, an account of the actual martyrdom in the amphitheatre at Carthage. The martyrs, except St Saturus, were all young people recently converted. St Saturus had been their teacher, and gave himself up, so that he might suffer with them. Of those arrested, Revocatus and Felicitas were slaves, but Perpetua was " well-born, liberally educated, honourably married, having father and mother, and two brothers, one, like herself, a catechumen, and an infant at the breast ". While she was in prison, St Perpetua wrote down what had happened to her since her arrest, and the visions which she had seen. St Saturus, encouraged by her example, did the same, and the North African church treasured the records, and for many years allowed them to be read aloud to the congregation during service time.

The " Passion " should be read as a whole, for neither extracts nor a summary can fully convey the simplicity, the genuineness, and the individuality of the narrative. Before her arrest, St Perpetua's heathen father was doing his utmost to dissuade her from declaring herself a Christian. Perpetua records a fragment of their conversation:

" ' Father ', I said, ' Do you see this vessel, for instance, lying here, waterpot, or whatever it may be ? '

" ' I see it,' " he said.

" And I said to him, ' Can it be called by any other name than what it is ? '

" And he answered, ' No.'

" ' So also I cannot call myself anything else than what I am, a Christian.' "

At this point her father lost his temper with her, but his

U

anger failed to shake her resolution.   During the next
few days, she and the other catechumens were hastily
baptized, and soon afterwards were lodged in prison.
What this meant to St Perpetua she tells in a few words:

" I was in great fear, because I had never known such darkness.
What a day of horror!   Terrible heat, thanks to the crowds!
Rough handling by the soldiers!   To crown all I was tormented
there by anxiety for my baby."

Later she obtained leave to have her baby with her in
prison, and she records her delight:

" My prison suddenly became a palace to me, and I would
rather have been there than anywhere else."

While they were waiting for their trial, St Perpetua had a
vision of the future that was in store for them.

" I saw a brazen ladder of wondrous length reaching up to
heaven, but so narrow that only one could ascend at once; and
on the sides of the ladder were fastened all kinds of iron weapons.
There were swords, lances, hooks, daggers, so that if any one
went carelessly or without looking upwards he was mangled
and his flesh caught on the weapons.   And just beneath the
ladder was a dragon crouching of wondrous size who lay in
wait for those going up and sought to frighten them from going
up.   Now Saturus went up first, who had given himself up for
our sakes of his own accord, because our faith had been of his
own building, and he had not been present when we were
seized.   And he reached the top of the ladder, and turned, and
said to me: ' Perpetua, I await you; but see that the dragon
bite you not.'   And I said: ' In the name of Jesus Christ he
will not hurt me.'   And he put out his head gently, as if afraid
of me, just at the foot of the ladder; and as though I were
treading on the first step, I trod on his head.   And I went up,
and saw a vast expanse of garden, and in the midst a man sitting
with white hair, in the dress of a shepherd, a tall man milking
sheep; and round about were many thousands clad in white.
And he raised his head, and looked upon me, and said: ' You
have well come, my child.'   And he called me, and gave me a

morsel of the milk which he was milking and I received it in my
joined hands, and ate; and they all that stood around said:
' Amen.' And at the sound of the word I woke, still eating
something sweet. And at once I told my brother, and we
understood that we must suffer, and henceforth began to have
no hope in this world."

The Good Shepherd and his flock in the garden of the
blessed are depicted again and again in the catacombs at
Rome, but never more beautifully than they are here in the
words of this Carthaginian girl.

All the prisoners were condemned and were reserved for
the forthcoming games. Their friends and relatives were
allowed to visit them, and the deacons of the local church
did what they could to render their imprisonment tolerable.
During this time, Felicitas, one of the martyrs, gave birth
to a child. Even the hardened crowd in the amphitheatre
were horrified, on the day of the games, when the young
patrician girl and the slave-woman straight from child-bed
were brought naked into the arena. Their scruples
vanished, however, when the attendants provided the
women with tunics, and they made no protest against seeing
them tossed by a mad cow, which had been thoughtfully
provided for the female Christians. The men among the
martyrs were exposed to leopards and bears. Only
Saturus was killed outright. The rest had their throats cut
by the soldiers at the end of the games, including St
Perpetua, who had to guide the hand of the nervous young
gladiator who had the task of despatching her.*

To some " not to be martyred is a martyrdom ". Tertullian's fiery zeal was baulked of fulfilment in the arena and
turned to rigorism instead. Ordinary, humdrum Christian
living, with its inevitable petty failures and trivial acts of
compromise with the world, the flesh, and the devil, seemed

* *Passion of SS. Perpetua and Felicitas*, trans. in *Some Authentic
Acts of the Early Martyrs*, by E. C. E. Owen, Oxford 1927.

INSCRIPTION ON THE TOMB OF SS. PERPETUA AND FELICITAS

to him no better than apostasy. He saw men about him
who professed to be Christians, and who yet earned their
living in employment which smacked of idolatry. There
were schoolmasters who taught their pupils stories of the
heathen gods, and who consecrated the first fee for each
pupil to Minerva; Christian plasterers decorated pagan
shrines and Christian painters gilded them; worse still,
there were believers who practised astrology, and image-
makers who had been admitted to the ministry. The plea
" But I must live ", Tertullian dismissed with scorn.

" In vain do we flatter ourselves as to the necessities of
human maintenance, if—after faith sealed—we say, ' I have
no means to live?' For here I will now answer more
fully that abrupt proposition. It is advanced *too late*. For
deliberation should have been made *before*, after the similitude of that most prudent builder, who first computes the costs
of the work, together with his own means; lest, when he has
begun, he afterward blush to find himself spent. But even now
you have the Lord's sayings, as examples taking away from you

all excuse. For what is it, you say? 'I shall be in need!'
But the Lord calls the needy 'happy'. 'I shall have no food.'
But 'think not,' says he, 'about food;' and as an example of
clothing we have the lilies. . . . Faith fears not famine. It
knows, likewise, that hunger is no less to be condemned by it
for God's sake, than every kind of death. It has learnt not to
respect *life*; how much more *food*? 'How many have fulfilled
these conditions?' But what with men is difficult, with God
is easy." *

A man of brilliant intellect and passionate convictions,
Tertullian had no use at all for half measures. He must
himself have abandoned the prospect of a great career at
the Bar when he became a Christian. To continue the
practice of law or to become a magistrate would have meant
continual compromise with idolatry; instead, Tertullian
devoted his skill as an advocate to the cause of Christianity.
The best known of all his writings is his *Apology*, addressed
to the Rulers of the Roman Empire, most probably during
the persecution in A.D. 197 under Severus. It has points in
common with the earlier Apologies, but its tone is very
different. Tertullian does not plead for toleration; he
demands it in the name of justice. He does not content
himself with defending Christians against false accusations;
he turns the tables on his adversaries. He does not sue;
he throws down a challenge.

"We are but of yesterday," he writes exultingly, "and we
have filled every place among you—cities, islands, fortresses,
towns, market-places, the very camp, tribes, companies, palace,
senate, forum,—we have left nothing to you but the temples of
your gods. For what wars should we not be fit, not eager,
even with unequal forces, we who so willingly yield ourselves
to the sword, if in our religion it were not counted better to be
slain than to slay? Without arms even, and raising no in-
surrectionary banner, but simply in enmity to you, we could
carry on the contest with you by an ill-willed severance alone.

* *On Idolatry*, Chap. XII.

For if such multitudes of men were to break away from you, and betake themselves to some remote corner of the world, why, the very loss of so many citizens, whatever sort they were, would cover the empire with shame; nay, in the very forsaking, vengeance would be inflicted. Why, you would be horror-struck at the solitude in which you would find yourselves, at such an ill-prevailing silence, and that stupor as of a dead world."

He demands evidence of the inhuman acts of incest and cannibalism which Christians were said to commit.

" Oh, how great the glory of the ruler who should bring to light some Christian who had devoured a hundred infants! But, instead of that, we find that even inquiry in regard to our case is forbidden."

He analyses the common procedure against Christians, and shows it to be contrary to the principles of Roman criminal law. Christians are condemned for the name of their religion without proof of any other crime; yet they are tortured, not to make them admit that name, but to force them to deny it. They could clear themselves of crime, but they are not allowed to plead in their own defence. He sums up:

" A law lies under strong suspicions which does not care to have itself tried and approved: it is a positively wicked law, if, unproved, it tyrannizes over men."

The rest of the *Apology* is devoted to refuting the charges made against Christians, showing that they are, in fact, ideas characteristic of heathen thought, and to describing the Christian faith and way of life. He ends with the famous defiance:

" The oftener we are mown down by you, the more in number we grow; the blood of Christians is seed."

The *Apology* is a great piece of writing: the fruit of a splendid but impatient spirit. Tertullian was aware of his own faults.   In a different mood from that of the *Apology*, he wrote:

" I, most miserable, ever sick with the heats of impatience, must of necessity sigh after, and invoke, and persistently plead for, the health of patience, which I possess not; while I recall to mind, and, in the contemplation of my own weakness digest, that the good health of faith, and the soundness of the Lord's discipline, accrue not easily to any, unless patience sit by his side." *

But, unhappily, his awareness did not save him from the danger to which he was temperamentally most prone. Angered by the laxity of orthodox Christians, he became convinced that the Montanists, with their far stricter discipline and their reliance on inspiration, were in the right. He adhered firmly to the Christian faith, but he parted company with the Church.   He became a schismatic.   Two centuries later, in the time of St Augustine, Tertullianists, as his followers were called, were still to be found in Carthage.   By this time they were few in number, and St Augustine records that they had returned to the communion of the Church and given up the basilica where they formerly held separate services.   But Tertullian, the originator of their sect, was never reconciled with the Catholic Church. His attitude became more uncompromising and his tongue grew more bitter as the years passed, for Montanism gave full scope to the harsh, critical side of his nature, and opposition fanned his fierceness into flames.   Nothing is known of the incidents which led up to this schism.   It is impossible to tell how much provocation Tertullian received, or how far his own impatient nature was to blame. What is certain is that his defection was a loss to the Church and a disaster for himself.   In spite of it, he is one of the greatest figures in the early Church, and his writings

* *Of Patience.*

moulded the language in which Christian thought found expression in the West, until the close of the Middle Ages.

If Tertullian had not joined the Montanists, probably some record of his life would have been preserved; as it is, hardly anything is known about him except what can be deduced from his writings. Fortunately most of these have been preserved. None of them, not even those written after he had become a Montanist, is, strictly speaking, heretical. The errors of the Montanists were in matters of discipline, not in faith. Tertullian's writings were therefore treasured and read, as they deserved to be, although their author was under a cloud. St Cyprian, the next great leader produced by the North African church, regarded Tertullian as his master and, in at least two instances, modelled his own writings on those of his predecessor—that is, in his treatises on *Patience* and on *The Lord's Prayer*.

Tertullian's writings show him in turn as the advocate pleading the cause of Christianity against the heathen, as the defender of the faith taking up the challenge of the heretics, and as the moralist counselling and reproving the faithful. Always, whatever his subject, his brilliant, witty, vigorous style makes him worth hearing, although as a moralist he harps too long upon one string. The *Apology* is easily the finest of the writings addressed to the heathen. *Ad Nationes* and *Ad Scapulam* are in the same vein, but *De Testimonio Animæ* is different. It is not concerned with persecution ; instead, it gives an argument such as Tertullian might have used to convince some heathen acquaintance of the truth of Christian teaching. Unlike the scholars of Alexandria, he lays aside literary evidence and calls as his witness the man in the street.

" Stand forth, O soul . . . stand forth and give thy witness. But I call thee not as when, fashioned in schools, trained in libraries, fed up in Attic academies and porticoes, thou belchest

forth thy wisdom. I address thee, simple and rude, and un-
cultured and untaught such as they have thee who have thee
only, that very thing pure and entire, of the road, the street, the
workshop."

Out of the mouths of ordinary men he quotes such
common expressions as " Which may God grant ", " If
God so will ", " God is good ", and " God shall judge
between us ". These he claims testify to the soul's natural
belief in God—in the God of Christian teachings, one,
righteous, omniscient, judge of the evil and of the good.

" There is not a soul of man ", he concludes, " that does not,
from the light that is in itself, proclaim the very things we are
not permitted to speak above our breath."

The challenge of heresy roused all that was best in Tertullian. His faith was simple and sincere, and he knew how
to defend it. Like a skilful general, he altered his tactics to
meet different forms of assault. Heretical attacks on the
authority of the Scriptures, on the humanity of Christ, and
on the resurrection of the body, he dealt with seriously and
deliberately; Valentinus and the other Gnostics he met
with ridicule; at Praxeas, he hurled all the bitter, satiric
gibes at his command. *De Præscriptione Hæreticorum*
takes its title from a legal term meaning a " demurrer ".
The heretics claim to prove certain points from Scripture,
and in answer Tertullian puts in a demurrer. He assures
the court that heretics have no right to use Scripture at all;
it does not belong to them. Until this objection is met,
their arguments cannot even be heard. On the face of it,
this is a mere legal quibble, but, handled by Tertullian, it
leads to the statement of orthodoxy's case against dissent.
Some heretics, in particular Marcion, had rejected any
books of Scripture which did not suit their tenets. Others,
such as the Gnostics, had used the device of allegory so that
they could interpret the words of Scripture in any sense they

pleased. Tertullian affirms that the Church's rule of faith
is the ultimate authority for the interpretation of Scripture,
and he quotes in substance the Apostles' Creed. This, he
says in effect, is a summary of the Gospel. It is the teaching of the apostles, preserved by the successors of the
apostles, that is, by the churches which they founded.
The fact that all the churches in the apostolic succession
profess the same creed, and agree in what they teach, is
proof that the tradition has not been corrupted. But
heretics, he argues, are those who do not " walk according
to the rule, which the Church has handed down from the
apostles, the apostles from Christ, Christ from God ".

" Thus, not being Christians, they have acquired no right to
the Christian Scriptures; and it may be very fairly said to them,
' Who are you? When and whence did you come? As you
are none of mine, what have you to do with that which is
mine? Indeed, Marcion, by what right do you hew my wood?
By whose permission, Valentinus, are you diverting the streams
of my fountains? . . . This is my property. I have long possessed it; I possessed it before you. I hold sure title-deeds from
the original owners themselves, to whom the estate belonged. I
am the heir of the apostles.' " *

Like St Irenæus, Tertullian appeals to the tradition of the
Church, preserved and guaranteed by a direct line of succession from the apostles, and embodied in the rule of faith,
the creed. His manner of dealing with heretics is different,
but the substance of his argument is the same.

While Christian scholars in Alexandria were labouring to
incorporate all that was sound in contemporary thought in
one vast system of Christian philosophy, Tertullian was
denouncing Greek philosophy as a snare and a delusion.
In his opinion, it bred idle discussion and was the nurse of
heresies. " What, indeed," he asks, " has Athens to do
with Jerusalem? What concord is there between the

* *De Præscriptione Hæreticorum*, VII.

Academy and the Church? . . . Away with all attempts to
produce a mottled Christianity of Stoic, Platonic, and
dialectic composition! We want no curious disputation
after possessing Jesus Christ, no inquisition after enjoying
the gospel! "

He lacked the Greek passion for abstract speculation, and
could not see the value of it. His own genius was practical,
Roman, juristic. He was strong where the Alexandrines
were weak, and weak where they were strong. He never
lost sight of the humanity of Christ, nor was he tempted to
explain away some of the facts of our Lord's life, as the
Gnostics did. *De Carne Christi*, his reply to those who
threw doubt on Christ's humanity, is evidence of his own
live and simple faith. For instance, in a well-known
passage, he answers Marcion's rejection of Christ's human
birth by parodying his opponent's argument:

" ' Away,' says he, ' with that eternal plaguey taxing of
Cæsar, and the scanty inn, and the squalid swaddling-clothes,
and the hard stable. We do not care a jot for that multitude of
the heavenly host which praised their Lord at night. Let the
shepherds take better care of their flock, and let the wise men
spare their legs so long a journey; let them keep their gold to
themselves.' " *

This is a piece of satire, but it is satire written by a man
to whom the scenes of Christ's nativity are as real as those
of his own childhood. It was Tertullian's keen sense of
the actuality of our Lord's earthly life which made the
theories of the Gnostics seem to him merely ludicrous. He
could not resist poking fun at them and, in one book,
Against the Valentinians, he mocked them to his heart's
content. Much of the humour has faded, as it is apt to
do in controversial writings, but here and there its freshness has lasted. No one who has attempted to grasp the

* *De Carne Christi*, II.

æon theory of the universe, which Valentinus elaborated, can fail to enjoy Tertullian's likening of it to a vast tenement block, such as could be seen then in Rome or now in any large modern city.

" As for our heretics, however, it is marvellous what storeys upon storeys, and what heights upon heights, they have hung up, raised, and spread out as a dwelling for each several god of theirs. . . . The universe, in fact, has been turned into ' rooms to let.' " *

But for the most part the Gnostic speculations had only to be taken literally, instead of allegorically, to appear utterly absurd without any exercise of wit by Tertullian, and the reader is haunted by the doubt that perhaps Tertullian was incapable of taking them, or anything else, in any way but literally.

What was perhaps the most important of all Tertullian's battles against heresy was fought after he had become a Montanist. A certain Praxeas from Asia Minor came to Rome at the end of the second century, and there propounded a novel doctrine. He asserted, to quote Tertullian, that " the Father himself came down into the Virgin's womb, was himself born of her, himself suffered, indeed, was himself Jesus Christ ". The attraction of this attempt to explain the doctrine of the Trinity was that it safeguarded the unity of God without denying the divinity of Christ. It seems that even the Bishop of Rome was favourably impressed. He also listened to what Praxeas had to say against the Montanists of Asia Minor, and decided against them. Tertullian opposed Praxeas from the first. He defeated him in person when he came on to Carthage from Rome; but, though the heretic was silenced, the heresy died hard. Modalism—the Son being thought of as a " mode " of God the Father's being—or Patripassianism,

* *Against the Valentinians*, VII.

as this particular form of the theory was called, was revived years later, and Tertullian then wrote his treatise *Adversus Praxean* to defend the true doctrine of the Trinity. With his gift for a telling phrase, he sums up the reckoning he has against Praxeas by saying:

" Praxeas did a twofold service for the devil at Rome: he drove away prophecy, and he brought in heresy; he put to flight the Paraclete and he crucified the Father."

But it is not his brilliant use of invective which makes this treatise great; it is that his own statement of the doctrine of the Trinity anticipates the conclusion eventually hammered out by the Church at the Council of Nicæa.

Faith is one half of Christian life, but conduct is the other, and Tertullian was tirelessly interested in both. He wrote against the heathen; he wrote against the heretics; but he also wrote on prayer and penitence, on patience, on popular entertainments, on women's dress, on a soldier's duty, on idolatry, baptism, fasting, chastity, and monogamy. He discussed whether girls should wear veils, whether Christians should flee to escape persecution, and whether he himself should or should not wear a toga. Of these books little need be said here. Their chief interest is in the light they throw on the daily life of Christians at the beginning of the third century, and that will be dealt with in the following chapter. As might be expected, they show Tertullian as a harsh critic of his fellow men and women. He was what later centuries would have called a Puritan in his moral standard, and as he grew older he became more and more severe in his demands. He condemned second marriages, and wished to impose a much stricter rule of fasting and of penance than the Church approved. He never wearied of preaching to women on the themes of chastity, modesty, and sobriety of dress. On charity and forbearance he had much less to say.

Whatever Tertullian's defects of character, he devoted his life and his great gifts to the service of Christ, and Western Christendom is deeply indebted to him. He was the first to express Christian ideas in terms of Roman thought and, in so doing, he created " ecclesiastical Latin, which was the chief medium of proclaiming the Gospel in the West for at least 1,300 years ".* Law was to the Romans what philosophy was for the Greeks—the mode of thought most natural to their genius. Tertullian, in attempting to express Christian doctrine in the terms of the law-courts, was interpreting it in the way most intelligible to Roman minds. He was translating it not merely into Latin, but into the spirit of his age. He coined phrases which have become accepted formulas of the Church: " Christus deus et homo " and " pater, filius et spiritus sanctus—unus deus ". He forged the very language of theology out of the terms of the law-courts. Speaking of the Trinity, he used the words " person " and " substance ", about which controversy was soon to rage. He took the word " satisfaction ", used in law of something which is accepted in place of a debt or in compensation for an injury, and applied it to penance and also to the Atonement. His writings are full of legal terms adapted to Christian use. Of course his medium was inadequate to express God's nature and his redeeming love for man; but the language of philosophy also had its limitations and defects, as would the scientific idiom of today if it were used to describe the Incarnation and the Atonement.

Each of the great city-centres where Christianity took root made its own special contribution to the life of the early Church. Each had its distinctive character, its particular gifts, its own approach to the Gospel. From its earliest days, the church of Carthage showed an unusual

* *Church Life and Thought in North Africa*, by Dr Donaldson, p. 41.

capacity for producing martyrs and visionaries.   Its character tended to extremes.   Glorious in its martyrs, but torn
by schism, troubled on the one hand by the rigorists and on
the other by the lax and worldly, Carthage had not the
stability of Rome, or the wisdom of Alexandria.   But out
of the tension of these inner struggles the North African
church brought forth three great Christian thinkers, Tertullian, St Cyprian, and St Augustine.   In so doing, it did
much to shape the ideas of Western Christianity.   As to
the language in which those ideas were expressed, ecclesiastical Latin appears to have been created by the North African
church.   The earliest Latin translation of the Scriptures
was evidently made in Carthage, where Latin, not Greek,
was the language of educated people.   This translation has
not survived, but Tertullian quotes from it, and so does
St Cyprian half a century later.   The fragments show that
it was a rough piece of work, yet the unknown translator
should share a little of the honour that belongs to Tertullian
for adapting Latin to the use of the Church.

Much has been written about Tertullian, for his is a
personality that attracts both praise and blame.   He is not,
of course, a canonized saint of the Church, but one of the
finest and fairest tributes paid to him was written by
Baron Friedrich Von Hügel, from the Roman Catholic
standpoint, in one of his letters to his niece:

" You will never forget, will you, Gwen, that Rome—that
official Christianity—deliberately and continually refused to
accept Tertullian's tone, or to endorse his rigorism?   He ranks
as the greatest of the Montanist heretics.   And most undoubtedly Rome was right in all this, and Tertullian was wrong.
Yet it remains simultaneously true, that Tertullian's is the first
mind and personality of the first rank, classable as Christian,
indeed heroically Christian in intention, that God gave or permitted to mankind, after the long break since St Paul." *

* *Letters from Baron Friedrich Von Hügel to a Niece*, p. 39.

BOOKS FOR FURTHER READING

Conflict of Religions in the Ancient World, by T. R. Glover. An excellent chapter on Tertullian.

Church Life and Thought in North Africa, by S. A. Donaldson.

Translation of Tertullian's works. A.-N.C.L.

Some Authentic Acts of the Early Martyrs, by E. C. E. Owen. Trans. of the Passion of SS. Perpetua and Felicitas. (Notice especially the frontispiece—a photograph of the inscription on the martyrs' tomb.)

Documents Illustrative of the History of the Church, ed. by B. J. Kidd. Vol. I, Nos. 87–104, inclusive.

CHAPTER XIV

EVERYDAY CHRISTIAN LIFE IN THE SECOND AND THIRD CENTURIES

ORDINARY men and women, who are neither exceptionally lucky nor exceptionally unfortunate, seldom find their names mentioned in the news of the day, still less often does any record of their lives survive to interest later ages. Yet one of the chief pleasures of reading history is that of living imaginatively in an age other than our own, and, in the case of Church history, it is particularly important to remember the ordinary Christians as well as the saints, confessors, apologists, and martyrs. The Church then, as now, was composed of all sorts and conditions of men, although in the first three centuries—the centuries of persecution—the indifferent or merely nominal Christian must have been comparatively rare. Living as they did in a hostile heathen environment, the early Christians were aware that they were a " peculiar people ", set apart by baptism from the world, the flesh, and the devil. In one sense, their everyday life was that of other men and women of their generation. In another and more important sense, it was quite different; for they had found a new meaning in life and a new standard of values. The expression of this new outlook in daily behaviour was the task of ordinary Christians in every walk of life. Patricians and slaves, shopkeepers, builders, schoolmasters, lawyers, matrons, and maid-servants, all alike took their share in the great experiment of working out the Christian way of life. It was given to them to lay the foundation of that Christian

civilization which in spite of many imperfections, became
the glory of Europe, and still survives, half-wrecked, as
our precarious heritage today.

Here and there, in records of martyrdoms or in episcopal
letters, individual Christians, otherwise unknown to
history, appear, like actors in minor parts, who enter, speak
a few words perhaps, cross the stage, and disappear for
ever.   Such glimpses are sometimes illuminating, but it
would be impossible to picture the life of the whole Christian
community from these few flashes.   Fortunately two
writers, St Clement of Alexandria and Tertullian, have said
a great deal, either about Christian conduct in their own
day or about what it ought to have been.   With their aid
it is possible to learn a good deal about the everyday life
of Christians in the second and third centuries A.D.

" Surely it is obvious enough, if one looks at the whole world,
that it is becoming daily better cultivated and more fully peopled
than anciently.   All places are now accessible, all are well
known, all open to commerce;   most pleasant farms have
obliterated all traces of what once were dreary and dangerous
wastes;   cultivated fields have subdued forests;   flocks and herds
have expelled wild beasts;   sandy deserts are sown;   rocks
planted;   marshes are drained;   and where once were hardly
solitary cottages, there are now large cities." *

So wrote Tertullian at the end of the second century,
with the pride of a Roman citizen.   Roman civilization was
in many ways as advanced as our own, and socially it was
quite as complex;   it is therefore a mistake to imagine that
most early Christians were simple folk to whom life presented few problems.   The majority of them were city-
dwellers, or attached to the huge households that belonged
to the Emperor and to a few wealthy men.   In some
districts, especially in Asia Minor, Christianity was already
widespread in the country;   but for the most part the peasants

* *De Anima*, Chap. XXX, Tertullian.

clung to paganism, which, with its fertility rites, had more meaning for them than it had for townsmen. A typical Christian gathering in any one of the many cities of the Roman Empire would have included some members of the local aristocracy, a large number of free citizens of lower standing, freedmen, some of them wealthy, and some slaves. Within the Christian fellowship these social distinctions were ignored. A slave or a freedman might become a bishop—several of the early bishops of Rome came from one or other of these classes—and no mention is made of rank in the early Christian inscriptions in the catacombs. But slavery was accepted as an institution of this world. A slave, when he became a Christian, was taught to obey his master for Christ's sake and give him better service than before. The modern reader will search in vain in early Christian writings for a denunciation of slavery, or for any hint that emancipation was one of the aims of the Church. Very little is said about slavery at all. It is simply taken for granted. Christians not only remained in slavery without protest, they also, if they were well-to-do, owned slaves themselves, and saw nothing wrong in it. St Clement, describing the ideal behaviour for a Christian gentleman, merely objects to his owning a large number of household slaves, as he objects to any other form of extravagant luxury. A Christian is not to be shoved up a hill by his domestics, " nor is a man in health to use his servants as horses to bear him ". St Clement continues:

" For as it is enjoined on them, ' to be subject to their masters with all fear, not only to the good and gentle, but also to the froward ', as Peter says; so fairness, and forbearance, and kindness, are what well becomes the masters." *

The Church's answer to the cruelty and injustice involved in slavery was not a programme of social revolution, but

* St Clement: *The Instructor*, Book III. xi, " Walking." Vol. IV, Clement of Alexandria I. A.-N.C.L.

the constant preaching of good will among men.   A Christian must treat all his slaves with consideration as fellow human beings; his Christian slaves he must, of course, regard as brothers.   It was an answer which cut at the root of slavery, which is an utter disregard of human personality. St Perpetua and St Felicitas, the Roman matron and the slave-girl, standing hand in hand in the arena, are symbolic of the new Christian attitude to life, which eventually made slavery an anachronism.

Slaves had little say in the direction of their own lives. They must obey orders, or else take the consequences. But when a freedman or a free labourer became a Christian, he often had a difficult decision to make.   His work might be wholly or partly connected with idolatry.   Must he give it up and risk starvation, or was a compromise possible?   A plasterer and decorator, for instance, could refuse commissions for adorning heathen temples or painting frescoes of the gods on the walls of private houses, and could still earn a living by mending roofs, polishing cisterns, laying on stucco, and painting harmless decorative designs. He would nevertheless be constantly tempted by fear of giving offence to a wealthy patron or incurring suspicion in a time of persecution, as well as by the wish to earn more money for his family, and it would never be easy for him to know just where to draw the line.   Tertullian was quite ready to draw it for him, and he ruled out everything that smacked at all of idolatry.   Worshipping idols, making idols, and equipping temples were all equally evil in his eyes.

" For it matters not whether you erect or equip: if you have embellished his temple, or altar, or niche, if you have pressed out gold-leaf, or have wrought his insignia, or even his house: work of that kind which confers not *shape*, but *authority* is more important." *

* Tertullian: *On Idolatry*. See this treatise for the whole of this section.

In practice, the choice must often have been a hard one; yet, in all these cases, there was alternative employment. The carver could make chests and boxes instead of images; the silversmith could produce cups and dishes for wealthy households; even the flower-sellers could make wreaths for banquets instead of for decking idols. Indeed, as Tertullian was careful to point out, supplying private customers meant more regular work for the craftsman, though the profits were smaller. " Shoe- and slipper-gilding is daily work; not so the gilding of Mercury and Serapis."

Besides these border-line occupations, which might be sinful or innocent according to circumstances, there were others which the Church condemned outright. Astrology was one of these, although some of those who practised that profitable art professed Christianity and endeavoured to justify themselves by appealing to the story of the three Magi, who were led to Christ by a star. The taint of magic, charlatanism, and heathen associations, however, was too strong to be cleansed by one citation from Scripture, and Simon Magus weighed heavily in the other side of the scales. Astrologers, sooth-sayers, spiritualists, and magicians of all kinds had to find fresh occupations if they were converted to Christianity. The same applied to actors and gladiators. St Cyprian mentions the case of an actor who left the stage when he became a Christian, but afterwards endeavoured to support himself by giving elocution lessons. St Cyprian's ruling is that this cannot be allowed. To train boys for the stage is as bad as to act oneself. ' But he sympathizes with the hardship of the man's case, and agrees that a small allowance shall be paid him from Church funds until he be able to earn his living in some other way. * The gross immorality of the theatre at this period fully justified the Church's condemnation of it, which sounds so strange to a modern reader.

* Letter LX in the A.-N.C.L. translation of St Cyprian's letters.

Both craftsmanship and manual labour were recognized as part of the Christian scheme of life. Had not St Paul worked for his living as a tent-maker? The Jewish custom of providing all boys with a trade suggested to St Ignatius the advice he gave to Christian fathers:

"Fathers, bring up your children in the nurture and admonition of the Lord; and teach them the Holy Scriptures, and also trades, that they may not indulge in idleness."

Celsus despised the Christians because so many of them were working men, " wool-dressers, cobblers, and fullers ", " uneducated and vulgar persons ", as he scornfully called them: but the Christians themselves were proud to carve the tools of their trades on their tombstones in the catacombs. Shop-keeping was also recognized as lawful, provided that the goods sold were not idolatrous and that the prices charged were fair. In the matter of price, Christians set a new standard of honest dealing by having fixed charges, in place of the mendacious bargaining which still prevails in Eastern countries. Even St Clement of Alexandria, academic as he was in thought and training, recognized that there was a " philosophy " of daily life as well as of the schools. Speaking to men of the market-place he said:

" It is in your power to listen to divine wisdom, aye, and to frame your life in accordance with it. Nay, you are not prohibited from conducting affairs in the world decorously according to God. Let not him who sells or buys aught name two prices for what he buys or sells; but stating the net price, and studying to speak the truth, if he get not his price he gets the truth, and is rich in the possession of rectitude."

Earlier still St Justin Martyr had noticed the impression which Christian business men made upon pagans:

" Many who were of your way of thinking", he wrote in his Apology, " have changed their violent and tyrannical disposition, being overcome either by the constancy which they have witnessed in their neighbours' lives, or by the extraordinary forbearance they have observed in their fellow-travellers when defrauded, or by the honesty of those with whom they have transacted business."*

Unhappily, there were some Christians, even in the first three centuries, who fell far below this standard. St Cyprian commented bitterly on the love of money shown by many Christians in the period of peace before the Decian persecution:

" Every one was applying himself to the increase of wealth; and forgetting both what was the conduct of believers under the apostles, and what ought to be their conduct in every age, they with insatiable eagerness for gain devoted themselves to the multiplying of possessions. . . . Numerous bishops, who ought to be an encouragement and example to others, despising their sacred calling, engaged themselves in secular vocations, relinquished their Chair, deserted their people, strayed among foreign provinces, hunted the markets for mercantile profits; tried to amass large sums of money, while they had brethren starving within the church, took possession of estates by fraudulent proceedings, and multiplied their gains by accumulated usuries." †

It was bad that such things should happen, but at least they were recognized to be evil, not defended as " sound business ". Usury was condemned in the early Church, as it had been in the Old Testament. Just before the last persecution, about A.D. 300, the Council which met at Elvira considered the question, and decided that a cleric found taking usury should be deposed and excommunicated. A layman might be pardoned, provided he repented and cancelled the debt; otherwise he too must be " cast out of the Church ". The same Council decided that clergy

* Kidd, op. cit., No. 40.
† Cyprian: *De Lapsis*, Kidd, op. cit., No. 132.

might engage in trade in their own province, but must not neglect their duties by going abroad in search of markets. *
The custom of paying small stipends to the clergy, which became usual during the third century, was doubtless intended to meet this evil by making it unnecessary for the clergy to become commercial travellers in order to earn a living.

Labourers, craftsmen, traders, even slaves, had their share in the public amusements of the Roman world. Family life counted for a good deal less than it does with us, and membership of some club or guild mattered more. Instead of looking forward to taking his wife and children to the seaside on August Bank Holiday, a Roman working-man would expect to have a good time on the feast day of his club. Instead of Christmas, he would have the licensed buffoonery and revelling of the Saturnalia. Instead of football matches, dog-tracks, and cinemas, he would have the circus and the amphitheatre. But all these amusements had their origin in idolatry. The public holidays celebrated the festivals of heathen gods; the shows at the circus and the amphitheatre began with sacrificial offerings; and so did the feasts of trade-guilds and clubs. A Christian had no part or lot in any of these things. He was cut off from the social life of his time, unless he chose to ignore the counsel of his bishop and the qualms of his own conscience. Undoubtedly, many Christians did join in heathen festivals and go to heathen shows. Writer after writer among the early Fathers finds it necessary to condemn the race-course and the theatre. Minucius Felix makes Octavius reply to his pagan friend, who reproaches Christians for avoiding what he calls " legitimate amusements ":

" We, whose reputation depends upon our decent mode of life, rightly abstain from evil pleasures, from your processions

* *The Canons of the Council of Elvira*, quoted Kidd, op. cit., No. 170.

and spectacles, which we know are derived from your religious rites, and whose pernicious allurements we condemn. At the curule games, who can help being horrified at the frenzy of the bawling populace and, at the gladiatorial shows, at the training for murder? On the stage, even, there is the same frenzy, while the range of vice is wider."

St Clement, Tertullian, St Cyprian, all echo the same sentiments. Tertullian, writing for a Christian, not a heathen, audience, makes it plain that temptation was too strong for many of the faithful.

" The Saturnalia and New-year's and Midwinter's festivals and Matronalia are frequented ", he complains, "—presents come and go—New-year's gifts—games join their noise—banquets join their din ! " *

He found it necessary to write a special treatise, " On Spectacles ", to remonstrate with those who tried to justify themselves for continuing to go to these entertainments after their baptism. He dwelt on the heathen origin of these shows, on their vicious character, on the delirious frenzy they provoked, on the cruelty they encouraged, and he condemned them as utterly unfit for a Christian.

" For ", he wrote, " how monstrous it is to go from God's church to the devil's—from the sky to the stye, as they say; to raise your hands to God, and then weary them in the applause of an actor; out of the mouth, from which you uttered Amen over the Holy Thing, to give witness in a gladiator's favour; to cry ' for ever ' to any one else but God and Christ ".

It was Gregory Thaumaturgus, bishop of Neo-Cæsarea in the middle of the third century, who found a practical solution to the problem of heathen festivals. He not only converted the pagans of his province, he converted their festivals, too, by giving them a Christian character. It was a method that proved extremely successful, and was widely

* Tertullian: *On Idolatry*, Chap. XIV.

adopted by the Church in the following centuries. As a result, many heathen customs have survived even to the present day, but their original significance has been forgotten. For example, we still give each other presents at the Mid-winter Festival, but now we do so in the name of Christ.

During the centuries of persecution, Christians were frequently accused of being enemies of the State, or at least of being indifferent to its welfare. This was mainly due to their refusal to worship the Emperor or any of the State gods; but it was also partly on account of their reluctance to undertake military service or any official duties. Their objection to military service was not so much due to pacifism (though some, like Tertullian, did hold that view), but to the realization that Emperor-worship formed part of much military ceremonial. Yet, in spite of this, there were plenty of Christians in the army, and they became more numerous as the years went on. The legend of the " Thundering Legion " assumes the presence of a considerable number of Christians among the soldiers of Marcus Aurelius, for it was their prayers that were said to have brought rain to the thirsty army. More certain evidence is afforded by the records of soldier-martyrs from the third century onwards. A particularly interesting account is given of St Marcellus, who was martyred in A.D. 298, during the reign of Diocletian.* Marcellus was a centurion of the Trajan legion, and evidently he had served in the army for some time without obtruding his religious beliefs on the notice of his senior officers. But on the feast of the Emperor's birthday, when special sacrifices were being offered, Marcellus astounded the whole legion by stripping off his sword-belt in front of the standards, declaring: " I serve Jesus Christ the Eternal King ". He then threw away his vine-switch, the sign of his rank as centurion, and refused

* E. C. E. Owen: *Some Authentic Acts of the Early Martyrs*, Sec. 11 & 12.

to worship idols, saying: " If such be the terms of service that men are forced to sacrifice to gods and Emperors, behold I cast away my vine-switch and belt. I renounce the standards and refuse to serve." He was immediately placed under arrest, and his commanding officer referred his case to Aurelius Agricolan, Deputy for the Prefects of the Guard. Aurelius gave the prisoner a fair hearing; but when he admitted his refusal to serve, and gave no reason except the fact that he was a Christian, Aurelius concluded that the man was insane, and condemned him to death. At that point, his staff secretary, who had been taking down notes of the case in shorthand, threw down his pen with an oath, saying that the sentence was unjust, for he, too, was a Christian. Aurelius lost his temper, to the amusement of Marcellus, who burst out laughing, and dignity was only restored to the court when Marcellus was hurried out to his death and Cassian, the secretary, removed to a cell to await trial. He, too, was shortly afterwards martyred.

Tertullian records with approval a similar case in which a soldier threw away his military crown on the occasion of an Imperial review of the troops, and was in consequence executed as a Christian. But these acts of provocation, the deliberate flouting of either civil or military authority, were not approved by the main body of Christian opinion. Christians were to endure martyrdom when necessary, but not to court it. Even so, there must have been many occasions when a Christian soldier could not in conscience carry out the duties assigned to him and died rather than do so. Others, like our own St Alban, suffered martyrdom in attempting to save fellow-Christians from persecution.

If it was difficult for a Christian to be a soldier, it was still harder for him to be a magistrate without acting against his conscience. Tertullian believed it was impossible. He catalogued some of the duties of State officials to prove his point: sacrificing, authorizing sacrifices, farming out victims, seeing to the repair of temples, collecting temple dues, giving shows in the amphitheatre, and presiding at them, and condemning prisoners to death or torture. In spite of this, Christians did sometimes accept office, and evade some of these duties during the intervals of peace in the third century.

There is still one important occupation among those condemned by Tertullian as unsuitable for Christians which has not yet been mentioned. It is that of the schoolmaster. Elementary schools were already numerous in the second and third centuries. There a boy, who might later become a potter or a builder, would learn to read and write, and so might chance to scrawl in wet clay one of the " graffiti " that have survived to interest modern archæologists. But the education given by these village schools did not go very far. Better-off people sent their sons to the grammar schools, where they were given a sound general education, mainly literary in character. It was this type of school that Tertullian had in mind when he said that teachers " are in affinity with manifold idolatry ". The chief trouble was that as the literature studied was inevitably pagan literature, the schoolmaster was bound to teach his pupils out of books written in praise of the heathen gods. In addition, he was expected to see to it that his school was wreathed with flowers on pagan festival days, and his own salary came to him in dues on these occasions. No wonder the Church soon began to organize schools of her own, where children might learn Christian doctrine from Christian teachers. Many children would go to pagan schools for their general education, and to a Christian class for cate-chumens as well. Later it became usual for bishops and others of the clergy to educate some of the boys born to Christian parents in their locality. From this small begin-ning, episcopal and other church schools grew up, and were already influential in the fourth century. The catechetical schools of Alexandria, and other large cities, were for adults, not for children, and at their best gave an education of university standard.

" We must now compendiously describe what the man who is called a Christian ought to be during the whole of his life."

With these promising words, St Clement of Alexandria begins his account of the behaviour proper to a Christian gentleman in every aspect of his daily life. He deals in turn with food, table-manners, furnishing, dress, laughter, sleep, exercise, personal adornment, the life of fashionable women, and many other topics. Here it is not possible to do more than quote a few passages to show the kind of behaviour that was usual in good society in Alexandria and other Græco-Roman cities, and, by contrast, the qualities which St Clement desired to encourage in his converts.

" Some men, in truth," writes St Clement, " live that they may eat, as the irrational creatures, ' whose life is their belly, and nothing else '. But the Instructor enjoins us to eat that we may live." *

Christians, he urges, should aim at a plain, wholesome diet and beware lest they vitiate their taste by the " unhappy art " of cookery. In particular, they should avoid pastry, which upsets the stomach. Into the great port of Alexandria poured luxuries from all over the world. St Clement contemptuously lists some of these imports: lampreys from the straits of Sicily, eels from the Mæander, kids from Melos, the mussels of Pelorus, and the oysters of Abydos, " not omitting the sprats found in Lipara, and the Mantinican turnip; and, furthermore, the beetroot that grows among the Ascræans ", and lastly, " the reddish-brown dried figs, on account of which the ill-starred Persian marched

* Clement of Alexandria: *The Instructor*. A.-N.C.L. Vol. IV. Clement I. Book II, Chapter 1, *On Eating*.

into Greece with five hundred thousand men." Thus, he says, men " sweep the world with a drag-net to gratify their luxurious tastes ". He has no use for these " gluttons, surrounded with the sound of hissing frying-pans, and wearing their whole life away at the pestle and mortar, who spoil plain food, namely bread, by straining off the nourishing part of the grain ". For Christians he recommends, besides whole-meal bread, fish, herbs, olives, milk, cheese, fruits, roast meat occasionally, and " all kinds of cooked food without sauces "; though he thinks the dishes that are simplest to prepare and need least cooking are best. Fancy sweets, such as honey-cakes and sugar-plums, he regards as luxuries sought after by those who are " all jaw and nothing else "; but a Christian may enjoy a honeycomb with no qualms of conscience, for this is good Scriptural food.

As with food, so with drink, St Clement's counsel is moderation in all things. Boys and girls, he says, should drink water, but their elders may take wine at supper-time, in the cool of the evening, when the serious reading of the day is over. " Those who are already advanced in life may partake more hilariously of the bowl, to warm by the harmless medicine of the vine the chill of age." But drunkenness, as one would expect, disgusts him. So do the table-manners of those who shovel their food greedily into their mouths, " as if they were stowing away their victuals for provision for a journey, not for digestion ", or who plunge their faces into the bowl and gulp down their liquor as though they fear it will be snatched away from them.* " In what manner do you think the Lord drank when he became man for our sakes?" Clement asks. " As shamelessly as we? Was it not with decorum and propriety? . . . For rest assured, he himself also partook of wine; for he, too, was man. And he blessed the wine, saying, ' Take, drink: this is my blood '—the blood of the vine."

* *The Instructor*, Chapter II, *On Drinking*.

From food and table-manners St Clement passes to table-ware and household furnishing. He rejects gold and silver cups as ostentatious and not really practical, for sometimes they are too hot to hold, and at others the metal spoils the liquor that is put in it. Glass breaks too easily, and common earthenware is best.

" Couches with silver feet and inlaid with ivory, and folding-doors of beds studded with gold and variegated tortoise-shell, and bed-clothes of purple and other colours difficult to produce, proofs of tasteless luxury, cunning devices of envy and effeminacy, are all to be relinquished, as having nothing worth our pains."

A Christian should have serviceable furnishings, suitable to his station in life; but senseless display is not for him.

" The Lord ate from a common bowl, and made the disciples recline on the grass on the ground, and washed their feet, girded with a linen towel—he, the lowly-minded God and Lord of the universe. He did not bring down a silver foot-bath from heaven." *

Neither St Clement nor even Tertullian, whose conception of Christian discipline was more severe, wished to debar Christians from all social contact with their pagan neighbours. Both thought it quite allowable to accept invitations to dinner-parties, or to weddings, or coming-of-age celebrations. On some of these occasions sacrifices would take place; but Tertullian ruled that a Christian might still accept the invitation, provided that it ran: " You are invited to be present on the occasion of my daughter's wedding ", and not " You are invited to assist at a sacrifice ". St Clement had doubts about one of the most popular institutions of his time—the baths. He strongly disapproved of mixed bathing, which is hardly surprising, since no bathing dresses were worn. He also thought that constant use of the baths was debilitating, and, as the Roman baths

* *The Instructor*, Chapter III, *On Costly Vessels*.

resembled what we call " Turkish baths " today, he was probably right. He gives a warning, too, against wasting time " in barbers' shops and taverns, babbling nonsense ".*

On dress and personal adornment, more particularly on women's dress, both St Clement and Tertullian have much to say. † They express strong disapproval of jewellery, elaborate hair-dressing, dyed hair, and the use of cosmetics. St Clement would allow women to make their clothes of softer materials than those in ordinary use for men, but he would ban the fashionable Indian silks, the flowered and gold-embroidered stuffs, and all the many dyes—green, rose-coloured, scarlet, purple, and saffron. His objection to dyed garments was partly that they were unnatural, and Tertullian took the same view, saying that God had not willed that sheep should be born with purple and sky-blue fleeces. But, besides this, these brightly coloured garments were associated with heathen festivals, especially with Bacchic initiation rites, whereas white robes suggested St John's vision of the redeemed in Revelation.

When dyed clothes were regarded as unsuitable for a soberly-minded Christian, it is no wonder that dyed hair was utterly condemned. At this period blondes were fashionable, and women used saffron to turn their hair yellow, as if, according to Tertullian's acid comment, they were ashamed not to have been born among the barbarians in Germany and Gaul. Tertullian, like St Clement, thought that Christian women should dress their hair simply. He disliked the frequent changes in fashion—the hair, now " bound, now loosed, now cultivated, now thinned out . . ." and padding, false hair, and elaborate curls, both exasperated and disgusted him.

* Book III, Chapters V—IX.
† St Clement: ibid., *On Dress*, etc., Book II, Chapters XI–XIII, and Book III, Chapters I–VII and IX, and Tertullian, *On Female Dress*, Book II, Chapter VII.

" I shall see (at the last day)," he writes, " whether you will rise with your ceruse and rouge and saffron, and in all that parade of headgear; whether it will be women thus tricked out whom the angels carry up to meet Christ in the air!"

HEAD OF A ROMAN LADY. BRITISH MUSEUM

Meanwhile, like the moralists of all ages, he and St Clement waged war on cosmetics, using the usual arguments, with, it is to be feared, the usual lack of effect. They pointed out that to paint the face was a presumptuous attempt to improve on the Creator's handiwork; that cosmetics injured the skin and aged it prematurely; that make-up was the sign, not of a lady, but of a courtesan.

Y

Many Christian women, however, continued to use ceruse, the ancient equivalent to face-powder, rouge, and eyelid-powder. In excuse, they pleaded that they must look pretty if they were to keep their husbands' affection, and, in any case, it would be no credit to their new faith if they went about looking dowdy. Such reasoning did not convince Tertullian or any who held strict views about Christian discipline in everyday life, and it is probable that the majority of Christians did, in fact, dress more quietly than their pagan neighbours and avoid artificial aids to beauty.

Vanity is a weakness not confined to women, and St Clement has an amusing description of the dandies of his day. He saw them idling about the streets of Alexandria, with their hair cut " in an ungentlemanly and meretricious way, clothed in fine and transparent garments, chewing mastich, smelling of perfume ". Tertullian also observed and listed what he dubbed the " deceptive trickeries " peculiar to the masculine sex, such as, " to cut the beard too sharply; to pluck it out here and there; to shave round about the mouth; to arrange the hair and disguise its hoariness with dyes; to remove all the incipient down all over the body; to fix each hair in place with some womanly pigment; then, further, to take every opportunity for consulting the mirror; to gaze anxiously into it." Christians should indulge in none of this. They should crop the hair of their heads and let their beards grow naturally. St Clement advises them, however, to clip the moustache with scissors for the sake of cleanliness in eating.

The wearing of expensive jewellery was another habit which a convert to Christianity was advised to abandon. St Clement wanted both men and women to be simple and truly childlike in all their ways, and he considered it a sign of luxury and ostentation. Besides, as he said, " How much wiser to spend money on human beings, than on jewels and gold! " But he allowed one exception to the general rule, and that was the use of the signet ring, not for ornament, " but for sealing things which are worth keeping safe in the house ". It is an interesting exception to a modern reader, for many Roman signet rings have been found in the course of excavating ancient sites, and some of them have designs of a Christian character. Designs showing the heathen gods were, of course, forbidden to believers, but there were many others they could choose from:

" Let our seals be either a dove, or a fish, or a ship scudding before the wind, or a musical lyre, which Polycrates used, or a ship's anchor, which Seleucus got engraved as a device; and if there be one fishing, he will remember the apostle, and the children drawn out of the water."

The life of women of fashion had little to recommend it in the eyes of St Clement. He saw their litters carried through the streets on the shoulders of stalwart Celts, and he noticed how boldly the occupants would part the curtains and stare out, liking to see and be seen. He saw them making the round of the temples, sacrificing, and practising divination, spending their time with fortune-tellers and sooth-sayers. They fluttered past him in bright, flimsy dresses, and he caught the flash of their jewelled slippers in the sun. At home he knew they were surrounded by slaves and need never do a hand's turn for themselves. This was not the way in which he thought Christian women should live. On the contrary, they should spin and weave their own clothes, superintend the cooking, fetch whatever was needed from the store-cupboard, and generally give themselves healthy exercise by doing a fair share of the work of the house. Men, too, he thought might handle the hoe or chop firewood without loss of dignity. But they should also have more active exercise, especially in their youth, either in the gymnasium or else wrestling and playing ball games. Older men might find walking sufficient.*

* *The Instructor*, Book III, Chapter X, *On Exercise*.

Presumably most of the men to whom St Clement's words were addressed were students, like himself, who spent a large part of every day in serious reading. His aim was to sketch the life, not so much of the ordinary Christian as of the Christian gentleman, "characterized by composure, tranquillity, calmness, and peace". It was an ideal to which men were to turn again centuries later, when civilization had recovered from the shock of the barbarian invasions.

The negative aspects of the Christian way of life were those most obvious to outsiders. To them, Christians seemed dour, gloomy people who rejected pleasure and morosely cut themselves off from society. What the pagan observer saw less clearly, or not at all, was the fellowship of the Church, which more than compensated the believer for what he lost in the world. Among themselves, Christians were gradually evolving a new standard of social behaviour, new customs, even new types of men and women. The core of this fellowship was the celebration of the Eucharist, and so church-going was recognized as being of vital importance, not to be abandoned even in times of persecution. Women were expected to go veiled to church, though they did not always keep to this rule, and naturally all were expected to behave soberly and quietly. St Clement was shocked to notice "how people change their fashions and manners with the place." Those who in church had appeared "so pious, so meek, so loving" were no sooner outside than they began to amuse themselves frivolously with their pagan friends. He likened them to sea-anemones, changing colour to suit the rocks they clung to. Worse than that, some would make the church resound with their kiss of peace, and yet have no love in their hearts towards their neighbours. But to say this is only to admit what is obviously true, that few men and women can remain for long upon the heights. Christians in the first three centuries were not by any means perfect, but they recognized the importance of worship and gave it the central place in their lives.

When a man became a Christian, the change would affect his home life most of all. The gods of the threshold and of the hearth would be thrown out and the familiar ritual abandoned. Instead, the Christian would bring home from the Sunday morning service a small portion of the consecrated bread, and this reserved sacrament he would taste after his morning prayers, before taking the first food of the day. On certain days he would keep a " station " or fast. Always he would say grace, not only before meals but also before going to the baths. Besides his morning and evening prayers he would try, if at all strict in self-discipline, to pray three times a day, at the third, sixth, and ninth hours. On numerous occasions he would make the sign of the cross.*

By the end of the second century, Christian customs had grown up. Some had been borrowed from Judaism, and some were not destined to survive. The habit of washing the hands before prayer (whether they were dirty or not) was certainly Jewish. Another curious custom, that of taking off your cloak before praying, Tertullian thought was pagan in origin. Christians stood to pray on Sundays and at Pentecost as a sign of triumph, but they knelt at other times. Already Christianity was an old-established religion with local customs as well as an authoritative tradition. The customs have changed in the course of centuries, the central tradition remains.

It is easy to understand the difficulties that must have beset a mixed marriage between a Christian and a pagan. The Church did not approve of a believer marrying a heathen, but this sometimes happened. In other cases, a convert might fail to convince his or her partner and have to make the best of the existing situation. Tertullian has

* See Tertullian, *De corona militis*, quoted on p. 238 above.

vividly described the position of a Christian woman
married to a heathen husband:

" If a station is to be kept, the husband at daybreak makes
an appointment with his wife to meet him at the baths; if there
are fasts to be observed, the husband that same day holds a
convivial banquet; if a charitable expedition has to be made,
never is family business more urgent. For who would suffer
his wife, for the sake of visiting the brethren, to go round from
street to street to other men's, and indeed to all the poorer,
cottages? Who will willingly bear her being taken from his
side by nocturnal convocations, if need so be? Who, finally,
will without anxiety endure her absence all the night long at the
paschal solemnities? . . . If a pilgrim brother arrive, what
hospitality for him in an alien home? If bounty is to be
distributed to any, the granaries, the storehouses, are foreclosed."

By contrast he paints a happy picture of the unity of
Christian marriage, where the flesh is one and the spirit is
one also.

" Together they pray, together prostrate themselves, together
perform their fasts; mutually teaching, mutually exhorting,
mutually sustaining. Equally are they both found in the
Church of God; equally at the banquet of God; equally in
straits, in persecutions, in refreshments. Neither hides aught
from the other; neither shuns the other; neither is troublesome
to the other. The sick is visited, the indigent relieved, with
freedom. . . . There is no stealthy signing, no trembling
greeting, no mute benediction." *

Most Christians then, as now, married; but some deliberately remained celibate. By A.D. 300, celibacy was recognized as the ideal for the clergy, as is shown by the Canons
of the Council of Elvira, but it was by no means an in-
variable rule in the second or even in the third century.
There was a recognized order of virgins, as well as of
widows, at this period. Tertullian was voluble about the

* Tertullian, *To His Wife*, IV and VIII.

question, much disputed in his day, whether virgins should
or should not be veiled in church.   These women refrained
from marriage in order that they might dedicate their lives
to God, but they were not under perpetual vows, nor did
they live apart from the rest of the community.   They were
thus subject to great temptation, and were sometimes the
occasion of scandal.   St Cyprian had to deal with a very
serious case of that sort, and Tertullian alludes to others.
The solution of this particular difficulty was not found
until religious communities for women were formed in
the fourth century.   The order of widows was open to
less objection, and had its origin in apostolic times.   These
were older women, devoted to good works, who received
small pensions from church funds for their support.   Second
marriages were not forbidden by the Church, but to remain
a widow was thought commendable.

The spirit of love which filled the early Church found
expression in numerous ways.   Christians were hospitable.
They welcomed brethren from distant churches, whether
they knew them or not, and they helped them if they were
in difficulties.   Christians were liberal in giving alms,
whether the money was needed for the poor, or for the
needs of prisoners, or for redeeming slaves.   They had
such a reputation for their zeal in visiting prisoners, that
the second-century pagan satirist, Lucian, made fun of them
for it.   The disreputable hero of his story, Peregrinus, was
in prison and, supposing him to be a believer, the local
Christians tried to set him free.   Lucian continues:

" Then, when this was found to be impossible, they looked
after his wants in every other respect with unremitting care and
zeal.   And from the first break of day old women—widows
they are called—and orphan children might be seen waiting
about the doors of the prison; while their officers, by bribing
the keepers, succeeded in passing the night inside with him. . . .
Indeed the alacrity they display is incredible, when any matter of

the kind is undertaken as a matter of public concern; for in short they spare for nothing." *

The orphans whom Lucian mentions were children adopted by Christians after their pagan parents had exposed them and left them to take their chance. This was one of the customary acts of mercy in the early days of the Church, and it was one of the ways in which Christianity slowly but surely influenced public opinion. Some Christians devoted themselves to the care of the sick, either as healers or exorcists, for mental illness was then, rightly or wrongly, attributed to the influence of evil spirits. In the terrible outbreaks of plague which devastated many cities of the Roman Empire in the third century, Christians nursed friends and enemies alike. Their behaviour was in striking contrast with the selfish fear which made pagan families thrust their sick and dying relatives into the streets. A new spirit was abroad in the world, and from it new customs and new social ideals were growing up.

The witness of ordinary Christians in their daily lives was as effective in its own way as the heroic faith of the martyrs. Tertullian, militant as ever, has summed up the matter in his *Apology*. Speaking of the money collected by voluntary contributions in church, he says that these funds are used

" for feeding and burying the poor, for boys and girls, without money and without parents, and for old men now house-ridden, for the shipwrecked also, and for any who in the mines, or in the islands, or in the prisons, become their Creed's pensioners, so that it be only for the sake of the way of God ".

And he continues:

" But it is the exercise of this sort of love which doth, with some, chiefly brand us with a mark of evil. ' See,' say they,

* Lucian: *De Morte Peregrini*, Kidd, op. cit., No. 51.

' how they love each other '; for they themselves hate each other: and ' see how ready they are to die for each other '; for they themselves are more ready to slay each other." *

It was in this way that Christians in the early Church fought and overcame the world.

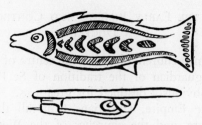

ROMAN BROOCH OF A TYPE PERMISSIBLE FOR CHRISTIANS

Found in London.

BOOKS FOR FURTHER READING

The Conflict of Religions, by T. R. Glover, the chapter on St Clement of Alexandria.
Clement of Alexandria, Vol. I. *The Instructor,* A.-N.C.L., Vol. IV.
Tertullian: A.-N.C.L., Vol. XI; Tertullian: *Apology; On Spectacles; On Idols; On Prayer; To His Wife; On Female Dress; On the Soldier's Crown.*
Documents Illustrative of the History of the Church, ed. by B. J. Kidd, Vol. I, Nos. 29, 40, 51, 61, 92, 132, 163, 170.
Christian Education in the First Four Centuries, by L. Millar.

* Tertullian: *Apology* cxxxix, Kidd, op. cit., 92.

CHAPTER XV

ROME: THE EARLY BISHOPS AND CONTROVERSIES
ON DOCTRINE

THE Roman church, placed at the centre of the civilized world, guardian of the tradition of St Peter and St Paul, was obviously destined for greatness. Being at the heart of the Empire, Christians from all the provinces resorted there, and the churches of the West inevitably looked for leadership to the Roman see, the only one among them which could claim apostles for its founders.

" The greatest, most ancient, and well-known Church, founded by two most glorious apostles, Peter and Paul at Rome . . . unto this Church, which holds a leading position among the Churches, must needs resort every Church—that is, the faithful who are everywhere—inasmuch as the apostolic tradition is always preserved by the faithful who are everywhere." *

So wrote St Irenæus towards the end of the second century, appealing to the authority of Roman tradition against the private speculations of heretical thinkers. His words give substance to the vision which the very name of the Roman church conjures up for those who know the history of succeeding centuries. Was this church, then, already in the second century the leader of all others? Was its bishop regarded as the supreme authority in the Church? Was he, in the modern sense of the term, a pope? Unfortunately, there is not very much reliable

* Irenæus, *Adversus Haereses*, iii. Quoted from Kidd, op. cit., No. 74.

evidence about the development of the Roman church in the first three centuries. Many of its bishops are hardly more than names to us, and the pieces of information we have got must be fitted together like a jig-saw puzzle, before a picture will appear. Even then the gaps are tantalizing and, naturally, scholars have been influenced by their own religious convictions in the reconstructions they have drawn. One thing is certain, no neat and tidy outline can do justice to the state of the Roman church in the second and third centuries. It was complex, many-sided, organic; for, like Topsy, it had " growed ". What St Irenæus says of the church of Rome in his day is true, and yet the impression a modern reader receives is misleading, because the statement is coloured for him by his knowledge of later developments. The facts revealed, even by the fragmentary records which have survived, show a state of affairs startlingly unlike that which existed in later centuries.

The earliest references to the church of Rome testify to its leading position and its reputation for faithfulness. St Paul writes:

" To all that be in Rome, beloved of God, called to be saints. . . . First, I thank my God through Jesus Christ for you all, that your faith is spoken of throughout the whole world." *

St Ignatius, early in the second century, directs a letter on his way to martyrdom " unto her that hath the presidency in the country of the region of the Romans ", " unto them that in flesh and spirit are united unto his every commandment, being filled with the grace of God without wavering, and filtered clear from every foreign strain ".

From the Roman side, there is the letter from the Roman to the Corinthian church, which a very early tradition ascribes to the hand of St Clement. It is a letter of ad-

* *Rom.* i. 7 and 8 (A.V.).

monition and the Roman church speaks with authority as the mouthpiece of the Holy Spirit:

" But if certain persons should be disobedient unto the words spoken by him through us ", says the writer at one point, " let them understand that they will entangle themselves in no slight transgression and danger; but we shall be guiltless of this sin."

But earlier in the letter, after pointing to the example set by St Peter and St Paul and by the martyrs in the Neronean persecution, St Clement is careful to add:

" These things, dearly beloved, we write, not only as admonishing you, but also as putting ourselves in remembrance." *

The general tone of the letter is in no way dictatorial. What is really remarkable is that in none of these three letters is there any mention of a Roman bishop. St Paul does not mention ministers of any rank in the Roman church. St Clement's letter says a good deal about the ministry and the duty of obeying those appointed by the apostles or by " other honoured men ", but he distinguishes only two orders, presbyter-bishops and deacons. If he was himself bishop of the church of Rome at the time of writing the letter, he never alludes to the fact. But that St Ignatius, with his burning conviction about the divine authority of bishops, should fail to greet the bishop of Rome is truly amazing. By the second decade of the second century, the distinction between the office of presbyter and that of bishop must have been generally recognized and Rome, like other churches, must have had a single bishop overseeing many presbyters. According to lists compiled at the end of the second century, the sixth bishop after the apostles would have been occupying the Roman see when St Ignatius sent his letter there. About the extent of his authority at this period there is no evidence at all.

* St Clement of Rome: *To the Corinthians*, section 7 trans. Lightfoot, *Apostolic Fathers*, Vol. II, Part I.

As early as the time of St Paul's letter the Roman church was composed of several separate congregations. St Paul sends greetings to five such groups: the church in the house of Priscilla and Aquila, the saints in the household of Aristobulus, those in the household of Narcissus, the brethren with Asyncritus, and those with Philologus. The catacombs have produced evidence which shows that the influence of the great families and the huge slave households affected the organization of the Roman church during the next two centuries. It could hardly be otherwise. Members of two or three of the great patrician families were converted to Christianity as early as Domitian's reign. The catacombs of Domitilla and Priscilla show that they provided places of burial for their fellow-believers; there can be no doubt that during their lifetime they provided places for meeting and worship as well. But this was not the only reason which encouraged the growth of separate congregations with distinctive characteristics of their own. Christianity in Rome spread most rapidly among the foreign Greek-speaking population, and not among the Latins. Besides the slaves attached to the great households, there were numbers of foreign residents in Rome, and these tended to group together according to the districts from which they came. Thus among those who were natives of Asia Minor, for instance, there would in course of time be a sufficient number of Christians to form a congregation. These would regard themselves as forming part of the Roman church; but they might well continue practices to which they were accustomed in Ephesus or Smyrna but which were not used by other Roman congregations. An actual instance of this will be mentioned later on.

Plainly the early Roman bishops can have had no easy task in co-ordinating the different sections of their church and in enforcing discipline. One custom, which was early established, must have been of great importance in impressing upon all the congregations their unity under one bishop. This was the practice of sending a fragment of the bread consecrated at the bishop's Eucharist to each of the parish churches in Rome. There the *fermentum*, as it was called, was placed in the chalice during the celebration of the Eucharist and, in this way, all congregations were reminded that they were taking part in the same service, presided over by the bishop. If it should happen that a presbyter in charge of one such group should defy his bishop's authority by teaching false doctrine, then the bishop might cut him off from communion, and the outward sign would be that the *fermentum* would no more be sent to him from the bishop's Eucharist.*

During the second and third centuries the Roman bishops had continually to face the challenge of visiting teachers from the provinces. Dr Prestige has likened the Roman church at this period to a mediæval university, in which " any Master of Arts had the right to set up his school and teach such pupils as he could attract ".† Some of these teachers were orthodox, like St Justin the Apologist, but many of them were not, and these sooner or later were condemned by the bishop and excommunicated. They then not infrequently set up rival churches of their own, and drew many of their hearers after them. In the first half of the second century, the Gnostics were the chief danger. According to St Irenæus, who wrote a treatise against them, Valentinus and Cerdon established themselves in Rome during the time of the eighth bishop, Hyginus. There they set up schools

" now teaching in secret, now making public confession anew, now being convicted of false teaching and removed from the assembly of the brethren ".

* Eusebius, op. cit., V. 24. 15. It is mentioned by St Irenæus as a custom of the early bishops of Rome.
† *Fathers and Heretics* by G. L. Prestige, Chapter II.

More alarming still, their schools often persisted when individual heretics died or went elsewhere. Marcion, for instance, succeeded Cerdon, enlarged his school, and taught a form of the same heresy which was the more dangerous for being shorn of many absurdities. False teaching would have been bad enough, but the Gnostics set up a separate church. They celebrated mysteries and they baptized their converts with a formula of their own. St Irenæus has described their practices:

" For some of them prepare a nuptial chamber and perform a rite of initiation accompanied by invocations over those who are being perfected; and they assert that this which they do is a spiritual marriage after the likeness of the heavenly unions. Others lead (the candidates) to water and as they baptize them say the following words: ' Into the name of the unknown Father of the universe, into Truth the Mother of all things, into him that descended upon Jesus.' "

The beliefs of the Gnostics, including Marcion, have been described already in an earlier chapter; what is of especial interest to notice here is that the Roman church took the full brunt of their attack. The details of the campaign are now lost, but there is not much doubt as to what were the main lines of defence. The Roman church held firmly to the creed derived from the apostles.

Already a simple form of the creed must have been in use, for from a very early date it was customary to deliver the *symbolum* or password, as it was called, to the catechumens before admitting them to baptism. In the second place, the Roman church must, during the second century, have come to a decision as to which books should be accepted as inspired and read at services. Marcion would have jettisoned the whole of the Old Testament and a large number of New Testament books. In reply the Church had perforce to define the canon, and much of the discussion, which was necessitated by this task, certainly took place in

Rome. A list of the books which the Roman church included in the New Testament has survived. It is known as the *Muratorian Canon*, and the original was written towards the end of the second century in Greek verse, so that Roman Christians could easily memorize it. Unfortunately, we have only a crude Latin translation, written at a much later date, the beginning and end of which are missing. The list evidently included all four Gospels, Acts, and St Paul's epistles. The Apocalypse, two letters by St John and one by St Jude were also accepted, but two letters forged by the followers of Marcion in the name of St Paul were firmly rejected.* Several books, such as Hebrews and 1 and 2 Peter, remained on the border line for many years, some churches accepting and others excluding them; but it was impossible for new writings to find their way into the canon. Thirdly, the church of Rome, in answering the arguments of the Gnostics, appealed to apostolic tradition and, to prove the tradition to be genuine, quoted the succession of Roman bishops from the time of the apostles onwards. Hegesippus, a Jewish Christian who toured the churches about A.D. 160 to assure himself that all professed the same doctrine, was much impressed by this evidence, and preserved in his memoirs a list of the bishops as far as Anicetus.

One obvious method of defence was to reply to the Gnostics in lectures and in writing. The Roman church, however, was not rich in scholars and theologians during the second century, and this part of the work fell chiefly to others. St Justin the Apologist was in Rome for two periods of some length, and he attracted many hearers to his lectures. His most bitter opponent was a Cynic philosopher called Crescens, who is said to have engineered his arrest; but St Justin spoke against the Gnostics as well as

* For a translation of the *Muratorian Canon* see *Documents of the Christian Church*, World's Classics Series, III, iii.

against the heathen, and wrote a treatise against Marcion. It was St Irenæus who undertook a systematic refutation of the heresies current in the second century, and he did this while he was bishop of Lyons. In his earlier years he had, however, spent some time in Rome, and it is not possible to say how far his later work reflects the debates he had listened to in Roman lecture-rooms. It was not until the third century that Rome found in Hippolytus a writer of real ability in her own ranks. Hermas, the author of *The Shepherd*, the only notable Roman Christian writer in the second century, was not a theological scholar, and was more concerned with morals than with heresies.

What evidence there is amply justifies the belief that from earliest times Rome held a leading position in the Church, and at least from the middle of the second century the Roman bishop was his church's recognized head and representative. The exact nature and extent of Rome's authority are much more difficult to estimate. A letter from Dionysius, bishop of Corinth, to Soter, who was bishop of Rome from about A.D. 166 to 174, is quoted by Eusebius, and it shows the great respect felt for the Roman church and for its bishop. Dionysius particularly mentions the generosity of the Romans in sending supplies to needy Christians in other churches, and he continues:

" and thus as Romans ye observe the hereditary custom of Romans, which your blessed bishop Soter has not only maintained, but even advanced, by providing in abundance the help that is distributed for the use of the saints, and by exhorting with blessed words, as a loving ' father his children ', the brethren who come up (to Rome)." *

This indicates the widespread influence of the Roman church, but the most useful evidence as to her authority is contained in the records of the Paschal controversy. The

* Eusebius, op. cit., IV, 23. 10. Text emended. Trans. by Lawlor and Oulton.

z

origin of this dispute and the course it took have been described in earlier chapters.* Victor, as bishop of Rome, was perfectly within his rights in insisting on uniformity of practice in the keeping of Easter within his own diocese. It also became him, as bishop of so important a see, to suggest to the bishops of other churches that they should hold synods to discuss the matter and endeavour to secure uniformity of custom throughout Christendom. But when the churches of Asia insisted on maintaining their own tradition, and Victor attempted to compel them to conform to the Roman practice, he was overstepping his authority. The bishops of other churches refused to join him in excommunicating the Christians of Asia, and St Irenæus expressed their sentiments in the vigorous protest in which he urged Victor " to have a mind for the things which make for peace and neighbourly union and charity ". Thus Victor found himself unable to exert authority over the Asiatic churches, nor could he obtain the co-operation of the bishops of other leading churches when they did not agree with his judgement.

Tradition has it that Victor was an African by birth, and this is likely enough, especially as his writings, which are now lost, were in Latin. By his time the Roman church had grown considerably, but the inscriptions in the catacombs show that it was still predominantly Greek-speaking. Persecution seems to have been confined to isolated cases. Commodus, who succeeded his father, Marcus Aurelius, in A.D. 180, had few virtues, either as a man or as an emperor, but he was not a persecutor of the Church. During the latter part of his reign he was under the influence of his mistress, Marcia, who had Christian leanings and who persuaded him to release the Christian confessors from the mines. Early in his reign, however, one martyrdom occurred in Rome which caused considerable stir. This was

* Chapter VI, p. 152 and Chapter XI, p. 259.

the trial and death of the Christian senator, Apollonius. Summoned before the senate to answer the charge of refusing to sacrifice to the gods, he answered that he was a Christian and would not sacrifice to empty idols. He then proceeded to defend his opinions until the prefect lost patience and exclaimed: " Surely thou wast not summoned hither to talk philosophy! " He gave Apollonius a day's respite in which to reconsider his decision, but when the trial was renewed the prisoner showed no change of purpose. On the contrary, Apollonius proceeded to expose the folly of worshipping idols until he was interrupted, first by the prefect, and then by a certain heathen philosopher who was standing by. The prefect made sincere efforts to understand his point of view, and, when Apollonius said that " the Word of God illumines the heart as the light gives sight to our eyes ", the prefect asked him to explain. In reply, Apollonius gave a brief account of our Lord's incarnation, and quoted the Greek philosopher's saying: " The just man shall be tortured, he shall be spat upon, and last of all he shall be crucified ". When he had finished, the prefect made a final attempt to persuade him to change his mind and, when he refused, reluctantly condemned him to be beheaded.*

There can be no doubt that the arguments of such men as Apollonius helped to overcome the prejudices against Christianity among intelligent Romans; but there were other speakers who did little good to the Christian cause, for they bred internal disputes and disunion. Some of these disputes were about church discipline; others were on matters of faith. Both were in a sense inevitable. Christian doctrine had not yet been adequately defined, and the Church's discipline had still to be tested by experience. But, while differences of opinion were bound to arise, greater charity on both sides might have prevented many of

* From *Acta S. Apollonii*, Kidd, op. cit., No. 81.

the schisms which actually occurred. Doctrinally, the chief problem at this time was that of reconciling belief in the unity of God with belief in the divinity of Christ. This led some men to assert that Christ was a man upon whom the Holy Spirit descended at his baptism; others held firmly to our Lord's divinity, but failed to distinguish between the Persons of the Trinity, saying that Christ was simply a mode of God the Father's Being. The Roman bishops had to decide whether to condemn one or both of these interpretations, and they had also to consider the claims of the Montanists who demanded a very strict standard of church discipline.

A few months after the assassination of Commodus, civil war broke out between the rival generals who claimed the throne. In the course of it the city of Byzantium was besieged and laid waste. It may have been the destruction of his city that brought a certain wealthy shoe manufacturer named Theodotus to Rome, or he may have come earlier because, as his enemies said, he had made his native city too hot for him. He professed to be a Christian, though he was said to have denied Christ during a time of persecution. The story is told of him that he met a fellowcountryman in the streets of Rome who charged him with apostasy, and that he replied: " I did not deny God, but only a man ". He certainly did not keep his views to himself, but openly taught that Christ's divinity descended upon him at his baptism in the form of a dove, and soon he had a following of those who accepted his opinion. Victor excommunicated him, but that did not end the matter. In the time of Zephyrinus, Victor's successor, Theodotus the shoe-maker was joined by Theodotus the banker, and by a mathematician named Asclepiodotus. These two approached a confessor named Natalius and offered him a salary if he would become the bishop of their sect. Natalius consented, but his conscience pricked him, and he was often disturbed by visions in the night. Finally one night he dreamt that he was being scourged by angels, and in the morning he rose at dawn, put on sackcloth and ashes, and hastened to the bishop Zephyrinus to implore him to receive him back. Zephyrinus, together with the Roman clergy and laity, was at length convinced of his penitence and he was taken back into communion. But Theodotus and Asclepiodotus persisted in their heresy. Like Marcion, they tampered with the text of the Scriptures, omitting whatever did not suit their own ideas. The author of *The Little Labyrinth*, a book written against a heresy derived from theirs, amused himself by collecting copies of their versions of the Scriptures, and found that they were not even consistent among themselves. Their criterion for judging the Scriptures appears to have been an unshaken belief in their own power of reasoning. They were devoted to the study of Euclid, Aristotle, and Galen, and when their opponents quoted texts against them they replied with syllogisms. This particular heresy seems to have died out in Rome before the middle of the third century. Artemon, its last notable adherent, is not heard of later than about A.D. 235. But in the East it made a fresh appearance with Paul of Samosata. Modern theologians have called this heresy Dynamic or Adoptionist Monarchianism, for its adherents attempted to assert the monarchy of God by saying that Jesus was a man adopted into the Godhead by means of the divine power (or dynamism) which descended upon him.

Praxeas, who fell foul of Tertullian, seems to have arrived in Rome at about the same time as the elder Theodotus. Unlike him, Praxeas succeeded in gaining the ear of the bishop, whom he encouraged both in condemning the heresy of Theodotus and also in rejecting the Montanists, who were endeavouring to obtain recognition. Praxeas came from Asia Minor with the reputation of having suffered for his faith, and earned the title of confessor. He was evidently a sincere believer and his ideas, though later condemned as heretical, were quite compatible with belief in the divinity of Christ. He thought of Christ as an aspect of God and startled thoughtful Christians by saying that God the Father suffered on the Cross. Such a confusion of the Persons of the Trinity was clearly at variance with the New Testament, for it made nonsense of our Lord's submission to his Father's will, his prayers and many of his sayings. Praxeas himself recanted his error after he had been defeated in argument by Tertullian at Carthage; but the same idea in a modified form was championed again in Rome by Noetus and later by Sabellius. It is usually known as the Sabellian heresy or " Modalism ", the Persons of the Trinity being thought of as three modes of One God.

The bishop who succeeded Victor, Zephyrinus, was not a man of learning. Hippolytus described him as " an ignorant and illiterate individual, and one unskilled in ecclesiastical definitions "; but Hippolytus was prejudiced. Zephyrinus found himself faced with a number of rival schools, some of whose adherents were in communion with him, whereas others were not. Among his own presbyters there was one very able scholar, Hippolytus; but he was a man of a harsh and intolerant disposition, and the new bishop may well have felt that if he took him for his counsellor he would alienate most of the rest. Instead, he came to lean more and more on the advice of another presbyter named Callistus, a man who had already had a curious and eventful history. The early life of Callistus is known to us only through an account written by Hippolytus, his undisguised enemy. Some allowance at least must be made for the writer's obvious intention to discredit Callistus, but it is hard to say how much should be discounted. The facts, as Hippolytus gives them, are as follows: *

* A.-N.C.L.: *The Writings of Hippolytus; Refutation of all Heresies*, Book IX, Chapters VI and VII.

Callistus was a slave belonging to a Christian named Carpophorus, who himself was in the household of Cæsar. On his master's instructions, Callistus started a banking business in the fish-market, a favourite quarter for money-lenders. Callistus was a Christian, like his master, and so in due course a number of the brethren, including some widows, deposited their savings with him. Either through mismanagement or, as Hippolytus suggests, through fraud, Callistus lost all the money that had been entrusted to him and, when his master demanded the accounts, he attempted to get away by sea. However, Carpophorus caught up with him before the boat sailed and, though he jumped into the harbour to avoid capture, he was taken and lodged in the treadmill where run-away slaves were punished. This was of no assistance to the unfortunate creditors, and they begged Carpophorus to release Callistus so that he might claim some money which he said was owing to him and pay at least part of the debt. This he agreed to do; but no sooner was Callistus free than he involved himself in fresh trouble. He went to a Jewish synagogue on the sabbath day and caused a disturbance there. The outraged Jews haled him before Fuscianus, the prefect of the city, and accused him of being a Christian. In spite of the protests of his master, who said he was no Christian but simply an embezzler, Callistus was convicted and sent to the mines.

Why Callistus should have insulted the Jews in their synagogue it is impossible to say. Hippolytus suggests that he was trying to commit suicide, but it seems a strange way of doing it. Probably the account is a garbled one, designed to show Callistus in a bad light. He certainly was sent to the mines on the charge of being a Christian, and in that miserable penal servitude he remained until Marcia secured from Commodus the release of all the Christian confessors. Hippolytus asserts that the name of Callistus was not on the list, and that he only obtained his inclusion by petitioning the governor; but this is highly improbable. Victor, who was bishop of Rome at the time of his release, sent the unfortunate man to Antium to recuperate and gave him a small allowance. While there, Callistus must have been ordained and, when Zephyrinus became bishop, he recalled him to Rome, gave him charge of the cemetery which now bears his name, and set him over all the local clergy in a position equivalent to that of archdeacon. It is hardly surprising that Hippolytus resented having Callistus set over him and his bitterness was increased by the theological disputes which followed.

Hippolytus had already been engaged in controversy with Noetus, who had revived the ideas of Praxeas, when a third and more formidable protagonist of this school appeared in the person of Sabellius. Sabellius was more plausible in his arguments than either of his predecessors, and Zephyrinus hesitated to condemn his views. There was evidently a real danger that the Roman church would split into two camps, with the supporters of Sabellius on the one side and those of Hippolytus on the other. Callistus apparently encouraged the bishop to temporize. On one day Zephyrinus would say in public: " I know that there is one God, Jesus Christ; nor except him (do I know) any other that is begotten and amenable to suffering." The Sabellian party would rejoice, being convinced of his support, and then on another occasion he would dash their hopes by stating: " The Father did not die, but the Son." Hippolytus was enraged by this wavering attitude which he attributed to mischief-making on the part of Callistus. His own position was much nearer the Catholic faith in three Persons in one God than was that of his opponent, but he said little about the Holy Spirit. This enabled his adversaries to charge him with being a ditheist, a believer in two gods, and, though the charge was false, it rankled. Open war was averted while Zephyrinus lived, but when he died and

Callistus succeeded him as bishop the split could be no longer avoided. Callistus excommunicated Sabellius, but even this did not serve to reconcile Hippolytus. He refused to recognize the authority of Callistus, and allowed his supporters, who must have numbered some local bishops among them, to consecrate him bishop of Rome.

Callistus had evidently a large following. He set up a school and taught that " Father and Son must be styled one God, and that this Person being one, cannot be two ". But he was careful to say not that the Father suffered, but that he suffered along with the Son. But what attracted numbers to his school was not his theology, but his new notions of church discipline. Hitherto, those who sinned after their baptism were subjected to severe and public penance before being readmitted to communion. But in the case of the most deadly sins, apostasy, adultery, and murder, absolution could not be given—that was the general view. Early in the second century, the author of *The Shepherd* had offered the hope of remission even of mortal sin once only after baptism. This had seemed shocking laxity to many, and the stricter sort, especially the Montanists, had vigorously opposed it. But Callistus went farther. He offered absolution to all who were genuinely penitent. He also relaxed the Church's rules about marriage, for he permitted clerics to marry, ordained men who had been married two or even three times, and recognized unions between free women and slaves, which were not valid in Roman law. Hippolytus was scandalized. He saw those whom he had excommunicated received and admitted to communion. Sinners who had been rejected by sect after sect in Rome became disciples of Callistus.

An over-rigorous policy in church discipline would no doubt have been disastrous, for the Church's aim is the redemption of sinners, not their condemnation. But there was danger in the other extreme as well. The Emperor

Severus had married an Eastern wife, Julia Domna, and through her and her sister's descendants, Heliogabalus and Alexander Severus, the tendency of the age towards religious syncretism was greatly increased. Heliogabalus was a Syrian priest of the Sun, and he introduced his oriental cult into Rome. Alexander Severus, a much saner and more attractive character, had a private chapel where he worshipped the deified emperors, Apollonius of Tyana, Abraham, Christ, and Orpheus. With such an example before them, many Romans must have thought it possible to pay honour to Christ without renouncing the gods of paganism. If at the same time the Church relaxed her demand for a high moral standard from her members, she might be inundated by the half-converted, until Christianity ceased to be a unique religion and became merely one ingredient in a mixture of all the cults. The successors of Callistus would no doubt have seen the danger in time and would have tightened the reins, but events prevented them. In A.D. 235, Alexander Severus was murdered, and his successor, Maximinus the Thracian, reversed his tolerant policy and issued an edict against the Christians. Both Hippolytus and Pontianus, the bishop who had succeeded Callistus, were sent to the mines of Sardinia. There the schism came to an end. In captivity the two were reconciled before they died, and both are now recognized as saints by the Roman church. An interesting relic of St Hippolytus was discovered in 1551: it is a contemporary statue of him, seated on his episcopal throne. The upper part was badly damaged when it was found, but the lower part is well preserved, and carved upon the throne can be seen the Paschal calendar, which St Hippolytus devised for determining the date of Easter, together with a list of his more important writings. *

* J. B. Lightfoot: *Apostolic Fathers*, Clement, Vol. II, pp. 440–442, *On Statue of Hippolytus*, pp. 388–405, *Literary Works*.

It was as a writer that St Hippolytus was chiefly remembered, for he was the first great scholar the church of Rome
produced. He had been a pupil of St Irenæus and, like his
master, he wrote a massive treatise against the heresies
current in his day. Besides this, he produced a large

STATUE OF ST. HIPPOLYTUS.   LATERAN MUSEUM

number of Biblical commentaries and theological writings.
But the book which was destined to have most influence on
the life of the Church was a short manual entitled *The
Apostolic Tradition*. There can be little doubt that Hippolytus wrote it for his own congregation, after the split with
Callistus, so that they might preserve the old tradition of
church order and discipline. In it he describes the ordina-

354 LIFE IN THE EARLY CHURCH

tion of bishops, presbyters, and deacons, the appointing of
those called to minor orders, such as widows and readers,
the rules for catechumens, baptism, the eucharist, the
ordering of love-feasts, rules for private prayer, and
various matters of a like nature. Like all his writings, it
was originally in Greek, and this may be the reason why it
was more valued by the Eastern churches than by Rome in
the years that followed, for Latin was gradually replacing
Greek as the language of the Roman church during the
third century.

Maximinus the Thracian shared the fate of most of the
later Roman Emperors. He was assassinated after a short
reign, and the persecution ended with his death. Fabian,
who was chosen to be bishop of Rome in A.D. 236, obtained
permission to bring the bodies of St Hippolytus and St
Pontianus back from Sardinia, and they were given honour-
able burial in the catacombs. Hardly anything is known
about the church of Rome during the next few years, but
there can be little doubt that this was a time of growth
when the number of Christians rapidly increased. Tradition asserts that Philip the Arabian, who was Emperor from
A.D. 244 to 249, was himself a Christian. However that
may be, there is contemporary evidence that when Rome's
millennium was celebrated in A.D. 248 there was an outcry
against the Christians, and Origen, who records it, says
that men were alarmed at the spread of Christianity. He
rightly interpreted it as a sign of persecution to come.
Meanwhile, during Fabian's long episcopate there is a good
reason to believe that the church's organization was improved. Three years after his death the Roman church
included: " forty-six presbyters, seven deacons, seven subdeacons, forty-two acolytes, fifty-two exorcists, readers,
and janitors ".* Fabian is traditionally credited with

* *Letter of Cornelius to Fabius*, Eusebius, op. cit., VI, xliii, 11.
Kidd, op. cit., No. 145.

having divided his church into seven districts, each under a deacon. All this strengthened the hand of the bishop, and it looks as though the factions which so troubled his predecessors had subsided. It was a time of peace and outward prosperity, when churches were built and the catacombs enlarged. Those who feared and hated Christianity watched and murmured, waiting for their opportunity.

In the summer of A.D. 249, Philip was succeeded by Decius. The Empire was in a precarious state, with the Goths pouring across the Danube and raiding the cities of the Balkan provinces. Decius decided not only to take the necessary military measures, but to restore public morale as well. To this end he revived the ancient office of censor and gave it to Valerian, an elderly and much-respected senator. Valerian was to deal with home affairs while he was at the front. He had already published a new edict against the Christians which came into force early in A.D. 250. This persecution was a well-planned, systematic attempt to stamp out Christianity, far more serious than any attack the Church had had to face since the days of Nero and Domitian. Decius aimed at killing the leaders and inducing the rank and file to apostatize. To this end he ordered that all suspects should be required to offer sacrifice to the gods on an appointed day. Those who refused were liable to be exiled and their goods confiscated, or else they might be imprisoned and afterwards tortured.

One of the first victims under the new edict was Fabian, the bishop of Rome. He died for his faith on the 20th of January, and others were thrown into prison. But numbers of the laity, and some of the clergy as well, failed to stand the test of persecution. On the appointed day they hurried to the Capitol and there made the required sacrifice on a heathen altar. This done, they were furnished with certificates, known as *libelli*, signed by the magistrate in charge. Some secured these certificates without actually sacrificing, and so saved themselves from the consequences of confessing their faith. The Church considered that these also were guilty of apostasy, though to a lesser degree than those who actually sacrificed. The persecution was widespread. Similar scenes were enacted in the great cities throughout the Empire, and many arrests were made. The bishops of Antioch and Jerusalem were martyred, and those of Carthage and Alexandria had to govern their churches from places of hiding. For over a year no bishop was chosen to succeed Fabian in Rome. Those presbyters who were not actually in prison managed the church's affairs as best they could. During this time they kept in touch with St Cyprian, the bishop of Carthage, by letter, and it is from this correspondence that most of our information is drawn. It will be considered in more detail in the next chapter, but the course of events in Rome must be summarized here.

The Roman presbyters found a leader in Novatian, one of their own number, a man of vigour and intellectual ability. He conducted the correspondence with St Cyprian and helped them to steer the Roman church in the difficult months that followed the death of Fabian. The treatment of the lapsed was the gravest problem. Those who had sacrificed or bought certificates were excluded from communion as apostates, but in a short time many of them were pleading their penitence and were begging to be restored to church membership. Some of them appealed to the confessors who were still in prison to plead their cause, and this put the presbyters in a difficult position. However, on St Cyprian's advice, they remained firm and reserved all cases until such time as a new bishop should be consecrated and a council convened. In this they were supported by Moyses the Confessor, a man of moderation and sense, as well as courage.

Decius had said that " he would far sooner hear of a rival

emperor than of a bishop set up at Rome ", but at the beginning of A.D. 251 he left to conduct the campaign against the Goths, and in his absence the persecution, which had probably never had much popular support, began to subside. In March A.D. 251, the Roman church took the bold step of electing a new bishop; but, to his bitter disappointment, Novatian was passed over and a much less brilliant man, Cornelius, was chosen. Encouraged by another malcontent, Novatus, who had come to Rome after scheming unsuccessfully against St Cyprian, Novatian set himself up as a rival to Cornelius. Moyses had died a martyr a few months before, but some of the other confessors, who had been released from prison, were persuaded into supporting Novatian. Three Italian bishops were induced to consecrate him, and the news was hastily carried to Carthage, in the hope that the Carthaginian church might recognize Novatian in place of Cornelius. This plan failed, for some of the Carthaginian clergy had witnessed the consecration of Cornelius, and they declared that it was valid. St Cyprian then used his influence with the Roman confessors, and after a short while they acknowledged their error and were restored to the Catholic Church. Dionysius, the bishop of Alexandria, endeavoured to persuade Novatian to do the same, but his advice was unheeded. Novatian claimed that he and his followers were defending the purity of the Gospel against those who would relax Christian standards by granting absolution to apostates and others guilty of mortal sin. He attracted the rigorists, who formed a permanent element in the Church, and the schism which he began in Rome spread throughout Christendom, especially in the East. Its adherents earned the title of Kathari, or the Pure, by the strictness of their discipline, and they were still quite numerous at the end of the fourth century.

In the summer of A.D. 251 Cornelius summoned a Council of the Roman church. Sixty bishops assembled under his leadership to consider the question of the lapsed and the Novatian schism. A Council at Carthage, led by St Cyprian, had already decided to restore all who were sincerely penitent to communion, at least on their death-beds, and sooner in most cases. The Roman council endorsed this decision. It also excommunicated Novatian. Before the end of the year, the news came that Decius had been killed in battle, and persecution was for a time at an end. The peace which followed, however, was uneasy and short-lived. Plague was devastating city after city in the Roman Empire, and it is said that at one time five thousand people died in a single day in Rome itself. The terror-stricken population was filled with superstitious fears, and attributed this and every other disaster to Christian influence. The authorities doubtless knew better, but in A.D. 253 Cornelius was exiled to Centumcellæ, where he soon afterwards died.

Lucius, the next bishop, died in less than a year, and was succeeded by Stephen. Cornelius had been glad to accept advice from St Cyprian, whose statesman-like handling of church affairs at Carthage had won him general respect. But Stephen was a man with strong opinions of his own and, as bishop of Rome, he believed that he was entitled to impose his ideas on others, rather than accept advice from them. Soon after he became bishop, St Cyprian wrote to him about the spread of Novatian's sect in Gaul. There were reports that Marcianus, the bishop of Arles, had joined the Novatians, and St Cyprian considered that it was the duty of Stephen to deal with the matter. The bishops of the great sees, Rome, Alexandria, Antioch, Carthage, and Jerusalem, had no actual jurisdiction over the bishops of smaller places, but it fell to them to summon local synods or councils when need arose, and it was natural for churches to appeal to them in cases of difficulty. How

Stephen dealt with this particular matter is not known. For the next fifty years Gaul was ravaged by repeated waves of invaders, and all records of the history of the church there have been lost. But in another case Stephen was appealed to by two Spanish bishops who had been deprived of their sees for apostasy during the Decian persecution. Stephen decided in their favour, apparently without making sufficient inquiries, and the churches concerned appealed against his decision to Carthage, where St Cyprian's fourth church Council was then sitting. The Council reversed the Roman verdict, and St Cyprian wrote to Stephen to inform him of the fact. These incidents paved the way for the serious dispute between the Roman and the Carthaginian churches over the question of second baptism.

This controversy will be dealt with more fully in the next chapter. The point at issue was whether Novatians and other schismatics or heretics should be baptized on entering the Catholic Church. The Roman church accepted any baptism as valid, provided it was performed in the name of the Father, Son, and Holy Ghost, and with water as the outward sign; but the church of Carthage denied that schismatics and heretics could admit men to membership of the Church, and therefore insisted on a second and orthodox baptism. Stephen not only upheld the Roman view against the decision of the Carthaginian church Council, which he was perfectly entitled to do, he also excommunicated St Cyprian when he refused to conform to the Roman ruling in the matter. It is clear that Stephen did indeed claim to be a " bishop of bishops ", a " pope " * in something like the modern sense, and he based that claim on authority derived from St Peter. St Cyprian, on the other hand, believed that all bishops alike inherited the authority of St Peter and the other apostles. He

---

* The title " pope " was, however, used of the bishops of Alexandria and Carthage before it was applied to the bishop of Rome.

A A

would not allow that one, even though that one were bishop of Rome, had the right to dictate to another. Firmilian, the bishop of Cæsarea in Cappadocia, emphatically supported St Cyprian, and St Dionysius of Alexandria, though he agreed with the Roman decision on baptism, disapproved of Stephen's attempt at coercion. In the face of such general opposition, Stephen was unable to win his point, and his successor, Xystus, removed the ban of excommunication.

The growing power of the Roman bishop, or pope, as he may from this time reasonably be called, was coloured in popular imagination by some romantic stories that found their way to Rome from the East early in the third century or at the end of the second. These are known as the " Clementine Romances ", and in them St Peter is glorified at the expense of St Paul. Clement, the hero of many wonderful adventures, is represented as a disciple of St Peter, by whom he is eventually consecrated bishop of Rome. The Clementine literature is not important in itself, but the popularity of these legends helps to explain the curious fact that, with the growth of papal power, there is a change of emphasis in the Roman claim to apostolic authority. In the first two centuries, St Peter and St Paul are usually mentioned together; later, the appeal is more often to succession from St Peter alone.

Valerian became Emperor in A.D. 253, the year before Stephen began his episcopate. According to St Dionysius, " not a single one of the emperors before him was so kindly and favourably disposed towards them (the Christians) . . . indeed all his house had been filled with godly persons, and was a church of God ".* Yet, in A.D. 257, at the instigation of his minister, Macrianus, Valerian launched another general attack against the Church as serious in its own way as that of Decius. The persecution opened with

* Eusebius, op. cit., VII, x.

an edict against the clergy, condemning them to exile and forbidding Christians to meet for worship. In the following year, the penalties were increased: death and confiscation of property for the clergy and laymen of the highest rank, exile or penal servitude for middle-class Christians. Access to the catacombs was also forbidden. On the 29th June, A.D. 258, just before the publication of the second edict, Christians in Rome secretly removed the bodies of St Peter and St Paul from their tombs at the Vatican and on the Ostian Way, and hid them in a place known as *Ad Catacumbas*, where they remained untouched until the persecution was over. As the civil service was riddled with Christians, it is no wonder that the information about the new edict leaked out. A little over a month later, early in August, Pope Xystus and four of his deacons were arrested in the catacombs, tried, and executed. The remaining three deacons, including St Lawrence, who is said to have been tortured on a gridiron, were martyred a few days later. As the deacons were responsible for the financial side of Church affairs and the administration of all charitable work, the loss of all seven deacons, together with the bishop, was a very serious blow. There were humbler martyrs as well. The best known of these is St Tarsicius, a young acolyte, who was carrying the Sacrament hidden beneath his cloak from one of the catacombs outside the city, where the Eucharist had been secretly celebrated, to Christians within the walls, when he was set upon by soldiers. In attempting to protect the Sacrament from desecration he was beaten to death. In the following year, there were martyrdoms in Africa and Spain and also in the East, though there the persecution was less intense than in the Western provinces.

In A.D. 260 Valerian was taken prisoner during his campaign against the Persians, and his son Gallienus reigned in his stead. In the following year, Gallienus published an edict of toleration, and the Church thereafter was left in peace for more than forty years. What little is known of the church of Rome during those years, and in the final persecution which followed them, will be told in a later chapter.

BOOKS FOR FURTHER STUDY

The Apostolic Fathers, Clement. Trans. by Lightfoot.

Ecclesiastical History, by Eusebius.

The Apostolic Tradition of Hippolytus, Translation and introduction by Burton Scott Easton.

Fathers and Heretics, by G. L. Prestige, Lecture 2, " Callistus."

History of the Church to A.D. 461, by B. J. Kidd, Chapters XIV, XVI.

Documents Illustrative of the History of the Church, Vol. I, ed. by B. J. Kidd. Nos. 74, 81, 82, 117–121, 142–146, 149–155, 158, 160–161.

CHAPTER XVI

CARTHAGE: ST CYPRIAN AND THE LAPSED

IN the year A.D. 246, a little more than half a century after the conversion of Tertullian, another distinguished lawyer was received into the Christian Church at Carthage. Thascius Cyprianus, now St Cyprian, was a middle-aged man at the time of his conversion, a man who ranked high in the city on account of his wealth, his learning, and his eloquence. Many of his letters have been preserved, and one of the earliest of these shows him, shortly after his baptism, writing to a fellow-neophyte of the transformation Christ is causing in their lives. Characteristically, St Cyprian writes among the trees and vine-branches of his garden, out of hearing of his household's noisy clatter. His serene and orderly mind loved the quiet of a garden, and his notion of a holiday was a day spent in some leafy shelter in his vineyard, reading the Scriptures and talking with his friends. But his thoughts, as he writes, contrast strangely with the peacefulness of his surroundings. He looks at the world in which he lives, and sees " the roads blocked up by robbers, the seas beset with pirates, wars scattered all over the earth, with the bloody horror of camps ".* The gladiatorial games and vicious theatrical shows disgust him, as they disgusted Tertullian before him. Even the law-courts he knows to be corrupt: the judge " sells his sentence " and " crimes are everywhere common ". Riches and the honours of rank have lost

* *The Writings of Cyprian*, translated by Robert Ernest Wallis, A.-N.C.L., Vol. VIII. Epistle I, *To Donatus*.

their splendour by being basely won. Magistrates are ruining themselves to appease the people with costly spectacles, while rich men are squeezing out the small-holders by buying up land and adding forest to forest. From this corrupt world he thankfully realizes he has been delivered by his baptism. He must still live in the world, but he is no longer of it. Instead he lives by grace. He has been born again and has passed from darkness into light.

" The one peaceful and trustworthy tranquillity," he writes, " the one solid and firm and constant security, is this, for a man to withdraw from these eddies of a distracting world, and, anchored on the ground of the harbour of salvation, to lift his eyes from earth to heaven; and having been admitted to the gift of God, and being already very near to his God in mind, he may boast, that whatever in human affairs others esteem lofty and grand lies altogether beneath his consciousness."

This man, with his studious tastes and his longing for a life of contemplation, God summoned to a bishopric at a time when the Church was endangered by persecution and rent by schism. St Cyprian obeyed the call, served the Church as bishop of Carthage with statesman-like wisdom for nearly ten years, and then died a martyr.

Within a short while after his conversion, St Cyprian was ordained priest and, when the bishop of Carthage died in A.D. 248, the laity insisted that he should be appointed to the vacant see. St Cyprian at first refused, urging that it was more fitting that a presbyter of older standing should be made bishop. But the people would take no refusal. They besieged his house and crowded all the avenues leading up to it. He tried in vain to escape by a window. Nothing would satisfy the people but his consent, and when at last he gave it they went wild with joy. Only a few looked on disapprovingly, among them five of the older presbyters. Some of those who doubted the wisdom of St Cyprian's election afterwards became his devoted friends, but others formed the nucleus of an opposition party which caused him serious trouble. St Cyprian's election, so different in its procedure from that of a modern bishop, was in accordance with primitive custom; for he was chosen by the laity and consecrated by neighbouring bishops by the laying-on of hands. As he himself wrote some years later about a brother bishop, Sabinus, " by the suffrage of the whole brotherhood, and by the sentence of the bishops who had assembled in their presence, the episcopate was conferred upon him, and hands were imposed on him in place of Basilides ".* In the Roman Catholic Church today the choice of a bishop rests ultimately in the Pope, and not even the reformed churches are as truly democratic in their procedure as was the Church of the first three centuries.

Early in A.D. 250, a bare eighteen months after St Cyprian's consecration, the comparative peace which the Church had enjoyed for half a century ended abruptly in the Decian persecution. The bishops of Rome, Antioch, and Jerusalem were martyred, but in all the great cities many of the laity and some even of the clergy hastened to the appointed temples to offer sacrifice. St Cyprian has described how Christians in Carthage queued for their damnation:

" They ran to the market-place of their own accord; freely they hastened to death, as if they had formerly wished it, as if they would embrace an opportunity now given which they had always desired. How many were put off by the magistrates at that time, when evening was coming on; how many even asked that their destruction might not be delayed! " †

People brought their baptized children to share in the heathen sacrificial feasts. In some cases husbands compelled their wives to sprinkle incense on the altars, even

* Cyprian, op. cit., Epistle LXVII, 5.
† Cyprian, op. cit., *On the Lapsed*, paragraph 8.

against their will.   Others compromised and endeavoured
to have the best of both worlds by buying *libelli* without
actually sacrificing.   Many of these were quite unaware
that they were committing mortal sin.   They regarded
their action simply as the evasion of yet another Government regulation, and such evasions did not lie heavy on their
consciences.   Others, again, went into exile of their own
accord, a perfectly justifiable course, unless they happened
to be priests abandoning their duties.   Yet in the midst
of this landslide many stood firm, and their faith and courage
saved the Church from destruction.

The bishops who were not immediately arrested, as St
Fabian was at Rome, were faced with a difficult choice.
One of the chief aims of the Decian persecution was the
elimination of the Church's leaders.   By courting martyrdom they would therefore be playing into the hands of the
enemy.   Moreover, their people and clergy would sorely
need their guidance, both during the persecution and afterwards.   On the other hand, to go into hiding looked like
cowardice, and might encourage some of the clergy, whose
duty was to remain with their parishioners, to say: " The
bishop has fled: why should we stand firm? "   As St
Cyprian wrestled with the temptation to vindicate his own
character at all costs, he must have remembered the bitter
words his master, Tertullian, had used of those who fled
from persecution.   Others within the church of Carthage
would still think the same.   But St Cyprian knew where
his duty lay.   He was a bishop, and his first consideration
must be the care of his church, let the rigorists among his
own people and elsewhere think what they would.   He
therefore chose to go into hiding, as did Dionysius the
Great of Alexandria.   They had good authority for their
decision.   It was the Montanists who courted persecution.
Orthodox Christians, like St Clement of Alexandria,
quoted our Lord's advice: " When they persecute you in

this city, flee ye to the other ", and counselled believers to accept martyrdom gladly, if it were forced upon them, but in no way to provoke it.

St Cyprian and Dionysius the Great continued to direct their churches from their places of exile, by means of letters and messengers. More than that, they kept in touch with the other churches as well, especially with the church of Rome, where the see was vacant and the presbyters were managing as best they could in difficult and dangerous conditions. Thus the persecution failed in both its main objectives: many Christians became apostates, yet the hard core of the faithful remained steadfast; some of the leading bishops were killed, but the Church was never without leaders, and her organization remained intact. A year later Decius was killed in battle, and the persecution came to an end.

By great good fortune, a large number of the letters which St Cyprian wrote in his exile during that year of persecution have been preserved. His hiding-place remained unknown to the civil authorities, as it does to us this day, but the way to it was very familiar indeed to certain members of the church of Carthage. A constant stream of messengers came and went between the bishop and his flock, and also between the bishop and the representatives of other churches. The months of his first exile were as active and important as any in his life. He was kept constantly informed of developments in Carthage, and he wrote, as occasion required to his clergy, to the laity or to the confessors in prison, advising, admonishing, and directing them in all the difficulties which arose. His advice was sought by the presbyters of Rome, and their policy during the critical months before the appointment of the new bishop was largely of his devising. Meanwhile, in the midst of all these cares he was leading a life of prayer and devotion. In this he was no hermit, withdrawn from the world, but a bishop leading his church in worship. In the spring of A.D. 250, when the persecution was at its height in Carthage, many confessors died under torture or were executed. Their names were enrolled in the Church's list of martyrs and St Cyprian remembered them constantly in his celebrations of the Eucharist. He also had a share in the work of relieving distress, for before he left the city he had made over a considerable part of his property to one of the presbyters for that purpose. From time to time, as there was need, he authorized the use of further instalments for the support of prisoners and of their destitute dependants. The church of Carthage was extremely active in visiting the confessors in prison, so much so that St Cyprian was constrained to send instructions that some discretion must be used. Too many should not go to the prison at one time, nor the same people go too often, for fear of exasperating the civil authorities. As the months passed and the persecution slackened, St Cyprian's cares grew greater rather than less. His clergy did not always obey him, some did not even answer his letters; the confessors were tempted to assume powers which they did not possess; some of the laity had been unfaithful, and others were misled by those who should have guided them. He must have longed for the day when he could return to Carthage to resume the direction of affairs in person.

St Cyprian's letters reveal the early Christians of Carthage as men and women like ourselves; some brave, some not; some magnificent in time of crisis, but exacting and unreasonable afterwards; some breaking under physical strain; some pitilessly critical of their weaker brethren; some heedless of Church discipline in their desire to meet penitents half-way. They reveal the writer also, a man with unusual breadth of vision, wise, moderate, and inexhaustibly patient. St Cyprian had ample opportunities for exercising his patience and moderation. He was not without personal enemies, some of them men who were jealous of his rapid rise to a position of great authority in the Church. His flight, necessary though it was, gave these men an opportunity. They wrote to Rome, reporting that their bishop had deserted them in time of danger, and the Roman presbyters, without waiting to ascertain the facts, wrote an injudicious letter in reply. St Cyprian dealt with the situation with tact and humour. He wrote a friendly letter to the Roman presbyters, enclosing the one they had sent to the Carthaginian clergy, saying that he hardly thought it could be genuine, even the paper gave him the impression that the letter had been tampered with.* Later, finding that the malicious reports continued, he sent them a full account of his actions and the reason for them, together with copies of his letters to his own clergy, which plainly showed that he was not shirking his duties, but was continuing to guide his church from his place of exile. The Roman presbyters were completely convinced, and afterwards turned to him for help in their own difficulties. The whole incident is characteristic of St Cyprian. It shows his openness, his confident habit of answering lies with truth, and his business-like thoroughness. The qualities he possessed were those which were most needed in an hour when the Church was endangered by dissension within, deliberately fomented by imperial enmity without.

When the date on which Christians were bidden to sacrifice had passed, the church in Carthage settled down to endure a state of chronic danger, as trying to the nerves as a siege or air attacks in a city. A number of confessors were in prison and these were liable at any time to be tortured and questioned, or else put to death. Meantime they lived in wretched conditions, although their friends were allowed to visit them occasionally, and could bring them food and other necessities. Many Christians who had

* Cyprian, op. cit., Epistle III.

escaped the notice of the authorities lived in constant fear that their hour of testing might yet come. Others were in exile, longing to return. But a large number were in a still more unhappy plight. These were Christians who had either sacrificed or burnt incense at the magistrate's order, or else had bought false certificates to that effect to save themselves or their families from persecution. By so doing, they had committed the sin of apostasy. They had denied Christ and had cut themselves off from his Body, the Church. No priest would give them communion, and the faithful shunned them. Among them there were many hard cases, fathers who had sacrificed to save their children, for instance, and women who had yielded reluctantly under strong pressure from their relatives. Some lapsed Christians no doubt drifted back to paganism contentedly enough, but many of them genuinely believed that only in Christ could they be saved, though they had not the courage to face torture or death for his Name. Soon they were begging, praying, and clamouring to be received back into the Church. They visited the confessors in prison, and implored them to intercede on their behalf. This some of the confessors were ready to do, either from genuine compassion or from vanity bred from the constant admiration they received. In the drab monotony of prison life the temptation to exercise power as a martyr was very strong, and one or two confessors yielded to it. They attempted to override the authority of both the bishop and the presbyters by themselves granting indulgences to numbers of the lapsed.*

The great respect felt in the early Church for those who had suffered for Christ's sake gave the opinion of the con-

---

* These certificates of pardon, like the certificates of conformity issued by the magistrates, were known as *libelli*. This double use is sometimes confusing, but the word *libellus* in itself simply means " a certificate."

fessors considerable weight. When St Cyprian received a letter, signed by a number of confessors, desiring that peace might be granted to certain of the lapsed who had repented, he was favourably impressed and willing to consider the question with his clergy, as soon as the end of persecution should make the calling of a synod possible. But when his clergy sent him specimens of certificates issued by con fessors, which read, " Let so-and-so be received to communion along with his friends ", he thought it was time to call a halt to a practice which was fast becoming an abuse. He wrote tactfully but firmly to the confessors, to the lapsed, and to his clergy, explaining that to admit men and women unworthily to communion, before they had purged their sin by penance and confession, was to profane the Body of the Lord, and a most mistaken form of kindness. He did not, as some did, deny all hope of restoration to the lapsed, but he did insist that a decision on a matter of such gravity must be taken by the whole Church—that is, by bishops, clergy, and laity—together in council, and not by individual priests or confessors. His ruling was supported by the majority of church people, both clergy and laity, though extremists in both directions continued to give trouble.

Official correspondence is apt to make dull reading, and St Cyprian's letters, interesting as they are in many ways, are for the most part of an impersonal and business-like kind. But occasionally, when he writes of some particular case, the men and women of the third century live again in his pages. No better example of this can be found than the case of Celerinus.* Celerinus came of a Carthaginian family which had been Christian for several generations, for his grandmother, Celerina, had died a martyr. He himself and his two sisters, Candida and Numeria, moved to Rome, and were there when the Decian persecution broke

* Cyprian, op. cit., Epistles XX–XXII.

out. Celerinus was among the first to be arrested, and was apparently tried before the Emperor, for he is spoken of as having " frightened back the great serpent himself, the pioneer of Antichrist " by his confession. For his boldness, he was thrown into prison, and was tortured for nineteen days, being racked and kept in irons, with only enough food and water to keep him from dying. In spite of his terrible sufferings, he survived, and was eventually released, broken in health and disfigured with scars. But his sisters were not made of such heroic stuff. Candida offered the required sacrifice to the gods, and Numeria decided to do the same. But, while she was actually on her way up to the Capitol she paused at the temple of the Three Fates, and there found an official who was willing to supply her with a *libellus*, for a consideration. No doubt the man was doing a brisk trade in these certificates, which enabled Christians to avoid persecution without actually sacrificing.

The news of the downfall of both his sisters was brought to Celerinus in prison just before Easter, and he mourned for them as dead throughout the festival. At last, in his despair, he bethought him of writing to his old acquaintance Lucian, now a confessor at Carthage. In a humble and pathetic letter, which is still preserved, he implored Lucian to intercede on behalf of his excommunicated sisters. The Roman presbyters had refused to reinstate any of the lapsed before a new bishop had been appointed to the see, but Celerinus hoped that the word of a martyr might be effectual. " I ask, therefore, my lord ", he wrote to Lucian, " and I entreat, by our Lord Jesus Christ, that you will refer the case to the rest of your colleagues, your brethren, my lords, and ask from them, that whichever of you is first crowned should remit such a great sin to those my sisters, Numeria and Candida ". Lucian was ready enough to comply. He sent an assurance of peace to the two sisters, saying:

" When the blessed martyr Paulus was still in the body, he called me and said to me: ' Lucian, in the presence of Christ I say to you, If any one, after my being called away, shall ask for peace from you, grant it in my name.' Moreover, all of us whom the Lord has condescended in such tribulation to call away, by our letters, by mutual agreement, have given peace to all." *

But a copy of his letter came into the hands of St Cyprian, who took a serious view of the breach of church discipline involved in this easy and unauthorized granting of indulgences. St Cyprian therefore wrote to the Roman presbyters, enclosing the correspondence between Celerinus and Lucian, as well as other letters he had himself written remonstrating with Lucian. He explained the difficulty he was having with this courageous, but ignorant and indiscreet confessor, and he praised the humility Celerinus had shown in the whole tone of his letter. St Cyprian evidently sympathized with "the good and stout confessor", as he called Celerinus, in his grief over his sisters, even though he could not support his request for their immediate reinstatement.

A few months later, Celerinus appears again in St Cyprian's correspondence. This time he is at liberty and has returned to Africa, bringing with him letters from Rome. St Cyprian writes to the clergy and people of Carthage to tell them that he has ordained Celerinus as reader, a step which he is sure they will approve. Of the later history of Candida and Numeria little is known. They devoted themselves to the relief of Christian refugees from Carthage, many of whom sought to hide themselves in the huge mixed population of Rome. Candida and Numeria met them at Portus, when they landed, and provided them with food and shelter. At one time they were caring for more than sixty of these hunted men and women.

* Cyprian, op. cit., Epistle XXI, sec. 2.

Despite their brother's passionate pleading, the Roman presbyters would not take the responsibility of restoring these two women, but deferred the case until the new bishop should be appointed. No record of his decision has survived, but there can be little doubt that they were ultimately granted the peace which their brother had so eagerly sought for them.

At the beginning of A.D. 251, the Emperor Decius left Rome to direct the campaign against the Goths in person. A rival claimant to the throne sprang up as soon as his back was turned, and in the general confusion the persecution was dropped. Had Decius returned to Rome he might have revived his anti-Christian policy, but he was killed in battle before the end of the year. Shortly after Easter, the situation was quiet enough for St Cyprian to return to Carthage, and in April his first Council of the local bishops, clergy, and laity met there to deal with a number of problems, the most important being the treatment of the lapsed. After long deliberation, the Council decided that the cases of those who had purchased certificates, the *libellatici*, should be carefully examined, and that those of the lapsed who had not actually sacrificed should be restored, upon application to their bishop and after a term of penance. But those who had sacrificed to heathen gods they declared should be admitted to communion only on their death beds. In practice, this ruling proved to be too strict, and a second council two years later further relaxed the conditions upon which the truly penitent might be restored.

Meanwhile, two other important matters came up before the Council. The first was the case of Novatus and Felicissimus. Novatus was a presbyter whose parish, known as the Hill, probably lay in a fashionable part of the town. He was strongly opposed to St Cyprian, and had admitted many of the lapsed to communion in deliberate disobedience to his bishop's orders. In this he had the support of

Felicissimus, whom he had appointed deacon. Felicissimus had control of considerable sums of money intended for charity, and his support was an asset. Serious moral charges were brought against him, however, and the Council had no hesitation in condemning both him and Novatus. Novatus left at once for Rome to see if he could secure the election of a bishop hostile to St Cyprian. Felicissimus remained in Carthage to watch for an opportunity to make further trouble there.*

The Carthaginian Council had not been long in session when two messengers arrived from Rome with letters for St Cyprian. One letter was from Cornelius, announcing that he had been consecrated bishop; the other was from Novatian, bitterly attacking Cornelius and denying the validity of his election. St Cyprian promptly sent two responsible members of his church to Rome to investigate the matter thoroughly, and, pending their return, he instructed all Carthaginian bishops to address any communications to the Roman church to the presbyters. Before the delegates could return, two African bishops who had been present at the consecration of Cornelius arrived in Carthage with adequate testimony to the validity of his election. The Council therefore sent letters of recognition to Cornelius, but hardly had they been despatched when four fresh emissaries arrived, who announced to the astonished Council that Novatian had been consecrated and was the true bishop of Rome. Novatus, the discredited Carthaginian presbyter, the chief organizer of this intrigue, wisely kept in the background. Without St Cyprian's guidance, the Council might have hesitated how to act, for Novatian had the support of certain Roman confessors, who were greatly respected, and he claimed to be upholding the faith against those whose laxity would destroy it. As it was, the Council rejected Novatian's claims. His four messen-

* Cyprian, op. cit., Epistles XXXVII–XXXIX.

B B

gers stumped the country in an attempt to win support for his cause, but had only very moderate success.   Meanwhile, St Cyprian wrote a moving letter to the Roman confessors who had joined Novatian, begging them to return to their true allegiance.   Dionysius of Alexandria sent a similar appeal and, having seen their action in true perspective, the confessors repented of their error and were received back into the Church.   But Novatian never returned, and the schism he originated lasted for centuries.

To St Cyprian the unity of the Church was as precious and as holy as her purity.   When his first Council was faced with the problem of the Novatian schism, St Cyprian produced for its guidance his great treatise *On Unity*, a study of first principles, not an analysis of the particular case before them.*   He had no doubt whatever about the wickedness of schism.   It was the work of the devil, who had " invented heresies and schisms, whereby he might subvert the faith, might corrupt the truth, might divide the unity ".

" He snatches men from the church itself; and while they seem to themselves to have already approached to the light, and to have escaped the night of the world, he pours over them again in their unconsciousness, new darkness; so that, although they do not stand firm with the gospel of Christ, and with the observation and law of Christ, they still call themselves Christians."

" Such men are strangers and enemies, whatever their pretensions.   ' He can no longer have God for his Father, who has not the church for his mother.' "

To modern Christians, accustomed to the numerous divisions of the visible Church today, these seem harsh words; yet St Cyprian was not writing from bitterness, but from an undimmed vision of the Church as the earthly expression of the unity of God.

* *On the Unity of the Catholic Church*, from Cyprian, op. cit., Vol. I.

" The Lord says, ' I and the Father are one '; and again it is written of the Father, and of the Son, and of the Holy Spirit, ' And these three are one '. And does any one believe that this unity which thus comes from divine strength and coheres in celestial sacraments, can be divided in the church, and can be separated by the parting asunder of opposing wills? He who does not hold this unity does not hold God's law, does not hold the faith of the Father and the Son, does not hold life and salvation."

The Scriptural foundation for this teaching he found in Christ's charge first to St Peter, and then to the other apostles. St Cyprian quoted the famous text: " Thou art Peter; and upon this rock I will build my church"; but he followed it with the charge to all the apostles: " As the Father hath sent me, even so send I you ". He then commented:

" Assuredly the rest of the apostles were also the same as was Peter, endowed with a like partnership both of honour and power; but the beginning proceeds from unity."

From this he deduced that all bishops had equal authority, the episcopate being one and undivided. It was as though they were holders of a joint account, upon which each of them could draw to the full.

" The episcopate is one, each part of which is held by each one for the whole. The church also is one, which is spread abroad far and wide into a multitude by an increase of fruitfulness. As there are many rays of the sun, but one light; and many branches of a tree, but one strength based in its tenacious root; and since from one spring flow many streams, although the multiplicity seems diffused in the liberality of an overflowing abundance, yet the unity is still preserved in the source."

Such was St Cyprian's conception of the unity of the Church, and upon it depended his practical conduct of church affairs. Believing as he did, he had to assert his episcopal authority against presbyters who would admit the lapsed to communion without sanction; on the other hand, he could not be a rigorist and drive men into schism.   The Church is *holy*, but she is also *one*, and a penitent within her ranks is better than a schismatic outside them.   Lastly, his views on episcopal authority affected his behaviour towards his fellow-bishops, especially the bishop of Rome. In later centuries, the text of his treatise, *On Unity*, was tampered with, in order to add his name to those of the supporters of papal supremacy.   But his actions, as well as his words, confuted this pretence.   He and Cornelius, the bishop of Rome from A.D. 251 to 253, addressed each other as " brother " and wrote as equals; the Roman presbyters addressed St Cyprian as " father "—that is, " pope ".   Cornelius made no attempt to claim authority over the bishop of Carthage, and Lucius, his successor, only survived his enthronement a few months.   It was during Stephen's episcopate that St Cyprian's theory was tested in practice.   Stephen was consecrated in May, A.D. 254, and in the following autumn, St Cyprian and his fourth Council, which was then sitting, received an appeal from the Spanish churches against a decision made by Pope Stephen.   Two Spanish bishops, Basilides and Martial, had been deprived of their sees for apostasy, during the recent persecution, and for lapsing into pagan practices.   Some time later Basilides had appealed to the newly elected bishop of Rome, and Stephen had declared them both to be the lawful occupants of their sees.   The churches concerned appealed to Carthage and the fourth Council unhesitatingly quashed Pope Stephen's verdict and declared that Basilides and Martial were excluded from the ministry, and that the bishops who had been elected to succeed them were to retain their sees. The letter in which St Cyprian conveyed this decision excused Pope Stephen's error, on the ground that he had not had sufficient evidence before him, and simply overruled the Roman judgement.   How Stephen reacted is not known, but that he claimed more authority than St Cyprian and the church of Carthage were willing to grant him was made plain in the next few years.*

The test came when a council at Carthage declared that anyone who had been baptized by a heretic or schismatic was outside the fold of the Church, and required a second, orthodox baptism. Pope Stephen disagreed with this decision. It was the custom in the church of Rome to accept any baptism as valid, provided that the proper form was used (" In the Name of the Father, and of the Son, and of the Holy Ghost "), and the proper matter, water. Stephen insisted that the African church should conform to the Roman practice, and when St Cyprian and his second Council on Baptism reaffirmed the former decision, Stephen refused to receive an African deputation, accused St Cyprian of being " a false apostle ", claimed the authority of the chair of St Peter, and wrote a circular letter in which he declared that he would not communicate with bishops who tolerated the use of second baptism. It was to deal with this situation that the seventh Council met in Carthage under St Cyprian, in September, A.D. 256. More than eighty bishops from the prosperous and civilized provinces of Africa, Numidia and Mauretania were gathered together with a large number of clergy and laymen. St Cyprian addressed them briefly:

" Our present business ", he said, " is to state individually our views of the particular subject before us, judging no one, nor removing from his rights of communion any one who may hold different views from ourselves. For there is none of us who constitutes himself Bishop of Bishops, or pushes his colleagues with a tyrannous terror to the necessity of compliance; since every Bishop according to the scope of the liberty and office which belongs to him has the decision in his own hands, and can no more be judged by another than he can himself

---

* Cyprian, op. cit., Epistle LXVII.

judge his neighbour, but we wait one and all the judgement of our Lord Jesu Christ, who one and alone has the power both to prefer us in the governing of his Church, and to judge our conduct therein." *

The bishops then expressed their individual opinions, and the Council unanimously decided against admitting the validity of heretical and schismatic baptism.

The history of this dispute over heretical baptism bears a remarkable resemblance to that of the earlier Paschal controversy. Both disputes arose because different customs had grown up in the churches with the passage of time. In both cases, the Roman bishop of the day attempted to compel the churches in other regions to adopt the practice customary in the church of Rome. In both cases he resorted to a threat of excommunication when persuasion failed. In the first instance it was Asia Minor, in the second Africa and Asia Minor together, that resisted dictation by Rome. On each occasion, a bishop of a church not immediately concerned came forward as peace-maker. In the Paschal controversy, it was St Irenæus of Gaul who persuaded Pope Victor to withdraw his excommunication. In the Baptismal controversy, Dionysius of Alexandria intervened, and urged that the dispute should be dropped for the sake of peace within the Church. Pope Stephen would not retract, but his successor, Xystus, removed the excommunication. For some time the difference in practice persisted, but gradually in the matter of second baptism, as in the time for celebrating Easter, the churches adopted the Roman custom of their own accord. All the western churches decided against second baptism at the Council of Arles in A.D. 314.

In the actual matter under dispute, both Stephen and St Cyprian had good reasons for the views they took. Stephen

* Quoted by E. W. Benson, *Cyprian, his Life, his Times, his Work*, p. 369.

was concerned to insist that " the unworthiness of the minister doth not hinder the efficacy of the sacrament ", and the opposite opinion is unworkable in practice. For instance, to believe that any priest who may happen to hold mistaken ideas about the doctrine of the Trinity is thereby incapable of baptizing a child is absurd. In point of fact, none of the human instruments used by the Holy Spirit in this world is quite free from either sin or error. But St Cyprian was not contending for any such foolish opinion. What troubled him about baptism by heretics and schismatics was not that the ministers were unworthy, but that they were incompetent. They were no longer members of the Body of Christ, the Church, and so they could not fulfil any of the functions of that Body. For them to attempt to do so was not a sacrament, but a mockery. Both men became heated during the dispute and expressed their views forcibly, but, unlike most controversial writings of the period, St Cyprian's letters are courteously worded and free from invective. In his love for the unity of the Church he endeavoured to exercise patience in order to preserve the peace. The conclusion of his letter to bishop Jubaianus speaks for itself. It was written in A.D. 256, when the baptismal controversy was at its height.

" So far as in us lies, we are not, for the sake of heretics, going to contend with colleagues and fellow-bishops: with them I keep Divine concord and the Lord's peace. . . . In patience and gentleness we hold fast by charity of spirit, by the honour of our college, by the bond of faith, by concord within the episcopate.

" To this end I have just composed a small book on ' The Good of Patience ', to the best of my small powers, under the permission and inspiration of the Lord." *

Stephen's attempt to use force to win his way in the baptismal controversy sprang, of course, from his idea that

* Quoted by E. W. Benson, op. cit., p. 439.

the bishop of Rome should be a "bishop of bishops". St Cyprian held the view that all bishops had equal authority, the bishop of an important see being simply the first among his peers, their leader, not their ruler. The church of Rome has persisted in Stephen's view of episcopal authority throughout her history. St Cyprian's conception seemed for a time to have been forgotten, but it was reborn at the Reformation, and can be seen today in practice in the Church of England and in all the churches of the Anglican communion.

During the interval of peace between the Decian persecution and that of Valerian, most of St Cyprian's time was naturally devoted to the internal affairs of the Church; but on two occasions at least events in the outside world forced themselves on his attention. The first occasion was when Berber tribesmen from the desert broke through the frontier posts and raided many prosperous cities in Numidia. Lambæsis, one of the places that suffered, was a garrison town, but, even so, the troops were unable to prevent the raiders from carrying off a large number of captives, among them some Christian women and children. There is a letter by St Cyprian addressed to eight Numidian bishops sympathizing with them in this calamity, and enclosing the equivalent of about eight hundred pounds for ransom money. This sum had been made up from numbers of small contributions given by Christians in poor churches, and St Cyprian particularly asked the bishops that the donors might be remembered in their prayers.* The incident is characteristic of this period when the defences of the Empire were beginning to give way. Barbarian raids were already a common calamity in most parts of the civilized world.

The Berber raid was in A.D. 252, and in the same year plague devastated Carthage. Plague in these years was

* Epistle LIX.

ranging the Roman Empire, appearing now in one city, now in another. Superstition ascribed it to neglect of the gods, and especially to the " atheism " of the Christians. An outbreak of plague was therefore doubly dangerous to the Christian community, for it was apt to be accompanied by persecution. In Carthage the plague ran its usual course. Many fled from the city, and those who could not leave went about in dread of what might happen to them. People turned the stricken out of their houses to die in the streets, and at the height of the pestilence the dead lay in heaps unburied. At the beginning of this time of terror, St Cyprian called the Christian community together and spoke to those present of the divine quality of mercy.* He told them that it was not enough to tend their own sick; they should love their enemies and take pity on the plague-stricken among the pagans who persecuted them. Under his direction, the Christians in Carthage did what they could to relieve the suffering around them, just as they did in Pontus and in Alexandria when the plague was raging there. Their efforts to meet the situation by nursing the sick and burying the dead were inevitably inadequate, and perhaps were unnoticed or misunderstood by many in that large, ignorant, and superstitious population. The refusal of Christians to offer sacrifices to Apollo, the giver of health, was bitterly resented, and for a time the " over-seer " of the Christians was proscribed by name, while crowds shouted in the circus that Cyprian should be given to the lions.

This danger seems to have passed with the plague which occasioned it, and several years of uneasy peace for the church of Carthage followed. Valerian became Emperor in A.D. 253, and his household was largely composed of Christians. It seemed that another large-scale persecution

* See E. W. Benson, op. cit., Chapter VI, sec. 2, and *Cyprian*, op. cit., *On the Mortality*.

was unlikely while he was on the throne. But towards the end of his reign he came under the influence of his minister, Macrianus, a man who believed in magic and hated Christianity. He persuaded the Emperor that the evils of the time—the barbarian invasions, outbreaks of plague, and natural calamities—were due to the decay of the ancient Roman religion. In A.D. 257 Valerian launched a new, carefully planned attack against the Church. It was aimed in the first place at the clergy and at the prevention of Christian worship.

It was on the 30th of August, A.D. 257, that St Cyprian was summoned to the Proconsul's secretarium, and there required to make a statement as to his religious position. The dialogue which followed is preserved in the Proconsular Acts:

"*Cyprian.* I am a Christian, and a Bishop. I know no other Gods but the one and true God who made heaven and earth, the sea, and all that in them is. He is the God whom we Christians wholly serve. Him we supplicate night and day for ourselves and for all men and for the safety of the Emperors themselves.

"*Paternus, the Proconsul.* In this purpose then you persevere?

"*Cyprian.* That a good purpose, formed in the knowledge of God, should be altered is not possible.

"*Paternus.* Well, will it be 'possible' for you, in accordance with the directions of Valerian and Gallien, to take your departure as an exile to the city of Curubis?

"*Cyprian.* I depart.

"*Paternus.* They have done me the honour of writing to me not about bishops only, but about presbyters too. I would therefore know from you who are the presbyters that reside in this city.

"*Cyprian.* You have by your own laws made good serviceable regulations against the very existence of informers. Accordingly it is not in my power to discover and delate them. However they will be found in their several cities." *

* Quoted by E. W. Benson, op. cit., pp. 465–466.

Having failed to extract any useful information from his prisoner, Paternus added that Christians were forbidden to hold assemblies, or to enter their cemeteries, on pain of death. He then passed sentence of exile on St Cyprian, who left shortly afterwards for a lonely little seaside town some fifty miles from Carthage. About the same time, Dionysius of Alexandria was ordered to remove himself to Kephron, a desolate place in the outskirts of the desert.

St Cyprian suffered no great hardship in his year of exile at Curubis. His devoted deacon, Pontius, who afterwards became his biographer, went with him voluntarily, and he described the place as a " sunny and suitable spot ". The brethren visited him freely, and the citizens went out of their way to supply him with everything he could want. But other African bishops and some of their clergy received much worse treatment. Many of them were condemned to hard labour in the mines, and St Cyprian did what he could to console them by sending them encouraging letters and money with which to buy food.* Other confessors were in prison, and some had suffered cudgelling and other ill-treatment. Most, if not all, these confessors, including men and women of the laity, had been found taking part in Christian worship after Valerian's prohibition had been published. But, stern as these measures were, they were quite insufficient for the suppression of Christianity. In the following year, Valerian took yet more drastic action. The events in Rome are related in another chapter. Pope Xystus with four deacons was martyred in accordance with a new rescript, which condemned all Christian clergy to death and punished all laymen of rank with confiscation of goods and banishment.

St Cyprian was back in Carthage when the news reached him. He had been ordered to return, and was living in his old home, until such time as the Proconsul should be

* Cyprian, op. cit., Epistles LXXVI–LXXIX.

sufficiently recovered from an illness to interview him. He had a premonition that his death was near, and, when the rescript was announced, he and his clergy prepared themselves for martyrdom. Some of his friends urged St Cyprian to escape, but this he refused to do. In the earlier Decian persecution his living leadership was needed, now he felt that the example of his death would do more good. But he was determined to die in Carthage, and so when guards were sent to take him to Utica he went into hiding for a while, until the Proconsul had returned to Carthage. For, as he wrote in his last letter to his people, " It is fit for a bishop, in that city in which he presides over the church of the Lord, there to confess the Lord ". When the Proconsul's arrival in the city ensured that his trial would be in Carthage, St Cyprian quietly returned to the gardens that he loved and there, on his own estate, he was found when centurions and troops were sent to arrest him. His trial on the following day could have only one result. He was accused of being a " pope to persons of sacrilegious views and of refusing to sacrifice to the gods ". He agreed that this was so. The new rescript was then read and, as the " standard-bearer " of the forbidden sect, St Cyprian was condemned to death. Followed by a large crowd of both Christians and pagans, he was led to an open space surrounded by trees. There he was beheaded, and, though the spectators swarmed even into the trees to obtain a view, they behaved quietly and did not attempt to interfere with the Christians who came at night with torches to bear his body with " prayer and a great triumph " to its resting-place.

The greatness of the North African church was to last only for a short period, very short compared with that of Rome, but the glory of the church which produced Tertullian, St Cyprian and, later, St Augustine, cannot fade.

BOOKS FOR FURTHER READING

Cyprian : his Life, his Times, his Work, by Edward White Benson, DD., D.C.L.   Macmillan, 1897.
Writings of Cyprian, translated by R. E. Wallis, Ph.D.   A.-N.C.L.
Documents Illustrative of the History of the Church, ed. by B. J. Kidd. Nos. 137–159, and No. 135, a translation of a typical Libellus found in Egypt.
Some Authentic Acts of the Early Martyrs, by E. C. C. Owen.   Translations of the *Acts of S. Cyprian* and of *Passion of SS. James and Marian*, being accounts of the martyrdom of St Cyprian and of other North African Christians who died in the same persecution.

CHAPTER XVII

Events in the East in the Third Century

WHEN Origen settled in Cæsarea after his expulsion from Alexandria, he brought new vigour to the Eastern churches. While the West could claim one great church of apostolic foundation, the church of Rome, the East could point to a dozen. Jerusalem, the mother of all the churches, had been reborn on the ancient site, some time after the destruction of the Jewish city; Antioch had an unbroken history from the day when the assembled brethren sent St Paul and St Barnabas forth on their first missionary journey; several of the churches of Asia could name St Paul as their founder; Ephesus preserved the tradition of St John, as well as of St Paul; Cæsarea had been the scene of the Pentecost of the Gentiles, when Cornelius and his household were converted by St Peter. But glorious as were the early traditions of the Eastern churches, no one of them played such a leading part as did the churches of Rome and Alexandria in the second century and the first half of the third. Now one church and now another in Asia Minor came into prominence on account of some exceptionally able bishop or apologist, some martyr, or, less happily, some heretic. Even Antioch lapsed into obscurity for a while after the martyrdom of St Ignatius, for the next bishop of whom anything is known is Theophilus, who wrote Biblical commentaries and books against heresy towards the end of the second century. Throughout this time, in the Eastern as in the Western provinces, the Church was waging a ceaseless battle against paganism. Of the many dearly bought victories, and the weary, heart-breaking defeats, little record is left.   But it is certain that Christianity spread far and wide throughout the Roman Empire and even beyond it.   History is inevitably, in the main, the chronicle of great men's lives, and it is only in imagination that these unspectacular periods, these times of quiet growth, formed of the labour of innumerable unknown men and women, can be seen to be splendid, not merely blank and dull.

" He was truly a paradise to us, after the similitude of the paradise of God ", said St Gregory Thaumaturgus of his master, Origen.   St Gregory and his brother came to Cæsarea by chance.   The two young men were escorting their sister, who was joining her husband there, and they intended to return through Syria to their home in the north of Asia Minor.   Instead, they fell under the spell of Origen, and stayed in Cæsarea to study under him for five years. Even then, St Gregory felt that he was leaving paradise when he obeyed the call of duty and returned to his native city of Neocæsarea to become its bishop.   The interior of Pontus, where Neocæsarea lay, was a wild mountainous region.   The northern boundary of the province was the Black Sea coast, and to the east lay Armenia, where as yet Christianity had hardly penetrated.   There were only a handful of Christians in Pontus when St Gregory began his missionary work there about A.D. 235.   When he died, about the year A.D. 270, the province was almost entirely Christian.   It is hardly surprising that legends gathered about his name, and that he became known as Gregory the Wonder-worker.   He had indeed worked wonders, but, presumably, not the kind of miracles attributed to him by his biographer St Gregory of Nyssa, who wrote only a century after his death.   These miracles included the drying-up of a lake and the transformation of his walking-stick into a tree.   Valueless as are the legends in themselves, they are evidence of the deep impression which St Gregory made upon the primitive imagination of the people whom he taught.

The years when St Gregory was converting the heathen in Pontus were not years of peace. In A.D. 249 came the Decian persecution, and he, like St Cyprian at Carthage, had to go into hiding for a while. His work was then only half done, and to have left his fresh converts leaderless would have been to court disaster. After the death of Decius, St Gregory was able to resume the task of organizing his diocese. Finding that his people clung tenaciously to their old heathen festivals, he hit upon the plan of appointing Christian feasts in commemoration of martyrs to take their place. By this means the festival remained, but its character and purpose were changed. There was little respite granted him in which to carry out such reforms. After the persecution came the plague, and after the plague came the ravages of the barbarians. The Goths had established themselves in the Ukraine, where " the temperature of the air, the aptness of the soil for every species of grain, and the luxuriancy of the vegetation, all displayed the liberality of Nature, and tempted the industry of man." " But," continues Gibbon, " the Goths withstood all these temptations, and still adhered to a life of idleness, of poverty, and of rapine ".* In the reign of Valerian they commandeered boats and crossed the Black Sea to raid the rich and ill-defended provinces of Asia Minor. Numbers of Christians were carried into captivity; worse than that, some so-called Christians seized the opportunity to loot the possessions of those who had been captured, and others even made common cause with the barbarians, out of spite or self-interest. It would seem that the conversion of Pontus to Christianity had been a mass movement inspired

* Gibbon: *Decline and Fall of the Roman Empire*, Vol. I, chapter X.

by the personality of St Gregory, and there had been little time for the people to assimilate the faith they had accepted. St Gregory dealt sternly with such serious offences, and encouraged his fellow clergy to do the same. A letter of his to another bishop in Pontus has been preserved, and in it he quotes the canons passed by a local synod which met to consider these evils. Already his missionary enterprise had become a well-organized church.

Of the rest of St Gregory's career little is known. Both he and his brother, Athenodorus, were present at the first Council of Antioch in A.D. 264, about which more will be said later. As he is not mentioned at the later Councils it is probable that he died a few years afterwards. His biographer records that he was buried in the church which he had built at Neocæsarea, and in the minds of his people his memory was cherished, until it sprouted miraculous legends as his staff was said to have sprouted leaves.

More will be said later of the stimulating effect which Origen's teaching had in Cæsarea, and indeed throughout Syria. But in the intricate pattern of the history of the early Church this thread is crossed by another of a different colour and from a different source. In the reign of Alexander Severus, in A.D. 226, a revolution took place in the great Eastern Empire which bordered on the dominions of Rome. Artaxerxes overthrew the Parthian kings and re-established the Persian Empire. He then proceeded to reform the traditional Persian religion, which was a form of dualism, based on the teaching of Zoroaster. Having won the support of the priests, the Magi, he embarked on a policy of persecution from which Christians and other dissenters suffered severely. Edessa, to the north, near the source of the Euphrates, was a Christian centre, and from there news of Christ came filtering down through the great river valley into Persia. Even in Edessa, where the church was in touch with Antioch and all the other churches

c c

of the West, Christianity wore an Eastern dress.   Just as
the churches in Africa today are seeing Christ with African
eyes and praising him in African ways, so in these early
centuries people in the East expressed their faith differently
from the Greeks and Latins of the West, and, when they
failed to understand, their failures were of an Eastern, not a
Western kind.   While the Greeks tried to fit Christ into
their philosophy and to turn the Church into a mystery
cult, Eastern heretics accepted the current Persian conception
of an eternal struggle between light and darkness, good and
evil, and interpreted Christ's saving mission accordingly.
Christianity was an ingredient in strange concoctions, one
of them so strange that theologians are undecided whether
to call it a Christian heresy or an independent religion.
This was Manichæism, hated alike by Persians and by
Christians, always persecuted and suppressed, yet spreading
like a peat fire underground, until it finally died out more
than a thousand years after it was first proclaimed in
Ctesiphon.

The gospel which Mani proclaimed in the streets of
Ctesiphon and Seleucia, the twin cities on the banks of the
Tigris, was other-worldly in the extreme.   This world, in
which good and evil are so inextricably mixed, he regarded
as an unfortunate accident, the result of the invasion of the
realm of light by the powers of darkness.   Men's hope lay
in the future, when all the elements of light in man and in
the universe would once more be separated from the elements of darkness.   Meanwhile, God, the Father of Greatness, Supreme Ruler of Light, had not left them without
guidance.

" Wisdom and deeds have always from time to time been
brought to mankind by the messengers of God.   So in one age
they have been brought by the messenger called Buddha to
India, in another by Zaradusht to Persia, in another by Jesus to
the West.   Thereupon this revelation has come down, this

prophecy in this last age, through me, Mani, messenger of the God of truth to Babylonia." *

Mani taught that those who would be perfect should make themselves channels by which the particles of light confined in matter might escape to their proper freedom. To do this, the elect must abstain from marriage, for to procreate children was to perpetuate the mingling of light and darkness; they must not take life either, so they might only eat vegetables, and these they might neither cultivate nor cook; they must also renounce property and devote themselves to prayer. Fortunately for the continued existence of the elect, and of Manichæism as well, a much less exacting standard of behaviour was required of the hearers, who formed the majority of the believers. They were permitted to marry and encouraged to work. They must not kill animals, indulge in any form of greed or lust, or worship idols. Certain religious duties were prescribed for them, and it was incumbent on them to feed and support the elect.

Mani was soon forced to flee from Persia and lead the life of a wandering prophet. He taught and gathered adherents as he went. About the year A.D. 276 he was lured back to Persia on some pretext, and was executed by order of King Bahram I. The king had his body flayed, and the skin, stuffed with straw, was set up over the city gate. In the persecution that followed, the Manichees were driven far afield, both to the East and to the West, and, wherever they went, they zealously preached their faith. By the fourth century Manichæism had become a serious rival to the Christian church, and by the time the struggle was over the Church had reproduced more than one of the characteristics of her defeated enemy, the most notable being

* *The Religion of the Manichees*, by F. C. Burkitt, p. 37. (Quotation from Mani's book *Shābūhragān* from Sachau's translation.)

the double standard of morality, one for monks and another for laymen.

In the third century, however, Christians living in Asia Minor were more concerned about Persian invaders than about Manichæan missionaries. When the power of the Parthians fell before Artaxerxes, the Arsacids retained one kingdom, Armenia, which had long been in the unhappy position of being a buffer state between the Roman and Persian Empires. About A.D. 258 Sapor, king of Persia, decided the time was ripe for an attack on Asia Minor. As a preliminary, he looked round for a man who would clear the road by assassinating Chosroes, the king of Armenia. He found the man he wanted in Anak, a Persian Arsacid, and, as events proved, the father of a Christian saint. Anak killed Chosroes, but the *satraps* who had failed to protect their king speedily avenged him. Anak was killed, and all his family with him, except an infant boy, who was smuggled out of the country to Cæsarea in Cappadocia. There he was brought up as a Christian and was named Gregory. Many years later, when Tiridates, the son of Chosroes, had recovered his father's kingdom with the help of Diocletian, Gregory returned there and took service under him. According to the account of his life which has survived, he suffered a long imprisonment and many tortures for his faith. Some of the details are certainly legendary, but the main outline of the story is credible enough. On his release he earned the title of St Gregory the Illuminator by his zeal in preaching Christianity. With his encouragement, churches were built throughout the length and breadth of the land. St Gregory was consecrated bishop of Armenia in the city of his adoption, Cæsarea in Cappadocia, about A.D. 302. Before he died, he had the satisfaction of baptizing the king and all his court in the river Euphrates, and Armenia thus became the first Christian country.

All this was still far in the future when king Sapor, having secured Armenia, proceeded to devastate Mesopotamia and to threaten Roman provinces farther west. To the fear of Goths from the north was added the dread of Persians from the east, and thousands of people living in the cities of Syria and Asia Minor must have felt profoundly relieved when the news came that the Emperor Valerian himself was on the way with reinforcements to drive back the Persians. Their relief was premature. Valerian was defeated and made a prisoner by Sapor, who was free for a while to ravage the Roman provinces across the Euphrates to his heart's content. Knowing that he could not hope to hold this territory, he treated the cities mercilessly. He surprised Antioch when the inhabitants were amusing themselves at the theatre. He carried off with him booty and captives, and he left behind a city of desolation, mourning for dead men and ruined buildings. Tarsus and several other famous cities in Asia Minor soon suffered a similar fate. Most of them put up little resistance, though Cæsarea in Cappadocia sustained a siege, and, with Gallienus as Emperor, no adequate measures were taken to check the Persian advance. Help came to the unfortunate inhabitants of Asia Minor from an unexpected quarter. Odenathus, a leading senator of Palmyra, gathered an Arab army from the desert tribesmen, and harassed Sapor's lines of communication until he was forced to retreat to the Persian side of the Euphrates. Odenathus followed up the advantage he had gained, and inflicted a decisive defeat on Sapor. For this he was rewarded with the title of Augustus by Gallienus, and became for practical purposes the ruler of the eastern provinces. His beautiful wife, Zenobia, who on his death succeeded to his power, played a part in a very curious chapter in the history of the church of Antioch.

It happened that the bishopric of Antioch fell vacant soon after Odenathus came into power. Whether Zenobia in-

c c 2

fluenced the election it is not possible to tell, but the man who was chosen, Paul of Samosata, became a favourite at her court. She gave him an important civil office which brought with it a salary of two hundred sestertia, and Paul was frequently to be seen strutting about the forum with his secretaries, reading and dictating his letters in public, so that everyone might see what a busy man he was. His vanity grew with the exercise of power, and so did his expenses. He gathered admirers and partisans around him, some of whom formed a bodyguard to attend him when he walked through the streets of Antioch. Though he had no private income, he gathered considerable wealth, not only by legitimate means, but also by taking bribes from people who had law-suits to bring before him. Such a man could not but bring dishonour to the church he ruled, yet it is doubtful whether any attempt would have been made to depose him had he not tampered with the church services and taught false doctrine. Paul had an exalted idea of his own eloquence as a preacher. He had a throne and a high pulpit erected in the cathedral church at Antioch for his own use, and during his sermons he had a habit of slapping his thigh and stamping on the floor of the rostrum to emphasize his remarks. His supporters were trained to applaud, and when Paul slapped his thigh, the church would resemble pandemonium, with men jumping up and shouting, while the women waved their handkerchiefs as they would at the theatre. Quiet orderly worshippers who did not join in these demonstrations were rebuked from the pulpit for their lack of zeal. As if this were not enough, Paul abolished the old time-honoured hymns to Christ, and trained a female choir to sing songs in honour of himself in church on Easter day.

Even before his vanity had brought him to this climax of blasphemous absurdity, the weight of sane Christian opinion had been brought to bear against him. Antioch already had a tradition of Christian learning to strengthen the Church's resistance to such an innovator as Paul, but it happened that one of the presbyters, Malchion, was a man of exceptional ability, a logician, and a teacher of rhetoric. He quickly perceived that Paul's teaching was dangerous, though Paul was an adept at evading the issue and covering his heretical ideas with a cloak of orthodox expressions, when taken to task about his statements. Zenobia was a Jewess, and also a remarkably intelligent woman. She had gathered round her some of the best intellects of the day, including the philosopher, Longinus. It is probable that Paul had the Court circle in mind, even when he was preaching to the faithful, and was more anxious that his views should be regarded as intellectually respectable by them, than that they should be strictly orthodox. He affirmed that in God there is only one Person and, shorn of its disguises, his teaching about Christ was that he was a man upon whom the Holy Spirit came, and who advanced in goodness until, after his triumph over sin upon the cross, his union with God became complete.

Four years after Paul's consecration, the opposition to his views had grown so strong that a synod met at Antioch, with Firmilian as president, to try the matter on the spot. It was an illustrious gathering. Besides Firmilian, St Gregory Thaumaturgus and his brother, Athenodore, were there, and so were the bishops of Tarsus, Iconium, Cæsarea, Jerusalem, and many lesser places. One great figure was absent. Dionysius of Alexandria had been invited to come, but was unable to take so long a journey owing to age and ill health. A pupil of Origen, successor to Heraclas, both as head of the Catechetical School and later as bishop of Alexandria, Dionysius the Great was a power in the Church. He had made his mark as a philosopher by emphasizing the importance of beauty in nature, as a proof that the universe is not the work of chance; in commenting on the Scriptures he had shown himself to be a remarkably sound literary critic; as a bishop, he had guided his church through the Decian persecution, the plague, and all the controversies which followed that terrible period. On this occasion, though he could not come, he sent a letter giving his opinion. Laymen and clergy in Antioch, and even local bishops, might be intimidated by Paul of Samosata, but this formidable assembly was not. However, Paul was wary and succeeded in side-stepping the charges of heresy which were brought against him. The synod dissolved without convicting him.

After a second synod had been equally unsuccessful in bringing Paul to book, a third was held in A.D. 269, and was attended by a very large number of bishops. This time Malchion's searching questions disclosed the true nature of Paul's opinions, and he was condemned by all as a heretic and " excommunicated from the Catholic Church under heaven ". Another bishop, Domnus, the son of his predecessor, Demetrian, was then appointed in his place. To make this decree was one thing, but to enforce it was another. Paul refused to consider himself deposed. He still had a strong following, and he retained possession of the cathedral church in spite of protests. But the tide had set against him. In A.D. 272 Aurelian, an energetic though short-lived Emperor, having dealt with a usurper in Gaul, turned his attention to the East. Zenobia's power by this time was so great that she appeared a serious rival, but Aurelian defeated her forces in a succession of battles and sieges, and eventually took the Queen herself captive. As he returned triumphant through Antioch, Domnus and his presbyters appealed to him for the restitution of church property to its rightful owners, for Paul was still in possession of the cathedral. Aurelian had no love for the Christians, but Gallienus had allowed them the right to hold property, and, as Emperor, he had to administer the law. He judged that the building should belong " to those with whom the bishops of the doctrine in Italy and Rome should communicate in writing ". Thus Paul who had been supported by one non-Christian monarch was finally ejected by another.* Incidentally, the Emperor's judgement provided the Roman church with strong support for her claim to exert authority over the rest of Christendom.

St Clement and Origen had established the reputation of Alexandria as a centre of Christian learning. Towards the end of the third century, Antioch gained similar renown. In addition to Malchion, there was a presbyter named Lucian, who lectured on the Christian faith and attracted students from far and wide, and Dorotheus, who had studied the Old Testament in Hebrew and was an authority on the interpretation of the Scriptures. These men and their fellow scholars established a tradition of Christian learning in Antioch with a character of its own. They rejected the allegorical method of interpreting the Bible, which Origen had used so freely, and instead they insisted on the literal meaning of the words, as scholars do to-day. Together with this went a firm insistence on the reality of our Lord's manhood. Christians in Syria were not easily tempted to deny the human nature of Jesus Christ, their danger lay in the opposite direction. While the Greeks in Alexandria were apt to doubt whether our Lord had really become a man and suffered on the Cross, the Syrians in Antioch often failed to grasp that he is truly God. Lucian's teaching, about which little is certainly known, seems to have erred in this way. He himself, having been out of communion with the bishops of Antioch for a considerable time, was restored to the fellowship of the Church when Cyril was bishop, and died a martyr during the Diocletian persecution. But some of his pupils went much farther

* Eusebius, op. cit., Book VII, pp. 27–30.

astray, and the teaching of one of them, Arius, split Christendom into two camps for a while during the next century. Yet the school of theology in Antioch had its strength as well as its weakness. Its scholars valued historical truth. They would not allow the literal meaning of the Scriptures to be lost in a maze of fanciful interpretations, or Christ's humanity to be called in doubt.

On the eve of the Diocletian persecution, the ancient churches of Antioch and Cæsarea were full of life and of promise for the future. Men were studying the Scriptures and striving to come to a fuller understanding of their faith. In doing this, they were preparing the way for the great councils of the next century, which had the task of formulating the Church's creed. In Cæsarea, during the closing years of the third century, scribes were industriously copying manuscripts for the magnificent library of Christian books which Pamphilus was assembling. Eusebius, his friend and disciple, was eagerly helping him in the task and, as he read, he was collecting material for his *Ecclesiastical History*. He was to write the book in sections, as he could find time, in the midst of persecution, when the very history he wrote was in the making. But before the storm broke, he had some quiet years in which to soak his mind in early Christian writings, many of which have since been lost. The library which Pamphilus collected was destroyed by the Arabs in the seventh century, and the lengthy quotations from his authorities, which Eusebius strewed thickly over the pages of his history, are in many cases all that is left of these earlier books.

As for the humbler Christians of the Eastern churches in these years of comparative peace, we can only imagine their lives, for no writer has recorded their history. While some were worldly, careless and indifferent, others had a faith in Christ which no torture could shake, and they were soon to prove what was in them in the last and most terrible of all the persecutions.

ROMAN LAMP IN THE FORM OF A CHURCH

BOOKS FOR FURTHER READING

Ecclesiastical History, by Eusebius, translated by H. J. Lawlor and J. E. L. Oulton. 2 vols. The second volume contains the introduction and notes.

Decline and Fall of the Roman Empire, by E. Gibbon. Vol. I. Chapters VIII, X and XI give the general history of the eastern provinces in this period.

Early Christianity outside the Roman Empire, by F. C. Burkitt.

The Religion of the Manichees, by F. C. Burkitt.

History of the Church to A.D. 461, by B. J. Kidd, Vol. I. To A.D. 313. Chapter XVII.

CHAPTER XVIII

THE FINAL PERSECUTION

LOOKING back on life in the early Church, there is one notable difference which distinguishes it from Christian life in our own day, at least as we know it in this country. For the first three centuries of the Church's existence, Christianity was a persecuted religion. A believer might at any time be challenged and compelled to choose between denying Christ and suffering imprisonment or death. Though thousands of Christians went quietly about their business without provoking question, the danger was always there. For that reason, the period is the Church's heroic age, and later generations have been inclined to romanticize it. It was no golden time, as some have imagined, with a united Church believing an uncorrupted Gospel and keeping herself unspotted from the world; on the contrary, the history of the first three centuries is darkened by schism, heresy, and moral failure, just as the history of every subsequent period has been. It cannot be otherwise, as long as the Church on earth remains a community of sinners who are being saved, not of just men made perfect. But the centuries of persecution have their own peculiar glory; for in them, and especially in the ten years from A.D. 303 to 313, hatred, prejudice, cruelty, and lust pounded against the Church like the waves of some monstrous sea, and were unable to destroy her. They broke in vain against the steadfast faith of thousands of ordinary Christians, who endured torture, death, or mutilation rather than deny their Lord.

402

When Diocletian became Emperor in A.D. 284, it seemed as if the downfall of the Roman Empire could not be long postponed. The senate had ceased to be a governing body, and the armies made and unmade emperors, according to their whim. Barbarian attacks from without, and political and economic disintegration within, seemed about to destroy the whole fabric of Roman civilization. Diocletian, however, had a plan by which he believed he could save the Empire. He moved his capital from Rome to Nicomedia, a city in Asia Minor, close to the straits of Constantinople. From there he had much better control of the eastern half of the Empire. He next associated with himself, as *Augustus*, a general called Maximianus, and gave him the government of the West. Maximianus made Milan his capital and, although he also ranked as Emperor, he obeyed Diocletian in matters of policy. With two Emperors dividing the vast Roman dominions between them, it was much harder for a rival to make a successful bid for power, yet Carausius did establish himself as an independent ruler in Britain. Diocletian then carried his scheme a stage farther. He appointed *Cæsars*, as subordinates to the two *Augusti*, and gave them charge of the frontier provinces where constant vigilance was needed to ward off barbarian attacks. The *Cæsar* for the western half of the Empire was Constantius Chlorus, the father of Constantine; in the East under his own control, Diocletian appointed Galerius, a bitter enemy of Christianity.

Diocletian's plan served its immediate purpose, for it secured a long period of peace in which the Emperor was able to deal with internal problems, while his subordinates beat back the barbarians and eliminated rivals. He thoroughly reorganized the administration of the Empire, in an endeavour to restore its finances and improve its economy. In the process he grouped the provinces into " dioceses ", a change which later influenced the organization of the

Church. For eighteen years, while these changes were in progress, Christians continued to enjoy the peace which they had been granted by Gallienus. There was no sign that Diocletian's plans included the elimination of the Church; on the contrary, his court was full of Christians, many of whom were trusted with responsible positions, and were even exempted from sacrificing on account of their religious scruples. Eusebius has described this period of prosperity and false security, when Christian assemblies everywhere were thronged with people, "by reason of which they were no longer satisfied with the buildings of olden time, and would erect from the foundations churches of spacious dimensions throughout all the cities". Looking back, Eusebius saw it as a time of slackness, when Christians quarrelled among themselves, took their prosperity for granted, and forgot their dependence upon God. The great persecution came, to his thinking, as a judgement, to bring back to the Church's remembrance the reality of her mission.

It was in the winter of A.D. 302–303 that the plan to destroy the Church was hatched in the vast imperial palace at Nicomedia. There is still a certain mystery about it, for though Diocletian undoubtedly gave his consent, the scheme is out of keeping with his temperate, organizing genius. It is much more characteristic of Galerius, the huge Dacian herdsman whom Diocletian had made a *Cæsar* for his military ability. Galerius had a broad streak of savagery in him, and he hated the Christians. He spent that decisive winter at Nicomedia with Diocletian, and it would seem that he found means to persuade the ageing Emperor that the Christians did actually menace the security of the State. Day after day, the two were closeted together, while the palace and the city buzzed with rumours. In the early spring certain civil magistrates and military commanders were taken into consultation, but still the secret was kept.   Even when a soothsayer was sent to in-quire the will of Apollo from the oracle at Miletus, the Christians suspected nothing.

On the 23rd of February A.D. 303, the persecution began. The day was carefully selected, for it was the festival of the god Terminus, and the Emperors hoped it would in future mark the terminus of Christianity.   At dawn the prefect of the prætorian guard with the chief officers of the city raided the cathedral church of Nicomedia.   They broke open the gates and ransacked the whole building in search of an image of the Christian god.   In this, of course, they failed, but they found copies of the Scriptures, which they burnt, and they looted all the fittings and church utensils. While this was going on, Diocletian and Galerius were standing on the roof of the palace, looking across at the church, which was built on a hill nearby; Galerius was for having it burnt to the ground, but Diocletian feared that the flames might spread to adjoining buildings.   Finally, he gave orders that not one stone should be left upon another, and the prætorian guard demolished it with axes.

Next day, the edict of persecution appeared upon the palace gate.   It enacted that all Christian churches were to be razed to the ground, all copies of the Scriptures burnt, Christian men in official positions degraded and deprived of civil rights, those in private life, together with Christian freedmen, reduced to slavery.   It had not long been posted, before an indignant Christian tore it down.   He was arrested at once, tried, tortured, and burnt alive.   But this savage sentence was a punishment for his act of treason in destroying the edict.   Diocletian did not intend to embark upon anything so unpopular and unwise as a massacre of a large minority of his subjects.   His first edict was carefully designed to avoid bloodshed, while cutting at the roots of Christian life.   By prohibiting Christian worship, destroy-ing the Scriptures, and degrading the adherents of this troublesome religion, Diocletian hoped to destroy the cult without killing useful citizens. Valerian had made a similar attempt, and it had not been successful, but this time there was a new provision, the destruction of the sacred books. Diocletian's own wife and daughter were cate-chumens, so he was aware of the great importance which Christians attached to their Scriptures. Take these from them and prohibit their assemblies, and the religion might slowly die for lack of the food which sustained it. The whole scheme is characteristic of the sober, calculating mind of Diocletian; there can be little doubt that Galerius was dissatisfied with it. As Mason has said: " Galerius did not see the good of burning the Bibles: he wanted to burn the men." *

Whether Galerius took a leaf from Nero's book, or whether chance played into his hands, it is impossible to say, but shortly after the publication of the edict a fire broke out in the imperial palace. A good deal of damage was done before it could be extinguished, and Diocletian was alarmed. The Christians were suspected of having started the fire and all Diocletian's household slaves were examined with torture to make them reveal what they knew. In spite of this, no evidence was forthcoming. Lactantius, a Chris-tian writer who was in Nicomedia at the time, suggests that if the servants of Galerius had been tortured, the origin of the fire would have been revealed, but they escaped all question. A fortnight later, another fire broke out in the palace, but was quickly extinguished. Galerius thereupon left the city in haste, saying that he would not stay to be burnt alive by the Christians. Diocletian was by then convinced that there had been a conspiracy, and he instituted a purge. He had his Christian chamberlains, men whom he had trusted for years, executed privately. He compelled his wife and daughter to sacrifice to prove

* *The Persecution of Diocletian*, by A. J. Mason, p. 118.

their loyalty.   Christians in the court and in the city were suspected of treason, and could only clear themselves by denying their faith.   According to Lactantius, " presbyters and other officers of the Church were seized, without evidence by witnesses or confession, condemned, and together with their families led to execution.   In burning alive, no distinction of sex or age was regarded; and, because of their great multitude, they were not burnt one after another, but a herd of them were encircled with the same fire; and servants, having millstones tied about their necks, were cast into the sea." *   Galerius, when he heard the news, must have felt that his winter at Nicomedia had not been wasted.

Meanwhile, the original edict against the Christians was being circulated throughout the Empire.   Maximian, who had a bloodthirsty disposition, received it with pleasure, and proceeded to give effect to it in Italy amd Africa.   Constantius, on the contrary, obeyed reluctantly.   In Gaul and Britain, which were under his rule, there were very few martyrdoms during the whole of the persecution.   St Alban, the young soldier at Verulamium (the modern St Albans), who was executed for sheltering a Christian priest, is the only British martyr of this period whose name and story have been recorded.   Constantius did not even order that copies of the Scriptures should be searched out and burnt.   He saw to it that a number of churches were destroyed, and considered that sufficient.   In the East, where the edict was strictly enforced, its proclamation coincided with disturbances in Syria.   Diocletian must have seen in this the realization of the fears which had made him so loth to attempt the suppression of Christianity, but he could not draw back.   Instead, he published a second edict, which followed hard on the heels of the first, ordering

* Lactantius: *The Manner in which Persecutors Died*, Chapter XV. Trans. A.-N.C.L., Vol. XXII.   Lactantius, Vol. II.

the imprisonment of all the clergy. By this means, he believed he would forestall any general rising which the Christians might be planning. Soon the prisons throughout the Empire were filled to capacity with bishops, presbyters, and deacons; yet, even so, many hid and continued to hold services for their people in secret.

In the first phase of Diocletian's persecution, the provision which caused most consternation among Christians was that which ordered that the Scriptures should be burnt. Every church had its precious library of sacred books, and in those days, when each word had to be painstakingly copied out by hand, even one codex or a single roll was valuable. It was conceivable that this ingenious scheme for suppressing Christianity might succeed, that all copies of the Gospels might be destroyed, that the faith might become a legend without historical evidence. The mere threat of such a loss was enough to rouse all but the most indifferent. It is no wonder that those who surrendered copies of the Scriptures to the authorities were regarded with detestation. A name was found for them: they were called *traditors*, a word akin to " traitor ". But not all those who handed over books to be destroyed deserved this title. Some bishops and priests very sensibly went through their church libraries, as soon as they knew the danger which threatened, and picked out a number of heretical books, which they either left in their churches or dutifully brought to the magistrate for burning. Bishop Mensurius of Carthage was one of these, and his plan worked admirably. But afterwards, when the heretical volumes had gone up in smoke, some members of the Carthaginian senate learnt of the trick and hurried off to inform the Proconsul, Anulinus. Anulinus, however, was not interested. He had done his duty as a magistrate in causing the church to be searched, and he refused to investigate any further.

It is likely that a good many magistrates were without

enthusiasm for the task of persecution which had been laid upon them, nevertheless, for the most part, they carried it out methodically and thoroughly. A detailed report has survived of a police raid upon the Christian church at Cirta in North Africa. It is not a record of martyrdom, for the clergy in this case handed over what was demanded of them, and so branded themselves as *traditors*, unfit for any sacred office. This particular account has been preserved by a fortunate accident, but similar scenes must have been enacted in hundreds of places in Italy, Africa, Greece, and the Eastern provinces. On 19th May A.D. 303, Munatus Felix, the high priest and warden of Cirta, with a posse of police came to the house where the Christians were accustomed to worship. Apparently there was as yet no special building for the purpose. There to meet him were Paul the bishop, his presbyters, deacons, and subdeacons and, when challenged, they made no difficulty about producing the church plate, which amounted to a considerable treasure. It included two gold and six silver chalices; six silver dishes; a casket, bowl and lamps, also of silver; two torches; bronze candlesticks and hanging lamps. There was, in addition, an assortment of clothing, probably intended for the poor. All this was confiscated, and the high priest then demanded that the scriptures should be handed over. Catulinus, one of the subdeacons, produced one large volume, but that did not satisfy Felix. Paul reluctantly admitted that there were other books, but said that the Readers had taken them home. Catulinus and Marculius, who were men of more spirit than their bishop, refused to disclose the names of the Readers, but this was a vain stand, for the men were known to the local authorities. Having finished their work at the church, the police called at the house of each of the Readers and demanded that they should give up all copies of the Scriptures that were in their possession. Felix, the tailor, produced five books; Victorinus handed over eight; Projectus gave up two big volumes and two small ones, and Victor, the schoolmaster, brought out two codices and four books in five rolls each. Eutychius declared he had none, and Coddeo was out, but Coddeo's wife gave them six codices and, though the police searched the house, they could find no more. If the losses in books had been on this scale in every church, the persecution might have had a large measure of success.*

Many Christians, however, were ready to die or to suffer unspeakable tortures rather than reveal where their copies of the New Testament lay hidden. St Felix, bishop of Tibiuca in North Africa, for example, admitted that he had some books and parchments, but refused to give them up. " It is better for me to be burned myself ", he said, " than for the Divine Scriptures, for it is better to obey God than men." The magistrate was reluctant to convict him, and sent him to Italy for trial there. St Felix could easily have saved himself by a subterfuge, but, like St Ignatius, he had a longing for martyrdom, which was eventually satisfied, for in Italy he was beheaded.

In November, A.D. 303, Diocletian went to Rome to celebrate his Vicennalia. It was usual on these occasions to liberate prisoners, but Diocletian had no intention of setting free the hundreds of Christian priests and bishops who were crowding his prisons after the second edict. In December the usual amnesty was published, with an additional clause to the effect that the clergy were to be freed only after they had sacrificed; if any refused, they were to be encouraged to accept this kind offer by the use of torture. By the time this third edict was published, Diocletian was lying ill at Ravenna. He insisted on being carried back to Nicomedia, though he could travel only in

* *The Persecution of Diocletian*, by A. J. Mason, Chapter V, and *The Shape of the Liturgy*, by Dom Gregory Dix, p. 24.

a litter, but before the long winter journey was over he collapsed. During the year that followed, his mind was affected by his illness, and he was incapable of attending to business. In A.D. 305 he consented to retire into private life, and induced Maximian to resign as well. This left Constantius as *Augustus* in the West and Galerius in the East. Constantius was in failing health, and, in far-off Britain, he could do little to influence political developments. Galerius appointed both the *Cæsars*, Maximinus Daza, an upstart soldier, and Severus. He ignored Constantine, the son of Constantius, who had been brought up at the court at Nicomedia. It is easy to guess what Constantine's fate would have been, had he not contrived to slip away from Nicomedia and travel post haste across Europe to join his father at York. This was in A.D. 306, when the future looked black indeed for the Church. Galerius and Maximinus Daza were doing their best to exterminate Christianity in the East, and Constantius, who had befriended Christians in the West, was dying. Yet that was the point at which the tide turned, for Constantine arrived in time to take over the command of the legions in Britain from his father. He proclaimed himself Cæsar, upon his father's death, and from that moment moved steadily forward on the road to power. But there were still six years to run before he was to lead his troops to victory at Milvian Bridge under the sign of the cross.

Meanwhile the persecution, especially in the East, was reaching a pitch of fury unknown before. In A.D. 304, while Diocletian was too ill to know what was being done, a fourth edict was published in his name, which added the death penalty to the punishments which could already be legally inflicted upon Christians who persisted in their " superstition ". Together with this edict, orders were circulated to all the towns that " the people one and all, without exception, should both offer sacrifice and also pour libation to the idols ".* How many Christians died for their faith in the terrible years which followed this pronouncement it is impossible to estimate. The number must have run into thousands. The record given by Eusebius, who was an eye-witness of many of the atrocities which he describes, is so full of insane cruelty that it would hardly be credible, were it not that our own generation has witnessed a similar outburst of sadism in Nazi Germany. Every refinement of torture that a perverted mind could think of was applied to those Christians who refused to sacrifice to idols. They were scourged, mutilated, roasted over slow fires, hung up by the heels, racked, and starved. Some endured the whole round of torments not once, but many times. Few were allowed the mercy of an easy death, such as beheading; instead they were thrown to wild beasts, crucified, burnt, drowned, or torn to pieces. With devilish ingenuity, the persecutors in the Thebais thought out a new method of execution. They bent down the tops of trees with pulleys, attached one leg of their victim to one tree and the other to another, released the trees, and let the condemned man be torn apart to the gratification of the watching multitude. Mass executions were common, sometimes as many as a hundred men, women, and children being killed in a single day. In one instance a whole town was wiped out:

" At this time armed soldiers surrounded a little town in Phrygia, of which the inhabitants were all Christians, every man of them, and setting fire to it burnt them, along with young children and women as they were calling upon God who is over all. The reason of this was, that all the inhabitants of the town to a man, the curator himself and the duumvirs with all the officials and the whole assembly, confessed themselves Christians and refused to give the least heed to those who bade them commit idolatry." †

* Eusebius, *Martyrs of Palestine*, III, 1.
† Eusebius, op. cit., VIII, 11.

The number of apostates among the Christians in those
provinces where the persecution was most severe must have
been very large indeed.   Many, perhaps most, of those
who sacrificed were sincere believers who lacked the
heroism necessary for steadfastness in the face of such a
terrible alternative.   They remained Christian at heart,
and were eager to be received back into the Church at the
first opportunity.   What is truly amazing in the circumstances is not that many quailed, but that such a large
number stood firm and endured unshaken to the end.
Their courage and their absolute certainty of belief made a
deep impression upon pagans of widely different character,
Arnobius, an African philosopher and professor of rhetoric.
was so moved by what he saw that he asked the Christians
at Sicca to prepare him for baptism.   Having heard his
slashing attacks on Christianity, they hardly knew what to
make of his request, and were with difficulty convinced of
his sincerity.   Lactantius, the author of the treatise on *The
Manner in Which the Persecutors Died*, was converted by
the scenes he witnessed at Nicomedia.   A man of a very
different type, Maxentius, the son of the retired Emperor
Maximian, was sufficiently impressed to think that Christian
support might be a valuable political asset.   When he made
himself *Cæsar* and, with his father's aid, dethroned Severus,
he was careful to adopt a policy of toleration.   In time, the
constancy of the Christian martyrs even filled their persecutors with superstitious fear.   When Galerius lay dying
by inches of a disgusting and incurable disease in A.D. 311,
he published an edict of toleration, permitting the Christians
again to enjoy legal existence and to rebuild their churches,
and he ended it with the strange request that they should
" beseech their own god for our welfare ".*   The sufferings
of the Church during the great persecution were preparing
the way for her triumph under Constantine.

* Eusebius, op. cit., VIII, 17.

In the West, the persecution was for a time severe in
Italy and North Africa, but it lasted little more than three
years.   In A.D. 306, the year when Constantine was proclaimed as *Cæsar* in Britain, Maxentius, the son of Maximian,
was hailed as Emperor by the Senate and the prætorian
guard in Rome.   In the following year he and his father
defeated and killed Severus and proclaimed themselves
Augusti.   This brought persecution to an end in the West,
for Constantine had favoured the Christians from the first,
and Maxentius had decided that it was good policy to do
the same.   But in the East the reign of terror continued
with hardly a respite for ten years.   Galerius had associated
with himself as Emperor his friend Licinius, as well as
Maximin Daza, and the edict of toleration which he published
during his last illness in A.D. 311 was in the names of
Licinius, Constantine, and himself.   It is significant that
Maximin Daza's name was not included.   Christians who
rejoiced that their afflictions were over soon learned that
they were mistaken; but at first all was jubilation.   Confessors released from the prisons and the mines poured back
into the cities, and were welcomed by thronging crowds
who bore them home in triumph, singing psalms and hymns
of praise as they went.   Churches which had been confiscated, but not destroyed, were handed back to their
rightful owners, and in every city they were filled to overflowing as the liberated bishops and priests began to celebrate the Eucharist once more in the customary manner.
Those who had worshipped secretly, in danger of their
lives throughout the persecution, now openly professed
their faith, and others who had given way came back,
pleading for forgiveness.

Maximin Daza no sooner heard the news of the death of
Galerius than he hurried across Asia and met Licinius in
Greece.   He was in a strong position, with the Syrian legions
supporting him, and he compelled Licinius to yield him the

whole of Asia Minor, as well as Syria and Egypt. He then returned to Nicomedia and began to work out his future policy. He evidently thought it inadvisable to reverse the toleration granted by Galerius straight away, but he may have dropped hints that a popular protest against the Christians would not be unwelcome. He aimed at a pagan revival, such as Julian the Apostate attempted to inspire half a century later, and in this he was ably supported by a Neo-Platonist named Theotecnus, who was Curator of the city of Antioch. The first move in the campaign was made by Maximin, who found some pretext in the autumn of A.D. 311, to forbid Christians to hold gatherings in their cemeteries. Next came a petition from the citizens of Antioch begging that Christians might be excluded from their city. The Emperor was so gratified by this expression of piety that, when he went on tour through the cities of Asia Minor in the early spring, numerous other places felt impelled to present him with similar petitions. These edifying documents, together with the Emperor's reply, were afterwards engraved upon bronze tablets and set up on pillars for all to see. Eusebius quotes the bulk of the Emperor's fulsome rescript in which he praises the piety of the petitioners, foresees that the gods will reward them with peace and prosperity, and agrees that those Christians who " persist in their accursed folly " should be driven into exile.

Theotecnus, meanwhile, was inaugurating the pagan revival with an impressive set piece at Antioch. He had a statue of Zeus Philius made, which had a cunning hidden mechanism, and with this he staged marvels to impress the populace. He elaborated the cult with an imitation of Christian baptism and gave it the character of a mystery religion. Maximin reached Antioch in March or early April, and at once began to work out his scheme for the reform of paganism. He realized that polytheism, with its diversity of cults and its lack of organization, could make no

D D

headway against Christianity, so, with the aid of Theotecnus, he drew up a scheme which would provide paganism
with a priesthood modelled on that of the Church. Each
city was to have a high priest, assisted by any existing
priests, whose duty was to offer daily sacrifice and who
corresponded to a bishop in the Christian order. Above
him was a pontiff, responsible for religious affairs throughout a single province. Both these officials were to wear
white priestly robes to make them more impressive, but
their most important function was to preside over ecclesiastical courts, newly created to make persecution of the
Christians more effective. They were, in fact, to be in-
quisitors rather than priests. These new courts had not
the power to inflict the death penalty, but they could order
blinding or the mutilation of ears and nose. Maximin
Daza introduced these innovations in the course of the year
A.D. 312, apparently in response to the anti-Christian
petitions with which he was being deluged, and it was not
long before persecution was again the order of the day.

In addition to these comparatively straightforward
measures, Maximin embarked upon a campaign of lies and
scandal-mongering, which he hoped would discredit
Christianity. Women of the streets were seized, threatened
with torture, and compelled to make slanderous accusations
against the Church. It is unlikely that this ruse met with
much success, but another of his devices was more dangerous.
Some anti-Christian writer, possibly Theotecnus, had produced a false and blasphemous version of the Gospel narrative under the title of the *Memoirs of Pilate*. Maximin
commanded that this book should be given the widest
possible publicity, and he ordered that copies should be
distributed to the primary schools as a text-book for the
children to learn by heart.

Christians in the East must have felt their hearts sink,
as the hope which the release of the confessors had aroused

died away and new methods of persecution succeeded the old. Peter, the Patriarch of Alexandria, who had been imprisoned during the Diocletian persecution and afterwards set free, was suddenly arrested and beheaded, together with a number of other Egyptian bishops. The bishop of Emesa in Phœnicia was thrown to the wild beasts with two other martyrs. Lucian, the famous Christian scholar, was summoned from Antioch to Nicomedia, and was there put to death. The loss of these leaders, in addition to those who had perished before, was a serious blow to the Church. But relief was in sight. Maximin had not pursued his policy of persecution for more than a few months before he found himself involved in war with the independant Christian kingdom of Armenia. Drought, famine, and plague added to his difficulties, and, by the autumn of A.D. 312, the boasts which he had had engraved on bronze tablets at Tyre and elsewhere were beginning to mock him. The grateful gods had brought him neither peace nor prosperity. At the same time a greater danger began to threaten him from the west, for Maximin had been secretly conspiring with Maxentius against Constantine, and in October Constantine defeated his rival and proceeded to cement an alliance with Licinius by giving him his sister in marriage.

It was on the eve of the battle in which he defeated Maxentius that Constantine had the experience which became known to legend as his vision. According to Lactantius, who was later tutor to his children and a member of his household, Constantine was directed in a dream to have the Christian monogram painted upon his soldiers' shields before they advanced to the attack. The fourth century was a superstitious age, and Constantine was as anxious to avail himself of a good omen before a decisive battle as a modern airman might be to carry his lucky mascot on a raid. He sent his soldiers forward marked with the symbol of the cross, and in this sign he conquered.* Maxentius and his army were driven back across Milvian bridge, which collapsed under the strain, flinging the defeated Emperor and numbers of his men to their deaths in the Tiber.   Constantine marched in triumph to Rome, where he was received with great rejoicing, and, after settling

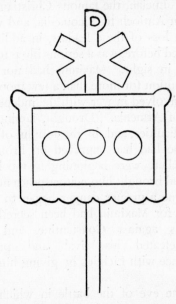

HEAD OF MILITARY STANDARD ADORNED WITH THE CHRISTIAN
MONOGRAM FROM A COIN OF CONSTANTINE

matters there, he went on to Milan, where he met Licinius in January, A.D. 313.   Besides celebrating the marriage of Licinius with Constantia, the two Emperors discussed matters of policy and came to an important agreement as to the future treatment of Christians.   Constantine was deter-

* Constantine's standard was not the simple cross, but the *labarum*, the cross added to Roman military symbols.   See Fig. above.

mined on nothing less than complete toleration and Licinius gave his consent. No copy of this famous Edict of Milan has survived, but its main provisions are known from the version published a few months later at Nicomedia, which is quoted by Lactantius. It marked a new era in the relations between the Church and the Empire. From then on, except for a brief period when Julian the Apostate endeavoured to revive paganism, the Church had no longer to fear the hostility of the State.

Maximin Daza, the only persecutor the Church had still to fear, heard the news of the alliance between Constantine and Licinius, and realized that it boded him no good. He decided to forestall his enemies and, though it was the depth of winter, he crossed Asia Minor with his Syrian army by forced marches, leaving a trail of dead behind him. He advanced across the Bosphorus, and had laid siege to Byzantium and Heraclea before Licinius had time to collect an army and engage him in battle. But at this point the tide turned against him, for he was heavily defeated, and had to retreat to Tarsus with the remnants of his army. Licinius promptly occupied Bithynia and, from the imperial palace at Nicomedia, where the great persecution had begun, he proclaimed the edict of toleration to which he had agreed at Milan. Maximin made a last-minute effort to conciliate Christian opinion by issuing a similar edict himself, with a lying preamble to the effect that he had never intended to injure his Christian subjects—his benevolent intentions had been misconstrued by provincial governors. But no subterfuge could now deliver him, for he was suddenly stricken by a fatal illness which has not improbably been supposed to have been *delirium tremens*. He was consumed with an internal fire, and wasted away to a shadow. In his final delirium he imagined that he saw God and the martyrs sitting in judgement on him, and he cried out for mercy like a man upon the rack. By the autumn of A.D.

313, Maximin was dead, and the churches of the East at last had peace.

"Thanks be to God, the Almighty and King of the universe, for all things; and abundant thanks be also to the Saviour and Redeemer of our souls, Jesus Christ, through whom we pray continually that peace from troubles without and troubles in the heart may be preserved for us steadfast and undisturbed."

So wrote Eusebius at the beginning of the panegyric which brings his *Ecclesiastical History* to a close. The Church indeed had reason to be thankful. The handful of believers upon whom the Holy Spirit came on the first Whit Sunday had become a great multitude whom no man could number. In spite of the hatred of the mob, the contempt of the intelligentsia, and organized persecution by the Government, Christianity had spread among all classes and in all lands. Public opinion had altered, almost imperceptibly, so that by the fourth century the old cry of "the Christians to the lions" was dying out. For it was Constantine and not Galerius who was the true representative of his age. He was not a Christian at the beginning of his reign, though his mother, Helena,* who according to one legend was a British princess, was a believer; but like many pagans of his day he was a monotheist at heart, and felt for Christianity the kind of respect which a modern unbeliever will sometimes express for the Society of Friends. His victory at Milvian Bridge certainly hastened his conversion, for to him it was a practical demonstration that Christianity is a faith which works. From that time forwards, his policy as Emperor was increasingly Christian in character. Not only did he at first tolerate and then favour the Church, but he also made Sunday a holiday and brought in laws to

* Many legends have grown round the name of St Helena. In sober fact she showed her devotion by causing churches to be built at the Holy Sepulchre and in Bethlehem.

ENGLISH MILES

100 200 300 400 500

200 400 600 800

KILOMETRES

MARE CASPIUM

S EUXINUS

Heraclea
PAPHLAGONIA PONTUS ARMENIA MEDIA
...NIA Neocæsarea ASSYRIA
GALATIA Nyssa Cæsarea
...lomelium Samosata Nisibis Nineveh
CAPPADOCIA MESOPOTAMIA R.Tigris PERSIA
Iconium Tarsus Edessa
CILICIA Seleucia R.Euphrates Dura Europos Ctesiphon
Antioch Seleucia
SYRIA Palmyra
Salamis Emesa BABYLONIA
...RUS PHOENICIA
Sidon Damascus
Tyre GALILEE
Cæsarea SAMARIA
Joppa Jerusalem

ARABIA

...PT
SINUS ARABICUS
R. Nile

prohibit such pagan abuses as gladiatorial shows, the exposure of children, and cruelty to slaves. Although he was not actually baptized until he was on his death-bed, he was to all intents and purposes a Christian Emperor, and the Church accepted him as such. Her triumph was as complete as any temporal triumph can be.

But the peace which Eusebius prayed for did not come. The Church still had to endure conflicts both without and within, for the old war against the world, the flesh, and the devil went on as relentlessly as ever in each succeeding generation. In some ways it was easier for a small persecuted minority to be faithful to Christ than it was for a Church flooded with new and half-converted members. The leaven seemed small when hidden in so large a lump. Yet the Church which had survived adversity, survived prosperity also. In spite of heresies and schisms; in spite of worldliness, moral failure, and lapses into superstition on the part of her members, she remembered her commission to preach Christ crucified and to show forth his death until his coming again. Roman civilization collapsed and the dark ages came, but Christian missionaries won new victories among the barbarians, and soon the Saxons and the once-dreaded Goths were building cathedrals to the glory of God. And so through change and decay, through revolution, and even through apparent dismemberment, the Church has survived down to the present day. Our task is no easier than that of any previous generation, but at least it is no harder. Christians in the first three centuries erred, failed, lapsed, and repented, just as we do. They struggled against materialism, indifference, and blind hostility, and for the most part saw little sign of victory in their day. Yet through them the Holy Spirit worked out his purpose and achieved the glory which is their crown.

" Wherefore seeing we also are compassed about with so great a cloud of witnesses, let us lay aside every weight, and the sin which doth so easily beset us, and let us run with patience the race that is set before us, looking unto Jesus the author and finisher of our faith."

BOOKS FOR FURTHER READING

Ecclesiastical History, by Eusebius, translated by H. J. Lawlor and J. E. L. Oulton. 1st Vol. text., 2nd Vol. notes. This edition also includes the *Martyrs of Palestine*.

The Manner in Which the Persecutors Died, by Lactantius. A.-N.C.L. Lactantius Vol. II.

These two books are the chief original authorities for the Diocletian persecution.

The Persecution of Diocletian, by A. J. Mason, 1876. A leisurely, readable book.

INDEX